Google Cloud Platform an Architect's Guide

D1673848

Part I – Google Cloud Platform Fundamentals

Chapter 1 - An Introduction to the Google Cloud Platform

In this opening chapter of 'Google Cloud Platform an Architect's Guide' we are going to present a brief overview of the Google Cloud Platform. In the following chapters in part 1 we will build upon this by introducing the four main categories of cloud services: compute, storage, Big Data and machine learning. However, we must not forget cloud security and networking as these are the essential glue that holds everything together in a robust and low latency manner.

Moreover, we will explain how GCP is flexible enough to provide you options for computing and hosting where you can choose a platform to:

- Work in a serverless environment – Function Engine
- Use a managed application platform – Apps Engine
- Leverage container technologies to gain lots of flexibility – Kubernetes Engine
- Build your own cloud-based infrastructure to have the most control and flexibility – Compute Engine

When you consider what technologies constitute Google Cloud Platform you should also contemplate the areas of shared responsibility. You can imagine a spectrum where, at one end, you have most of the responsibilities for resource management, which is Compute Engine. At the other end of the spectrum is Cloud Function Engine, where Google retains most of those responsibilities as it is a fully managed service often called a serverless environment. Regardless, the GCP gives you options for both hands on managing of resources or to take advantage of Google's managed services, it's up to you.

Figure-1

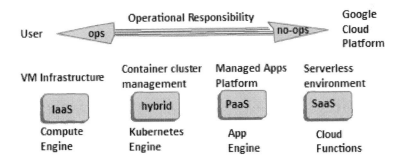

In this chapter we will start by focusing on the VM infrastructure within the compute and storage services together with the topic of networking. Networking is important to us as we cannot effectively use any of the cloud's resources without using the Cloud Networking services. However cloud networking is often the least understood component of cloud computing as it differs in several ways from the traditional on-premises networking that you may already be familiar with.

As a result we will through the course of this book build upon the overview we present in this chapter by providing deeper and wider discussions on cloud networking in subsequent chapters. The same can be said of security. Similarly we will first introduce some basic security concepts that pertain to the cloud before going into greater detail later in the book. But for now let us start with some basic concepts on cloud computing.

Cloud Computing Concepts

Cloud computing is about the seamless delivery of computing services—including infrastructure such as virtual servers, large scale storage, databases, and networking, as well as platforms for Big Data, advanced analytics, and artificial intelligence— all over the Internet ("the cloud"). These services provide you with the means for faster innovation through flexible infrastructure and rapid deployment of resources, with the benefits of economies of scale. You typically will pay only for cloud services you use; this helps you lower your capital expenditure, run your infrastructure and operations more cost efficiently, as well as the capability to scale to meet your business requirements.

Cloud computing platforms have become very popular over the last decade due to some fundamental principles:

- First, the cloud is a very cost-effective and highly efficient place to rapidly develop, deploy, run your applications and store your app data. This is mainly because it reduces any upfront capital investments in servers and other infrastructure but also because it greatly reduces the operational burden if not the overall cost because it means you are no longer burdened with many time consuming tasks such as provisioning servers, then having to maintain them or even backing them up so it frees you from a lot of housekeeping chores.

- Secondly, scale, Cloud services scale dynamically both growing and shrinking resource consumption as required. This type of dynamic or elastic scaling of resources can result in reasonably priced access to high performance and almost infinite infrastructure resources.

- Thirdly, performance, cloud computing provides truly global access which enables the delivery of your services and products closer to your customers across the cloud provider's own global-scale infrastructure. This vast network inherently provides global load balancing and the distribution of content closest to the customer resulting in lower latency and economy of scale.

- Fourthly, reliability, Cloud computing makes data backup, disaster recovery, and business continuity easier and less expensive because data can be mirrored at multiple redundant sites on the cloud provider's network at a fraction of the cost of an on-premise solution.

- Last, but not least, productivity, as on-premises data centres typically require a lot of manual installation of hardware, application and stack provisioning on top of hardware configuration, software and security patching, and many other support duties. Cloud computing removes the need for many of these tasks, so IT teams can spend time on achieving more innovative and business orientated goals.

Those are the main features and benefits of cloud computing in general but how is Google's Platform organized and what differentiates it from the competition?

Google Cloud Platform

As we have just seen, the five drivers behind cloud computing that
enthuse customers to migrate their IT systems to remote service
providers, relates to cheaper and more efficient availability of
resources. This also provides for disaster recovery and business
continuity solutions that come at a fraction of the cost of redundant
data centres. However, although this explains the attraction for
companies with limited budgets, technical resources, little in-house
IT skills, or only a local presence, it doesn't address the needs of
SME or larger organizations where IT skills are in abundance and
where there are multiple locations for business continuity.
Furthermore, with these large enterprises it is control, security and
management that are the key concerns. Indeed for many large
organisations the actual cost saving that are so apparent to the
smaller organisation and the startup are possibly going to prove
neutral or even negative. This is simply because the cloud financial
model shifts the burden away from one-time capital expenditure
(CapEx) onto operational recurring costs (OpEx). Consequently, a
large organisation with thousands of applications and servers may
find that the cloud is not the cost effective nirvana they have been
led to believe. Thus, to understand why the cloud is still so
attractive and compelling to these types of organizations we have
to consider some history.

The fact is that many medium to large organizations have been on the path to cloud for many years, they just didn't realize it. For instance, colocation has been around for decades as companies strived to reduce data centre costs by sharing facilities. Indeed many large companies would offset the huge costs of operating their data centres by providing colocation services to medium sized companies as a very cost effective solution that served both party's needs. Consequently, many smaller non-technology based companies would much rather collocate than start investing scarce capital into running their own power hungry and operationally intensive data centres. Instead they could simply rent space in another large organization's shared facility and this was known as colocation.

For many businesses, running data centres are not core business goals so colocation frees up capital for more business centric initiatives such as research and development or improving their products and services rather than pouring all their hard earned cash into paying huge cooling and electricity bills.

However, for the large enterprise collocation was very attractive as it contributed to the upkeep of their essential data centres. Indeed we can look at colocation as being just one of the stages along the road to cloud computing.

Virtualization appeared on the scene in the first decade of the 2000s. Server virtualization was hugely popular as it addressed the inefficiencies of single servers running a single application, which were common best practices at the time. This practice however led to the proliferation of small servers that were run using barely a fraction of their capabilities and that resulted in escalating energy costs and huge inefficiencies. This led IT departments to adopt server virtualization as a priority as it led to much needed efficiencies and superior provisioning times. Virtualization allowed IT to do a lot more with fewer servers and other infrastructure components with little trouble as a virtualized data center match the architecture of a physical data center. But now there was a problem as virtual servers that were separately manageable from the underlying hardware created an issue as it meant that the technical expertise of the support staff was critical but also in short supply.

Virtualization lets us all use resources more efficiently and just like colocation, it lets us be more flexible too but it made troubleshooting an individual application vastly more difficult. This was because before with the one application one server models the tiresome conflicts of what was software and what was a hardware issue was easily sorted. However, with virtualization you made efficient use of shared server resources and capabilities by running many low-resource applications on the same server. This was done in order to reduced waste and reduce the proliferation of physical servers. But there was the downside and that was that data centre support needed to know exactly how virtualization worked. They also needed to know the exact requirements of each application so maintaining the infrastructure became far more complex. Thus, virtualisation resulted in less capital and energy cost but that benefit was wiped out in higher operational costs such as wages for experienced support staff.

Moreover, previously capacity planning had been considered to be an unattractive but relatively straight forward task. With virtualisation it became an essential role in server and network management. After all, with virtualisation it's even more important that you determine how much resources each application may need and how each might scale. Thus, you'll need to predetermine all these factors before you deploy them on a host server. One solution was to run a single VM on a server but that negated the benefits of virtualisation. But running several VMs on a single server requires detailed understanding of each VMs operational requirement. Indeed before deployment of an application it was often the case that you had to perform detailed capacity planning and then present the results to the change control board or the project management team. This negated much of the flexibility and rapid provisioning benefits.

The advent of the internet in the early 90's and its subsequent proliferation globally in the early 2000's made the huge internet providers aware that virtualization was not a solution in its self as the ability to scale became paramount. Network issues and in particular latency brought about through traditional layer three routing made them look towards Software Defined Networks (SDN) and a shift away from virtualization towards SDN and container based architecture.

As a result, these internet-scale businesses like Google understood that traditional networking and server architecture with virtualisation would not scale to their global demands. Consequently, large internet-scale organisation switched to a container based architecture based upon an automated SDN elastic cloud built around automated services. With this model all the services are automatically proactively provisioned and seamlessly configured so that the infrastructure is optimized to run stacks, environments and popular applications.

But, what was most important is that the pioneers of cloud computing such as Google when developing their revolutionary SDN networks didn't have a vendor roadmap to follow so they created their own SDN global networks and developed their own routers, switches and servers to meet their own world-wide criteria. Moreover, some of the pioneers realized that these new networks could support not just their own global ambitions and scope but also the requirements of others. What Amazon in particular realised early on was that their vast pool of resources could now be shared reliably, efficiently and cheaply over the internet just like co-location. The Amazon cloud then made colocation and in-house virtualisation now a poor alternative as cloud became very attractive for small organizations that lacked their global scale.

Further, around the late 2000's the cloud delivered a much easier way to manage applications through Software as a Service (SaaS). This way of delivering cloud hosted software over the internet was fantastic as it disconnected on-premises technicians from being application experts. Indeed, all you needed was a robust internet connection to benefit from an enterprise-class hosted software solution.

The CRM platform Salesforce was one of the pioneers and it dislocated IT in many respects from desktop and application support. But SaaS was also the instigator of Infrastructure as a Service, (IaaS), and Platform as a Service, (PaaS) as these offerings soon followed.

IaaS though hard to comprehend at the time provided raw compute, storage, and network services that are organized in ways that are far cheaper to provision and more efficient than on-premises servers. In contrast, the PaaS offerings were more suitable for developers that needed a platform on which to run their application code. Moreover, PaaS provides developers with software libraries that give easy access to run-times, drivers and interfaces that run seamlessly on a transparent underlying managed infrastructure.

Whereas, SaaS had been a huge success the introduction of IaaS by cloud providers was met with far more reticence. Many larger companies thought that giving up control and management of their infrastructure was not an attractive proposition. Indeed, the larger organisations were already running their own version of the cloud via colocation in their large data centres. Hence, they didn't see any benefits of moving operations to the cloud all they saw was the potential hazards mainly regards loss of control and security.

Security was the main obstacle to cloud adoption for larger organisations. Indeed even with SaaS there had been concerns regarding the multi-tenant models and data segregation between cloud customers. Another concern for big companies was regards the added complexity of running multi, hybrid or private clouds as there was not one single solution for businesses operating proprietary technologies. This can be demonstrated through the understandable concerns of moving mission critical databases or applications to a single cloud provider. It simply couldn't be done; for example, the easiest and generally best solutions would be the migration of the proprietary solutions such as Oracle, IBM and Microsoft databases and applications to their respective vendor clouds. This is because for large enterprises these databases and applications are not just mission-critical they also tend to be huge. This makes them unsuitable for running within a VM due to their scale and performance requirements. But of course, a multi-cloud solution raises more issues as these applications and databases often need to communicate with one another so this added another layer of network latency and security complexity.

On the other hand for small companies migrating to the cloud made perfect sense once they could be reassured of any security concerns. They could migrate their Oracle, IBM DB and SQL Server solutions easily as they could run them intact within VMs on the same cloud. This mitigated many of the security and inter-communications latency issues. But for the enterprise there still was significant hurdles to be overcome, such as decomposing vast monolithic applications and huge databases, would take a lot of time and money with little in the way of obvious rewards. The major issue being was that organisations thought of moving to the cloud simply in terms of technology upgrade and an expensive upgrade at that. They did not see it as a business or cost differentiator as there was no barriers to entry, if you could do it so could anyone else. Furthermore the much heralded cost-efficiencies didn't really work at their scale.

The re-emergence of interest around 2010 in SDN, microservices and containers changed the enterprise IT mindset. For now the focus was on moving away from the 3-tier data centre structure and moving to faster layer-2 architecture. The former was how data centres were previously designed and client/server applications built and deployed. This model supported monolith applications and huge data bases on massive server clusters. However the 3-tier model also added latency between the layers as traffic had to pass through physical routers and often firewalls at the layer boundaries. The layer-2 model however was faster as there was no inter-layer communications as everything was on the same flat Ethernet network. This meant everything could communicate directly with everything else – if it was permitted - on a common network with the security and virtual firewall rules enforced centrally by the SDN network.

The obvious improvement in on-premises performance and reduced latency between applications encouraged the use of microservices, which are single function modules of code. Microservices encouraged the decomposition of monolithic applications as it brought the benefits of faster development and the promise of agile development, continuous improvement through frequent updates and rapid deployment. Now large organisations' business teams were beginning to pay attention. Next came containers and this is where the modern cloud technologies and large enterprise data centre technologies would eventually converge on a common architecture. Don't get me wrong though the introduction of microservices, containers and flat networks have made cloud migrations feasible but it is still not easy. This is because decomposing a mission critical application into microservices or sharding vast databases into manageable components takes time and effort. However, the rewards are now scalability, flexibility, speed, redundancy, centralised security, global-reach, multi-regional caching, network efficiency and infrastructure cost effectiveness, amongst many others. But the drivers now for modernisation or as it is called digital transformation came from the business teams and the c-suite. This turn-around from an IT-push to a C-suite and business-team's pull came-about because the need to modernise to a more pervasive digital, flexible, agile and rapid business environment was now deemed to be business critical. This is because the business teams could now translate the cloud benefits to real business objectives such as wider market visibility, better customer identification and personalisation, informed and dynamic decision-making, faster time to market and advanced capability-building.

Framing the ROI

Consequently when framing any questions regards return on investment for moving to the cloud for all but the smallest of companies or startup we should avoid stressing the cost saving benefits. The reason for this is two-fold, one it may not actually be true for larger or well established organizations. Two, it is better to concentrate on composite ROI whereby you take a three tier approach. The lower tier would be regards the infrastructure Total-Cost-of Ownership (TCO) and capital investments in modernisation. For a startup the value generated at this tier could be significant but for most larger organizations the CapEx and OpEx ratio will typically be neutral or even negative over 3-5 years. Then we should consider the second tier which concerns Human Resources (HR) with regards to the operations and maintenance and this is where organisations can make some positive ROI due to offshoring much of the operations, management and maintenance burden and thus reducing staffing, training and administration requirements. However, even at this HR tier the ROI is typically only around 5%. It is at the third tier, which measures business value that we will typically see significant return on investment. Indeed when we consider business benefits in the ROI this is where we start to see ROI in excess of 50%.

Therefore, when considering ROI for moving to the cloud you should take a holistic approach by considering infrastructure, HR and business value to reach a composite value. This will require involving the business-teams in technology decision making as well as elevating IT to a become a business function with responsibilities to create business value. After all this is what digital transformation is all about.

Spoilt for Choice

In the last section we discussed how and why ROI and the benefits of moving to the cloud can vary depending on the size and maturity of the organisation. Indeed we learned that cost-savings are not always the predominant driver and that increases in business flexibility, increased business capability and speed to market are often the key drivers. However for smaller businesses and certainly a startup where preserving precious seed capital is essential if they hope to survive then reducing infrastructure CapEx is hugely important. So switching perspective we can now view the benefits from a SMB or start up point-of-view.

In years gone-by there were several internet providers that filled the market demand for outsourcing a data centre and to meet the needs of financial managers looking to offset the huge IT costs of investing in a data centre by outsourcing the service. Indeed there were internet service providers that provided hosted web services that delivered all the advantages that we have already mentioned, touch of a button provisioning and monthly bills at a set monthly subscription. There was no need for on-premises experts, as these were managed services focused on the SMB or small companies that had no technical experience so they charged every month even though you had barely used their service.

On the other hand, today's cloud providers like Google provide a service which is billed based upon the resources that you use. Indeed Google introduced billing by the second, which can reduce operational expense significantly. Thus some companies can make considerable saving using cloud services, which deliver a variety of functions and applications for running a network, managing the infrastructure and getting the best possible value from capturing, storing and processing data.

The problem was that when cloud computing came to the attention of business the terms were not really intuitive; even IT who certainly embraced the more pervasive SaaS didn't actually understand the difference between IaaS and PaaS.

To get a better understanding of these cloud service we need to contemplate the IaaS model at some high level. What the concept of IaaS relates to is you pay for the use of cloud hosted infrastructure, but you only pay for the resources that you use or reserve and no more. This is very advantageous for business as it means you can forget about detailed capacity planning as should you get the forecasting wrong and your product or service goes viral you will still scale to meet demand but still only pay for the resources your application uses. In contrast, when using on-premises infrastructure you would have had to predetermine and set the resources to scale and overprovision the servers and network bandwidth with a safety margin in order to scale to your most ambitious and affordable goals. In contrast IaaS is very forgiving as it is dynamically scalable so it expands and shrinks to meet the current resource requirements of the application.

This is also true of the PaaS model; in so much as you pay for what you use. Again this must be considered preferable to having to forecast your capacity and usage beforehand and pay up front for resources you may not use. Cloud computing has become very popular with SMB because of this pay-as-you-use model. Further, Cloud Computing has eventually become dominant in many SME IT environments due to the shift towards automated configuration, provisioning and deployment and all with no human intervention. It may seem unintuitive but the IT leaders that first railed against cloud computing eventually came around to finding that the autonomous managed infrastructure and automated managed services was a good thing.

Thus we are now seeing more enterprises moving their IT operations to the cloud, but the old question persists, to what cloud? The question is difficult to answer as it depends on circumstances. As we discussed earlier if you are heavily dependent on a particular technology say Oracle, IBM or VMware then it makes sense to lift-and-shift your operations straight up to the respective vendors cloud. However, for the vast number of Microsoft business clients it makes more sense to deploy to Microsoft Azure cloud. This is simply due to the respective vendors knowing their products better than anyone else. For SMB and SME with more general requirements and open source solutions then Amazon AWS is by far the most popular and largest cloud environment. AWS has the largest global reach and number of points-of-presence; it also has by far the largest portfolio of cloud services. So, why would an SMB, SME or large enterprise want to migrate their operations to specifically Google Cloud Platform?

The Google Cloud Platform

Google has built one of the largest fibre optic networks in the world and they have invested billions of dollars over the years to build the network to meet their own global requirements. As a result, the network has been designed to deliver the highest throughput with the lowest possible latencies for their internet based applications. To meet their own specifications required that Google designed an SDN network unlike any vendor's roadmap at the time.

Google's cloud network global scope may not be as large as AWS but Google is investing heavily and catching up quickly. For example, the global scale of the network requires interconnects at more than 90 Internet exchanges, which ensures fast efficient connection with low latency. What is more Google has more than 100 points of presence worldwide that are geographically and strategically placed. This global distribution of PoPs ensures redundancy and high availability. Thus, if an Internet user sends traffic to a Google resource that is temporarily unavailable, Google will detect the request and will respond via the closest edge network location. This method provides the lowest latency and provides the best customer experience.

In addition, Google's Edge-caching network also provides geographical caching of content so that it always delivers content closest to the end user. A distributed cache will minimize latency and increase customer experience by reducing connection and download times as well as provide a measure of business continuity.

Although Google may be considered to have been slow of the mark to benefit from sharing their global network they have tried over the last few years to catch up with Amazon's AWS cloud platform. Consequently, they have invested billions of dollars building their own cloud platform and global network fibre links to ensure its networks are low latency, resilient and highly efficient.

Today, Google strives to make their cloud platform attractive, affordable and available to their customers. This change in strategy appears to come about as Google has come to believe like Amazon, that presently and in the future data is and will be integral to all businesses, regardless of size or industry. This was not always the case, as even quite recently IT was often considered to be a service function of a business. After all manufacturing or product development, sales, marketing and finance were the core profit generating business units. IT was simply a service department that generated no new money or profit. But as technology has become integrated and almost inseparable with all these traditional business functions cloud providers have come to realize that the way a company will differentiate itself from its competitors will be through leveraging cost effective advanced IT technology in order to create new business value from its data. Google's belief is that future companies will largely deal in data, through advanced analytics, Artificial Intelligence and its subset of machine learning. Hence, Google's focus is on providing cloud services for businesses that focus on data and analytics, but also for companies that need to reimaging there data centres in the cloud to extend their scale and global reach. As, in the future, companies must have the ability to service customers around the globe. Hence, customers that build on-premises solutions will be at a severe disadvantage as the cost are simply prohibitive. What is worse it is crucial capital that is wasted as it should be spent on core business functions that generate profit.

Thus, Google believes that every company will have a need to rely on data analytics as well as have a global presence and this will require a global partner that can provide them the infrastructure to scale to their ambitions. Ultimately, this strategy will allow them to release their cash and energy to be spent on developing digital processes that permeates the entire organisation and its value and supply chains. It is by following this road-map that places an emphasis on pursuing affordable, scalable, global and highly-advanced technology that will enable organisations to differentiate themselves and become digital leaders and the creators of innovative business value.

Cloud Native Architecture

Google's network is designed to support its eight key web-based products which each have in excess of one billion subscribers so it must be designed to be robust, scalable and efficient. But how does it differ from traditional network design?

At a high level, we can consider cloud-native architecture to mean a design that adapts to take advantage of the many new possibilities—but also the very different set of architectural constraints—offered by the cloud compared to traditional on-premises infrastructure. If we look to some of the high level elements that you as a network architect will be trained to consider, such as:

- The functional requirements of a system
- The non-functional requirements
- The architectural constraints

What we actually will find is that the cloud is not much different from the on-premises data centre. This is simply because the cloud is made of the same fabric of servers, disks and networks that makes up traditional infrastructure. This means that almost all of the principles of good architectural design still apply for cloud-native architecture.

While many of the functional aspects remain the same regardless as to on-premises or cloud the latter is often more challenging when it comes to the non-functional aspects. These do often result in design constraints. Indeed, some of the fundamental assumptions about how the infrastructure fabric performs do change when you're in the cloud. The differences are in speed and flexibility. For instance, provisioning a replacement server can take weeks in traditional environments, even in VM environments it still takes a day, whereas in the cloud, it takes seconds. Hence in the cloud it's much easier to provision a full application stack with fully automated scaling and fail-over scenarios than on-premises. However in order to take advantage of these properties it is a requirement that the cloud provider has many application and vendor partners. To this end Google Cloud Platform support a very large partner network, which allows you to provision both proprietary and open source solutions with a single click via the Cloud Launcher service.

Google's SDN network facilitates a cloud-native design, which also tends to focus on key metrics such as resilience, horizontal scaling, distributed processing, and automation. So we need to take these characteristics into account when you are evaluating other cloud-native architectures that are not based on Google's own SDN cloud network.

Google Software Defined Network

The Google Cloud Platform is organized as a software defined network, now that might sound confusing but it's not really and we will consider the architecture later in some detail. But for now all you need to know is that Google's global network is defined by segments and its smallest entity is a Zone, which can be defined as a deployment area for Google Cloud Platform Resources. It could be simplified to mean a data centre but that is not always the case as a zone could have several points of presence within a local zone. However a zone works as one large switch operating within a common subnet so entities within a zone communicate at layer-2 or the Ethernet data layer – which we will cover later – but it means latency is minimal and configuration negligible.

When you launch a virtual machine for example, in a GCP zone using Compute Engine, you will be prompted to select a local zone. This is the local area where you wish the application or service to run. Hence you would select the closest zone to where you want the application or service to run. This will ensure that the associated compute, storage and network resources are local and close to the area they serve to deliver low latency and high performance. However zones, as we have seen, can be large geographical areas that contain several data centres which are many kilometres apart and this allows for a measure of redundancy and business continuity planning. For instance you could mirror your infrastructure across two zones perhaps 100 km apart to give you a measure of mitigation for disaster recovery or business continuity should one zone's data centre suffer a natural catastrophe.

Zones are grouped into regions

As we have seen zones are segments in larger independent geographic areas called regions. This means that you can select what zone and region you're GCP resources reside in. Importantly, all the zones within a region have very fast and very low latency interconnected network connectivity among them as they operate much like an Ethernet switch at layer-2 in the data communications protocol stack. Intercommunication between Zones within a region will typically have round trip network latencies of under-five milliseconds, which is very fast when you consider the devices may be 100 km apart or more.

What this means is that zones within a region can be considered to be from a data network perspective both a single broadcast domain as well as a single failure domain. This is important when you contemplate building a fault tolerant application, as you can easily spread the application's resources across multiple zones within a region. This is because they share a common subnet so the fail-over from one server to another will be seamless. Sharing a common layer-2 domain helps protect against unexpected failures as well as greatly assist in real-time synchronization or replication of data between cluster peers or master/slave models despite the fact they may be 100s of miles apart.

Furthermore, you can run synchronised or mirrored resources in different regions if you want greater security against natural disasters. However it is not just for business continuity or disaster recovery that you may want to mirror infrastructure across regions as many organizations choose to do this in order to deliver content to customers' at the most convenient point of presence. Thus you may choose to use regions to deliver content closer to your customer base. For example this is how Google brings their applications closer to their users wherever they may be in the world. Diversifying across regions also protects against the loss of an entire region, say, due to a submarine fibre cable being severed or some natural disaster.

Sometimes you will find that some Google Cloud platform services do support placing resources in what we call a Multi-Regional configuration. Currently the GCP is configured to support 15 regions. What this means is that data may well be stored across regions within the parent region. For example data may be redundantly stored across several geographically diverse locations within the US Multi-Region. In practice this means that there is a copy of the data stored in at least two geographic locations, separated by at least 160 kilometres within the US. You may want to look into this if you are located in Europe or Asia for example as some nations despite being in the same broad geographical region may not wish or be allowed to store data out with their own borders. If that is the case then you can easily stipulate the regions and zones you wish your data to be backed-up that meet your nation's regulatory compliance.

Sustainable Cloud Networks

In the era of the new green deal and the awakening of public awareness that demands a future based upon sustainable and carbon neutral industry, enterprise data centres have come under the spotlight. It is hardly surprising as computer networks consume vast quantities of energy and produce equal amounts of wasted energy in the form of heat. Indeed, the internet is built on physical infrastructure, and all those servers consume vast amounts of energy and produce heat as a by-product that has to be controlled or dissipated. Around the world today data centres consume around two percent of the world's electricity supply; hence there is a responsibility for the major data centre providers to provide sustainable and eco-friendly energy plans. To this end Google strives to make their internet-scale data centres run as energy efficiently as possible.

As a result of their efforts Google's data centres were the first cloud providers to achieve ISO 14001 certification, which is the gold standard for improving resource efficiency and reducing waste. In order to achieve this certification Google is one of the world's largest corporate purchasers of wind and solar energy, which means that Google has been 100 percent carbon neutral since 2007, and will shortly reach a 100 percent renewable energy sources for its data centres.

Today many of Google's customers pursue environmental goals as part of their mission statements, for sustainable and green business practices and they can responsibly live up to those ideals by running their workloads in GCP.

Cloud Efficiency Model

The most commonly used list of benefits for adopting cloud computing is the one created by the US National Institute of Standards and Technology. In their definition, cloud computing is considered to be a model for efficiency in remotely hosting and running I.T. services, which have typically five equally important components.

First, Google Cloud Platform provides you with access to online remote computing resources; these are delivered as an on-demand and self-service model. Hence, GCP is ideal for small medium business (SMB), small medium enterprises (SME) or for those matter companies of any size. This is because all you have to do is to use a simple interface to access all the processing power, storage, and network resources that you require. Importantly though you can have access to all the infrastructure, services and resources without the need for any of your own infrastructure or in-house skills as access to most GCP managed services requires no human intervention at all.

Second, because GCP resources are distributed around the globe and accessible on the internet you access these resources over the net from anywhere you have an internet connection. Furthermore, your customers can also access your applications or services from anywhere in the world with low latency and high availability. As a result you or your customers don't need to know or care about the exact physical location of those resources. What this means is that you can mirror your IT environments not only across zones but also regions and even continents to ensure business continuity in the case of a local or regional disruption of service. Previously, that would have required vast expense establishing multiple data centres and moreover in keeping them synchronised.

Third, Google has their own internet-scale network infrastructure, which provides a vast pool of resources that are allocated dynamically to their clients on a pay-as-you-use basis. That model allows Google to dynamically service their customer with only the resources they require at any given moment so Google can get vast efficiencies by balancing their pool of resources across their demand driven network of customers. The elastic nature of the allocation of resources means that should you quickly need more resources such as CPU, memory, network bandwidth or storage you will get allocated them seamlessly and rapidly without any human intervention being required. However, if the demand were to fall you can then scale back. The consequences of this are that you only pay what you use or reserve so if you no longer use a resource, you will no longer be charged for it.

Fourth, Security, Google supports a wide array of vendor software and hardware but they also use their own securely built servers. These secure servers have Google's own Titan security chips and secure-boot processes, which makes Google's cloud infrastructure highly secure.

Fifth, Google like other internet-scale providers takes advantage of economies of scale by buying and building infrastructure, licenses and services in bulk and then passing the savings on to the customers. However, Google has the largest partner network, which manifests itself through a wide array of open-source and proprietary software, which is pre-provisioned and available at a click. Thus, the considerable ease-of-use advantages when provisioning servers and application stacks or environments. What is more each will have the correct versions, dependencies and libraries installed automatically doing away with a lot of the troublesome tasks when deploying stacks. For example, a LAMP (Linux, Apache, MySQL, and PHP) stack can be provisioned in just a click of a button and the same is true of other environments such as Java. In addition networking becomes easier as it is configured automatically in most cases meaning the requirement for in-house expert-level networking skills is no longer a requirement.

GCP Charging Model

A key reason for migrating IT to the Google Cloud Platform is to reduce costs and typically GCP offers several ways to reduce operational spending and overall costs. For start-ups and Greenfield companies cloud computing greatly reduces the capital expenditure required as there are no upfront investments in servers and network equipment. Established businesses however can also benefit by reducing maintenance, administration and operational costs of running a data room/centre. This is primarily due to clouds typical pay-as-you-use model, rapid provisioning of servers, and reduced time to profit in product/service development, which translates to tremendous saving if managed correctly.

Indeed, all cloud providers follow this pay-as-you-use model but it was Google that first introduced billing by the second rather than rounding up to the minute for the virtual machines that you configure as part of the Compute Engine service.

Initiatives such as charging by the second can have a large impact on monthly billing if you are running thousands of VM instances. However, the per second model for billing is not restricted to the use of virtual machines through the Compute Engine as it is also available for several other services as well such as;

- Kubernetes Engine, which is GCP's container managed Infrastructure as a Service,
- Cloud Dataproc. which is GCP's open source Big Data system Hadoop as a service, and
- App Engine Flexible Environment which is GCP's platform as a service.
- Cloud Spanner, which is GCPs vastly scalable SQL relational database

Moreover GCP has several other cost reducing or cost management initiatives that you should be aware of and take into consideration when planning deployments of services. For example, Compute Engine offers you discounts based upon consistent use of a VM resource. These discounts are automatically applied to reward sustained usage, i.e. these are automatic discounts for running a virtual machine for more than 25% of the billing month.

This discount translates to a significant saving for every incremental minute you use it over the 25% threshold.

Savings can also be made through diligent sizing of the VM that you create. This is because when you initially provision a VM you will select among other things, the memory size and how many virtual CPUs you require. In most cases customers will pick a reconfigured VM from a drop down menu but you can customize your VM. Because Compute Engine allows you to select the required memory or virtual CPUs when provisioning the VM this enables you to fine-tune the VM to tailor the pricing to match your workloads. Moreover, if you are in development you might want to take advantage of the micro VMs that GCP offers within Compute Engine. These are minimal VMs that are ideal for building prototypes or proof-of-concept models. By using micro VMs in development you can reduce the cost significantly. Another way is to use pre-emptive VMs to reduce costs. A pre-emptive VM is one that Google can reclaim at any time so they are only suitable for certain applications but the pricing is significantly reduced.

Avoiding Vendor Lock-In

Earlier in this chapter we highlighted some of the reasons why customers are moving their IT operations to the cloud and to Google Cloud in particular. However not every IT customer was initially enamoured with the prospect of potentially losing control of their data's security and integrity. That was the major factor amongst customers for not migrating operations to the cloud but there was another common reason and that was the fear of vendor lock-in.
Many companies were concerned that if they migrated their workloads to the cloud they might become so dependent on the providers service that they became effectively locked into a particular vendor. This is a common concern amongst IT leaders.

Google recognizes this concern and provides customers with the ability to run their applications elsewhere should the GCP no longer be the most suitable service provider.

For examples of how GCP allows customers to avoid being locked in Google has designed the GCP services to be compatible with open source products.

For example, if we consider GCP's Cloud Bigtable, which is a massive database, which we'll discuss later in detail. But for now what is important is that Cloud Bigtable uses the same interface as the open source database Apache HBase, which gives customers the benefit of code portability. Another example is GCP's Cloud Dataproc, which offers the same open source Big Data environment Hadoop, as a managed service.

In addition Google is committed to the open source community and projects and regularly publishes key elements of technology using open source licenses. By doing so Google participates in creating and supporting open source ecosystems. These open source communities and systems provide customers with options other than Google.

For example, TensorFlow, which is an open source software library for machine learning was originally developed inside Google, but is now a robust open source ecosystem.

In addition to Google's commitment to the open source paradigm they are making efforts to integrate open source projects into GCP in order to provide maximum interoperability.

For example, Kubernetes provides GCP customers with the tools to mix and match microservices running on-premises or even on other clouds. There is also Google Stackdriver, which is GCP's monitoring and management application, which is a collection of open source tools that allows customers to monitor workloads across multiple cloud providers, such as Amazon's AWS.

Summary

In this chapter – An Introduction to the Google Cloud Platform we described the benefits of cloud computing in general and then specifically the GCP, We were introduced to some of the GCP core service offerings which can be broadly categorized as compute, storage, Big Data, machine learning, networking, security, operations and tools.

Hence, GCP's services can be leveraged to utilise computing, storage, Big Data, machine learning and application services and functionality for your web, mobile, analytics and backend solutions.

We also demonstrated that GCP is an internet-scale solution, that has global reach, high availability and reliability yet it is still cost effective,

Furthermore GCP is open source friendly and it's designed for business continuity and security in mind.

In the next chapter we will take a deeper dive into each of the compute services and the storage services, how these services and how customers can best use them. Also because Google has itself seven major cloud services supporting over a billion users then this makes security in the GCP paramount and ensures that the GCP is designed with security in mind.

Use Case: 1

A start up business ABC Technology, has sent you an RFC for a proposal for architectural change to accommodate growth, business continuity and disaster recovery for the business, their applications, and data. Their entire operation is presently dependent on on-premises hardware that supports a three-tier web application consisting of webserver, application server and a database. They have three set-ups one for production and another for development and testing and another for data storage/archive. They are looking for a cost effective and high performance solution. What can you propose when answering the RFC.

Solution

As a first stage you could propose that the client mirrors their on-premises architecture to Google Cloud Platform by using VMs in Compute Engine. This is readily achievable and can be quickly prototyped for demonstration. All that would be required is for you to reproduce their current architecture to GCP using VMs and lift and shift the code and data. By mirroring and then replicating the databases to the cloud you will have solved their business continuity and disaster recovery requirements with an easy to implement solution but is it a cost effective solution? To address the cost effectiveness we would need to ascertain the desired level of continuity requirement. For example how much down-time and data loss can the business accept? If the client can be flexible regards the recovery time objectives (RTO) then it would be possible to build and test a warm DR cloud environment. In this case we would build the cloud infrastructure replicate the databases and leave them active but tear down everything else after copying the configuration into a deployment manager template. This would mean that you could rapidly recreate the environment on demand. If however the RTO is zero then we would need to build and run the entire cloud architecture 24/7 but that would have not insignificant financial consequences. However you still have to address the issue with accommodating growth and scale. In order to do this you might suggest that after the first stage is complete and the client is happy that they switch over to using the cloud infrastructure and only use the on-premises as the backup site for local storage and archiving of data. As the GCP is elastic and highly scalable this would provide the automatic scalability of the hardware needed for the forecasted growth. You could also detail a third stage whereby they later retire the on-premises data centre altogether and replicate everything in the cloud and mirror the infrastructure and storage across two zones or regions. This solution would meet all of their objectives for handling growth, business continuity and disaster recovery in an efficient and cost effective manner.

Chapter 2 – Introduction to Cloud Security

GCP – Security by Design

Security or rather the opaqueness of the security controls in place in the cloud was a major inhibitor to cloud adoption a decade or so ago. However cloud providers have gone to great lengths to address this issue so you will find that security is both pervasive and transparent throughout the infrastructure that the GCP and Google services run-on. In this chapter we will introduce some of the high-level security features build-in to GCP. However, a deeper dive into security will be covered in detail later in the book. But for now we just want to introduce some basics. So let's consider some of the approaches Google takes to protect the privacy and integrity of their customers' data.

Google's Bottom-Up Approach to Security

When contemplating an overview of the key security controls and functions inherent in the GCP it is helpful to start at the bottom of the security stack and work up. At the lowest layer in the stack are the data centre buildings that houses Google's infrastructure. Google designs and builds its own data centres and they protect physical access to these buildings by deploying multiple layers of physical security protections. This layered approach has increased levels of security controls applied at each layer as we work our way from the perimeter gates into the core of the data centre. For example at the perimeter gates access will only be given to data centre staff or pre-booked visitors however at the data centre server room access there is via an air lock door. These security doors only allows one person to pass at a time as sensors in the floor detect the presence of more than one person so this prevents tail-gating. In addition, the air locks can only be enabled through biometric sensors such as an iris scan, which also mitigates an authorized employee scanning in an unauthorised guest. Also access to these data centres is limited to only a very small fraction of Google employees on a work requirement basis. In short if you don't have a specific work requirement and an authorised permit to work you will not get access.

But the physical security doesn't stop there as within the server rooms the entire hardware infrastructure in Google data centres, such as the server boards and the networking equipment, are custom designed by Google. These are not off-the-shelf commodity servers they are custom designed and built with security in mind during the design process.

In addition, Google also designs many of its own custom chips, which includes a hardware security chip called Titan, which is baked into each server. This custom designed security chip is currently being deployed on both servers and network equipment and peripherals. But this is not just security by obscurity as Google goes much further to protect their infrastructure.

Secure Infrastructure

When we consider the security by design approach we can see that Google takes the integrity of their server machines very seriously. The servers use their custom Titan chips to instigate a secure boot process whereby the servers use cryptographic signatures to verify the software, drivers and firmware at every stage of the boot process this makes sure they are booting only clean authenticated and verified software. Also to minimize the threat-footprint Google servers are hardened to remove any potential software vulnerabilities and developers are supplied with secure libraries that are free of commonly known bugs or vulnerabilities.

In addition to Google's servers' secure boot and their proprietary Titan security hardware Google's infrastructure is also protected by cryptographic privacy and integrity at the data and network layers. This layer of security is for the protection of software remote procedure calls (RPC), which is called data-on-the-network. This is the way that **networks** allow sharing of files, **data**, and other types of information. Google services communicate securely with each other using RPC but the infrastructure automatically encrypts data traffic in transit between applications, servers and data centres as data is encrypted by default at rest and in flight.

Identity and Access Management (IAM)

Google Cloud Platform also has robust identity and access management functions (IAM), which provides the central identity service. IAM controls authentication, access permission and authorization. In simplistic terms this can be seen by end users as the Google log in page, but it reality it goes well beyond simply asking for a username and password. The IAM service will intelligently challenge users for additional information based on risk factors such as whether they have logged in from a known device or from a similar location in the past. Identity and Access Management will be discussed in detail later.

However, an authentication control you are probably familiar with is 2-factor authentication as this is when Google prompts the users of its services such as Gmail to use a registered mobile phone when signing in. This can be any registered phone but this can include other devices which are based on universal second factor standard (U2F).

Encryption at rest and in flight

Most applications access physical storage indirectly via storage services so GCP has encryption built into those services. Google also enables native encryption support in hard drives and SSDs. That's how Google manages to encrypted all of the customers' data at rest. On the other hand when data is in flight data is also encrypted using TLS or HTTPS. Google services that want to make themselves available on the Internet have to register with an infrastructure service called the Google frontend (GFE). The GFE is responsible for checking all incoming network connections for correct SSL/TLS certificates and adherence to security best practices.

In addition the GFE applies mitigation techniques against denial of service attacks. These are common brute force attacks typically deployed by an attacker attempting to swamp the available open TCP connections by repeatedly attempting to open a connection but never completely the process, which results in tens of thousands of incomplete sessions. Once the server runs out of available TCP sessions no one can connect to it hence the term, denial of service.

However the internet-scale of Google's infrastructure enables their network to simply absorb even the most determined of the distributed denial-of-service (DDOS) attacks. But even still, behind the GFEs there are additional multi-tier denial-of-service fortifications that mitigate any denial of service impact.

AI and Incident Response

Inside Google's infrastructure, machine intelligence and rule-based algorithms analyse at wire speed any traffic and warn of possible incidents. To ensure both proactive and reactive response Google conducts Red Team exercises that simulated network attacks in order to improve the defences and the effectiveness of the security operation centres responses. Hence the security NOC will monitor servers and network infrastructure 24/7 and in addition Google aggressively limits and actively monitors the activities of employees who have been granted administrative access to the infrastructure. Some other notable security procedures Google has in place are:

- To guard against phishing attacks against Google employees their accounts are protected by and require use of U2F compatible security keys.

- To help ensure that code is as secure as possible Google stores its source code centrally and requires two party review of new code.
- Google also gives its developers secure libraries that keep them from introducing certain classes of security bugs.
- Google also runs a vulnerability rewards program, where they will pay a bounty to anyone who is able to discover bugs in the infrastructure or their applications.

Security Trust Model

Google's security philosophy is based upon the premise of building the most trusted cloud available. To that purpose Google is striving to provide security on the cloud by building a robust and secure infrastructure on which customers can host and run their cloud applications and services. Also they are striving to take the next step by addressing security built in the cloud, which addresses security for applications, data and services. Last but not least they are provisioning security services which customers can use to deploy security tools and functions across their on-premises or other clouds.

In their pursuit of building the most trusted cloud Google look to establish several key factors:
- Establish a verifiable secure platform
- Deliver unparalleled visibility and transparency into operations
- Verification through trusted third-parties
- Simplify security controls
- Continuous improvement and investment

The GCP approach is to minimise the potential attack service and thus increase the customer trust surface. The way they increase trust is based upon increased transparency as to how the GCP works. Hence Google's desire to not only deliver a secure verified platform but to create the trust for a shared security model by providing the transparency, knowledge, and tools that the customers need to secure their applications that run on top of the GCP.

To understand Google's motivations in developing a shared security model we have to recognise that Google considers that a) the data belongs to the customer, b) that Google respects the customers data privacy, c) Google will not use customer data for advertising/marketing purposes or allow access to a third party, d) Google will provide the user with visibility and transparency into its security controls and methods.

Visibility and Transparency

Data integrity, which is today a major concern for customers due to compliance and privacy regulations, is ensured by encryption at rest and in travel. This ensures customers data is protected to the highest standard at all times. Google manages visibility and transparency which we see as being the core elements underpinning trust in five key ways:

1. Operations – Google make available to customers white papers and documentation as to how security controls are applied throughout the GCP operations everything is open and available for the customer or third party security vendor to scrutinize
2. Request and Reporting – Google provides documentation for legal and regulatory use to ensure compliance with

national laws. Google was also the first to produce a transparency report that details how many requests for access to customer data they have had from government or regulators and the actions taken

3. Contractual Commitments – Google doesn't just claim to be transparent they are contractually obliged to do so. Google makes themselves legally obliged to provide operational and security processes and procedures they commit through contract with you

4. Privacy – Google will provide detailed reports as to who in Google has access to your data, what they did, and why they did it.

5. Regulatory Compliancy –Google is audited by third parties for regulatory compliancy for relevant international standards such as those in force in the Americas, Europe/Middle East and Asia

Introduction to the GCP Hierarchy

In the previous section when we introduced security within the GCP we took a bottom-up approach as it was easier to visualise the placement of the different controls. So now when we introduce the GCP structure and hierarchy we will take that same approach as understanding the hierarchy is crucial in you playing your part in securing the CGP – remember Google's shared security model means that you also have a responsibility in securing your data. Therefore we feel that may find it easiest to understand the close bonds between security and the GCP resource hierarchy if we consider them consistently from the bottom up.

Projects and Folders

When you start to build your GCP virtual cloud infrastructure you will start off creating a project. Projects are essential as they are the administrative and billing domains for all of the resources you use. Every resource you use will be stored and billed against that project - whether they're virtual machines, cloud storage buckets, SQL tables or anything else in GCP they must reside in a billable project. There are some CGP basic rules concerning projects:

- All of the Google Cloud platform resources that you deploy must belong to a single project.
- Projects are the mechanism for enabling and using the GCP services like managing APIs, enabling billing and adding and removing collaborators and enabling other Google services.
- Each project is a separate compartment and each resource belongs to exactly one.
- Projects can have different owners and users, they're built separately and they're managed separately.
- Each GCP project has a name and a project ID that you assign. The project ID is a permanent unchangeable identifier and it has to be unique across GCP.

Project IDs are used in several contexts within GCP to enable it to support multi-tenancy as the project ID establishes unambiguously which project you are working in. For example when using storage buckets for your data you will create a bucket with a unique global identifier, which for convenience is typically based upon your project ID. The unique ID then provides complete segregation of the projects data from any other project. Project IDs are assigned by CGP at project creation and cannot be changed. Also project IDs are made to be human readable strings and you'll use them frequently to refer to your projects. On the other hand, project names are simply for your administrative convenience they have no deeper system relevance so you can assign and change them to something meaningful yourself.

GCP also assigns each of your projects a unique project number and you'll see that displayed to you in various contexts. Project numbers are like project IDs as they cannot be changed by the user.

Now you could have a different GCP project for each department or IT project undertaken, for example, an application development initiative, a digital transformation initiative or an IoT deployment initiative. This is fine for a small start-up company with flat organisational structures and fluid roles. However, for larger organisations with many departments and strict hierarchal policy control then managing individual projects which may eventually run into the thousands is unsustainable.

Another secure approach would be to assign projects to a single administrative unit called a folder. One caveat is though, is that to use folders you will need to have an organization node at the top of the hierarchy but we will come to that later.

Now you can organize projects into folders although you don't have to it is just easier to administer and manage. Nonetheless, folders are simply an elegant way of segregating projects it can be thought of as an organisational tool that CGP provides to make your life easier. For example, you can create a folder to represent each functional department to provide separation, let's say HR, Finance, IT, and as they are also hierarchal this means other nested folders can be made for their own individual teams, applications or development environments, within the parent's department folder. The advantage of using folders is that permission and access controls can be applied to the folder. This means when you place the appropriate projects into the parent folder the project will automatically be segregated from other folders but not its own sub-folders and they will inherit the folders permissions policy. As I'm sure you can image this can save a lot of tedious and repetitive work should changes be required in policy across many projects. But with folders the change will only need to be done at the highest hierarchal folder level instead of on every individual project or sub-folder. For example, a big advantage of having folders is maintainability as it provides departments and project teams with a level of autonomy to delegate administrative rights or determine their own access policy within their own projects that over-rides organisational policy. As the resources in a folder inherit IAM policies from the parent folder then if several projects are administered by the same team, you can put IAM policies into the parent folder instead of on the individual projects or resources. Trying to accomplish this without folders would require putting duplicate copies of the policy on each project and resource in turn, which would be very tedious and error prone.

The Organizational Node

Most organizations will want to use an organisational node to bring diverse projects and folders under one single administrative umbrella that provides full visibility and a place for centralised policy control over the entire organizations cloud infrastructure domain. This is not always the case when companies start investigating moving to the cloud. However it soon becomes obvious that recreating the organisations structure in the cloud is the most rapid path to migration. Therefore it is a good idea to organize all those diverse and autonomous projects and sprawling folders in your company under a single hierarchal structure. This can be considered the organization node as it provides the starting place to locate the domain administration, which allows you to apply policy centrally as it sits at the very top of the hierarchy.

To understand the benefits of reproducing the organizational node based hierarchy in the cloud we need to consider some of the features that it brings you. An organizational node has some special roles, for example, you can designate an organization policy administrator. Having centralized administration can enforce company administrative policy such as Identity and Access Management (IAM) across the organisation i.e. the policy can establish default behaviour across all folders and projects. It also ensures that only people with organisational administrative privileges can change company-wide policies.

You can also assign a project creator role, this allows the organisational administrator to delegate responsibility to an individual project manager, which is a great way to allow them autonomy and to manage the resources they consume and control the money they spend.

However, if you have an organizational node, with a hierarchy of folders and projects below then you need to understand the flow of policy and permissions. For example there are some GCP resources such as data storage buckets, which let you apply access policies at the individual resource level. Therefore, we must understand how policies are inherited and how some seemingly conflicting policies are resolved.

The first key point is that the organization unit is at the top of the hierarchy and the place for central administration of policies. Importantly these centralized policies are inherited downwards in the hierarchy. Therefore, setting policies at the organizational unit level will automatically be inherited by all the hierarchy – the underlying folders, projects and resources. But that doesn't mean they are definitive in fact it is far from it. Indeed, policies applied at the lower folders or even at the resources level may take precedence. To understand why this happens we need to take a closer look at the hierarchy starting with the organisational node.

So how do you get an organization node?

If you are an existing G Suite customer then you will have a G Suite domain and as such an organizational node therefore any GCP projects will automatically belong to your organization node. But if you are not a G-Suite customer then you can use Google cloud identity to create one.

However once you get your new organization node, the default operation is to allow anyone in the domain to be able to create projects and billing accounts. This is necessary to prevent disruption during a transition so everyone retains the same rights as before.

Thus the first step must be to apply the organizational administrative policy to the new organization node.

Once you have an organization node, you can create folders underneath it and put in projects.

Here's an example of how you might organize all your GCP resources:

Figure-2

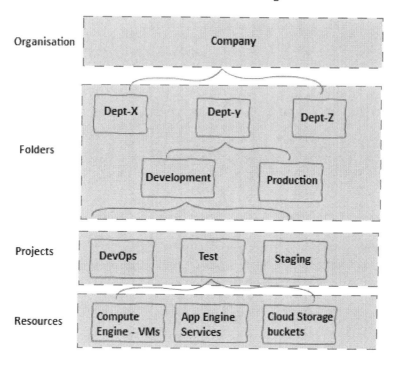

There are three folders directly beneath the organisational node labelled Company they are; "Dept-X", "Dept-Y", and "Dept-Z". In this example, if we consider the folder for "Dept-Y" we can see that it has been separated into two folders, Development and Production. Each folder contains their own projects or other child folders, and within the Development folder, there are three projects, DevOps, Test, and Staging and each will contain the resources needed for the specific project. Thus we can see that the Test project contains the resources; Compute Engine-VMs, App Engine Services and Cloud Storage buckets. What is crucial to remember here is that folders are just like any other resources in that they inherit the policies of their parent.

For instance, if you set a policy at the organization level, it will automatically be inherited by all its children folders as well as their folders and projects and ultimately the projects own resources. This means that the inheritance is transitive and that is one important rule to keep in mind.

However, that is great for applying general organizational policy across the board but many departments may need autonomous control of their access policies on their own projects and resources. This means that they could potentially provide access to resources that contradict the organizational unit's access policy. Therefore we need to understand which rules take precedence. In CGP the policies implemented at a higher level in this hierarchy can't take away access that's granted at a lower level.

For example, suppose that a policy applied on the Test GCP project gives a user the right to modify a cloud storage bucket, but an inherited policy at the organization level says that the user can only view cloud storage buckets and not change them. Then there will be a clear conflict. Therefore the second rule to understand and remember is that the more generous policy is the one that takes effect. In this example the user will have access to modify the cloud storage bucket despite this grant being applied lower down the hierarchy it is the more generous policy.

Identity and Access Management (IAM)

Many enterprises and large companies today deploy their own on-premise Identity and Access Management solutions in order to assist them in applying robust and coherent identity and access polices across the entire organization's infrastructure. Moving all or part of their operations to the cloud will require that they have the same consistent policies across the virtual parts of their business. Google Cloud Identity & Access Management (Cloud IAM) thus lets administrators apply the same granular polices so that they can authorize who can take action on what resources. In short Cloud IAM gives you all the granular control and visibility to manage cloud resources.

Cloud IAM is designed to scale to meet the requirements of even large enterprises with complex organizational structures, hundreds of workgroups, and potentially thousands of projects. Cloud IAM provides a central and unified view into applying security policy across your entire organization, with additional auditing capabilities to ease compliance processes.

Cloud IAM is the service that administrators use to authorize who can take action on specific resources within the GCP. An IAM policy whether on-premises or in the cloud typical has two parts. One part determines and identifies the user, which is the identity function in so much as it is responsible for the identification and authentication of the user. There is then the access part, and this determines what the user is authorized to do and on what resource.

The identity part of IAM will name the user or users you're addressing in the policy rules and in Cloud IAM policy this can be defined by a Google account, a Google group, a Service account, an entire G Suite, or a Cloud Identity domain.

The access policy which is what rights and permissions that the user has been given is defined by an IAM role. Thus a Cloud IAM policy will define by a Google account or ID combined with a Role.

The Purpose of an IAM Role

If you have ever considered applying access permissions in windows or Linux at the file system levels you will undoubtedly recognise that to do any meaningful work you need to apply a combination of permissions. This is no different in IAM.

For example, to manage instances in a project, you will need to have the permissions to create, delete, start, stop, and change an instance. Of course other users may need to have only read access, others read, write and modify, while managers and administrators would require full access across many of the resources within the project. However, that is only manageable on a per user basis in very small organizations.

The typical way around this conundrum is to group the permissions that are typically needed for a job function all together into a role. This then makes IAM much easier to manage and much less error prone.

Cloud IAM Role Types

There are three kinds of roles in Google's Cloud IAM service, which you can use depending on your requirements. The categories of role types are primitive roles, predefined roles and custom role types.

Primitive Roles

The first type is what is known as the Primitive roles as these are very broadly defined. You apply them to a GCP project and they affect all resources in that project. The broad roles are; the Owner, Editor, and the Viewer.
Thus, If you're designated the role of a viewer on a given resource, you can examine it but not change its state.
On the other hand If you're designated the role of an editor, you can do everything that a viewer can do, plus change its state.
Finally, if you are privileged to have an owner role, you can do everything an editor can do, plus they can manage rolls and permissions on the resource. Moreover, the owner role on a project also let you do one more very important task and that is to set up billing. However that might not be compatible with your company's internal policy.

The reason that the owner is also given the billing task is that they are typically in charge of the resources and responsible for the budgets. But in many organizations there are strict rules governing finance and spending. Therefore, a new role is created that of the Billing Admin role, which allows the administrator to delegate the authorisation for billing for a project to a user without giving them the right to change the resources in the project. In this way we can separate the owner's access permissions from the billing permissions. For example, you may want to grant someone other than the owner the billing administrator role, such as the project manager or a finance employee.

A word of warning though about primitive roles as they may be too coarsely defined and not granular enough to provide the separation of duties required in most teams. This is especially true if you have several people working together on a project that contains sensitive data. In that scenario, primitive roles are probably too course to be fit for purpose.

Predefined Roles

In order to address this shortfall, GCP Cloud IAM provides a finer grained version of role types that cover many more job types and task scenarios. These refined GCP services offer their own sets of predefined roles and they define where those roles can be applied.

For example, Compute Engine, which offers virtual machines as a service offers a set of predefined roles. You are then able to apply these refined roles to Compute Engine resources in a specific project, a folder, or across an entire organizational unit.

By applying refined roles for example those provided for the Compute Engines VMs such as the InstanceAdmin Role lets you pass the required permissions to anyone designated that role to perform a certain set of actions on virtual machines. Thus they will be able to list all VMs within that project, read and modify their configurations, as well as change their state by starting and stopping them.

Custom Roles

However, as we have seen if you designate a user to be in the InstantAdmin role for VMs that will apply to all instances of VMs within that project. In many cases this may still be too broad and you may need something even finer-grained. To address the requirements for highly specific and fine grained roles Cloud IAM introduces custom roles. The requirement for custom roles is driven by many companies adhering to a least privileged access model in which each person in the organization has the minimum amount of privilege needed to do his or her job. So, for example, maybe you will need to define a Role that has the inherent permissions to allow a user to start and stop Compute Engine and virtual machines, but not be allowed to reconfigure them. This would be a suitable case for an InstanceOperator role.
Because of this requirement Cloud IAM allows us to make custom roles, which allow you to customise a similar role by adding or removing some permission as we just saw when changing InstanceAdmin to the more restrictive InstanceOperator role.

There is however a couple of caveats we need to be aware of when using custom roles. First, if you decide to use custom roles you will need to manage their permissions manually. This is very like the manual granting of individual permissions to a group or resource as the interaction between permissions can be complex and unpredictable. This can make custom roles error prone and even security risks.

As a result, some companies require any custom roles to be thoroughly audited by a third party or a peer review before being assigned. Others have simply decided they'd rather stick with the predefined roles than accept the risk.

Another thing to be aware of is that custom roles can only be used at the project or organization levels, which rules them out at the folder level.

Service Accounts

So far in our discussion regards the Cloud IAM we have been addressing the situation where a user or a group of users require identification, authentication and then given access to a resource to perform tasks compatible with their role. However, there is also the very common scenario where one resource needs to interact and communicate with another resource. For example you may need to give permissions to a Compute Engine virtual machine, rather than to a person, in order to automate a process.

The way this is done is by the use of a service account.

For instance, you may have an application running in a virtual machine, such as a web server, that needs to communicate with another VM, which runs the business logic for the application. This VM in turn needs to store data in Google Cloud Storage, but you have to lock down the access so that only that virtual machine can directly access the data. In this scenario, you would create a service account to authenticate your VM webserver to the VM application and then only the VM application to the cloud storage.

The way that Service accounts work is that they are set up with an identity that corresponds to an email address. That is pretty straightforward but the authentication is less so as a VM cannot enter a password as we certainly do not want to be hard coding a password. Therefore, instead of hard coded passwords, the service accounts use cryptographic keys to access resources.

A simple example is if you consider that you have created a service account, which you have granted the InstanceAdmin Role. By having this role the service account could effectively be used to permit an application running in a VM to create, modify, and/or delete other instances. But the interesting thing about Service accounts are they are more than just identities as they are also resources so they can have their own IAM policies attached to it. This is very handy because service accounts also need to be managed. An example, is maybe Alice needs to manage what can use a given service account, while Bob just needs to be able to view them. Thus, you can give Alice an editor role in a service account and Bob can have the viewer role. This is just like granting roles for any other GCP resource.

However another thing to be aware of is that you can grant different groups of VMs in your project with different identities by creating different service accounts for each distinct group of VMs. Another convenience is that you can also change the permissions of the service accounts without having to recreate the member VMs.

If we consider a more complex example we can see this principle in action. So let us say that we have a very common design whereby we have an application that's implemented across a group of Compute Engine virtual machines.

However the design criteria demands that one component of your application needs to have an editor role on another project, but the other components must not have access.

In this case it is possible to manage both design criteria by creating two different service accounts, one for each subgroup of virtual machines.

Only the first service account will be granted privilege on the other project and this reduces the potential impact of a miscoded application or a compromised virtual machine affecting the other project.

Blended Security

In practice security is applied across the GCP through the blending of resource management, organisational policy and IAM rules. It is by combining strategically the policy, rules and privileges at those different tactical levels that we can obtain the fine grained policies that deliver the security principles of separation, maintainability and simplicity.

Cloud Security Principles

Many companies that move to the cloud are concerned by the lack of transparent security controls and they wish to see a clear methodology that adheres to the basic cloud security principles of separation, maintainability and simplicity. However, what does that mean in real terms?

Ideally the principle addresses the security in the cloud where there may be issues with separation of data in multi-tenant environments. It might also raise security concerns due to its obscurity, which makes it difficult for administrators to maintain and reproduce a coherently policy that can be applied consistently without errors. Finally, there are concerns that simplicity in the cloud amounts to an incomprehensible web of security controls. The way that GCP addresses security is through blended controls that delivers on separation through the use of IAM, folders, projects and firewall ACLs to segregate multi-tenant data. Also it uses the strengths and flexibility of IAM to provide granular permissions tied to roles for users and groups to access or be denied access to resources. Finally, the blending of these GCP security controls demonstrates the simplicity of administration and in applying RBAC, firewall rules, subnets and user authentication constraints at granular level across the organisation to fine tune the access policy. For an example of blended security control let us take a brief look at a common use case where we could apply these important security principles;

A business wishes to move to the cloud but they have concerns due to their business model, which demands collaborating with partners and supply chain democratisation. They want to open up some of their resources to their partners but not all. They also want to be confident that the partners can only access what they grant them and no more. However, the issue is that some individuals need further access to other departments such as IT for posting project documentation as well as HR to post their timesheets.

The way the company could address this is through a blend of security controls. Initially they could contain the shared project within its own folder that would provide separation from other business units in both directions. Then they could provide IAM access rights to that folder and assign them to a specific group that had specific access only to the project folder and no others. The problem comes when some employees need cross reference access across projects but for only one purpose. In this case we could create a GCP IAM group that had access to read/write to their home project but also access to post to a specific resource for the timesheet repository as well as to the IT code repository but with no access to any other resource. We could do this in other ways, which we will learn later but for now this is an elegant solution.

Study Use Case -2

The client ABC returns to you with a request for more details on your proposal; 1) to provide cloud based business continuity and disaster recovery solution. This time they are concerned more about the security of the GCP cloud and how they could convince their management and stakeholders that the data was secure and stored under conditions compliant with regulatory best practices. Point 2), they are also looking at automation and how the solution could work autonomously rather than having IT copying data across from the production servers to the storage/archive servers. Point 3), how can they ensure the principles of separation, maintenance and simplicity with regards security in their cloud environment? How can you answer their concerns and also provide a workable solution for an automated hands free solution to data archiving.
Solution
There are a number of security controls that you can address to reassure the client regards the security of data stored in the cloud such as data by default is encrypted within GCP at rest and in flight. Hence data is encrypted when in the database and archived storage and also when traversing the network. Moreover a secure VPN is used to encrypt and provide for privacy when traversing the internet. These controls ensure the integrity of the data at all times. Should the client still have concerns you could suggest that they encrypt their data before sending to the cloud or bring their own encryption keys but that's not really advisable unless they have experience in key management.
The second concern regarding automation can be fulfilled using service accounts to manage the archiving of data using IAM. A service account allows a VM instance to be granted privileges and so its application can then perform autonomous actions such as handling a data archive process without any user intervention.

When addressing point 3, you could stress the importance of taking a blended view towards security controls such as merging hierarchy controls such as folders with IAM. You could explain how together they could control the separation, authentication and authorization of users while enforcing the access permission they are entitled too and no more. You could also explain about how projects and folders enforce separation by default. But also how you can relax that separation by allowing restricted privileges and access for employees. This can be accomplished by placing them in an IAM group, which has access to both the Production and Development environments despite them being in different projects or folders. This can be demonstrated quite readily through a prototype in GCP.

Chapter 3 - Interacting with Google Cloud Platform

Introduction

There are perhaps four ways you can interact with Google Cloud Platform, some are easier than others and you will be introduced to each in turn but we will in this book tend to stress the shell code method. These diverse methods of interaction are led by specifically the Console, this is the most interactive way for someone to control and configure the Cloud infrastructure. The problem is that as a web interface it requires the user to understand the steps required in order to configure a resource as well as to find their way about the GUI, which can be slow and time consuming.

On the other hand the SDK and Cloud Shell provides a way to configure the GCP through using command line scripts and this means that you can develop a library of scripts that can be easily customized to create any resource you require. Once you have such a library of configuration scripts you can provision infrastructure in seconds.

In addition there is the Mobile App, which is simply another device orientated method for utilising the web or script methods of configuration. The final method is far more interesting as it uses APIs to provide the software templates that are required to input the crucial operational data that is required to trigger the Application Programmable Interfaces (APIs). An interesting point is regardless of whether you are using the console, cloud shell or the mobile app you are ultimately interacting with GCP cloud through the APIs.

The GCP Console

The GCP Console is a web-based administrative interface and dashboard, which provides an administrator with a graphical user interface with an easy point and click action. The console is designed for administrative use only, so if you build an application in GCP, you'll most likely use the console or at least at first, but the end users of your applications do not have access to it. This is because the console lets you as the administrator view and manage all your projects and all the resources they use. It also lets you enable, disable and explore the APIs of GCP services. Also from the console GUI you can conveniently access Cloud Shell.

Cloud Shell

The Cloud Shell is a command-line interface to GCP that's easily accessed from your browser. From Cloud Shell, you can use the tools provided by the Google Cloud Software Development kit (SDK) without having to first install them somewhere. Whereas the console is a great graphical interface for creating and modifying resources as it is based upon check boxes and drop down menus to assist you in configuration options. However, it can be slow and tedious if you have to configure or modify many resources. This is where the Cloud Shell command line excels as it can run shell scripts. This means you can execute a customised shell script to create resources such as several VMs very quickly and automatically.

Unfortunately many administrators that are new to GCP work through the console but conversely you will find that experienced professionals work almost exclusively using Cloud Shell. This is not them showing off, it's just once you have built up a library of basic functional scripts say for creating VMs or storage buckets, its far quicker, less tedious and a much more efficient way of working. In this book we will concentrate primarily on Cloud Shell running the SDK commands because once you understand and become familiar with customising scripts and handling the configuration options then reverting back to using the console GUI becomes highly intuitive. Also explaining scripts doesn't require hundreds of screenshots.

The GCP Software Development Kit

The Google Cloud SDK is a set of command line tools that you can use to manage your resources and your applications on GCP. The easiest way to get to the SDK commands is to click the Cloud Shell button on a GCP Console.

The SDK includes the gcloud tool, which provides all the main command line interface commands for Google Cloud Platform products and services. These are all the functional commands you will use when creating and administering VMs and containers. In addition there is also the gsutil set of commands, which is for Google Cloud Storage and there is another specialized bq command set, which is for BigQuery.

The SDK is stand-alone software that you can download and install anywhere, such as on your laptop or on-premises server or even in another cloud, it doesn't matter. The SDK is also available as a docker image, which makes it really easy to download and install in a VM. The most convenient way is to access it via the command line in your console web browser on a virtual machine with all these commands already installed.

Using APIs

The important thing to understand is that the services that make up GCP provide application programming interfaces (APIs) so that the code you write can access and control them. Hence, when you write scripts and execute them in the Cloud Shell you are directly interfacing and consuming the APIs of the relevant GCP services.

These APIs that the services offer are what are called RESTful, which means they adhere to the representational state transfer model. For now all we need to know about RESTful APIs are that they are the standard way of passing information between an API and a client, which simply means that your code will consume Google services using the same methods that web browsers talk to web servers i.e. through URLs.

Therefore we find that because they are based on RESTful the GCP APIs will reference the resources and GCP services using URLs. This is a convenient way to connect and pass your code and any information to GCP.

The APIs present or offer preconfigured services that you write your code to interact with. But although this is programming and its code that you are writing you cannot just pass them anything for the code must adhere to a strict form, which is much like a template. This makes customizing templates very easy even for non-coders as it just requires the substitution of key parameters. What is more is that the APIs use JSON which is very readable for humans so it is a popular way of passing textual information over the web.

As the SDK is very powerful you will need to secure access to it and there's an open system for user log in and access control. You can also conveniently browse through the library of available APIs within the console browser and this is where you can turn on and off any APIs. By default many APIs will be switched off as many are associated with quotas and limits.

By having the APIs deactivated by default protects you from inadvertently using resources. Therefore, it is a best practice to enable only those APIs you need and then you can request increases in quotas if or when you need more resources. However you must be careful when using APIs for managing quotas and system resources as they can be quite tricky to predict. For example, if you're writing an application that needs to control GCP resources, you'll first need to experiment with the correct APIs to ensure you get the adjustments just right. Fortunately GCP has a tool for this and it's called the APIs Explorer.

Using the API Explorer

The GCP hosts many APIs and as we have just seen some of these are used to control limits and quotas so need careful planning. However the GCP console includes a tool called the APIs Explorer that enables you to interactively try out the APIs and learn about their use even with just basic user authentication. API Explorer also lets you see what APIs are available and in what versions. But as we saw earlier APIs expect parameters and some will be required while other may be optional so to understand the APIs functionality and whether it is appropriate for our use we need access to the documentation. Fortunately, all the GCP API documentation is built in and accessible through the explorer.

API Client Libraries

If we consider the scenario that you have explored GCP for a suitable API and you are confident that you can provide it with its required parameters so now you're ready to build an application that uses it. Now the great thing about APIs is that you can build applications using APIs and some glue code so you don't have to start coding the application from scratch.

Indeed to make life even easier for non-coders Google provides client libraries that take a lot of the skill out of the task of calling GCP services via the APIs from your code.

The GCP contains two kinds of libraries. Google clouds latest and recommended libraries for the GCP hosted APIs are called the Cloud Client Libraries and they adopt the native styles and idioms of each language.

On the other hand, the Google API Client Library is available for your desired language if for some reason a Cloud Client Library doesn't support the newest services and features.

Regardless of which you use you will find that these libraries are designed for generality and completeness. You will also find that utilising these libraries to bring GCP APIs into your code will take a lot of the drudgery out of coding your application.

Finally, to return back to administration there is one more tool that is of interest in today's mobile world, the mobile App for Android and iOS. This mobile application lets you view and manage the resources you're using at GCP by allowing you to build your own custom dashboards so that you can get all the information you need at a glance.

Google Cloud Launcher

A key advantage to cloud over on-premises is the time it takes to provision an application server. After all it might take all day to build a real server with the OS and the environment and software stack. But with cloud many application servers can be provisioned in minutes. Hence, if you would like to try out Google Cloud Platform and a quick way to get started with GCP, with minimal effort is to use the Cloud Launcher tool.

The Google Cloud Launcher enables you to get started quickly by deploying functional software packages on Google Cloud platforms. Everything is provisioned automatically; including the software stack, the optimal environment settings and all dependencies so there's no need to manually configure the software, virtual machine instances, and storage or network settings. Although, you can still do that by modifying many of the settings before you launch if you have specific custom requirements.

Moreover, not only do these application packages come preconfigured with the latest versions and security patches. Many of the latest software packages in Cloud Launcher are provided at no additional fee so long as they are open source. However, there will be some proprietary software packages within Cloud Launcher and they do charge user's fees, particularly those published by vendors who require a commercial license for their software. However, before you provision the software the Cloud Launcher will show you estimates of the monthly charges, so make sure you are comfortable with the fees before you launch the software image.

Moreover, you should be aware that these estimates are for the software it doesn't take into account network usage as that depends a lot on how you use the application which cannot be determined prelaunch.

In addition, GCP will continuously manage updates and security patches to the base images for the software packages to fix critical issues and vulnerabilities. However, it does not update the software after it's been deployed this is necessary to prevent any disruption or breakage of a deployed and working application.

Therefore you may need to check that your application works on the latest version and update level before you deploy any upgrade. Despite those caveats however using Cloud Launcher is a way to expedite the provisioning of applications and to ensure a consistent stack throughout your environment.

Use case -3

Things are going well with your proposal to ABC and you have been asked in again to answer some awkward questions such as how do we as the client organisational administrators allow other departments to have autonomy over their respective projects so that they can interact with their own GCP project infrastructure? Now you have to answer a serious question as to how you give project administrators and developers the same rights and privileges that are inherent in their on-premise environments but also restrict the access rights of other team members. The problem being is that as a startup company employees multitask and have several job functions dependent on the project or task. Therefore it is not easy to identify a specific role and then delegate a role to an individual so they need something more flexible as job roles are fluid. There is also the problem of how do they directly interface with the Cloud Infrastructure as there are several potential solutions and they are not sure which the best way is.

Solution

One approach you could take is to propose the company deploys IAM using custom roles. In this way you could assign each employee the actual base privileges that they need to do their job but still restrict them access to all other areas. For example, you could grant permissions for custom access to roles then apply these to specific groups that have will have access to both the Production and Development environments but deny these groups access to HR and Finance. Although creating custom roles and groups per individual is not recommended as it soon becomes unsustainable in large organization. However, in a startup company with few employees it can be the preferred method of deploying IAM. Creating custom roles for each employee that performs multi-roles within the business is the best way to provide the access required while still maintaining the principle of least privilege.

With regards interacting with the GCP you could inform them of the benefits of each of the methods; the console, Cloud Shell, which is the command line using the SDK, APIs for programming, and templates and scripts for automating tasks or for running batch tasks using Cloud Shell.

Chapter 4 - Compute Engine and Virtual Machines

Introduction

The way that most organisations migrate their applications to the cloud is by using a lift and shift methodology. By doing so the architects are trying to replicate the on-premise environment in the cloud by using virtual machines to mimic real world servers. This is the most common way to run workloads in the cloud. Indeed this is the most intuitive way as Compute Engine lets you replicate your data centre configuration and then run your applications within virtual machines on Google's global infrastructure. In this chapter, we'll learn how Google Compute Engine works with a focus on Google virtual networking.

Now for those of you that are new to virtual computing the best thing about virtual machines is that they have the power in generality of a full-fledged server with an operating system running in each instance. This is how in on-premise servers you could run several VMs with each one running a different OS, such as Windows Server, Ubuntu, Linux Red Hat, etc. and all share the common hardware resources such as CPU, I/O bus, network, memory, disk, etc.

We saw previously that a quick and clean method for getting started with GCP is to use Cloud Launcher to provision applications and a proprietary software stack as a package along with the underlying virtual infrastructure that they need to run. In the cloud this is how Google uses the same technique of virtualisation to make the most efficient use of shared hardware through multi-tenancy models whereby many diverse customers may be hosted on the same physical server.

Hence, you will configure a virtual machine much like you build out a dedicated physical server by specifying its amounts of CPU power and memory, along with the desired amounts and types of storage and its operating system. You can flexibly reconfigure them, however, and a VM running on Google's cloud has then got global network connectivity.

Virtual Private Cloud (VPC)

Cloud Launcher has its uses but the other way a lot of people get started with GCP is to define their own Virtual Private Cloud (VPC). In this context we consider a VPC as being your own cloud virtual network. It is an on-demand configurable pool of shared computing resources allocated within the GCP environment. This shared pool does however provide a certain level of isolation between the different organizations using the resources.

Figure-

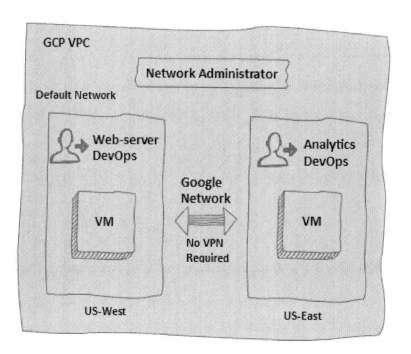

Another important component of a VPC is it provides the critical internetworking between resources, such as VMs. It does this in a global and flexible way to ensure that all your cloud based resources and services can interact with one another. Thus a popular way to get started in GCP is through creating a VPC.
 When you start out you can create the PVC inside your first GCP project, or you can simply choose the default VPC and use that. Regardless, your VPC provides the networking capabilities and services to connect your Google Cloud platform resources to each other and to the internet.

Basic Cloud Networking

Google's GCP provides you with the concept of the VPC which to all intent and purposes resembles your own private network. It also provides the underlying networking required to connect your cloud resources to each other and the internet. This networking service is typically automated and requires no intervention from you. However if you like you can do many of the network tasks that you perform on your on-premises network such as you can segment your networks, use firewall rules to restrict access to instances, and create static routes to forward traffic to specific destinations. However there is a key difference between your on-premise networking and Google GCP networks. Google's GCP is built upon a Software Defined Network which can be considered to be one vast layer-2 network with global reach. Thus the Virtual Private Cloud networks that you define will have global scope. This means that they can have subnets in any GCP region worldwide and importantly the subnets can span the zones that make up a region. This architecture makes it easy for you to build redundancy into your design as there will be very low latency between resources in different zones as they are on the same subnet and communicating at layer-2 much like they were connected to the same switch. This is perfect for business continuity as a failure in one zone can be addressed seamlessly by the resources in another zone. Moreover the SDN architecture makes it easy to define your own network layout with a global scope as in addition to supporting resources in different zones on the same subnet, you can dynamically increase the size of a subnet in a custom network by expanding the range of IP addresses allocated to it without affecting the already configured VMs.

In this example, your VPC has one network.

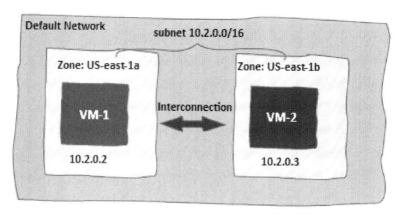

Figure -4

So far, it has one subnet defined in GCP us-east1 region. Notice that it has two Compute Engine VMs attached to it.

They are neighbours on the same subnet even though they are in different zones.

You can use this capability to build solutions that are resilient but still have simple network layouts.

The Fundamentals of Compute Engine and VMs

Compute Engine is the GCP service that allows you to create and run virtual machines on Google infrastructure. In contrast to on-premises servers there are no upfront investments and you can provision and run thousands of virtual CPUs on a system. Moreover the systems are designed to be fast and to offer consistent performance.

You can create a virtual machine instance by using the Google cloud platform console or the gcloud command line tool and you can run Linux and Windows Server images that are provided by Google or use your own customized versions of these images. For example you can even import your corporate custom server images from your physical servers.

Creating a VM

CPU

When you create a VM, the first decision is to pick a machine type which determines how much memory and how many virtual CPUs it has. These selectable choices range in size from micro to behemoth but if you can't find a suitable predefined type that meets your needs perfectly, you can always make a custom VM.

Speaking of using custom processing power, if you have workloads like machine learning and heavy data processing that can take advantage of GPUs and even TPUs, then you should be aware that GCP provides GPUs as well as Google's own TPUs (Tensor Processing Units) and these are also available for you to use.

The Google developed TPU is their custom application-specific integrated circuit (ASIC) tailored for machine learning workloads on TensorFlow it was developed as a cloud based rival to Nvidia's GPU for handling heavy machine learning workloads.

Storage

The next decision is what type of storage you want your VM to use. VM are like physical computers they need disks to store persistent data. You can choose two kinds of persistent storage, standard or SSD.

The importance of the term persistent is that it lets us know that the data will survive the termination or deletion of the host VM. For example, a persistent drive is actually an external storage area which we can separate from the VM itself. For example we can elect to delete a VM but to retain its data i.e. the persistent disk.

However there is another type of disk storage that is very fast and should you have a requirement in your application for very high performance scratch space, you may want to attach a local SSD. However, a local SSD is part of the VM so be sure to store data of any permanent value somewhere else because local SSD's content doesn't survive when the VM terminates. Because of this you cannot separate a VM and a local SSD disk as you can with a persistent disk. Anyway, most people will begin with using the standard persistent disks and that's the default.

Another convenient aspect of VM is taking backups. Once your VMs are running it is easy to take a durable snapshot of their disks. These are useful as backups but they also are required when you need to move a VM to another region.

The Boot Image

The next step is that you choose a boot image. As we have discussed already GCP offers a wide selection of Linux and Windows versions that are pre-configured but if you want you can import your own images. Indeed, a common request made by GCP customers is that they want their VMs to always boot with a specific configuration, such as installing specific updates or packages at boot time.

Therefore it is common for people to use GCP VM start-up scripts that will control the start process by following the commands in the script. But you can via the scripts also pass into the VM other kinds of metadata.

Pre-emptive

Another factor you might want to consider is if you want to make your VM pre-emptible. You can save a lot of money if you choose to use pre-emptible VMs where they are appropriate. However pre-emptible VM are only suitable in certain use-cases as they behave differently from ordinary VMs. The difference is that with a pre-emptive VM you are effectively agreeing to allow the Compute Engine to terminate the VM should its resources be needed elsewhere and you will only get around 30 seconds warning. Furthermore a pre-emptive VM is guaranteed to be terminated after 24 hours if it hasn't already been pre-empted. However, if deployed wisely you can save a lot of money - around 80% discount - using pre-emptible VMs in the right scenarios, but be sure to make sure that your workloads are able to be stopped and restarted gracefully.

Auto-scaling

Auto-scaling is another factor to consider because despite the fact you can create huge VMs - the maximum number of virtual CPUs in the VM is 96 and the maximum memory size in beta is at 624 gigabytes – and these huge VMs are great for workloads like in-memory databases and CPU intensive analytics but you may not want to start off at that size.

For example, most GCP customers start off by scaling out, not scaling up. What that means is they add more standard sized VMs to loadbalance across, this is called horizontal scaling, rather than increasing the size of their existing VMs, which is known as vertical scaling.

When it comes to horizontal scaling VMs Compute Engine has a feature called auto scaling that lets you add and take away VMs from your application based on load metrics.

However to get that to work effectively there is a need for a robust load balancing function that can handle the intelligent balancing of the incoming traffic across the group of VMs. To help with this Google VPC supports several different kinds of load balancing, which we will cover in detail later.

Cloud Networking Revisited

Much like physical networks, VPCs have their own routing tables that are populated with the shortest routing information that we will use to forward traffic from one instance to another instance within the same network, across sub-networks and even between GCP zones without requiring any external IP addresses. By using private RFC1918 addresses rather than routing external IP addresses to communicate between VPCs ensures lower latency. VPCs routing tables are built in to the VPC so you don't have to provision or manage a router. Moreover, with GCP you don't have to provision or manage a firewall instance as a VPC comes with a global distributed firewall. However even though you do not manage a firewall instance you can still control or restrict access to instances for both incoming and outgoing traffic. The way that this is done is by defining firewall rules or you can use metadata tags on Compute Engine instances, whichever you find is more convenient. For example, you can tag all your web servers with a tag, web, and then write a firewall rule, which states that all traffic arriving on ports 80 or 443 with the tag, web, is allowed into all VMs, no matter what the source or destination IP address happens to be.

Something that may cause some initial confusion is that VPCs belong to specific GCP projects. That is fine if your company only has one project or if projects are required to be strictly segregated but more often a company will have many GCP projects and the VPCs do need to communicate.

If that is the scenario then you may simply want to establish a peering relationship between two VPCs so that they can exchange their routing information – subnets by default – so that they can then exchange traffic, that's what VPC peering does.

On the other hand, if you want to have finer control such as you want to utilise IAM to control who and what in one project can interact with a VPC in another project then that's what a shared VPC is for.

A shared VPC allows an organization to connect resources from multiple projects to a common VPC network. The goal is to allow the VPCs to communicate with each other securely and efficiently using internal IP addresses. If or when this happens you use what is known as a shared VPC. In this case you designate one project (VPC) as the host project and then attach one or several other service projects to it in order to share resources. A shared VPC also allows the organization administrator to delegate responsibilities, such as creating and managing instances to the service project admins, while maintaining centralized control of the network.

Load Balancing

Earlier when we discussed VMs and how VMs could auto scale under fluctuating loads by scaling sideways by increasing the number of available VMs we didn't address how do your customers get to your application. The issue is that with horizontal scaling the number of available VMs will change so it might be provided by four VMS one moment and 40 VMS at another? We briefly explained that it would require intelligent load balancing but what it really requires is Cloud Load Balancing.

Cloud Load Balancing

Cloud Load Balancing is fully distributed software and a defined managed service for all your traffic. Because the load balancers are a managed service and they don't run in the VMs that you have to manage, you don't have to worry about scaling or managing them. Therefore you can place Cloud Load Balancing in front of all your traffic, HTTP and HTTPS, other TCP and SSL traffic, and UDP traffic too.

With Cloud Load Balancing, a single 'anycast' IP front ends all your backend instances in regions around the world. The Load Balancers in the region closest to the traffic source will receive the traffic as its using anycast and this also provides the cross-region load balancing, including automatic multi-region failover.

In addition to its anycast functions Cloud Load Balancing reacts quickly to changes in users, traffic, backend health, and many network conditions, which will result in traffic being gently moved in small fractions if the backends start to become unhealthy.

Although you do not have to manage or administer the load balancing as it is a managed service you do need to select the correct type of load balancer to match your traffic. For example if you want a cross-regional load balancing for a web application, then you would want to use HTTPS load balancing.

However, there are several types of global load balancers available so you would want to use the global SSL proxy load balancer for Secure Sockets Layer traffic that is not HTTP.

Or if its TCP traffic that does not use Secure Sockets Layer, then you would want to use the global TCP proxy load balancer. But those two proxy services only work for specific port numbers, and they only work for TCP.

So if you want to load balance UDP traffic or traffic on any port number, you can still load balance across a GCP region with the regional load balancer.

Additionally, all those versions of the load balancing services are intended for traffic coming into the Google network from the internet. Therefore if you are looking to load balance traffic within the GCP such as between the presentation layer and the business logic layer of your application then you would need to use another type called the internal load balancer.

The internal load balancer will accept traffic on a GCP internal IP address and load balance it across Compute Engine VMs. We will discuss how to deploy and use the internal load balancer later.

Google DNS Service

A good example of Google's cloud infrastructures reliability and global reach is demonstrated via the Google DNS service on IP address 8.8.8.8 which provides a public domain name service to the world.

Google's global DNS is the public network service that translates the internet host names used in URLs to public IP addresses. It does this by looking up the registry for the public IP addresses that the network needs to be able to establish communications.

DNS is one of those unsung heroes of the internet because without it everything just stops working. Despite this DNS has been rather neglected over the years but came to more widespread attention when several of the main DNS providers came under denial of service attacks rendering large portions of the internet unreachable.

Google has a highly developed DNS infrastructure that by its global scale protects it against denial of service attacks. Google makes 8.8.8.8 a freely available managed service so that everybody can take advantage of it and Google is so confident in this service that it is the only one that they provide with a 100% SLA.

DNS servers resolve registered hostnames to public IP addresses so this begs the question as to how will the internet host names and addresses of applications you build in GCP be registered if the IP addresses are register to Google but assigned to you.

This why GCP offers the Cloud DNS service, it is to help the world find your applications and services. Cloud DNS is another managed DNS service running on the same infrastructure as Google so it has the same global reach, low latency and high availability making it a cost effective way to make your applications and services available to your users. The way it works is that although the Cloud DNS is a managed service it is also programmable. This enables you to publish and manage millions of DNS zones and records using the GCP console, the command line interface or the API. The DNS information you publish will be served from Google's data centre locations around the world.

Content Delivery

Google has infrastructure and network locations in regions and zone around the globe and this gives it a global system of geographically diverse edge caches. You can use these edge caches to accelerate content delivery in your application using Google Cloud CDN. What this means is that if your services are built in a US zone then customers in another region such as Asia will need to traverse the globe to reach your content in the US. However as Google have data centres in many zones in Asia or any region for that matter, it can host your content in a cache close to the customer. By presenting your content closer to them means your customers will experience lower network latency.

Furthermore, your original content services will experience reduced load as requests are now offloaded to the regional caches and so you can save money on network charges too.

Also it's another managed service which means it is easy to deploy as all you have to do is set up the HTTPS load balancing and then simply enable Cloud CDN with a single checkbox.

You may already be using CDN from a third party provider as there are lots of other CDNs out there. But that should not be a problem as Google runs the CDN interconnect partner program so if your CDN provider is a member then you can continue to use it.

Connecting to the GCP

One attraction of the cloud is that you can spin up VMs quickly and cheaply and that allows you to build a development infrastructure that is segregated from your production network. This is the reason that many organisations start with cloud deployments as it gives the development or project teams their own space to experiment and try out proof of concept or build prototypes cost effectively. However, eventually you may want to create a production environment and many GCP customers want to do that. The problem of course is that you will eventually need to interconnect your on-premises or other cloud networks to the Google VPCs. This causes a significant issue as when you first build the PVC you can operate and test it out using just an internet connection. However, when you want to move to production you will need to be able to replicate your on-premises infrastructure in the cloud. This will mean constructing cost-effective communication channels between your network and Goggles cloud. After all you may need to transfer 100's of gigabytes of date from an on-premises data base to cloud storage.

In order to meet the requirements of organisations GCP offers a selection of technology choices. For many customers the starting point will be through a web browser with the GCP environment segregated from the company's internal network. Running a development network in the PVC and accessing it via a browser is fine. However when you shift to production you will often find the need to upgrade to a Virtual Private Network (VPN) secure connection that runs over the internet using the IPSEC protocol. This will not only secure the connections but it will allow you to transport data, administer resources and interconnect as if the cloud is an extension of your own on-premises network.

A basic SSL browser connection is a very good starting solution when using Goggle cloud as it allows you to work in a development area that is segregated from your on-premises network. If you do wish to interconnect then all you have to do is install some static routes that point towards the subnets used in either network. For small deployments using static routing this is very desirable as it removes all of the complexity of dynamic routing protocols. After all it only requires one static route in each direction to direct traffic to a given network. The problem is that if you start to go to production then you may need many static routes installed that are continually changing.

To make the routing updates dynamic, then you have to use a router and a routing protocol and GCP uses a feature called cloud router. The managed service that is cloud router will analyse traffic and using algorithms learn and work out the best paths from your network to other connected networks. It will do this automatically and update your Google VPC exchange route information with any newly learned networks over the VPN using the Border Gateway Protocol (BGP).

BGP is however an external routing protocol that is only really required for internet scale networks. For instance, if you add a new subnet to your Google VPC, your on-premises network will automatically exchange routes with it and vice versa. This may or may not be what you want as some customers don't want to use the internet, either because of security concerns in so much as they do not wish to advertise their networks or because they feel they need more reliable and secure bandwidth.

If you do not want to use a VPN or a Cloud Router then you can consider peering with Google via a direct peering arrangement. PVC peering relates to collocation where you put your own router in the same public data center as a Google point of presence and then directly connect, share routes and exchange traffic. In order to facilitate this Google has more than 100 points of presence around the world, there are also many Internet Exchanges such as in London, New York and Frankfurt amongst many others that provide the same interconnect services.

However, for the many customers who are not located close to a point of presence there is still the possibility that they can contract with a partner in the carrier peering program to get connected. This would mean again collocating but at a closer and more convenient geographical zone.

A caveat of peering though is that it isn't covered by a Google service level agreement.

For customers who require five 9's reliability and availability for their interconnection with Google then they should consider using a dedicated interconnect in which customers get a direct private connections to Google.

The advantage here is that if these connections have topologies that meet Google's specifications, they can be covered by up to a 99.99 percent SLA. These connections can be backed up by a VPN for even greater reliability to provide a strong measure of business continuity.

Use case - 4

The client ABC returns with a request for more details on how they can give access to their different development sub-teams to the main Development project. These teams typically work autonomously on a single function or topic so are deployed within independent projects but they obviously need access to the main Development project that hosts the application.

Solution

The proposed solution that you could present is based upon using a shared-VPC for the main development project and allowing the other projects to share its resources. In this way their main Development project that hosts the app will be designated as the host project. The other projects that are configured to share those resources will be designated as service projects.

Figure -5

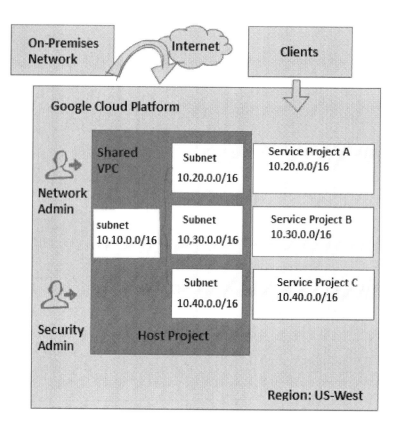

There are several caveats that you need to consider such as making sure that all projects are within the same folder – if you are using folders – you will also need to create a central administrator to manage all the projects. This means creating a central administrator role and giving them permissions to create new service projects as well as having the instant.admin role in each service project so that they can configure the networking.

To secure this environment you should recommend disabling the service projects external access so they can only access and be accessed by internal resources.

Chapter 5 – Cloud Data Storage

Application will almost always need to store some data, whether that be media to be streamed or sensor data from devices or customer account balances, or maybe simply the fact that they need to maintain session information via cookies. Moreover, we can see that different applications and workloads will often require diverse storage quotas, limits and solutions.

However in the cloud the available data storage options are quite diverse and you need to be specific about the type you select. You already know from earlier that you can store data on your VM's persistent disk or on SSD local disks.

But, Google Cloud Platform has other storage options to meet your needs as not all data is the same. Indeed data can be categorized into several groups; structured, semi-structured, unstructured, transactional, and relational data and they are best stored in a different format.

Cloud Storage Options

In this section we will discuss the core the diverse GCP storage options that have come about to address modern needs, these are: Cloud Storage, Cloud SQL, Cloud Spanner, Cloud Data Store and Google Big Table.

Why do we have different storage types you may ask? Simply it is because each storage type is best suited to the type and quantity of the data. This is due to data having some basic characteristic such as being structured or unstructured.

Figure -6

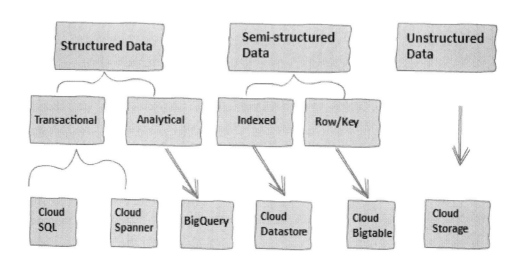

Structured Data

Structured data fits a predefined schema, which makes it possible for search engines to search, organize, and display your content. Structured data is representable, is in a standard format so is understandable and can communicate to search engines what your data means.

Examples of structured data include numbers, dates, and groups of words and numbers called strings that fit a predefined record. Structured data accounts for about 20 percent of the data that we handle and is the data you're probably used to dealing with. It's usually stored in a relational database.

Unstructured Data

Unstructured data is defined as being information that does not have either a pre-defined data structure or is not organized in a pre-prepared manner. Unstructured information is typically of an undetermined size; it can be text-heavy but may also contain data such as dates, numbers, and facts as well.

Examples of Unstructured Data often include text and multimedia content, such as e-mail messages, news articles, videos, photos, audio files, presentations, webpages and many other kinds of business documents of an undetermined size. As these data types size are typically unpredictable they are stored as data objects or rather as data blobs.

Whereas structured data is stored in predefined fields and records in an orderly database schema, unstructured data, due to its unpredictability is stored as an object, a lump of data, in a region of storage. In this case each data object can be accessed using its unique identifier or a more complex expression through attached metadata that refers to the object. In addition, each object has a unique data type.

As we will see each type of Google storage is designed for a specific purpose to store a type of data and perform a function that depends on your applications requirements. Therefore, you might want to use one or several of these services in combination to meet the storage requirements that best suits your data.

Google Cloud Storage

This is GCP's object file storage which means that instead of storing data in a schema or a file system it stores your data as an arbitrary bunch of bytes – a blob - and the storage system lets you address it with a unique key. Typically these unique keys are in the form of URL's which means object storage interacts nicely with Web technologies.

This is how Google's Cloud Storage works and as it is a form of object storage you don't have to provision capacity or develop a schema before you use it. What this means is that you simply make objects and the service stores them with high durability and high availability and references them via a URL.

Cloud Storage is suitable for many types of data storage requirements such as when serving website content, storing data for archival and even for storing data for disaster recovery.

Cloud Storage as we have seen is very web friendly as each of your objects in Cloud Storage has a URL this makes it an ideal method for making available to your end users large data objects via web download.

Google's Cloud Storage is a managed service and it stores your data for you in storage areas called buckets. You will initially create and configure your unique storage bucket then use it to hold your storage objects. The storage objects stored within a bucket are actually immutable, which means that you cannot edit them in place but instead you create new versions. In addition Cloud Storage always encrypts your data on the server side before it is written to disk and you don't pay extra for that.

Furthermore, in a Cloud storage bucket encryption is applied by default at rest and when data is in-transit using HTTPS. This makes it a convenient and secure way to initially move data from your on-premises servers or your computer into GCP. In this way Cloud Storage acts as an ideal landing post for your data before you move it onwards to other GCP storage services.

This is a good way to upload data into GCP as your Cloud Storage objects will be securely stored and organized into buckets. When you create a bucket, you give it a globally unique name and you specify a geographic location where the bucket and its contents are to be stored and you choose a default storage class.

Therefore, you need to consider a few things before you go ahead and pick a location as ideally you will want a location close to your customer base that will minimizes latency for your application and your end users.

In other words, if most of your users are in Europe, you probably want to pick a European location. There are also in some countries legal restriction about where your customers' data can be stored so for example in the European Union you must store their data within the EU unless you have their explicit permission to store it outside the EU. Therefore, it's best if you operate in Europe or have a large European user base to store your data in a region and zone in Europe.

Securing your Data

Your objects will be stored as encrypted data when it is at rest or in-flight but there will usually be others that need to access the data. Therefore, GCP provides several ways to control access to your objects and buckets. The preferred way to control access and assign user permissions is to use Cloud IAM. When you deploy IAM to authenticate and authorize users the most efficient way is for you to assign roles and the permission attached to each of the roles is inherited from project to bucket to object.

In some case you feel that you need finer control, in that case you can create access control lists (ACLs) that offer greater granularity for specific users. Typically you will use ACLs to define who has access to your buckets and objects and then what they are authorised to do. Hence, each ACL you configure will consists of a scope which defines who can perform the specified actions and this can be a specific user or group of users and a permission which defines what actions can be performed. For example, read or write. However when data is stored in a bucket then that Cloud Storage object becomes immutable so if you do need to change the object you have to create a new version. To help you keep track of the versions you can turn on object versioning on your buckets. If you do activate versioning, then Cloud Storage keeps a history of modifications. You can list the archived versions of an object, restore an object to an older state or permanently delete a version as needed. If you don't turn on object versioning, a new version always overrides an older version.

However with versioning there is the risk of junk accumulating so Cloud Storage also offers life-cycle management policies. In this case you could instruct Cloud Storage to keep only the three most recent versions of each object in a bucket that has versioning enabled. But the polies can be flexible so you could also delete objects older than 365 days or you could create a policy that will delete objects created before a certain date.

Cloud Storage Classes

Another important consideration when using Cloud storage is that you must choose the type of storage class that best suits your needs. There are four different types of storage classes: regional, multi-regional, nearline, and coldline. All of the storage classes are accessed in comparable ways using the cloud storage API and they all offer millisecond access types. However that's where the similarity ends.
Multi regional and regional are high performance object storage designed for frequent access, whereas nearline and coldline are designed for infrequent access for backup and archival storage and as we will learn they are priced accordingly.
You must be clear on the storage classes or you could pay over the odds for the wrong service class.

Regional vs. Multi Regional

Regional storage allows you to create your bucket and store your data in a specific GCP region for example, in US Central one, Europe West one or Asia East one. It's cheaper than multi regional storage but it offers less redundancy.

Multi regional storage on the other hand, is more expensive but it provides geographical redundancy. That means that when you pick multi-regional storage you select from a broad geographical location like the United States, the European Union, or Asia and cloud storage will then store your bucket and data in at least two geographic locations separated by at least 160 kilometres.

You would tend to want to use Multi regional storage for frequently accessed data such as for, website content, interactive workloads, or data that's part of mobile and gaming applications. Regional storage on the other hand is best for storing data that requires frequent access with high performance and low latency for data intensive computations. This make regional storage that is located close to their application running on their Compute Engine virtual machines a better option.

Nearline vs. Coldline

In GCP Cloud Storage there are two much cheaper options for storing infrequently accessed data. The options are Nearline and Coldline.

  Nearline storage can be considered to be a low cost, highly durable service for storing infrequently accessed data. Remember in all classes there is low latency access so lower performance is not an issue. The differences are in cost, which is based upon frequency of access i.e. data base read.

The Nearline storage class is a better approach to either multi regional storage or regional storage in scenarios where you plan to read or modify your data once a month or less.

A typical use case for Nearline storage class is when you want to run monthly analytics against a batch of data. In this scenario you can continuously add log files to your cloud storage bucket on a daily bases as there is no restrictions on adding data – restrictions apply to egress or read access - and then access the aggregated data once a month for analysis.

On the other hand, we have Coldline storage, which is a very low cost, highly durable service for data archiving, online backup, and disaster recovery. You can consider Coldline to be the best choice for data that you plan to access (egress/read) very rarely, less than once a year at most.

However Coldline has some caveats you must contemplate such as it has slightly lower availability, 90-day minimum storage duration, higher costs for data egress access, and higher networking costs for egress accessing of your data.

These additional costs are there to deter Coldline being used much like Nearline for monthly access as the additional egress access and data transport network costs would negate any cost benefit.

However when used correctly Coldline is a very low cost option as the addition access and network charges are insignificant when incurred annually. This makes Coldline storage ideal if you want to archive data but still have rapid access to it in case of a disaster recovery event.

Availability of these storage classes varies with multi regional having the highest availability of 99.95 percent followed by regional with 99.9 percent and then Nearline and Coldline with 99 percent.

As for pricing, all storage classes incur a cost per gigabyte of data stored per month, with multi regional having the highest storage price and Coldline the lowest storage price.

Egress and data transfer charges may also apply.

In addition to those charges, Nearline storage also incurs an access fee per gigabyte of data read and Coldline storage incurs a higher fee per gigabyte of data read.

Data Transfer into Cloud Storage

The availability, flexibility, cost effectiveness and scale of Google cloud storage offers the potential to solve a wide range of enterprise technical challenges. But not all on-premise infrastructure will be easy to integrate into cloud technology. It is very attractive to first use GCP for development and proof of concept but eventually we will want to take advantage of the financial and operational benefits and shift production systems into the cloud but how do we do that without major upheaval? Shifting production to the cloud requires careful planning as not all areas of IT are so easily accomplished when migrating operations to the cloud. There are obvious candidates such as backups and real time replication of databases for business continuity, which makes sense. But there are others such as large scale monolithic applications or mainframes that simply are not suited to a cloud environment. Nonetheless, there are areas in a modern IT environment where cloud is hugely beneficial and we can examine some of them now.

Where cloud data deployment is beneficial

Many of our applications need to be delivered with speed, at scale and while reducing costs and these are the common challenges many of us face in our enterprise when deploying new systems. These operational criteria are often difficult to achieve with more traditional approaches, but this is where cloud excels as it has vast scale, geographical reach, agility and flexibility – so how can we utilise the GCP to meet enterprise demands, such as low latency, high performance and security?

Why Cloud Native?

While our existing enterprise on-premises technology maybe restrictive, it is deeply ingrained into in the way we operate. Enterprise IT are typically expert in developing and running applications on-premises and operations teams are skilled in running their data centres at highly efficient levels. IT is also skilled in running their networks in order to optimise service delivery. However when we contemplate shifting to native cloud services – those designed and built to run in the cloud – it is not a trivial task. Indeed reimagining applications and services may require the rewrite of applications, workflows and retraining of staff. This is not a trivial pursuit as all of these efforts will cost time and money, and have the potential to introduce risk.
However, integrating cloud technology with familiar enterprise technologies can help simplify use of the cloud, and allow us to more easily and widely adopt it. We will discuss cloud native design later.

Designing Cloud Tiers

The ever-increasing amounts of data we hold has become a real challenge as it is not just for historical records or analytics it is also due to regulatory demands. However, as well as production and regulatory compliance data, there are also archives, backups and other "cold", infrequently-accessed data. What is more, we will often need to keep a mirror image of all our operational data for business continuity so that we can switch over operations at a flick of a switch to another diverse geographical region in case of a local catastrophic failure. All of this cold storage data will need to be archived but accessed quickly in the case of a disaster recovery scenario.

Where to store different classes of data, so that it is held on the most cost-efficient tier – including on-premise or in the cloud – presents a real technical and business issue. We have already considered the GCP options of Nearline and Coldline but the question still remains, how do we size our data storage requirements accurately and easily grow our capacity on demand? How do we manage our data so that backups and infrequently used data are placed in cold storage so that they do not consume expensive frequent access storage but still remain accessible? Fortunately, Google's cloud storage options with its scalability and attractive pay-as-you-use model has created the almost perfect long-term repository. However, this technology as compelling as it is, is not without its challenges. Cloud storage cost are not the only expense as we need to consider the issues of retrieving data from a cloud repository, as there are always network charges but the benefit that a cloud storage tier delivers make it worthy of consideration.

Data protection in the cloud

One of the single most stubborn obstacles that enterprises state as preventing them from adopting a cloud deployment is that they will lose control over their data security and the data integrity. In this scenario enterprises feel that their responsibility for data protection is a high priority that cannot be readily compromised. Hence in many enterprises today they see this as a challenge as they feel responsible for protecting much more data and for even longer lifespans. They also have to meet ever more stringent regulatory compliance legislation and all of this puts a huge strain on their existing data protection infrastructure.

Data protection suppliers have seen how large-scale, relatively low-cost repositories such as Google Cloud Storage can help lessen some of these problems with the scale and flexibility that the GCP data protection provides for your data. Such cloud based functionality allows for data to be moved to a cloud location based on policies defined to meet the needs of the enterprise and do it as part of your standard backup operations.

A caveat however is that you should be aware the limitations of this approach. Associated cloud costs such as network data transfer costs, and egress read access to data, need to be taken into consideration when pricing the service. Similarly you must consider the impact on your recovery capability of restoring large amounts of data from a public cloud.

Geographic data sharing

One of the longest-standing issues many organisations face is finding an effective way to share data across multiple locations in order to minimise latency and provide high customer levels of experience.

The challenge is complex with on-premises as it involves synchronising transactions as well as potentially moving large amounts of data while maintaining file integrity. Traditionally, this issue of synchronicity has been accomplished via a distributed file system, which typically relied on the replication of databases across a network. This however has its own problems as there may be replication lag if a database is overwhelmed. It also comes with management issues like maintaining a single source of truth or ensuring the security and integrity of the data through global file locking. But spreading and replicating data over large geographic areas is a staple capability of cloud. But the problem still persists how do we get those large data sets to the cloud?

Importing Data into the Cloud

Regardless of which storage class you choose, whether that is regional, multi-regional, Nearline or Coldline, there are issues that you need to overcome. The most significant is how you import all the relevant data into the cloud storage. With GCP there are several ways to bring data into cloud storage. The most commonly used way especially for operations with smaller data sets is simply to use gsutil, which is the cloud storage command from the GCP Cloud SDK.

However, you can also move data in with a drag and drop in the GCP console, if you use the Google Chrome browser but that only works for small data sets. But what can you do if you have to upload terabytes or even petabytes of data?

If you have to move vast quantities of data then Google Cloud platform offers the online storage transfer service and the offline transfer appliance to help. In the case of the online storage transfer service it lets you schedule and manage batch transfers to cloud storage from another cloud provider from a different cloud storage region or from an HTTP(S) end point.

On the other hand if you need on-premises data transfer then the transfer appliance is a physical and rack mounted device, which is a high capacity storage server that you lease from Google Cloud. You simply connect it to your network, load it with data and then ship it to an upload facility where the data is uploaded to cloud storage. This may seem primitive but it is still probably the fastest and cheapest way to upload vast amounts of data into the cloud. Using this service enables you to securely transfer up to a petabyte of data on a single appliance.

There are other ways of getting your data into cloud storage as this storage option is tightly integrated with many of the Google cloud platform products and services. For example, you can import and export tables from and to BigQuery as well as Cloud SQL. You can also store App Engine logs, Cloud Datastore's backups, and objects used by App Engine applications like images. Cloud storage can also store instant start-up scripts, Compute Engine images, and objects used by Compute Engine applications.

In summary, cloud storage is often the ingestion point for data being moved into the cloud from on-premises or other cloud locations and because of this it is frequently the long term storage location for most user data. Consider using Cloud Storage if you need to store

Immutable blobs that is larger than 10 megabytes such as large images or movies.

This storage service scales up to petabytes of capacity with an upper limit of five terabytes per object.

Cloud Bigtable

Cloud Bigtable is Google's NoSQL, Big Data database service. What the term NoSQL with regards database technology means is that it is 'Not Only SQL' and the difference between NoSQL and the traditional SQL relational database is that the former is better suited to today's application data loads and development lifecycles. Relational databases require that schemas be defined before you can add data. A schema is a collection of relational tables that consist of records and fields. For example, you might want to store data in a customer record that hold data in fields, such as phone numbers, first and last name, address, city and postcode. Hence, an SQL database needs tables, records and fields in a DB schema to be preconfigured in advance in order to store the data into the relevant customer record.

However, this pre-configuration and planning of the database schema fits poorly with modern agile development approaches, because each time you complete new features, the schema of your database often needs to change. If the database is large or reiterations frequent, this can involve significant downtime. Also it is unlikely that, using a relational database, you would be able to effectively accommodate data that's completely unstructured or unable to fit a pre-defined schema.

The modern approach is to use NoSQL databases, which are built to allow the insertion of data without any predefined schema. That makes it easy to make significant application changes in real-time, without worrying about service interruptions – which means development is faster, code integration is more reliable, and less database administrator time is needed.

Despite this SQL and relational databases do excel in certain areas such as in transactional processes as an enforced schema is a big help for some applications but it is also a big hindrance for others. This is simply because many modern apps require a much more flexible approach, hence the move towards the NoSQL schema. These applications do not need all the rows to have the same columns. And in fact, the database might be designed to take advantage of that by sparsely populating the rows.

That's part of what makes your NoSQL database in Bigtable what it is as its tables are sparsely populated so that they can scale to billions of rows and thousands of columns allowing you to store petabytes of data.

Fortunately Google GCP offers Cloud Bigtable as a fully managed service so much of the technology complexity and data schema is transparent to you, so you don't have to worry about configuring and tuning it. Therefore you can just look upon it as being an ideal place for storing large amounts of data with very low latency. As such it is also perfect for storing data that has a single lookup key and it also supports high throughput, both read and write, so it's a great choice for both operational and analytical applications including Internet of Things, user analytics and financial data analysis.

Cloud Bigtable is offered through the same open source API as HBase, which is the native database for the Apache Hadoop project. Having the same API enables the portability of applications between HBase and Bigtable.

However Cloud Bigtable has a few advantages most notably with regards scalability. For if you have worked with and managed your own Hbase installation, you will know that once you hit a certain rate of queries per second scaling gets difficult. But scaling with Cloud Bigtable is easy as you can just increase your machine count which doesn't even require downtime.

Also, Cloud Bigtable handles administration tasks like upgrades and restarts transparently.

Furthermore, security and privacy in Cloud Bigtable is robust and inbuilt as all data is encrypted by default both in-flight and at rest. Also to control authentication and authorisation to access the data you can use IAM permissions to control who has access to your Bigtable data.

As Cloud Bigtable is part of the GCP ecosystem, it can interact with other GCP services and third-party clients. Thus, from an application API perspective, data can be read from and written to Cloud Bigtable through a data service layer like managed VMs, the HBase rest server or a Java server using the HBase client to serve data to applications, dashboards and data services.

Data can also be streamed in through a variety of popular stream processing frameworks, like Cloud Dataflow Streaming, Spark Streaming and Storm.

However, if you prefer to do batch processing rather than streaming then data can also be read from and written to Cloud Bigtable through batch processes like Hadoop map reduce, Dataflow or Spark. Often summarized or newly calculated data is written back to Cloud Bigtable or to a downstream database.

Finally, should you remain unconvinced here is a stellar reference to its ability as Cloud Bigtable is actually the same database that Google uses to host many of its core services including search, analytics, maps and Gmail.

Consider using Cloud Bigtable if you need to store a large amount of structured objects.

Cloud Bigtable does not support SQL's queries nor does it support multi-row transactions.

This storage service provides petabytes of capacity with a maximum unit size of 10 megabytes per cell and 100 megabytes per row.

Relational Databases

In the previous section we covered NoSQL databases but there is still a demand for traditional relational database services. Remember, relational database services use a predesigned database schema laid out in tables in order to help your application keep your data consistent, and correct. This makes relational database services great for handling transactions. Without database transactions, your online bank wouldn't be able to offer you the ability to move money from one account to another. Typically, relational databases require an expert to design, configure, maintain, manage, and administer.

However if you want the transactional power along with the protections of a relational database, then you can use GCP's Cloud SQL.

Cloud SQL offers you the choice of database engine such as, MySQL, PostgreSQL and SQL Server as a fully managed service, which again decouples a lot of the complexity associated with setting up and managing these types of databases.

But you don't have to use Cloud SQL as you could always run your own database server instance inside a Compute Engine virtual machine which a lot of GCP customers do but CloudSQL offers MySQL, SQL Server and PostgreSQL databases that are capable of handling terabytes of storage.

There are some other notable benefits of using the CloudSQL managed service instead of managing your own database instance within a VM.

- Firstly, CloudSQL provide several replica services like read, failover, and external replicas. This means that if an outage occurs, CloudSQL can replicate data between multiple zones with automatic failover.

- Secondly, CloudSQL helps you backup your data with either On-Demand or scheduled backups.
- Thirdly, CloudSQL can scale both vertically by changing the machine type, and horizontally via read replicas.

Moreover, if we consider Cloud SQL from a security perspective, you will get as part of the managed service, network firewalls, encrypted data on Google's internal networks, and when stored in database tables, temporary files, and backups.

Another benefit of CloudSQL instances is they are readily accessible by other GCP services and even external services. This means you can easily authorize Compute Engine instances to access CloudSQL instances and configure the CloudSQL instance to be in the same zone as your virtual machine for low latency and high performance. Finally when it comes to administration you can manage CloudSQL just like on-premises database as it supports other applications and tools like SQL Workbench, Toad, and other external applications that use standard MySQL drivers.

Cloud Spanner

If CloudSQL does not fit your requirements because you need a horizontal scale capability, then consider using Cloud Spanner as it can provide petabytes of capacity. In addition to its scale Spanner can also offer transactional consistency at a global scale, it also supports relational schemas, SQL, and even synchronous replication for high availability.

You might want to consider using Cloud Spanner as opposed to Cloud SQL if you have outgrown your present relational database, or require sharding your databases in order to scale horizontally, have a demand for higher throughput and higher performance, or need transactional consistency at a global scale and strong consistency, or just want to consolidate your databases. Natural use cases for Cloud Spanner include financial applications, and inventory applications. You would be well advised to consider using Cloud SQL for relational database support especially if you use MySQL or PostgreSQL or if you require vast scale then try Cloud Spanner. If you need full SQL support for an online transaction processing system then Cloud SQL provides terabytes of capacity, while Cloud Spanner provides petabytes of capacity. If Cloud SQL does not fit your requirements because you need horizontal scalability not just through the replicas, consider using Cloud Spanner.

Cloud Datastore

Google Cloud Platform also supports another data storage service, Cloud Datastore, which is a highly scalable NoSQL database and its primary use cases is to store structured data from App Engine apps. You can also utilise Cloud Datastore as the integration point when you build solutions that span App Engine and Compute Engine VMs.
As you would expect from a fully managed service, Google handles all Cloud Datastore administration as it is designed to shard and replicate, providing you with a highly available and durable database that scales automatically to handle your workload. Unlike Cloud Bigtable, it also offers transactions that can affect multiple database rows, and it lets you do SQL-like queries.

To get you started, Cloud Datastore has a free daily quota that provides storage, reads, writes deletes and small operations at no charge. Consider using Cloud Datastore if you need to store unstructured objects or if you require support for transactions and SQL like queries. This storage services provides terabytes of capacity with a maximum unit size of one megabyte per entity. There is another type of storage called BigQuery, which it sits on the edge between data storage and data processing, and it is used predominantly in Big Data and Machine Learning in the Cloud. The usual reason to store data in BigQuery is to use its Big Data analysis and interactive query capabilities. You would not want to use BigQuery for example as the backend store for an online application.

Considering the technical differentiators of the different storage services does help some people decide which storage service to choose. Others like to consider use cases. In which case:

- Cloud Datastore is the best for semi-structured application data that is used in App Engines applications.
- Bigtable is best for analytical data with heavy read write events like AdTech, Financial or IoT data.
- Cloud Storage is best for structured and unstructured, binary or object data like images, large media files and backups.
- SQL is best for web frameworks and in existing applications like storing user credentials and customer orders.
- Cloud Spanner is best for large scale database applications that are larger than two terabytes, for example, for financial trading and e-commerce use cases.

But it may well be that depending on your application requirements that you use several of these services to get the job done.

Use case – 5

Now that they have committed to a cloud infrastructure solution it only remains for them to choose suitable cloud storage. They would also like to know whether to stick with MySQL residing on VMs or to migrate to CloudSQL to derive many of the benefits of the cloud. What solutions can you propose that is simple to implement and cost effective?

Solution

You have proposed in the original design that the backup/archived data be stored in Cloud Storage as Coldline as this will be cheaper and easier to manage due to versioning and other management tools. This is still the preferred option if they insist on archiving their data in the cloud. However they should be aware that this will take a lot of time to recover and restore the data over the internet and bear costs and significant network charges when they retrieve the data. It will also use up a lot of internet bandwidth so you will need a dedicated channel just for this data migration. It might therefore be better to leave the backup/archived data where it is and continue with their existing backup and offsite storage method. Once they have switched over and the cloud infrastructure is active then they can start using the Cloud Storage coldline storage as that will no longer require internet transfer as it will all be handled across Google's network.

Before making a cloud storage decision, be sure to answer the following questions:

- What are your workload performance characteristics?
- What type of cloud media is appropriate to meet those performance demands?
- What levels of resilience are needed?
- How often do you need to access the data?
- What would be the cost of moving data out of the cloud?

- Do you fully understand the public cloud cost model?

Moving to CloudSQL will be relatively straightforward as it is itself MySQL so it will be a like for like swap. This makes transferring the schema and data straightforward as a simple sqldump that is uploaded into Cloud Storage is all that is required. Cloud SQL can then build the schema and data using the sqldump object in the Cloud Storage bucket. There might be an issue with down time or service disruption but replicating the on-premises master to the CloudSQL MySQL instance will keep the two synchronised without the need for any service disruption.

Chapter 6 - Containers and Kubernetes Engine

In this chapter we will shift the focus away from GCP storage portfolio to containers and the Google Kubernetes engine. We will describe in this chapter why you want to use containers, what their benefits are and how to manage them in Kubernetes engine.

An introduction to Containers and Kubernetes

In an earlier chapter we introduced you to the Compute Engine, which is GCP's Infrastructure as the Service offering (IaaS), with access to servers, file systems, and networking through the deployment of VMs. We will also discuss the App Engine service, which is GCP's Platform as a Service (PaaS) offering in the next chapter. However for now, it is time to introduce you to containers and Kubernetes engine, which is a hybrid service that conceptually sits between the Compute Engine and App Engine, and as you will see provides benefits from both of the services. Compute Engine and its functions that deliver automation and elasticity introduce the model of programmable infrastructure. Indeed using IaaS or PaaS such as App Engine makes your applications self-aware and allows them to scale-out and scale-in dynamically.

Nonetheless, technology doesn't stand still and a new wave of technological innovation has arrived in the form of immutable infrastructure and micro-services. At the forefront of this change is a popular Linux-based technology called containers, this is where a single kernel has the ability to run multiple instances of a VM upon a single underlying operating system.

When we use Compute Engine VMs we are utilizing the benefits of Infrastructure as a Service, which allows you to share compute resources with other developers by virtualizing the hardware using virtual machines. In this case, each developer can deploy their own application environment. Thus they can build their applications in their own self-contained environment with access to an operating system, RAM, file systems, networking interfaces, and so on. This is one of the several benefits of using virtual machines as they provide you with a self-contained environment where you can install your favourite applications, run-times, tools, web server, database, middleware, and so on. Also in addition to being able to custom configure the operating environment you are also able to configure the underlying system resources such as disk space, disk IO, and networking.

But that isolation and flexibility comes at a cost as the smallest unit of compute is an app with its VM. Remember that a VM is a virtualised server that will contain its own guest OS and that will be large; perhaps gigabytes in size, and also it may take several minutes to boot the OS. That may not be a problem when you are starting out and perhaps building a development location in GCP but as you move to production and the application grows you will need to scale horizontally by adding replica VMs to meet the demand.

However, this is where some issues arise, because as demand for your application increases, you will have to copy an entire VM, and boot the guest OS for each instance of your app, which can be slow, costly and inefficient.

However, one way around this was to use the App Engine services, as you get access to programming services. Hence, all you had to do was use those services to write your code and your self-contained workloads including any dependent libraries. This meant that when demand for your app increased, the platform would scale your app seamlessly and independently by workload and infrastructure. This solution scales rapidly, but you sacrifice the benefit of being able to fine tune the underlying architecture to save cost but that is where containers come in to play.

What are Containers?

The idea of a container is to give you the independent scalability of workloads, but with an abstraction layer of the OS and hardware. Therefore what you effectively get is a VM without a dedicated guest OS. Indeed the container acts just like its name suggests as a box around your code and its dependencies. However the container also comes with limited access to your own partition of the file system and hardware. This means it doesn't require its own guest OS so It only requires a few system calls to create and start, which means it doesn't have to boot an OS so it can be up and running as quickly as a process.

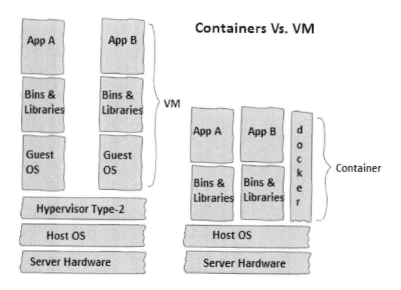

Figure -7

To run your application in a container all you need on each host is an OS kernel that supports containers, and a container runtime. In essence, you're virtualizing the OS; it scales well and also gives you nearly the same flexibility as IaaS.

However a huge benefit with containers is that through this abstraction of the underlying OS, your code is now highly portable, so you can deploy it readily on any OS or hardware. This means you no longer have to make different versions of your app to support different OS, which means you can rapidly and continuous deploy your application. Thus you will go from development, to staging, to production, and deployment to the cloud without reconfiguring or rebuilding the application. This is a tremendous boon for rapid and continuous deployment in DevOps environment but it gets even better.

Containers scale well horizontally so if for example you were running a web server, you can scale your application in seconds and as many containers as you need, depending on the size of your workload, on a single host. Nonetheless, that's not the best way to go about it.

With containers you'll want to shift away from running an application on a single container as you will benefit more by building your application using lots of containers each performing their own function like microservices. If you take this approach to building your app using single function microservices or micro-apps and deploying them in containers connected via the network this will make them modular, easy and quick to deploy, and they will scale independently across a group of hosts.

Building Containers

The first thing you will need to know is how to build a container and then run it and the most common way us to use an open source tool called Docker or you could use Google Container Builder. These tools define a format for bundling your application, its dependencies, and machine specific settings into a container.

When you use the docker build command to build the container it builds and stores the container locally as a runnable image. You can save and upload the image into a container registry service, and share or download it from there. Then, you will use the docker run command to run the image.

Nonetheless, the tasks involved in building and packaging applications into containers is only a small part, the vast majority of the work is associated with application configuration, service discovery, managing updates, monitoring and orchestration.

Potentially when you use containers a host can scale up or down and start and stop the containers on-demand as demand for your application changes, or if a host fails. But you will need tools to orchestrate and control the provisioning process and that is where Kubernetes comes in.

The Role of Kubernetes

Kubernetes acts as the orchestrator managing many containers deployed on many hosts and scaling them as microservices. Kubernetes also plays an important role in automatic provisioning and deploying rollouts and rollbacks.
To understand how and why we need Kubernetes as an orchestrator we have to comprehend that deploying and managing containers manually is not really feasible. This is due to fact that there is a lot more too just building and running containers there are the other tasks associated with service discovery, managing updates, monitoring, and provisioning, which are the essential components of an automated, reliable, scalable, distributed system.
To assist us in automating the management and provisioning of our container base we can use Kubernetes, which is an open source orchestrator that abstracts containers at a higher level so you can better manage and scale your applications.
Kubernetes can be thought of as a set of APIs that you can use to deploy and manage containers. The Kubernetes system is organised as a set of master components that run as a control plane, and a set of nodes that run containers. In Kubernetes, a node represents a computing instance like a virtual machine. Specifically in Google Cloud, Kubernetes nodes are virtual machines running in the Compute Engine.

At a very high level of operations, you describe a set of applications and how they should interact with each other, and Kubernetes figures how to make that happen.

Nodes, Pods and Clusters

Kubernetes uses the concept of a cluster which is basically a set of containers. Hence once you have built your container, the first thing you will need to do is deploy it into a cluster.

However, Kubernetes clusters can be configured with many options and add-ons, which can be complex and time consuming so instead, you can use the Kubernetes Engine, or GKE.

GKE is hosted Kubernetes by Google. Within GKE clusters can be customized, they can support different machine types, numbers of nodes, and network settings. Kubernetes is also able to launch containers in existing VMs or to provision new VMs and place the containers within them. Kubernetes goes well beyond simply booting containers as it also provides the tools to monitor and managing them. With Kubernetes, administrators can create Pods; these are logical groups of similar or tightly coupled containers that are related to an application. Pods are duly provisioned within the Compute Engine VMs.

When using Kubernetes Engine, it will deploy containers on Compute Engine VMs using a wrapper around one or more related containers called a pod. This is the smallest unit in Kubernetes that you can create or deploy. Logically a pod will represent a running process on your cluster. It can be either a component of your application, or the entire application.

Typically, you only would place one container per pod, but if you have multiple containers with a hard dependency, you can package them into a single pod, and share networking and storage. The pod provides a unique network IP and the containers inside a pod can communicate with one another using the 'localhost' interface and the ports will remain fixed as they are started and stopped on different nodes.

Starting a Deployment

One way to run a container in a pod in Kubernetes is to use the 'kubectl' run command. This starts a deployment of a container running in a pod. A deployment represents a group of replicas of the same pod and keeps your pod running even when nodes they run on fail.
It could represent a component of an application or an entire app. By default, pods in a deployment are only accessible inside your GKE cluster.

Exposing a Deployment

To make them publicly available, you can connect a Load Balancer to your deployment by running the 'kubectl' exposed command. In GKE, the Load Balancer is created as a network Load Balancer and Kubernetes creates a service with a fixed IP for your pods. Any client that hits that IP address will be routed to a pod behind the service.

The Kubernetes service defines a logical set of pods and a policy by which to access them. It is an abstraction that enables you to separate the deployments - to create and destroy pods, allow them to get their own IP address, - from the complexity of individual administration. However, those addresses don't remain stable over time. To get around this issue we use service groups.

Service Groups

A service group is set of pods, which provides a stable endpoint or fixed IP for them.
For example, if you create two sets of pods called front-end and back-end, and you put them behind their own services, back-end pods IP addresses may change over time but the front-end pods are not aware of this, nor do they care, as they simply refer to the back-end service by name rather than by IP addresses.

Scaling a Deployment

To scale a deployment, run the 'kubectl' scale command. In this case, three pods are created in your deployment, and they're placed behind the service and they will share one fixed IP.
So far you have learned to run imperative commands like run, expose and scale. This works well to learn and test Kubernetes step by step. But the real strength of Kubernetes comes when you work in a declarative way. Instead of issuing commands, you provide a configuration file that tells Kubernetes what you want your desired state to look like, and Kubernetes figures out how to do it.

Use Case -6

A client has come to you requesting your advice on whether they should build their apps using containers. They explain they are keen to take advantage of container technology as they want to embrace a continuous improvement and rapid deployment culture. The problem is that their current infrastructure isn't very flexible and they are not sure how to manage the change, would a cloud development environment be fit for purpose?

Solution

There are actually two parts to this question, first there is the issue of building apps using containers and secondly whether to build a development environment in the cloud. If we address the second point first we can propose that creating the development environment in the cloud would be a highly flexible and agile solution. This is because developers can spin-up VMs and other resources in seconds without any capital outlay or provisioning delays. This makes development fast and flexible. Moving the development to the cloud also lessens the internal burden on networks and IT as they no longer will need to be involved every time a developer wants to spin up an instance. So long as it is managed and audited frequently to ensure there is no proliferation of zombie VMs around it can be a cost effective solution.

Regards the point about containers, we need to take a few things into consideration. One of the points is whether the development team has the required skills or any experience in creating and managing containers. That of course is not for us to say so we can only advice on which platform they could use that supports containers. Here they have a choice of App Engine Flexible Environment, Compute Engine or of course the specialist platform Kubernetes Engine. Each has their place but if they are serious about containers then Kubernetes is the optimal platform for handling and managing containers at scale.

Chapter 7 - App Engine

So far we have discussed two GCP products that provide the compute infrastructure for applications: virtual machines for Compute Engine and containers for Kubernetes Engine.

But perhaps you just want a Platform as a Service so that you can focus on your application code and not have to concern yourself with infrastructure. Well that is why there is Google's PaaS, the Cloud App Engine.

App Engine is what is known as a platform as a service. In GCP, the App Engine platform manages the hardware and networking infrastructure required to run your code. What this means is that when you want to deploy an application on App Engine, you just handle the application's code and the App Engine service will give you access to the platform runtime and libraries of your choice and provision and manage the infrastructure on your behalf.

To accomplish this, App Engine provides you with the built-in services that many web applications require by default, such as a NoSQL database, in-memory caching, load balancing, health checks, logging and a way to authenticate users. But there are no servers for you to provision or maintain as everything is handled transparently within App Engine.

The concept behind App Engine is that you code your application to take advantage of these services and App Engine will provide them for you. Moreover, App Engine will automatically scale your application's resources in response to the demand and amount of traffic but you will only pay for those resources that you use. The billing model and the automated and elastic scaling is why App Engine is especially suited for variable workloads or unpredictable applications such as web and mobile backends.

App Engine offers two choices of environments, standard and flexible. Of the two App Engine Environments, Standard is the simpler. It offers a simpler deployment experience than the Flexible environment. However the most notable difference is that with the Standard Environment your low utilization applications might be able to run at no charge as it offers a free daily usage quota for the use of some services.

In order to assist in the deployment of code to the cloud App Engine Google provides an App Engine SDK. These are available in several languages and provide you with simple commands for deployment and an environment for testing your application locally before you upload it to the GCP's App Engine service.

Now, what often intrigues people is the question of what does the application code actually run on?

App Engine Standard Environment

The short answer to that is it runs in App Engine on an executable binary called a runtime.

In App Engine Standard Environment, you use a runtime provided by Google. Also the Standard Environment provides runtimes for specific versions of Java, Python, PHP and Go. As well as the libraries that supports all the App Engine APIs.

For many applications, the App Engine Standard Environment runtimes and libraries may maybe all you need. But, if you code your application in another language then the Standard Environment is not the right choice so you will need to use the Flexible Environment.

The Standard Environment also has some other caveats that you may need to contemplate such as it runs in a Sandbox. That's a software and security construct that enforces independence of the hardware, operating system, file system or physical location of the server it runs on and it also enforces the segregation and isolation of the code.

Running your code in a sandbox is not necessarily an issue as one of the reasons why App Engine Standard Environment can scale so effectively and manage your application in a very fine grained way is because of the sandbox. They are also very secure as the code is isolated from the OS, other applications, and the file system.

Nonetheless, sandboxes can and do impose some constraints such as your application can't write to the local file system. Therefore, your application will have to use a database service if it needs to store data persistently. As a result, Cloud Datastore is tightly coupled with App Engine standard edition to provide that service.

Also, all the requests your application receives will have a 60-second timeout, and because code is segregated by design you can't install arbitrary third party software in a sandbox.

If these constraints will adversely affect your development then that would be another pointer towards using the Flexible Environment.

Here's a brief roadmap of how you'll use App Engine Standard Environment in practice;

- First you develop your application and run a test version of it locally using the App Engine SDK.

- Then you use the SDK commands to deploy it.
- Each App Engine application runs in a GCP project.
- App Engine automatically provisions server instances and scales and load balances them.
- Your application can make calls to a variety of services using dedicated APIs.

App Engine Flexible Environment

If you find the constraints of the App Engine standard environments sandbox model is just too restrictive or you need to code in another language not supported in the standard environment, then you may want to consider the Flexible Environment version.

A notable difference is that instead of using a sandbox, App Engine flexible environment lets you run your application inside Docker containers on Google Compute Engine Virtual Machines, VMs. In addition it lets you specify the container your App Engine runs in and the App Engine manages these Compute Engine virtual machines for you.

Furthermore, the VMs are monitored, health checked, healed as necessary, and you select the geographical region that you want them to run in. Another feature of the flexible Environment is that App Engine will apply automatically any critical backward compatible updates to their operating systems. All this works transparently so that you can just focus on your code.

App Engine apps use standard run times that can access App Engine services such as data store, memcached, task queues, and so on. The simpler standard environment starts up instances of your application faster, but because of the sandbox you get less access to the infrastructure in which your application runs.

Flexible environment, however, lets you SSH into the virtual machines on which your application runs. It lets you use local disk for scratch base, and it lets you install third-party software. Flexible Environment also lets your application make calls to the network without going through App Engine. On the other hand, the standard environment can save you a lot of money as the billing can drop to zero for any idle applications. This is very attractive in a DevOps environment.

An interesting thing is that in the Flexible Environment the App Engine uses Docker containers instead of a sandbox. So how does App Engine flexible environment compare to Kubernetes Engine? Here's a quick comparison of use-cases for App Engine with Kubernetes Engine.

- App Engine Standard Environment is for people who want the service to take maximum control of their applications deployment and scaling.
- Kubernetes Engine gives the application owner the full flexibility of Kubernetes orchestration.
- App Engine flexible edition is somewhere in between.
- App Engine Flexible Environment treats containers as a means to an end, but for Kubernetes Engine, containers are the fundamental organizing principle.

A common use case for App Engine is to host API services. This is because they can be quickly uploaded to App Engine and it will manage any scaling and authentication issues. API's are a very common way of opening an application up to the outside but in a strictly limited way. Indeed all our interaction with the GCP so far whether that was via the console or the SDK has been ultimately via the APIs that Google expose for your use.

Application Programming Interfaces, APIs

We have mentioned Application Programming Interfaces, APIs, several times already as a method for connecting to a service. However, let us now give them a description and definition that is more precise.

The problem that persists in software services implementation is that they can require precise interfaces that become complex and they are frequently changeable.

The issue is that integrating services requires connecting other pieces of software and that requires knowledge of the code and also the internal details about how they work. This would make local integration with in-house applications very difficult but integration with third parties nigh on impossible.

Nonetheless, integrations with third parties, even banks do go ahead, as instead application developers write software that abstracts away all the needless internal details to provide templates for the delivery of necessary parameters. This presents a clean, well-defined interface. Then they document that interface as an API.

API Management

Now that we know what an API is we can consider how Google Cloud Platform manages their library of APIs. A feature of the API concept is that the underlying implementation can change as long as the interface remains working. Thus, other pieces of software that use the API don't have to change anything.

However, sometimes you will have to change an API to add or deprecate a feature. In this case then the clients or other software that use that API will have to know about the changes. Therefore, developers need to version and track their APIs.

In order to manage and make this transition as clean as possible developers need to document the changes so that client and other developers know that an API has been depreciated or functionally upgraded. In the latter case the developers should document that version two of an API contains additional functional calls that version one does not.

This means that applications that consume the API can specify the API version that they want to use in their calls.

Managing and supporting an API is very important task and Google Cloud platform provides two API management tools. The first approach is related to issues where you're developing a software service and using one of GCP's backends. The criteria you would like to meet are that you'd like to make it easy to expose this API but you'd like to make sure it's only consumed by other developers whom you trust. Thus you'd like for the API to know which end user is making the service call. In addition you would like the API to be monitored and the usage logged.

Cloud Endpoints

In this scenario you would use Cloud Endpoints as it implements these capabilities and more using a proxy that is easy to deploy in front of your backend services. It also provides you with an API console to wrap up those capabilities in an easy to manage interface. Cloud Endpoints supports applications running in GCPs compute platforms in your choice of languages and your choice of client technologies.

Apigee Edge is also a platform for developing and managing API proxies but it has a different approach as it is primarily focused on business problem such as rate limiting, setting quotas, and providing analytics.

However, because the backend services for Apigee Edge need not be in GCP, engineers often use it when decomposing a legacy application into microservices or micro-apps.

It is advantageous and a less risky way to move a monolith application into the cloud. By doing it this way you avoid replacing the entire application in one risky move. Instead they can use Apigee Edge to peel off its services one by one, standing up micro services to implement each in turn until the legacy application can be finally retired.

Use Case – 7

The client likes the idea of building a development environment in the cloud but they would like to know which platform to use App Engine or Kubernetes?

Solution

The issue here is that both Google Kubernetes Engine (GKE), which is a cluster manager and orchestration system for running your Docker containers and Google App Engine (GAE), which is a Google managed container service can be the right choice it depends on the degree of control that you need.

They will both provide you with the same benefits such as scalability, redundancy, rollouts, rollbacks, etc. However, the difference between them is in their management. This is because GKE gives you the fine grained control over everything about your cluster. On the other hand GAE manages the containers on your behalf with as little configuration or management as possible. Of course this also restricts your control.

So if you choose GKE then you will have more fine control, but also more work for you to do. For example, you may need to configure the network, security, software updates etc. On the other hand with GAE most of this is done for you leaving the developers to focus on their app.

However GKE does provide you with more freedom as you can change cloud providers easier than if you are using GAE so there is less risk of vendor lock-in.

Chapter 8 - Cloud Functions

In the previous chapter we discussed App Engine and how as a PaaS it was designed for application development environments. The object was to abstract the underlying infrastructure for the application code, thereby allowing developers to focus solely on their code. App Engine either ran application code and typically API services in a runtime or within a container depending on the version of App Engine being used. However, some applications use even smaller segments of code for micro-applications, which are typically one function apps, much like microservices. For this type of development you can further abstract the underlying infrastructure and applications and utilise Google's serverless platform, Cloud Functions.

Many applications contain event-driven components that are triggered by some criteria being met, for example, maybe you have an application that lets users upload videos.

Whenever that happens, you need to know so that you can process that video. An event can trigger the application to process the user's uploaded video and perform a transcription of the video into various text files, and then store each file in a repository.

You could always integrate this function into your application, but then you have to worry about capacity planning and providing all the compute resources necessary to meet the demand. The issue with a new application is you don't know whether user uploads will happen once a day, once an hour or once a millisecond.

But, what if you could just ignore the tedious task of capacity planning and forecasting and simply make that provisioning problem irrelevant?

What would be required is a single purpose function that could perform, in this example, all the necessary video transcription and storage tasks. Then you would only need it to be triggered to run automatically whenever a user uploads a new video.

And that is exactly what cloud functions lets you do.

Introducing Cloud Functions

The beauty of cloud functions is that you just pay whenever your functions run in 100 millisecond intervals. Also you don't have to worry about servers or runtime binaries. You just write your code in JavaScript in a Node.js environment that GCP provides and then you configure it to be triggered by an event. Cloud functions can trigger on events in cloud storage, Cloud Pub/Sub, or in an HTTP call. We will introduce Pub/Sub to you in detail later.

However, you only get billed when your event triggers your function and only then for the duration that it runs. Therefore, you no longer need to be concerned – from a capacity planning perspective - whether it runs once a day, once an hour or once a millisecond as GCP is responsible for managing and providing the required resources.

The way that you can deploy cloud functions is quite simple as you start by setting up a cloud function and choose which events that you wish to acts as triggers. For each event type, you declare to the cloud functions that this is the event that they react to.

Then comes the difficult part as you will need to write and attach your applications JavaScript functions to your triggers. This ensures that should an event of interest trigger your function that it will subsequently be executed.

After you have set up your applications functions with corresponding events and suitable triggers, your functions will run whenever the event occurs.

Some applications, especially those that are based upon microservices architecture can be implemented entirely in cloud functions, which make it very cost effective. This makes deploying cloud functions a very efficient and easy to deploy application. Specifically when you are seeking to enhance an existing application, which may have variable demand as it removes the worry about scaling.

Why Cloud Functions?

If we cast our memory back to the first chapter we mentioned the design issue whereby at one end of the scale there is managed infrastructure and at the other end an extreme dynamic infrastructure. However, you will often come to the conclusion that you can choose where you want to be along that line. For example, you may choose to be further towards the Compute Engine if you want full control to deploy and manage your application in virtual machines that run on Google's infrastructure. Similarly, if you need control but want to use containers then you can use the Kubernetes Engine as these clusters define a measure of control. On the other hand you may well choose to relinquish much of the control and management burden and select to use the App Engine service as it is ideal if you just want to focus on your code and leave infrastructure provisioning and management to Google. Conversely, standard environment may be too restrictive as you may want to retain some control of your custom runtime environment and that is what the App Engine flexible environment lets you do. Of course to relieve yourself from the chore of managing infrastructure, capacity planning and to build or extend your application, then you can use Cloud Functions.

When you deploy applications through Cloud Functions, you only need to supply chunks of code for business logic, you set the event triggers and attach the code and it will get spun up on demand in response to specific events to create functions.

Microservices and Service Mesh

Adopting microservices architecture in order to decompose large monolithic applications can bring many benefits, including increased flexibility, independence and modularity. However these benefits often come at the expense of added complexity as the process of decoupling a single-tier monolithic application into many smaller service modules introduces many design hurdles. For example, when you decompose a monolith down to 1000s of autonomous microservices how do you know what's running? Indeed, if you don't have visibility into what microservices are running how do you monitor, update or secure your microservices? To address to these significant challenges, you can always deploy a service mesh. This is a software solution that helps you discover and make sense of all those thousands of interconnections between services. A service mesh also helps you with orchestration, security, and in collecting telemetry data across distributed microservices and containers.

The way that a service mesh works is that it decouples your applications dependency from the network. Thus it can monitor all traffic for your application, typically through a set of network proxies or sidecars that sit alongside each microservice. These sidecar proxies provide for individual policy implementation and even language independence at the microservices level. This in turn, allows local and remote development teams to work independently and be language agnostic.

Google Cloud Platform has its own GCSM which is a fully managed service that is built on the high-performance Envoy sidecar proxy and the open source Istio service mesh provides the overlay on your microservices running in Kubernetes for container API support. The Google Cloud Service Mesh supports end-to-end encryption between services using mTLS (mutual TLS), as well as a granular traffic control, routing, and authorization policy. It also integrates with Stackdriver to monitor and alert on key metrics. Further, this is all achieved with no change to your application code.

Istio on GKE provides a managed, mature service mesh that you can deploy that spans both the Cloud and on-premise networks with just one click. However the real utility of the Istio service mesh is in the context of the cloud-native ecosystem as it provides a path towards infrastructure abstraction and process automation in a cloud or a hybrid cloud environment.

Automation

Organizations are increasingly moving toward automation as it delivers efficiencies, velocity and quality in the development process. Today many organisations strive for continuous improvement and rapid deployment to deliver their products. Hence development has become a pipeline-based approach for automating application upgrades and rapid deployment.

Google Cloud Service Mesh based on Istio integrates seamlessly with continuous delivery systems and the deployment pipelines. For example, you can configure your pipeline to deploy Istio VirtualServices in order to manage granular traffic management or even in-flight A-B testing without any manual intervention. Istio can also work with modern GitOps workflows due to its declarative configuration model. In this scenario it is the source control that serves as the central source of truth for both your application and infrastructure configuration.

Traffic Director

Traffic Director is GCP's fully managed traffic control plane for service mesh. It is an abstraction that's used to deliver microservices and modern applications. The service mesh data plane, is deployed through service proxies like Envoy and it controls the flow of traffic and the control plane enforces policy, configuration, and intelligence. With Traffic Director, it is easy to configure traffic control policies. You can also use Traffic Director to deploy simple load balancing as well as deploy it across multiple regions as VMs or containers and use Traffic Director to deliver global load balancing with automatic cross-region overflow and failover. Some advanced features like request routing and percentage-based traffic splitting enables seamless scalability within Compute Engine and Kubernetes Engine environments.

Serverless, with Service Mesh

Today, serverless computing transforms your source code into workloads that are executed only when called or triggered by an event. Organizations are adopting the serverless approach as it decouples code from infrastructure, which in turn reduces infrastructure costs, increases efficiency while simultaneously allowing developers to focus on writing code that delivers more business value.

However, today most organisations are typically running heterogeneous development environment so are not solely running serverless workloads. Indeed they are also likely to have stateful applications, including microservices apps within containers on Kubernetes infrastructure. Therefore, the GCSM allows Kubernetes users to deploy container applications and serverless functions onto the same cluster.

Further, the ability to work with serverless functions in the same way that you work with your traditional containers helps you to provide a uniformed standard methodology between your serverless and Kubernetes environments. This means that you can use the same Istio traffic rules, certificate issuance, authorization policies, and metrics uniformly across all your workload pipelines.

Portability

Organisations are increasingly adopting more complex cluster configurations as they reap the benefits of code portability. But this requires lower latency, security, and the need for tools that span both cloud and on-premise. Hence, Google's Cloud Services Platform is there to provide the interoperable environment, which can combine complementary solutions that include Google Kubernetes Engine, GKE On-Premise, and Istio. The goal is to move towards creating a seamless Kubernetes experience across hybrid development environments.

Use Case - 8

The client ABC is looking over your proposal with interest but they are becoming confused when they do their own research into GCP as they cannot differentiate between the services and how they are used. They request that you provide a high-level summary of each with perhaps some use-cases?

Solution

In order to meet the clients request you can summarise the difference between the services in a brief summary. Such as the one below:

Summary of Platform Properties
App Engine Standard

PROS

- This is a cost effective way to host development apps or for production platforms for APIs or low throughput apps.

- This is a low maintenance platform as App Engine manages the infrastructure for you
- App Engine also handles auto scaling on your behalf and it is fast and lightweight as it is based upon instance classes
- Additional functions such as version management and **traffic splitting** are built into App Engine standard and flexible environments
- Native access to Datastore as it has co-location with App Engine Standard environment
- There is also built-in access to Memcache
- Standard environment runs in a secure sandbox. This is inherently more secure way of working compared to Compute Engine where you need to do your own security controls.

CONS

- The secure sandbox prevents interact with the file systems and persistent storage and there are other constraints such as the instances are kept smaller so they can benefit from the fast autoscaling.
- There is no networking with the standard edition's sandbox so there is no support for Cloud Load Balancer
- Limited to supported runtimes: Python 2.7, Java 7 and 8, Go 1.6-1.9, and PHP 5.5.

App Engine Flex

PROS

- Not limited to the standard runtimes as it can support custom runtimes
- Integration with GCE networking
- In built version and traffic management

- larger instance sizes makes it more appropriate for large applications or Java applications that consume a lot of memory

Cons

- No internal load balancers or support for shared VPCs
- No native integration with Memcache

Google Kubernetes Engine

PROS

- Natively integrates with containers, which allows for custom runtimes
- Tight coupling with containers for better management and cluster configuration
- Enforces best practices for virtual machines,
- Provides for easy roll back of VMs too previous versions
- Containers provide a flexible and platform neutral deployment framework
- Open source Kubernetes, provides a method for portability between on-premises and the cloud
- Private Clusters, now in beta, eliminate the need to expose public IP addresses
- Version management through Google Container Registry

CONS

- There is no native traffic management
- There is some management overhead
- Not really intuitive so there is a learning curve due to many new concepts such as pods, deployments, services, ingress, and namespaces
- Public IPs need to be exposed to locations where you want to run 'kubectl' commands
- Monitoring tool integration is limited

- No L7 internal load balancing so you have to use third party solutions

Compute Engine

PROS

- Intuitive and will little learning curve this is what makes Compute Engine the most popular method
- You have almost total management and administrative control so you can load whatever tools or third party add-ons that you want
- No need for public IPs
- You can run docker containers using the container-Optimized OS

CONS

- As you have total control it can be complex to manage and control as you have to do most things yourself
- More management overhead
- Autoscaling is slower than App Engine
- Installing software on custom GCE instances can be difficult to maintain

Chapter 9 – Using GCP Cloud Tools

Google Cloud Development Tools

There are many popular third-party tools for development, deployment and monitoring that will work natively in GCP. However, apart from the myriad of open source tools that work out of the box you also have the option of using the in-built tools that are tightly-integrated with GCP.

In development and DevOps environments that are utilizing the Cloud App Engine there is a requirement for managing code, libraries and repositories. This will often require many tools to assist in managing code versioning, libraries, and source code trees. To do this many GCP customers use the well-known repository Git to store, distribute and manage their code. What that entails is them running their own Git instances or using a hosted Git provider.

Cloud Source Repositories

Running your own Git instance is a great way of managing a code repository because you have total control. On the other hand using a hosted Git provider may mean some loss of control but it is a lot less work. A potential solution to this dilemma is that GCP provides its own way to keep code private to a GCP project. Further, it can also use IAM permissions to protect access to it. But the good part is that you do not have to maintain the Git instance yourself.

That's what Cloud Source repositories is all about. When you use the Cloud Source Repository the managed service provides Git version control to support your development of any application or service that are running on App Engine, but it can also be used on Compute Engine and Kubernetes Engine.

In addition, Cloud Source Repositories, lets you handle any number of private Git repositories, which allows you the freedom to organize and manage your code as you see fit. Further, the Cloud Source Repository also contains a source viewer so that you can browse and view repository files from within the GCP console.

Initially setting up your environment in GCP can entail many steps, such as configuring the compute network and storage resources, as well as keeping track of their configurations.

This is considered an imperative method as you issue direct commands. You can do it all by hand if you want to but if you want to clone your environment, you have to replicate all those commands again. A better way is to take a declarative approach and proactively work out the commands you need to set up your environment and then make a template as this is more efficient.

This is good if you already have a strong idea of how you wish the environment to be and later should you want to change your environment, you can readily reconfigure it. However this does mean you have an idea of what the environment should look like but not necessarily know how you want the environment to be configured so it's declarative rather than imperative.

GCP provides Deployment Manager to let you do just that.

Deployment Manager

Deployment manager is an Infrastructure Management Service that automates the creation and management of your Google Cloud Platform resources for you based upon a template.

To use deployment manager, you will create a template file using either the YAML markup language or Python that will describe what you want the components of your environment to look like. You don't need to imperatively state the commands just what you want it to finally represent.

Then, you give the template to Deployment Manager which figures out how it can achieve your design and then does the actions needed to create the environment your template describes.

If you need to change your environment, edit your template and then tell Deployment Manager to update the environment to match the change.

Here's a tip, you can also store and version control your Deployment Manager templates in Cloud Source Repositories.

Stackdriver

There is little doubt that in order to run an application reliably and with any stability you need to have robust monitoring.

Managing is only possible with diligent monitoring of the application as it passes you the information about how the system is working and handling demand and traffic fluctuations and provides early warnings as to potential flaws. It also indicates where potential changes may be required to mitigate issues and then subsequently whether the changes you made are working or not. Monitoring of an application also lets you respond to issues through informed decisions rather than with guesswork or in blind panic mode.

Stackdriver is the built-in GCP tool for monitoring, logging and diagnostics and it provides the low level tools, which gives you access to many different kinds of signals from your Infrastructure platforms, virtual machines, containers, middleware and application tier, logs, metrics and traces. By providing access to this system level signals it also gives insight into your application's health, performance and availability. So if issues occur, you can fix them before a condition escalates to a serious problem.

The core components of Stackdriver consist of components responsible for detecting the Monitoring, Logging, Trace, Error Reporting and debugging.

Stackdriver monitoring checks the endpoints of Web applications. This also occurs with other Internet accessible services, such as those running on your cloud environment. Using Stackdriver you are able to configure uptime checks, which you can link to particular URLs, groups or specific resources that you wish to monitor such as specific VM instances or load balancers. In addition Stackdriver allows you to configure alerts on interesting criteria, like when health check fail or up-time checks fall to levels that need immediate action. Furthermore you can combine Stackdriver to work with a lot of popular notification tools so you can create dashboards to help you visualize the state of your application. Stackdriver logging lets you view logs from your applications and filter and search on them.

Logging also lets you define metrics, based on log contents that are incorporated into custom dashboards and alerts. You can also export logs to BigQuery, Cloud Storage and Cloud Pub/Sub.

By incorporating Stackdriver into your existing network management system or Network Operation Centre software you can leverage its in-depth error reporting to notify you when new errors are detected. It can also track, group and categorise error in your applications.

But you can also use Stackdriver trace to proactively sample the latency of App Engine applications and report on per-URL statistics so you can be notified ahead of time of a gradual degradation in a specific service.

How about when tasked with the dreaded debugging of code? A tedious method in debugging code in an application is to go back into it code and enter lots of logging statements.

Stackdriver debugger reduces a lot of this drudgery by debugging code and logging errors in a different way. It does this by connecting your applications production data to your source code. In this way it allows you to inspect the state of your application at any code location in production. That means you can view the application state without adding logging statements.

Stackdriver Debugger works best when your application source code is available, such as in Cloud Source repositories, although it can also work if your code is held in other repositories too.

Anthos

Anthos is an application management platform that provides a consistent development, operations and security experience for use on both cloud and on-premises environments. Anthos is different from other public cloud services. It's not just a product but a fully software based umbrella for multiple services aligned with the themes of application modernization, cloud migration, hybrid cloud, and multi-cloud management.

Anthos is a collection of complementary services, which helps manage containers in either cloud or on-premises environments. Anthos brings benefits to all areas of the business. From a developers perspective we can consider Anthos as supplying a Kubernetes container management platform. It enables developers to deploy containers and microservices based architectures. It does this though providing Git-compliant management and CI/CD workflows for configuration. It also provides the code for deploying Anthos Configuration Management as well as code-free protection of services via mTLS and instrumentation using Istio and Stackdriver. However it has also got inbuilt support for GCP Marketplace so that a developer can easily drop off-the-shelf products into clusters.

Now when we consider Operations then Anthos provides centralized, efficient, and deployment templates as well as the management of clusters. The benefit to operators is that Anthos enables them to use single command deployment of new clusters with GKE and GKE On-Prem (gkectl). It also provides a platform for the centralized configuration management and compliance as well as simplified deployment and roll back via Anthos Config Management and Git check-ins. As a result Anthos provides operators with a single pane of glass visibility across all clusters from infrastructure through to application performance and topology with Stackdriver.

From a security perspective, we can consider Anthos to enforce security standards on clusters, deployed applications, and even the configuration management. Anthos provides a central point for audit and a secured workflow via Git compliant repositories. It also provides for compliance enforcement of cluster configurations using namespaces and labels as well as inherited configurations and the securing of microservices via Istio and in-cluster mTLS certificates.

Furthermore with Anthos Migrate you can now let Anthos auto-migrate your VMs from on-premises, or other clouds, directly into containers in GKE. This new migration technology lets you easily and quickly migrate your infrastructure without modifications to the original VMs or applications. This frees-up operations from managing housekeeping tasks like VM maintenance and OS patching, so it can focus on managing and developing applications.

Istio

Istio is an open source service mesh that reduces the complexity of microservice deployments. A service mesh is often necessary to describe and manage the network of connections that proliferate when applications use microservices. A service mesh is therefore a centralised interconnect a patch panel for services that handles all the interactions between modules and applications. As a service mesh grows in size it grows exponentially in complexity, so it becomes much harder to understand and manage. Developers and administrators thus need methods that enable microservice discovery, load balancing, failure recovery, metrics, and monitoring. Istio provides this visibility and connectivity by layering transparently onto your existing distributed applications. It is also a platform with its own range of APIs so it integrates into any logging platform, or telemetry or policy system. Istio enables you to operate a distributed microservice architecture, which provides you with a uniform way to secure, connect, and monitor microservices. However what makes Istio so popular in cloud environments is it makes it easy to create a network of deployed services and container clusters with load balancing, service-to-service authentication, monitoring, and even canary testing, with few or no code changes in service code. You simply add Istio support to services by deploying a special sidecar proxy throughout your environment. The sidecar (Envoy) intercepts all network communication between the associated microservices or clusters, which then allows you to configure and manage the services using Istio. Some of Istio's functionality includes:

- Automatic load balancing for HTTP, gRPC, WebSocket, and TCP traffic.
- Fine-grained traffic control with routing rules, retries, failovers, and recovery.

- A policy and configuration API supporting access controls, rate limits and quotas.
- Support for metrics, logs, and traces for all traffic within a cluster, including cluster ingress and egress.
- Secure service-to-service communication in a cluster with strong identity-based authentication and authorization.

Istio is essential for traffic management, security and observability in cloud and hybrid environments when using microservices or containers via Istio Connect, Istio Secure and Istio Monitoring respectively.

In GCP Istio is integrated with GKE and you simply have to install Istio on Kubernetes Engine with the Istio on GKE add-on. You can also integrate Compute Engine VMs into an Istio mesh deployed on Kubernetes Engine. Furthermore, Istio can be used with Google Cloud Endpoints service.

Use Case -9

The client ABC has raised concerns regards how their in-house support teams can monitor the new cloud environment. They need to be able to configure alerts and notifications as well and build dashboards that provide data on performance KPIs for reporting purposes. In addition they want to explore ways for moving their existing virtualisation environment consisting of VMs to the cloud container platform GKE.

Solution

The obvious solution for this proposal is to configure Stackdriver for uptime, application and system monitoring. To achieve this you can configure uptime checks using HTTP, HTTPS, UDP or TCP on URLs, applications, load balancers and most resources. In addition to simple uptime checks you can also delve deeper using application level monitoring. In this case you are interested in alerts about the health of the application rather than the VM. If you are using App Engine you can even get latency checks performed. Then there are the system checks whereby you configure alerts for such things as CPU and memory usage, network traffic utilisation or open TCP connections. However you can also configure for processes such as to audit which processes are running, sleeping or are zombies. Stackdriver also provided a method for logging, which support teams will require when troubleshooting. Logging is inbuilt into Stackdriver and App Engine and it can capture some GKE events. However for Compute Engine you will have to install the agent. Stackdriver Logging UI supports several methods for searching such as by time interval, response code, log level, log source amongst other things. However, if the standard search capabilities of the Logging UI are not enough, you can export your logs to Google BigQuery, which can quickly query, aggregate or filter several terabytes of data.

With regards migrating or managing containers on-premises then Athos is something you might want to consider. Although a relatively new product it is designed for hybrid environments as well as multi-cloud ones so would be a good fit for the clients' purpose. Indeed the Anthos' hybrid functionality is available both on Google Cloud Platform (GCP) with Google Kubernetes Engine (GKE), and there is now a data center edition with GKE On-Prem. This software solution also lets you manage workloads running on third-party clouds like AWS and Azure, so you can deploy, run and manage your applications on the cloud or premises that you want. Anthos will give the client a unified management view of their hybrid deployment and a consistent platform to run their workloads. However if you are deploying on GKE and using clusters or microservices then you would want to look at deploying Istio for GKE as it can provide the necessary discovery, connectivity, monitoring and traffic control you will need in that environment.

Chapter 10 - Cloud Big Data Solutions

Google believes that in the future every company will be a data driven company and making the best use of information will be a critical competitive advantage. To that end Google Cloud provides a way for every business to take advantage of Google's investments in infrastructure and data processing innovation. By doing so, they have abstracted the complexity of building and maintaining data and analytics systems from the inherent constraints of expertise and financial restrictions.

In this chapter we will learn how to leverage Google's technologies for the fastest and most cost effective way to deliver competitive advantage by using the GCP Big Data services.

Whether the business initiative is to strive for real time analytics or pursue machine learning these Big Data tools are intended to be simple and practical to use. Google has designed them for you to readily embed in your applications so that you can get those business critical insights faster.

Google's Cloud Big Data solutions help you transform your business and user experiences with meaningful data insights without you having to have multi-million dollar on-premises infrastructure or a team of in-house data scientists.

Big Data Solutions

Google likes to describe Big Data Solutions as an Integrated Serverless Platform. Where a Serverless platform means you don't have to worry about provisioning compute instances to run your jobs. As with App Engine and Service Functions this is a fully managed service, so it provisions the required infrastructure and resources seamlessly and transparently when needed and you pay only for the resources you consume.

The platform is integrated, so that GCP data services work together to help you create custom solutions.

Big Data Solutions is built around and compatible with Apache Hadoop, which is an open source framework for Big Data. You may often hear the term Hadoop used informally to mean the Apache Hadoop and all its associated services such as Spark, Pig, and Hive. Regardless, Hadoop is built on the MapReduce programming model which Google invented and subsequently published. The concept behind the MapReduce model is that it works on two functions. The first function is called the Map function, which runs in parallel with a massive dataset to produce an intermediate set of results. Then a second function called the reduce function will use the intermediate set of results as a source from which to build a final result set.

Cloud Dataproc

Cloud Dataproc is a managed service that enables you to use the open source data tools for tasks such as batch processing in batch and streaming modes, querying and machine learning.

Cloud Dataproc is a fast, easy, and managed way to run Hadoop, Spark, Hive, and Pig on Google Cloud Platform. All you have to do is request a Hadoop cluster. It will be built for you in 90 seconds or less on top of Compute Engine virtual machines whose number and type you may control. If you need more or less processing power while your cluster is running, you can scale it up or down at will.

You can use the default configuration for the Hadoop software in your cluster or you can customize it. Also you can monitor your cluster using Stackdriver. However a significant attraction to running Big Data and Dataproc is that when running Hadoop on-premises it will require a major capital hardware investment and considerable operational costs. On the other hand running these Hadoop jobs in Cloud Dataproc, allows you to only pay for hardware resources used during the life of the cluster you create so there is no capital investment (CapEx) and little in comparison to on-premises operation expenditure (OpEx) as Dataproc is a managed service. This makes it very efficient and cost effective.

Although the rate for pricing is based on the hour, Cloud Dataproc is built by the second.

GCP's Cloud Dataproc clusters are built in one second clock time increments and subject to a one minute minimum billing. So, remember when you're finished using your cluster, you should delete it as then the billing stops. This is a much more agile use of resources than on-premise hardware assets.

You can also save money, by telling Cloud Dataproc to use pre-emptible Compute Engine instances for your batch processing. However you must make sure that your jobs can be restarted cleanly if they're terminated. But if they can be stopped gracefully restarted then you can get a significant discount in the cost of running the VM instances - around 80 percent cheaper.

Be aware though that the cost of the Compute Engine instances isn't the only component of the cost of a Dataproc cluster, but it's a significant one.

Once your data is in a cluster, you can use Spark and Spark SQL to do data mining.

And you can use MLib, which are Apache Spark's machine learning libraries to discover patterns through machine learning.

Cloud Dataproc is great when you have a data set of known size or when you want to manage your cluster size yourself. But what if your data shows up in real time or its arrival is of unpredictable size or rate?

That's where Cloud Dataflow is a particularly good choice.

Cloud Dataflow

The GCP service Cloud Dataflow is a fully-managed ETL (Extract, Transform and Load) service that is equally capable of handling streaming data in real time and/or historical data in batch mode. Cloud Dataflow is serverless, which means there is no need for resource provisioning and management, Google handles all this for you. However, with Dataflow you still have access to almost infinite capacity to leverage against your toughest data processing and analysis challenges.

You can use Dataflow to build data pipelines via expressive SQL, Java, and Python APIs in the Apache Beam SDK, and these pipelines work for both batch and streaming data with equal reliability. There's no need to spin up a cluster or to size instances as Cloud Dataflow will fully automate the management of whatever processing resources are required.

Cloud Dataflow frees you from operational tasks like resource management and performance optimization.

You use Dataflow to build really expressive pipelines where each step in the pipeline is elastically scaled. Some of those transforms you see are considered to be map operations and some are considered to be a reduce operations. Furthermore, there is no need to launch and manage a cluster as the service provides all resources on demand.

People use Dataflow in a variety of use cases as it's a data pipeline as well as a general purpose ETL tool. Hence it has use case as a data analysis engine, which comes in handy in things like fraud detection in financial services, IoT analytics in manufacturing, healthcare and logistics as well as click stream, point of sale and segmentation analysis in retail.

And because those pipelines can orchestrate multiple services even external services it can be used in real time applications such as personalizing gaming user experiences.

Nonetheless, what if instead of a dynamic pipeline, your data needs to be analysed more in the way of searching by trawling through a vast ocean of data. For example you want to make ad-hoc SQL queries against a massive data set – well then the GCP has a solution for that and it is called, BigQuery.

BigQuery

This is Google's fully manage petabyte scale, low cost analytics data warehouse.

Because there's no infrastructure to manage, so you can focus on analysing data using the popular and commonly understood SQL command syntax to find meaningful insights.

It is also easy to get your data into BigQuery as you can load it direct from cloud storage or cloud data store, or stream it into Big Query at up to 100,000 rows per second.

Once the data has been loaded, you can run SQL queries against multiple terabytes of data in seconds making queries run super-fast. In addition to running SQL queries, you can also easily perform read and write in BigQuery via GCP's ETL service called Cloud Dataflow, or even use the Big Data open source Hadoop, or Spark.

BigQuery is built upon and uses the processing power of Google's infrastructure to deliver its high performance and vast scale so it can be used by all types of organizations from startup to Fortune 500 companies. Indeed, smaller organizations will often take advantage of Big Query's free monthly quotas, while larger organizations like its seamless scale, capacity, SQl queries and it's available of 99.9 percent service level agreement.

Google's infrastructure is global and so is BigQuery, which lets you specify the region where your data will be kept. This can be an important decision based upon technical criteria such as latency and network traffic or by regulatory compliance such as GDPR. So, for example, if you want or are required to keep data only in Europe, you don't have to go set-up a cluster in Europe. Just specify the EU location where you create your data set. The US and Asia locations are also available.

Regardless of where you store your data you still retain full control over who has access to the data stored in BigQuery. This includes sharing data sets with people in different projects. Moreover, if you do share your data sets with other projects that won't impact your cost or performance, people you share with pay for their own queries, not you.

On another billing topic, because BigQuery separates storage and computation, you pay for your data storage separately from queries. That means you pay for queries only when they are actually running.

In addition there is long term storage pricing, which is an automatic discount for data residing in BigQuery for extended periods of time. So for example if your data exceeds a storage time of 90 days in BigQuery, then Google will automatically apply a discount to the price of the storage.

As BigQuery is a data analytics warehouse its natural use cases are applications such as real-time inventory systems, large-scale events and log analytics, IoT, predictive maintenance, digital marketing and data distribution with large scale commercial or public data sets.

Pub/Sub Messaging Service

For modern applications that require the analytics of data streams from many distributed sources such as the IoT, especially if these are event-driven processes working in real time, it is necessary in order to scale to have a messaging service.

The GCP uses the Cloud Pub/Sub service as its messaging service and this model is designed on the publish/subscribe pattern that is commonly found in software and networking design.

The concept of the Pub/Sub messaging service is that it designates entities as being a publisher of a message and others as explicit subscribers –this means that a publisher will only send a message to an entity that has subscribed to the message - this makes it an efficient, simple, reliable, scalable foundation for stream analytics. Moreover, the Pub/Sub service allows you to interconnect independent applications you build or interface with to efficiently send and receive messages but importantly they remain decoupled so that they are able to scale independently.

The way the Pub/Sub works is that an application can publish messages in Pub/Sub and one or more subscribers will subscribe for those specific messages in order to receive them.

However, sending and receiving messages doesn't have to be synchronous and it's designed to provide at least once delivery at low latency, which makes Pub/Sub great for decoupling systems. However when we say at-least-once delivery, we mean that there is a small chance some messages might be delivered more than once. This is very important to understand when you write your application. For example, you don't want double or triple transactions to go through in a financial or trading application.

You can configure your subscribers to receive messages on a push or pull basis. In other words, subscribers can get notified when new messages arrive for them or they can check for new messages at intervals.

Cloud Pub/Sub builds on the same technology, which Google uses within its own global products for messaging and in event-driven applications. It is an important building block for applications that handle ingress data traffic that arrives at high or unpredictable rates like Internet of Things systems. Cloud Pub/Sub offers on demand scalability to one million messages per second and beyond but you simply choose the quota you are comfortable with.

If you're in the business of analysing streaming data, Cloud Dataflow as a streaming pipeline is a natural pairing with Pub/Sub. Applications built on GCP's Compute Engine platform are also good candidates for and easily interfaced using Pub/Sub.

We will revisit Pub/Sub later in more detail in subsequent chapters as it is such an important component in Cloud architecture.

Cloud Datalab

Scientists have long used lab notebooks to organize their thoughts and explore their data.

For data scientists they also use web-based applications called notebooks because it is a natural way to aggregate their data analysis with their comments about their results in one accessible place.

A popular environment for hosting those is Project Jupyter as it lets you create and maintain web-based notebooks containing Python code and you can run that code interactively and view the results. In GCP the Cloud Datalab service addresses this need and it also takes the management work out of maintaining lab notebooks. Datalab runs in a Compute Engine virtual machine, so to get started, you simply specify the virtual machine type you want and what GCP region it should run in. When it launches, it presents an interactive Python environment that's ready to use. As it is tightly integrated with BigQuery, Compute Engine, and Cloud Storage, you will find that accessing your data doesn't run into authentication issues. Moreover, Datalab also orchestrates multiple GCP services automatically, so you can focus on exploring your data.

Once you have Datalab up and running, you can visualize your data with Google charts or map plot line. Also if you want tips or learn more there is an interactive Python community, which publish their notebooks. There are also many existing packages for statistics, machine learning, and so on. With Datalab, you will only pay for the resources you use so there is no additional charge for Datalab itself.

Use Case -10

A client has an API hosted on GKE and they wish to log the events into a database for later analysis. They don't require any transformation just straight insertion as-is so they have considered; option 1, inserting the events directly into BigQuery using its API, or option 2, using Pub Sub to stream events into Dataflow for insertion into BigQuery. What would you propose?

Solution

Option 1 may be the simplest solution as you don't need to transform the data but they must be aware that it won't scale and they won't be able to handle errors properly i.e. back-off-and-retry. Therefore the recommended method is to use the following configuration: App -> Pub Sub -> Dataflow (streaming) -> BigQuery. That's the way to get the solution to scale and handle errors correctly and it is the most fault-tolerant and scalable solution.

Chapter 11 - Machine Learning

Machine learning is an exciting branch of the field of artificial intelligence that has really caught the imagination over the last decade though it has been around for much longer than that. Machine Learning has huge potential in business and industry as it is a way of solving problems without explicitly coding the solution or even knowing the solution beforehand. Instead, human coders build machine learning systems using algorithms that are designed to be highly iterative and self-learning so they can improve themselves over time through repeated exposure to sample data which we call training data.

One of the issues with machine learning is that it requires vast amounts of data and the corresponding infrastructure to handle it. That doesn't just mean storage but also the networks, processing power, software and servers to operate at the required scale. This constraint meant many SMEs felt that machine learning at any serious scale was beyond them. However, the Google Machine Learning Platform is now available as a cloud service so that you can add innovative capabilities to your own applications without having to build your own infrastructure and applications.

Indeed, Google applications that rely on machine learning such as YouTube, Photos, Google mobile App and Google translate have shown what machine learning can achieve when using Google's internet-scale infrastructure.

In addition the Google Machine Learning Platform gives you the necessary tools to run machine learning exercises using pre-trained models or to generate your own custom models.

As with other GCP products, there's a range of services that stretches from the highly general and pre-configured to the highly specialized and pre-customized in order to suit all needs.

Google not only provides the internet scale infrastructure and services that will enable you to run machine learning it also provides the applications, algorithms and libraries. TensorFlow is Google's own open source software library that's exceptionally well suited for machine learning applications like neural networks. TensorFlow was developed for Google's internal use and then made available to the open source community. As a result you can use TensorFlow wherever you like but GCP is an ideal place for it because machine learning models need lots of on-demand compute resources and lots of training data.

Moreover when it comes to machine learning you start to move into the realms of huge processing power and the need for GPUs. However Google has developed a processor especially designed for TensorFlow. These TPU's, Tensor Processing Units, which are hardware devices designed to accelerate, machine learning workloads with TensorFlow can be thought of as cloud based rivals to the GPU.

GCP makes the TPU available in the cloud with Compute Engine virtual machines and each cloud TPU provides up to 180 teraflops of performance.

But, because you pay for only what you use, there's no upfront capital investment required in order to get your hands on the potentially infinite resources you may require for your machine learning adventure.

Nonetheless, machine learning is not for the faint-hearted and even with all the Google resource on-tap many business want a more managed service. Hence, Google Cloud Machine Learning Engine will let you construct machine learning models that will work on any type or any size of data set. Also, the Machine Learning Engine can take any TensorFlow model and perform large scale training on a managed cluster.

Moreover, if you want access to add various machine learning capabilities to your applications then Google Cloud also offers a range of machine learning APIs suited to specific purposes. This provides you with access to machine learning functions and services without you having to concern yourself with the details of how they are provided.

Organizations in all sorts of fields use the Cloud Machine Learning Platform for lots of diverse applications. But they can almost always fall into two categories depending on whether the data they work on is structured or unstructured.

Based on structured data, you can use ML for various kinds of classification and regression tasks like customer churn analysis, product diagnostics and forecasting.

It can be the heart of our recommendation engine for content personalization and cross-sells and up-sells.

You can use ML to detect anomalies as in fraud detection, sensor diagnostics or log metrics.

On the other hand if your machine learning is based on unstructured data, you can use ML for image analytics and many popular use cases in commerce and industry, such as, for identifying substandard components on a conveyor belt, identifying damaged shipments, or for automated inventory and stock control.

But you can also do text analytics too, which opens up opportunities for automating processes such as validating forms, blog analysis, language identification, topic classification and even advanced sentiment analysis.

You will likely find that beneath the hood of many innovative applications are machine learning systems that contain several of these kinds of applications working together. The Google Cloud machine Learning Platform makes that kind of interactivity well within your grasp.

GCP Managed Services

In the last few chapters, we have focused on how to create, use and manage cloud infrastructure in GCP. However there is an alternative to creating, running and managing infrastructure in the first place and that is to integrate an existing solution into your application design. If you would rather spend your time working on the development of your applications rather than on building the architecture that they run on, then you should consider GCP's built-in managed service.

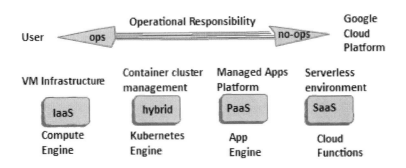

Figure -8

In short, if we consider Compute Engine to be at the hands on IaaS end of the spectrum then we can consider managed services to be at the Serverless end of the spectrum as it is typically a partial or complete zero-touch range of managed solutions offered as a service.

However not all managed services are completely serverless so in practice they actually exist on a continuum between platform as a service and software as a service, which is

Determined by how much of the internal methods and control are actually exposed to the user. Generally though, if you choose to deploy a managed service you are in effect outsourcing the provisioning, running and lifecycle management of the service and all its dependencies to Google. For a lot of companies whose core businesses is something other than network design, management and support this approach makes a lot of sense. Focusing on the core business releases a lot of precious resources and passed the administrative and maintenance burden to Google.

If this sound likes a match with your business model then instead of setting up an infrastructure to support specific types of workloads, you may want to take advantage of some of the many services that Google have to offer on GCP as managed services.

In this chapter we will be covering some fully managed services such as Dataproc, Dataflow, BigQuery, and some other managed services of interest. Most of these are Big Data, machine learning and data analytics orientated, which is really where most small to medium businesses lack skills but where Google excels, especially on their own cloud infrastructure.

Let's take a look at the continuum of solution options.

On-premises	IaaS	PaaS	SaaS
Application	Application	Application	Application

Data	Data	Data	Data
Runtime	Runtime	Runtime	Runtime
Middleware	Middleware	Middleware	Middleware
OS	OS	OS	OS
Virtualisation	Virtualisation	Virtualisation	Virtualisation
Servers	Servers	Servers	Servers
Storage	Storage	Storage	Storage
Networking	Networking	Networking	Networking

In the table above you the user are responsible for looking after the blue coloured functions and Google is responsible for the orange functions.

As you can see with IaaS you can pretty much build everything you want by building your own infrastructure using the console, cloud shell, and virtual machines. We'll also learn a little bit later about automating our infrastructure using Cloud API in programmatic deployments using Deployment Manager. However, when you start to deploy managed services you begin to move from Infrastructure as a Service towards Platform as a Service and then eventually to Serverless Computing, so you don't have to worry about programmatically automating processes.

Compute Engine and Deployment Manager provide you with the means to actively control and architect your environment and allows you to hands-on build your infrastructure. However when you move to adopting managed services such as Dataproc and Dataflow you are now well into Platform as a Service territory. What this means is that you have less control but also less administrative burden. When you move further towards BigQuery, which is GCP's vast data warehouse, it is a fully embracing managed service more akin to Software as a Service.

There is a continuum of services and platform options available in GCP. Several can perform a similar function but you should consider all options in a particular context. Now, contemplating the diagram, we can see that the solutions to the left offer greater outsourcing of management and administrative overhead, but with a loss of control. On the other hand, the solutions to the right offer greater hands-on control but with increased responsibility and management overhead.

We can look to three of the managed services we discussed earlier to see how this works in practice. For example, if we look at the data processing managed services we can see that they comprise three core services.

The first one is Dataproc, which is a managed service which lets you spin up a Spark Hadoop cluster quickly and cost effectively with both Hive and Pig in-built capabilities. Now, what you have to consider is just how long and at what expense would it take to accomplish that on-premises? But in GCP you can spin up this environment that utilizing a preconfigured deployment manager process we call Dataproc in a matter of minutes.

The second data processing managed service is Dataflow and it is of interest as it is GCP's ETL batch and streaming processing pipeline. Dataflow is based on the Apache Beam open SDK framework. This means it is compatible with Apache Beam and so you can create your own ETL jobs. You can submit them yourselves on your own platform, or you can push them to Google Cloud's Dataflow. In this case Dataflow will handle all that automatic scaling and realtime streaming, in order to speed up the ETL processing.

Finally, the third service is Google's BigQuery. Now as we know BigQuery is a fully managed data analytic service that can scale to the petabyte scale. Further, BigQuery is also a fully -fledged Software as a Service. However to better understand each of these data processing components we need to learn a little bit more about each of them in turn.

DataProc

Cloud Dataproc, is a managed Spark and Hadoop service that lets you take advantage of open source data for batch processing, querying streaming and machine learning. Indeed as a managed cloud service DataProc has a number of interesting features probably the most notable is it is very affordable. This is due to GCP having automated the deployment process and by utilizing Google's vast compute network and infrastructure to derive cost at scale. These benefits also include per second billing, sustained use discounts, the ability to use pre-emptible virtual machines, amongst several other discounts.
Nonetheless, DataProc is also outstanding with regards to its technical features. Despite these high technical capabilities DataProc is actual very quick and easy to deploy. Further it is easier to provision and maintain these resources because Google is responsible for most of the maintenance burden.

Another compelling feature with regards DataProc is that GCP supports all of the major third party ETL data analytics software packages whether they be open source or proprietary. This means they are likely to support the packages that you may already be utilizing on-premises or feel that you might want to utilize in the cloud.

GCP also integrates as you would expect very tightly with a number of other related Google products, including Google Cloud Storage, Bigtable and BigQuery. Indeed, you can output or even ingest data directly from Bigtable because it's using a compatible HBase API. With reference to performance DataProc is notably faster when data processing workflows because less time is wasted having to wait for clusters to provision and start executing applications. To connect to your Dataproc cluster, you can use the web-based user interface to submit jobs. You can also use the YARN Web UI, HDFS web user interface, as well as SSH through a SOCKS proxy.

When it comes to starting a cluster, DataProc doesn't just spin up a bunch of VMs using its own logic, though it can do if that is what you want. Instead DataProc remains controllable, so by using the G-Cloud tool and the Cloud Dataproc API you can interact and control clusters in a programmatic fashion.

Moreover, if you are looking for more granular control you can always deploy and configure Stackdriver to assist in the management, notification, alerting and monitoring of DataProc.

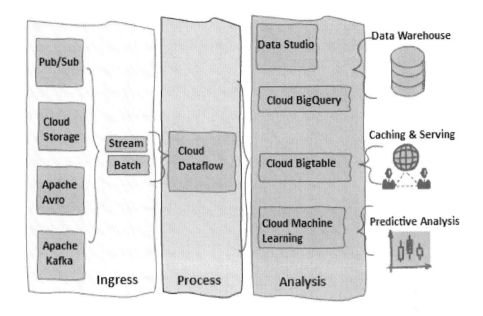

Figure - 9
Dataflow

Dataflow is GCP's online batch and stream ETL processing service. It is based on the open source based Apache Beam SDK. The data process of Extract, Transform, and Load (ETL) are the three key functions that are applied to data being extracted from one source, transformed into a new format and then loaded into another sink database, typically a data warehouse.

ETL thus is the process that acts as an interface and translator facilitating the conversion and separation of data. It is simply part of the data processing function and hence, Dataflow helps retrieve, order, and format the data as its being streamed in to the data processing environment.

Indeed, you may input data from many different sources both on-premises or from other clouds. Typically though it would be from Cloud Datastore but you could output the reorganised data or input it directly into cloud storage such as BigQuery, Bigtable or Cloud Datastore.

The way that this works is that Dataflow creates Pipelines, PCollections, Transforms, and I/O Sources and Sinks.

- Pipelines are a series of computations that accepts data and transforms it, outputting to an external or to an internal Sink. The input source and output Sink can be the same in a Pipeline, as this allows for data format conversion.
- PCollections are a specialized container of nearly unlimited size that represents a set of data in the Pipeline.
- Transforms incoming data to a format suitable for an outgoing process such as our data processing operation.
- I/O Sources and Sinks are different data storage formats. Cloud Storage, BigQuery, Tables, and more, as well as custom data source/sinks.

The following examples give you a sense of the processing capabilities of Dataflow. In this simple model Pipeline data is input from a source into a PCollection, transformed and then output.

In diagram 9 we can see each of the components that make up a pipeline of data processing jobs from multiple sources.

Figure -10

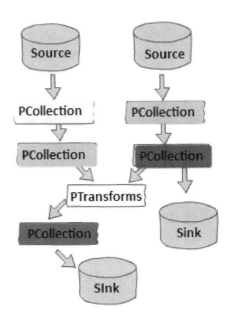

Pipelines: these are data processing job that is made up of a series of computations including input, processing and output.

PCollections: These are bounded (or unbounded) data sets which represent the input, intermediate and output in pipelines.

PTransforms: These are when data processing steps merge in a pipeline and one or more PCollections serve as both an input and output.

I/O Sources and Sinks: APIs for reading and writing data which can be considered to be the roots and endpoints of the pipeline.

In the multiple transform pipelines, data is read from BigQuery then filtered into two collections based on the initial character of the name.

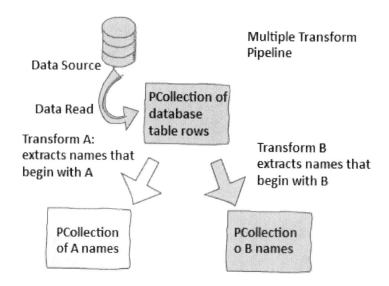

Figure-11

In the merge pipeline example, the purpose is to collect all sorts of data that maybe you've ingested from BigQuery or another data source. We can transform those different names as well, so we can split everything back, and then flatten those out.

In the multiple input pipeline, you're doing joins from different data sources. There are different ways to connect the pieces, but Dataflow's job is to ingest the data in parallel as fast as possible, scale out and then of course output an ETL that's friendly for whatever the normal source it's going to.

BigQuery

BigQuery is a powerful Big Data analytics platform used by all types of organisations. BigQuery is Google's fully managed enterprise scale data warehouse for analytics. BigQuery is low cost, serverless and considered to be Software as a Service (SaaS). Therefore, with BigQuery there is no infrastructure to manage and you don't need a database administrator.

So you can focus on preparing and analysing the data to find meaningful insights using familiar techniques and processes. BigQuery allows you to analyse all your batch and streaming data by creating a logical data warehouse over managed columnar storage. BigQuery has in-built Business Intelligence (BI), and Machine Learning (ML) capabilities that let carry out geospatial analysis on gigabytes to petabytes of data using simple SQL to produce analysis dashboards, spreadsheets, datasets and reports. On performance, BigQuery is very powerful streaming ingestion captures and analysing data in real time, ensuring insights are always current. Nonetheless, probably BigQuery's biggest selling point is that it can be setup in minutes and then scale seamlessly across its serverless architecture without you having to provision any environment resources or invest in on-premises hardware. BigQuery is a fully managed service so it eliminates the entire operational and maintenance burden by automatically replicating your data for redundancy and to guarantee business continuity. Also, for those wanting to try their hand at Big Data analysis or machine learning you can analyse up to 1 TB of data and store 10 GB of data for free each month.

If you are planning venturing into machine learning or advanced analytics then you may want to look to some other GCP managed services that are available. Cloud Datalab is a managed service for data analysts and data scientists that runs on iPython Notebooks, and it combines both a Python library, in which you can write Python code, with real time visualization.

If you're writing Python code to run queries from BigQuery, then you can output those visualizations directly within the Cloud Datalab interface. Because these are Jupyter Python notebooks you can actually save these notebooks and share them with colleagues. Cloud Datalab doesn't just support Python; it also supports interactive SQL and JavaScript.

When we consider data visualisation we mustn't overlook another managed service for data scientists, Data Studio, which lets you create dynamic, visually compelling reports, and dashboards. With Data Studio, you can easily connect to a variety of data sources, visualize your data through attractive, dynamic, and interactive reports and dashboards, and share and collaborate with others, just as you can in Google Drive.

Cloud Vision

Following on from image detection there is the Cloud Vision API which enables developers to understand the content of an image. This API classifies images into thousands of categories, bus, car, traffic lights, sailboat, cat, and so on. It is designed to detect and identify individual objects within images, which is difficult for machines but easy for humans. Nonetheless, it is now advanced enough to also be able to find and read printed words contained within images.

The Cloud Vision API encapsulates powerful machine learning models behind an easy to use API. Therefore, you can use it in your applications to build Meta data on your image catalogue, moderate offensive content or even do image sentiment analysis.

Cloud Speech API

Many of the use cases for Image API can also work with the cloud speech API as it too enables developers to convert audio to text. This can have high utility in business and commerce as the internet brings an increasingly global user base.

Some natural use cases are, transcribing the audio to text in videos, enable command and control through voice command in smart devices, or more mundanely transcribing dictated audio files. Leading on from the Cloud Speech API we have a natural progression from transcribing audio to text to actual language translation.

Cloud Natural Language API

This service offers a variety of natural language understanding technologies to developers. The API recognizes over 80 languages and variants and it can do a lot of great things such as; syntax analysis, by breaking down sentences supplied by our users into tokens, identify the nouns, verbs, adjectives, and other parts of speech and figure out the relationships among the words.

It can also do entity recognition whereby it can parse text and flag mentions of people, organizations, locations, events, products, and media.

Another function is that it can understand the overall sentiment expressed in a block of text. This is becoming a popular use case in call centre use of sentiment analysis on, email, web blogs and text messages.

Furthermore it can perform these capabilities in multiple languages, including English, Spanish, and Japanese.

Cloud translation API

This API provides a simple, programmatic interface for translating an arbitrary string into a supported language. Google translate is an example of machine learning and natural language APIs working in tandem to learn and improve. This is clearly demonstrated by the huge leaps in accuracy and quality in the translation service over just the last few years. It still isn't perfect but it's continuously improving and what's more if you don't know the source language, the API can automatically detect it for you.

Cloud Video Intelligence

The Cloud Video Intelligence API lets you annotate videos in a variety of formats.
It helps you identify key entities that are nouns within your video and when they occur.
You can use it to make video content searchable and discoverable within search engines such as Google.

Dialogflow

The service Dialogflow is considered to be a development suite that you can use when creating conversational interfaces for websites, mobile applications, popular messaging platforms, and IoT devices. Dialogflow is an end-to-end service based upon a build-once deploy-everywhere use case to create UI interfaces such as chatbots and conversational IVR that enable you to build a natural and rich interaction between interactive users and your business infrastructure. Dialogflow is what is known as a Knowledge Connector, which allows you to aggregate large volumes of data from your enterprise to your agent, such as when building FAQs and knowledge-based resources.

Chapter 12 - Google Cloud Networking

In this chapter we will learn how to interact with Google Cloud Platform and you will also be introduced to the concepts behind virtual networking and learn how your virtual machines connect to each other. This is especially important if you are hosting applications that are used by customers all around the globe. If that is the case then you will need to understand how Google does the networking as it differs from the traditional routing that you are probably used to. This is because as we discussed earlier the Google network is essentially a single, flat SDN network that spans the globe.

Now integrated within the Software Defined Network, we have features such as auto-scaler, load balancers, routers, firewalls but these are not physical devices they are essentially rules that Google has distributed to control the flow of traffic across its global SDN network.

Then finally, we will conclude with virtual machines. We will discuss how they work in the cloud environment? We will also discuss what needs to be done when you contemplate moving to the GCP from your own physical environment and physical servers. For example how to you transpose or lift and shift your physical network to what GCP has on offer?

The interesting thing about virtual machines is that they are, in case you don't know, essentially a collection of memory, CPU, storage and network connectivity. We build VMs in the Google Compute Engine. So in this chapter we will see how we build custom VMs that meet your exact needs and billing requirements and how applications can scale and what choices we have.

GCP Infrastructure Fundamentals

Getting started with GCP requires that we get a good understanding of what it actually is because it is far more than just the services we have already highlighted. Indeed, Google Cloud is just part of a much larger ecosystem, which consists of, providers, partners, developers, third-party software, open-source software and other Cloud providers. So, the Google Cloud Platform or GCP is part of the larger Google Cloud ecosystem that consists of Chrome, Google Devices, Google Maps, Google Drive, Gmail, Google Analytics, G Suite, Google Search, amongst others. Therefore, GCP is just one component in the Google Cloud and it can be considered to be a computing solution platform that really encompasses three core features; infrastructure, platform and software.

Google Cloud Platform core services spans from infrastructure as a service, through platform as a service, to software as a service. Now this typically means that there are several ways to accomplish a given task. The alternative solutions on this continuum have different requirements like managing components, systems or resources. This means that selecting the correct service will change the role of your operation staff, some services will require intervention and the management of things like CPUs, memories and disks while others are managed services that Google manages on your behalf and they will require zero intervention by you. By the end of this chapter you will have a good understanding of the alternative solutions on offer and how to best implement them to suit your needs.

Virtual Networks

GCP is one of the largest and fastest networks in the world and it runs upon a software defined network that is built upon Google's own global fibre infrastructure. The important thing to understand is when we talk about resources within the GCP we should really consider them as services. This is because these resources are not hardware, for example, when you choose a persistent disk type and capacity for your VM it isn't really a physical device you are getting. Instead it's a service that you acquire from GCP and you connect and interact with it over a network.

Therefore we need to have a good understanding of how GCP has implemented networking.

Hence, we will start by taking a deeper dive into the Virtual Private Cloud or VPC which we introduced at a high level earlier as it is Google's managed networking functionality for your Cloud Platform resources.

Virtual Private Cloud

With Google Cloud Platform a VPC is your private cloud network, where you can provision your GCP resources, interconnect them or isolate them from one another in a virtual private cloud. Essentially, a VPC is a comprehensive set of Google managed networking objects, which provide isolation, segregation and security in a multi-tenant environment. A VPC can also give you the agility to control how your workloads can connect either locally, regionally or globally. When you connect your on-premises or remote resources to GCP, you will automatically have global connectivity to your VPCs without you having to make configuration changes in each region. You can define fine grained networking policies within the PVC, and between GCP and on-premises or other public clouds.

Global Reach

VPC are global resources so a VPC can span multiple regions by communicating across Google own internal network infrastructure without having to cross the public Internet. For example, you can share a connection between the VPC and your on-premises network without the need for a connection in every region.

Expandable

Google Cloud VPCs are expandable as you can easily increase the IP space of any of the subnets within the VPC without any disruption to running workloads. This means you can make IP configuration changes on the fly without any downtime and provides you with flexibility and future growth options.

Shareable

With a single VPC for an entire organization, teams can be segregated within projects and each has their own separate billing and quotas applied. However, they can still share a private IP subnet and have shared access to services such as VPN or to a Cloud Interconnect.

A Virtual Private Cloud (VPC) is therefore a global private and isolated virtual network partition. The VPC provides managed networking functionality for your Google Cloud Platform (GCP) resources. Hence, you can think of a VPC as a virtual version of your traditional physical network. VPC provides IP addresses for internal and external use along with granular IP address range selections. Networks come in three different types, default, auto mode and custom mode. You use sub-networks to allow you to divide or segregate your network environment.

Types of Network

There are basically three types of networks, the default, auto-mode and custom. However the default network is actually an auto-mode network that is created for you unless you disable it. So in practice there are two main types;

- Auto-mode – when this type of network is created a subnet is assigned in every region from a predefined CIDR block of private IP addresses in the 10.128.0.0/9 range. If or when new regions appear a subnet will automatically be created for the auto-mode network so you don't have to do anything. You can however add your own subnets outside of the 10.128.0.0/9 range if you want.
- Custom mode – with this type of network no subnets are allocated upon creation, which gives you full control of what subnets you want to use. With custom mode networks you have to allocate a subnet in each region where you want to have resources.

Something to note is that you can convert an auto-mode network to a custom-mode, but not vice versa.

Auto-mode networks are easy to setup and they will not clash or overlap with any existing subnets you are using, say for a VPN, as they use a predefined CIDR block. However as they use the same predefined address block of IP you are unable to connect these networks together, for example in VPC peering.

Custom mode is far more flexible but you have to do the subnet allocation in each region yourself. However, if you don't need automated subnet allocation in every region and want more granular control that allows you to use Cloud VPN and VPC network peering then this is the mode you will use.

Primary and Secondary Address

A network in GCP can have a primary and a secondary subnets allocated. You can select any private address range for both of these addresses so long as they are different. Primary addresses are the main address space that the VMs will use to communicate over. Secondary addresses are used as aliases for example to reference different services within a VM.

One thing of note though when using custom mode networks is that GCP reserves 4 addresses within the subnet. The first and last addresses in the subnet range are like in traditional networks reserved for the subnet address and the broadcast, respectively. However, in GCP it also reserves the second and second-last addresses in the subnet for the default gateway and for future use respectively.

Projects, Regions and Zones

Google Cloud Platform (GCP) use projects as the foundation for creating, enabling, and running all GCP services. This includes, enabling billing, adding and removing collaborators, and managing APIs and IAM permissions for GCP resources.

A region is a specific geographical location where you can run your resources. Each region has one or more zones; most regions have three or more zones. For example, the US Central one region denotes a region in the central United States that has four zones, such as US Central 1A, US Central 1B, US Central 1C, and US Central 1F.

Zones can be thought of as Google's data centres, although that is not strictly true as some zones may well have several, but its close enough. A collection of zones reside in a region and they have an interesting feature whereby a subnet can be shared across zones making them ideal for continuous data protection and high availability.

Projects, Networks, and Sub-networks

Projects are the key method for organizing and holding all your infrastructure resources. A resource can be in only one project because a project associates objects and services with billing. Nonetheless, projects can contain up to five entire networks. Interestingly these networks do not have IP ranges assigned, but instead are simply a construct of all of the individual IP subnets, or services that are contained within that project. GCPs networks are global in their reach across all available regions around the world. What this means is that in GCP a single VPC network covers the entire planet. Hence, it is only the IP subnets that are attached to a specific region. But as the virtual machines communicate between subnets using private IPs (RFC1918 addresses) over Google's internal global network—therefore no extra routing is needed.

So, for example, if you have servers in the USA, Singapore and Europe all you have to do to make your servers communicate across continents on GCP is to:

1. create a VPC network
2. create a subnet in the US, put your US servers in it
3. create a subnet in Europe, put your Europe servers in it
4. create a subnet in Singapore, put your Singapore servers in it

That's all there is to it. Your VPC network will naturally, due to the SDN architecture, span the three continents so it is already functional. This global reach means that you have effectively one network that exists anywhere in the world, Asia, Europe, America and what is more, simultaneously.

Alternatively networks can be used to provide segregation in a multi-tenant environment. This is due to the fact that even though there are VMs in the same region and zone they are logically separated from one another by being in different networks.

As we have just seen inside of a network, you can also segregate your VM resources using sub-networks. Subnets can also be used to isolate systems inside the same GCP network.

We can see how this is done by studying the accompanying diagram of a project that contains two networks.

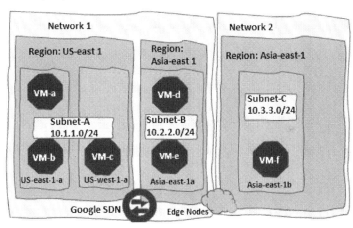

Figure -12

In the diagram, we can see that each network contains some virtual machines. Now in Network 1 we can see that it has two subnets, A and B, but even though they are in different regions they can still communicate over their internal IP addresses across the Google SDN fibre infrastructure, which , makes those two subnets and their VMs appear as though they are on the same layer-2 switch.

However, if we consider the subnet C and its VM-f, we can see that they are not in the same network. Thus, VM-f cannot communicate directly even though they are in the same region as VM-d and VM-e they cannot communicate using their private IP addresses so they must communicate over external IPs. But a notable thing is that this traffic doesn't traverse the internet as you would probably think. Instead the traffic between VMs, C and D, is going through the Google Edge routers, which incidentally have different billing, latency and security criteria that we need to take into consideration.

The diagram has a region, region 1 with two zones, Zone A, and Zone B. Subnetworks can extend across zones within the same region such as subnet 1. The subnet is simply an IP address range, so you can carve up IP addresses within that range into smaller groups.

Just like in traditional IP networks the first address in the subnet is reserved for the router address. The last address in the subnet is reserved for the broadcast address. Even though the two virtual machines in this example are across different zones, they will still communicate with each other using the same subnet IP address. Essentially, a single firewall rule will apply to both VMs even though they are in different zones.

Typically in the data centre you might design your IP plan to be divided into sub-networks in the traditional way based on a top-down hierarchy. For example you may have a master network 172.168.0.0, and then you segment it into smaller blocks called subnets. Essentially, these subnets have been segregated from one another to minimise the broadcast traffic. You could then deploy a different subnet to each department giving them some rudimentary security from one another. Each of these subnets might then represent different departments such as, sales, finance, marketing, or development.

The difference though is that in GCP, networks do not have IP ranges so you just simply set up a network. Then you create multiple subnets for sales, finance, marketing, and development. But because there is no parent IP address range assigned to the network the sub-networks don't need to fit into an address hierarchy.

While sub-networks can be used to provide some rudimentary levels of security and manage resources, there are other more flexible ways of doing this such as with Cloud IAM, labels, tags, and managed instance groups.

IP Addresses

A virtual machine in GCP can support two IP addresses. One of the IP addresses is allocated via DHCP internally and is used as an internal IP address. Every VM that you make and then any service, such as App Engine, that depends on virtual machines gets an internal IP address. Hence upon creation of the VMs their symbolic name is registered by GCP with an internal DNS service. The DNS is scoped to the network so that it can translate the symbolic name to the internal IP address. Using DNS it can translate web URLs and VM names of hosts in the same network, but it can't translate hostnames from VMs in a different network.

The other IP address that can be assigned is the external IP address which is optional.

You would only need to assign an external IP address if your device or machine is accessed publically over the internet. The public or external IP address can either be assigned from a pool, making it dynamic and ephemeral or it can be statically assigned a reserved external IP address. The point to understand is that you will be billed for reserving external IP addresses this applies even when they're not attached to a running VM.

Also, whether you use an ephemeral or static IP address, the external address is unknown to the OS of the VM. This is because the external IP address is mapped to the VM's internal address transparently by VPC. You can demonstrate this yourself by running the internal command 'IP Config', within a VM in GCP; you will find that it only returns the internal IP address. To understand why this is we need to understand how the DNS service works.

As we know, each VM instance has a symbolic name, used as the hostname, which can be resolved by DNS to an internal IP address. Moreover, there is also an internal fully qualified domain name, or FQDN for the VM that uses the format hostname.c.project-id.internal.

However, should you delete and recreate a VM instance, the internal IP address can change as it's assigned dynamically by DHCP. This change in IP address can cause disruption in active connections from other Google Compute Engine resources as if their connection is lost they must obtain the new IP address via DNS before they can connect again. Hence, the DNS name always points to a specific instance no matter what the internal IP address is.

The way that this works is that each VM instance has a metadata server that handles all DNS queries for local network resources, so it acts as a DNS Resolver for that instance.

The metadata server also handles all other non-internal queries by sending them to Google's public DNS servers for public name resolution.

However, as we have already noted, the VM instance is not aware of any external IP address assigned to it. Instead, the network stores a look up table that matches the external IP address with the internal IP address.

A VM instances with an external IP addresses is allowed to accept connections from hosts outside of the project. Indeed that is how users outside the project access your application by calling it directly using the external IP address.

However there are a few caveats here as for one, the public DNS records pointing to instances are not published automatically. Indeed, by default an admin has to publish these using existing DNS servers.

But you can host Domain names in GCP using Google Cloud DNS. This is a managed service for those that don't want to create their own BIND server on another VM.

Another networking feature of GCP is alias IP ranges. Alias IP ranges let you assign a range of internal IP addresses as aliases to a virtual machine's primary network interface.

This is useful if you have multiple services running on a VM and you want to assign each service a different IP address.

In essence, you can configure multiple IP addresses representing containers or applications hosted on a VM without having to define a separate network interface. You just draw out the alias IP range from the local subnets primary or secondary CIDR ranges.

Routing Traffic

So far we have covered projects, networks, sub-networks, IP addresses and DNS.

Now we need to pull this all together to understand how GCP routes traffic. In GCP each network has its own virtual router that collects and maintains the routes that let instances in the network send traffic directly to each other even across subnets. The virtual router by default only works in regional dynamic mode whereby it only shares routes within its own region. There is an alternative, global dynamic routing mode whereby the virtual router will share routes it learns with every region. Also, each network has a default route that directs packets for an unknown destination to a default gateway that handles IP addresses that are outside the network. Although these routes will typically cover most of your needs, you can also create special routes that override them should the need arise.

However, just because a VM has a route to a packet destination does not mean that the packet can get there. Routes match packets by destination IP address but no traffic will flow without it matching a firewall rule.

Therefore in addition to a valid route a firewall rules must also allow the packet. Therefore, the default network has preconfigured firewall rules that allow all instances in the network to talk with each other. But the manually created and custom networks do not have any preconfigured rules you will need to create them yourself.

Firewall rules

To understand how to make firewall rules we must first understand the routing process. By default, a route is created in the routing table when a network is created, enabling traffic delivery from anywhere. Also, a route is created when the subnet is created. This is what enables VMs on the same subnet to communicate internally.

However a route in the routing table may apply to one or more instances. A route applies to an instance, if the network and instance tags match. For example, if the network matches and there are no instance tags specified, the route applies to all instances in that network.

Compute Engine then creates individual read-only routing tables for each instance.

Therefore within GCP there is a virtual router at the core of each network and every virtual machine instance in the network is directly connected to this router. In practice all packets leaving a virtual machine instance are first directed to and handled by the network's own virtual router. It is only then they are forwarded on their next hop on their path.

The virtual network router selects the next hop for each packet by consulting the individual routing table for that instance.

GCP firewall rules on the other hand exist to protect your VM instances from unapproved connections in both the inbound and outbound directions – in firewall terms this is often know as ingress and egress respectively.

However a firewall is not a physical device it is essentially the VPC network itself that functions as a distributed firewall. This is because the firewall rules are applied to the network and connections are allowed or denied at the instance level.

Therefore you should consider the firewall as existing not only between your VM instances and other networks, but also between individual instances within the same network.

Also, if for some reason all firewall rules in a network are deleted, there's still an implied deny all ingress rule, and an implied allow all egress rule for the network.

You can express your desired firewall configuration as a set of firewall rules. Conceptually, a firewall rule is composed of the following parameters;

- The direction of the rule - Inbound connections are matched against ingress rules only, and outbound connections are matched against egress rules only, the source of the connection for ingress packets or the destination of the connection for egress packets.

- There is the protocol and port of the connection, where any rule can be restricted to apply to specific protocols only or specific combinations of protocols and ports only.
- There is the action of the rule, which allows or denies packets to match the direction protocol port and source or destination of the rule, the priority of the rule which governs the order, in which rules are evaluated, the first matching rule is applied, and the rule assignment is made.
- By default, all rules are assigned to all instances, but you can assign certain rules to certain instances only.

GCP firewall use cases for both egress and ingress

Firstly let us consider the way the Egress firewall rules work to control outgoing connections originated inside your GCP network;

- Egress allow rules are set to allow all by default
- Egress allow rules permit a VM to initiate a connection that match specific protocols, ports, and IP addresses
- Egress deny rules, are used to prevent instances from initiating connections that match non-permitted port, protocol, and IP source or destination ranges
- For Egress firewall rules, destinations to which a rule applies may be specified using IPs or ranges

You can also use destination ranges to protect from undesired connections, initiated by a VM instance, toward an external destination. You can also use destination ranges to protect from undesired connections, initiated by VM instance toward specific VMs in another subnet.

On the other hand Ingress firewall rules protect against incoming connections to the instance from any source. Ingress rules are set as 'deny all' by default. Therefore you need to apply specific rules to allow ingress traffic;

- Ingress allow rules, allow specified protocol, ports, and IP addresses to connect in
- The firewall prevents instances from receiving connections on non-permitted ports and protocols
- Rules can be restricted to only affect particular sources
- Source CIDR ranges can be used to protect from undesired connections coming to an instance either from external networks or from GCP IP set of ranges

In addition, source tags can be used to protect an instance from undesired connections coming from specific VM instances that are tagged with a matching tag. This enables a VM to receive a connection from an external address and deny another VM from receiving a connection from a VM in the same network.

You can control ingress connections from a VM instance by constructing inbound connection conditions using source addresses, protocols, ports, and source tags on instances. However, Source Tags can only be used for VM to VM connections.

Load Balancing

The GCP offers a variety of ways to load balance in-bound (ingress) traffic from sources across the internet. You can use the default Global HTTPS load balancing service to put your Web application behind a single anycast IP address across the entire Internet. The way that works is simply that you deploy the same public IP (an anycast address) across all the diverse Google points of presence (PoP).

The way that anycast works is that the address is advertised as the unique address for a service across the global network. The thing is it is not unique as it is presented, advertised and replicated across every region in the global network. The idea being that due to the vast distances and latency involved a user will always connect to the closest PoP advertising that external IP address. The other geographically diverse PoP instances of that IP address will serve as automatic failover for redundancy. This is because; the user will always connect to the closest geographical point of presence that the IP address determines, so they will also get the best customer experience and lowest latency. Moreover, the network will load balance traffic for the application among all your back-end instances in the closest region but if necessary it can reach other backends around the world.

Load balancing is tightly integrated with GCP's Content Delivery Network. This gives you the option to cache many types of content close to your regional customers around the globe. To take advantage of Content Deliver Network all you have to do is set up HTTP(S) Load Balancing and then simply enable Cloud CDN with a single checkbox.

However you may well be wishing to load balance protocols other than HTTPs. In that case you can use the regional load balancer for global TCP for traffic on many other optional ports. For UDP traffic or for the SSL Proxy you will also use the regional load balancer. Finally, to load balance the internal ingress traffic within the VPC for example between tiers of a multi-tier application you will use the internal load balancer.

Interconnectivity

GCP also offers a variety of ways for you to interconnect your on-premises or other cloud networks with your Google VPC. It's simple to set up a VPN but you will have to manually update the routing when you add subnets. But if you want to use dynamic routing so that all new subnets will be auto-discovered and propagated then you will need to use, cloud router. This option makes the update of routing tables dynamic as it will manage the BGP routing updates between your site and the GCP.

You can also peer with Google, through many worldwide points of presence either directly or through a carrier partner. Or if you need a service level agreement and can adopt one of their required network topologies, then you are best to use the Dedicated Interconnect.

Network Billing

It is important that you understand the usage conditions you will be billed for on GCP's network;

- First of all, ingress or traffic coming into GCP's network is not billable it's free of charge. In addition, all egress traffic within the same zone, to a different GCP service within the same region, or to other Google products like YouTube, Maps, Drive, and Gmail from a VM in GCP with a public or private IP address is not charged either.
- However, there is a charge for egress between zones in the same region and between regions.
- These rules apply to charges only for egress traffic through internal IP addresses.

It is important to realise that there are different billing charges for egress through external IP address, regardless of whether the instances are in the same zone. Hence there is no free transfer of egress traffic between VMs in the same zone when using public external IP addresses.

Another thing to consider when designing your network is your throughput and round-trip latency between virtual machines. This is going to vary by location, so check your applications requirements against the current specifications for the VPC when choosing where to place the VMs.

For example, VM to VM communication within a single zone has much more consistent performance than VM to VM communication between regions across continents.

Keep in mind that as VPC is constantly evolving, there are some features that are marked BETA. These features do not have a service level agreement or SLA and the online documentation states which features are currently in BETA.

If you make design changes, you might have to delete networks and subnetworks.

If that is the case, start by deleting your VMs and any related firewall rules. Then, depending on whether you have an auto type network or a custom type network, you might only be able to delete the entire network or you might be able to delete the sub-networks independently.

Designing the Network Architecture

We learned so far about projects, networks, subnetworks, regions, and zones now let's see how they are specifically used in common network designs. The goal here is to get an appreciation of how they all can work together to deliver a robust network design architecture. After all they do provide us with alternatives for managing groups of resources with varying availability and access control requirements. This means that not only can you manage resources at a very granular level, if you need to work things globally; you also have that capacity to do so.

A key design criterion for any network design is availability, as a network is of no use to us if we cannot access it so let's take a look at the options at our disposal for delivering availability.

Google Cloud Platform excels in the areas of reliability and availability because of its own highly reliable and robust SDN infrastructure that underpins all of Google's own applications and business activities but also due to its hierarchal design of regions and zones.

The fact that the SDN infrastructure allows subnetworks to communicate across zones makes creating a highly available application easy. Hence, should your application need increased availability for high business continuity, you could simply place two virtual machines into different zones within the same region and using the same subnetwork. This is very simple to deploy and very effective way to instantly create high availability and automated fail-over. However, it is not just simple to deploy it is very convenient to secure as using a single subnetwork allows you to create a single firewall rule that is assigned across both zones. Therefore, by deploying identical VMs on a single subnet on separate zones, you will get high-availability without any more security complexity.

However if we want to present our application to users around the world then we need to look to solution that have global scale. In the high availability solution we proposed earlier, we placed resources in different zones within a single region, which provided the required improvements in reliability and availability for business continuity. The solution also provided you with the required isolation from many types of infrastructure, hardware and software failures. Nonetheless, when we consider globalization then putting our resources in different regions provides an even higher degree of redundancy and failure mitigation. Indeed if we replicate our applications and resources across different regions this will allows us to design highly robust systems with resources spread across different geographical diverse failure domains. Also, by replicating resources across geographical regions we can make use of global or regional load balancer, which we can use to route the traffic to the region that is closest to the user.

Globalization does give us global redundancy and high availability worldwide but unfortunately we no longer benefit from the simplified security that we got with the multi-zone, single subnetwork model. However, if the VMs are in a single network, then they can still communicate through GCP's internal global network.

If we now take this decomposition of our design and resources one step further by placing our application and resources in different regions within different networks and different projects, we will benefit from further segregation.

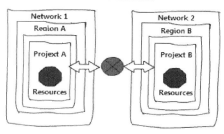

Resource Isolation

In this model our resources are now isolated, which prevents compromise of one part from spreading to other parts, but also prevents them communicating with each other over private IP addresses. However, we can get around that inconvenience by using VPC network peering to allow these resources to communicate over a private address space.

Finally, in this last case, the VMs are isolated into separate projects, but within the same zone. This can be useful for identity and access management.

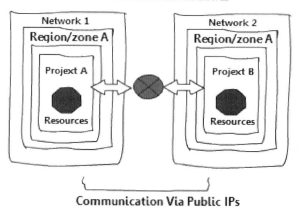

Resource Isolation in Zones

Communication Via Public IPs

For example, if software development is Project A, and test engineering is Project B, you can assign different people to different roles in the projects for management separation or what is called separation of duties. To achieve this you should consider segmenting the system up into multiple projects to enable more granular access control. The issue here is that a network cannot span across different projects. So using separate projects implies that the VMs must communicate via external IP addresses across the Internet.

Bastion Host

Another common network design makes use of a bastion host to provide internal resources and VMs with isolation from the internet. Bastion hosts provide an external facing point of entry into a network containing private network instances. In this scenario only the bastion host is configured with a public external IP address on its interface all the other internal VM instances use the private internal address space addresses. The Bastion host is therefore acting like a proxy or gatekeeper for internet access for both ingress and egress traffic.

This bastion host model can also be deployed to provide a single point for fortification or for network audit purposes, which is controllable as its SSH services can be either started or stopped to permit or block any inbound SSH connections coming from the Internet. For example, should you have an application or service running on an internal VM instance that is provided to an internal corporate audience but requires remote administrative access then there is no need to provide this instance with an external IP address.

In order to gain access to this instance, the admin can create a maintenance host known as a bastion host with an external IP on an internet facing interface. The admin could then restrict access to the internal VM instance by creating a firewall ingress rule to allow SSH traffic on port 22 to the private address IP of the VM.

A similar but technical variation of the bastion host network design is a network address translation, for NAT gateway isolation. Similar to the previous design we have VM instances that do not need an external IP address for their primary purpose but remote maintenance is frequently required. In this case, rather than give each instance an expensive external IP you can configure another VM instance in the same network with an external IP and have it serve as a NAT gateway configured with IP forwarding to serve the entire network.

Use Case – 12

A client ABC wishes to allow collaboration with other organisational unit in different zones and regions. These units are independently controlled and in their own VPCs, which are isolated from the ABC VPC. The other business units are keen to collaborate with ABB via their VPC but would like to remain isolated from one another. How can you allow these different business units to interconnect with ABB but retain their isolation from each other without going across VPNs and the internet?

Solution

You could propose to use VPC peering. By using VPC peering you effective form interconnects across the Google internal network using private IP addresses. A VPC can peer with several peers but only directly peered VPC can communicate there is no transitive communication allowed. Because peering is set up independently at either VPC both retain their autonomy and remain administratively separate. VPC peering also works on GCE, GKE and GAE –Flexible. One caveat is auto-network types cannot peer as their IP address ranges could clash so they will need to be converted to custom-mode first. Another is that when VPC peer all subnet routes are exchanged if this is not desirable you may need to set up firewall rules to filter access.

Part II - Essential Cloud Infrastructure Core Services

Chapter 13 - VMs in Compute Engine deep-dive

In this chapter, we will take a deeper dive into some of the core services that we introduced in Part 1, which provided you with a high level introduction to Google Cloud Platform. The first core service that we will examine in far more detail than previously is Compute Engine's VMs.

Compute Engine VM

In GCP when it comes to compute and processing options the most commonly used is the traditional virtual machine instance. This is typically because Compute Engine gives you the utmost in flexibility when making a VM instance. For example you are free to run whatever OS or language that you want as this is a pure IaaS - infrastructure as a service - model.

With IaaS, you get a VM and an operating system and it's up to you to manage it and handle aspects such as auto-scaling and the firewall rules.

The primary work-case of Compute Engine is pretty much any general workload, especially enterprise applications that were designed to run on a server infrastructure. This makes Compute Engine very portable and easy to run in the cloud.

Earlier you learned that when using Compute Engine to make a new VM instance you can use either predefined or custom machine types, the former offers you a selection of commonly used models, the latter allows you to choose how much memory and how much CPU you want. You can also select the type and capacity of disk you require, such as standard hard drives, SSDs, or local SSDs. You can even configure the networking as well as run a combination of Linux or Windows machines. In this chapter, now that we understand more about security, networking and load balancing, we're going to cover several of the other features that we can configure differently such as, start-up scripts, machine rightsizing, firewall rules, availability policies, pricing options as well as the usage discounts.

Customizing the VM

A good starting point when discussing VMs is to consider how many CPUs you will require. To this end the Compute Engine provides a large selection of predetermined machine configurations that would be suitable for most use cases. Specifically, there are predefined micro, medium or high CPU, low to high memory, and standard and shared-core machine types. But importantly, should those machine types not be suitable, you can also customize your own machine.

CPU

To assess your requirements you might like to contemplate that typically for most applications that your choice of CPU will affect your network throughput. To be more specific, your network will scale at two gigabits per second for each CPU core that you choose, up to a maximum of 16 gigabytes per second throughput. The maximum throughput you can achieve is if you go for a VM with eight virtual CPUs.

However, if you are coming from an on-premises world, you will need to be aware of some essential difference when it comes to CPU cores. In the on-premises world you would count the number of physical cores in a CPU as well as the number of hyper-threads. However in the cloud thinks work differently as in GCP, the vCPU cores are not equivalent to physical cores. In GCP you can consider that one vCPUs or virtual CPUs are equivalent to one hyper-thread core. Thus, if you compare single-core hyper-threaded CPU on-premises against a cloud vCPU then you must realise that the former would be equivalent to two virtual CPUs. So keep in mind 4 cores on-premises does not match 4 CPUs in the cloud you may need to go for as many as 8 virtual CPUs to have equivalence.

Disk Storage

Once you have chosen your compute options and the number of CPUs you will want to select your storage options. You have three options for disk; standard, SSD, or local SSD.
Hence you have the choice of hard disk drives (HDD), or flash memory solid-state drives, (SSDs).

Both of these options provide the same amount of capacity in terms of disk size but they have different use cases. Therefore, the quandary is do you go for raw performance or go for cost efficiency?

Basically, the SSDs are designed to deliver high performance as they support a far higher number of IOPS per dollar than the hard disk drives, which provide a higher amount of capacity for your dollar. If you require really high performance then you might want to look at Local SSDs as they have significantly higher performance and throughput measured in IOPS and have even lower latency than SSD persistent disks. This is because local SSD as their name suggests are directly attached to the physical hardware.

However, be careful what purpose you use local disks for as the data that you store on a local SSD does not persist; it is maintained only until you stop or delete the VM instance then it is lost. So if you do use local SSD then make sure you copy any important data to a persistent storage device before you close or terminate a VM. Typically, because of its temporary nature a local SSD is used as a swap disk in Windows environments just like you would if you wanted to create a RAM disk. So if you need more scratch pad capacity, and it is only temporary, then you can store those extra data on a local SSD.

However there are limitations to the number of SSD a VM can support. Currently you can make a VM instance that can support up to eight 375 gigabyte local SSD partitions. This is a total capacity of three terabytes for each instance. On the other hand you can deploy Standard HDD or non-local SSDs up to a total capacity of 64 terabytes for each instance. Also, the performance of these disks improves with each extra gigabyte of capacity that you add.

Networking

When it comes to choices for networking then we can select the different types of networks and then created custom firewall rules using IP addresses and network tags. You can also choose between regional HTTPS load balancing and network load balancing. Because these are not physical devices this type of traffic engineering are applied as basic traffic forwarding rules. The traffic entering into Google's network and VPC destined for your IP address subnet range is subject to your firewall ingress rules.

Virtual Machine Billing

When it comes to billing for the usage of virtual machines, GCP offers a variety of different options in order to keep the prices low. First, virtual machines are billed per second, on a one minute minimum basis. This means that you only pay for the usage but they must still be managed to prevent unchecked VM proliferation which became common in on-premises VM deployments in development environments.

Nonetheless, for those VMs that are active and productive Google offers sustained use discounts. These are automatic discounts to monthly billing awarded for running a VM instance for more than 25% of a month, Compute Engine automatically – no action is required by you - gives you a discount for every incremental second you use for that instance. The discount increases with usage, and you can get up to 30% net discount for instances that run for the entire month.

For some infrequent tasks or for development purposes you might want to consider pre-emptible instances, which come with up to an 80% discount. However, as the name suggests Google can pre-empt or terminate these instances with a 30 second notification, if it requires access to those resources for other tasks. Furthermore, Compute Engine actually always terminates pre-emptible instances after they run for 24 hours, so be aware of that.

The ability to customize the amount of memory and CPU used through custom machine types allows further billing reductions. Also when it comes to sizing your virtual machine, you at first might not know exactly what your requirements are so Compute Engine provides VM sizing recommendations. These are available after a GCP has had time to research the used resources – typically 24hours - of your virtual machine instances becoming active. Then based upon the historical data GCP will provide recommendation for resizing the instances for optimal minimum billing.

When you create a new instance, recommendations for the new instance will appear 24 hours after the instance has been created but for most applications you may want to leave it for a week or more to get a more representative picture for capacity planning.

There is also a type of VM called an inferred instance. This means that when it comes to billing all similar type of machine used in the same zone will be combined into a single charge. The results is that you get the most discount available, for example, GCP aggregates the billing time of all instances so you get the largest discount as it appears to be one machine in use the whole time.

Also, when combining resources over several VMs this means that memory and virtual CPU of the same type are aggregated for billing purposes, so that you will get the discount on the greatest resource consumption.

For those wanting to try out Compute Engine there are also free usage limits. These free usage quotas provide one f1-micro instance, with up to 30 gigabytes of HDD persistent disk and up to one gigabyte of network egress traffic, per month. At the other end of the usage spectrum there are more attractive discounts for VM usage when you purchase committed use discounts.

VM Security

When we contemplate security issues with VMs it is important to remember that the creator of a VM has full root privileges on that instance. For example, if you consider a Linux VM, the creator will have SSH capability and they can then use the GCP console to grant SSH capability to other users.

Similarly, when creating a VM using a Windows OS, the creator can use the GCP console to generate a username and password. After that, anyone who knows the username and password can connect to the VM's OS using a remote desktop protocol or RDP client.

A point to remember is that if you are using the default network type listed then you don't need to define any firewall rules to allow access to the VM. However if you are using manual or custom network types you will have to add the required firewall rules for both SSH and RDP in order to allow access to the instance.

IAM Roles

When you use IAM with Compute Engine this gives you very granular control over the permissions that you can give a project, user, group or resource. Indeed, every API method in Compute Engine will require that the identity that is making the API request does have the prerequisite privileges to use the Compute Engine resource. Privileges take the form of permissions, which you can grant to others by setting an IAM policy. The purpose of the IAM policy is to grant roles to a member (user, group, or service account) of your project in a consistent and reproducible manner. In addition to legacy roles (viewer, editor, owner), and the custom roles that you can configure yourself there are the Compute Engine predefined roles. Predefined roles are normally sufficient for most projects as they have more granularity than primitive roles and are more convenient to use than custom roles. Indeed, predefined roles allow you to can grant multiple roles to a project member on the same resource, which provides a large measure of flexibility. For example, if you want to give an admin full control of all Compute Engine resources you could give a user roles/compute.admin. However, you want to be only providing permissions on the least required principles so you may want to select a role that serves more specific job functions. Compute Engine has many specific predefined roles such as;

- roles/compute.instanceAdmin - Permissions to create, modify, and delete virtual machine instances. This includes permissions to create, modify, and delete disks.
- roles/compute.loadBalancerAdmin - Permissions to create, modify, and delete load balancers and associate resources.
- roles/compute.networkAdmin - Permissions to create, modify, and delete networking resources, except for firewall rules and SSL certificates.

- roles/compute.networkUser - Provides access to a shared VPC network once granted, service owners can use VPC networks and subnets that belong to the host project.
- roles/compute.orgSecurityPolicyAdmin - Full control of Compute Engine Organization Security Policies.
- roles/compute.storageAdmin - Permissions to create, modify, and delete disks, images, and snapshots.

These are just some of the predefined roles within Compute Engine there are many more that serve specific job functions and roles. However, you can combine several roles and give them to a user or group. For example, if your networking team is responsible for managing the network and applying the firewall rules, you can grant roles/compute.networkAdmin and roles/compute.securityAdmin to allow the networking team to do only those specific tasks.

VM Lifecycle

It is important to understand the lifecycle of a VM so that you know the exact status of the VM at any given time – for billing at least. The lifecycle of a VM is represented by different stages and their related status.

The initial stage is the provisioning state and this is after you have configured all the properties of a VM such as CPU, memory, disk, OS and then you click create. Once the VM goes through the internal build process it enters the provisioning state. At this point all the VM's resources such as CPU, memory and disks are being reserved, but the VM itself isn't running at this stage.

The next stage is when the newly provisioned VM moves to the staging state. This is the VM state where the resources have, moved from being reserved to acquired, and the instance is prepared for launch. It is in this staging state that the Compute Engine is configuring the resources and adding IP addresses, as well as starting the booting up process for the OS image.

Once the staging stage completes and the system has booted the VM is now in the running state. This is the state where it will start doing useful work such as executing pre-configured startup scripts and enabling SSH or RDP access. The running state is where the VM is fully operational and can do all the tasks that any physical server could manage. However a VM can do a lot of things that you can't achieve on a physical server. For example, you can live-migrate your virtual machine from one host to another host in the same zone instead of requiring an instance to be rebooted.

This feature is not only beneficial to you as it also allows Google to perform maintenance tasks critical to keeping the infrastructure running. Indeed the live migration feature maybe working transparently to you as Google works behind the scenes to keep the infrastructure protected and reliable without any interruption to your service on any of your VMs.

The great thing from an administration perspective is that there are many tasks you can complete while the VM is running. These include, the ability to move your VM to a different zone, take a snapshot of the VMs persistent disk for backup or for VM migration purposes, exporting the system image, or re-configuring metadata. However not all admin tasks can be performed on the fly as some actions require you to stop your virtual machine. Some of the tasks that will require you to enter the stopped state are if you want to upgrade your machine by adding more CPUs.

When the instance enters the stopped state, it will run through any pre-configured shutdown scripts and then transition into the terminated state. From the terminated state, you have the options to either restart the instance which would bring it back to its provisioning state, or you can delete it.

When you are in the running state you also have the option to reset a VM. This task is comparable to pressing the reset button on your computer. Hence, be aware that like resetting your computer the memory contents of the VM will be lost. Reset also returns the virtual machine to its initial state.

There are several ways in which we transition a VM state from the running state. The most common method for admins is through the GCP console or through the gcloud command.

However other tasks which may be OS specific are performed from within the OS such as for reboot and shut down.

It's important to know that changing state due to a shut down or reset is not instant so if you are rebooting, stopping, or restarting an instance, then the process will take about 90 seconds. However, there is a caveat that you should be aware of and it concerns pre-emptible VMs specifically. With a pre-emptible VM if the instance does not stop after 30 seconds, then Compute Engine will force the shutdown. It does this by sending a hard 'off' signal to the operating system. So you need to be aware of this behaviour when writing shutdown scripts for pre-emptible VMs.

Availability Policies

A VMs availability policy determines how the instance behaves under certain tasks such as during a live migration event. We saw earlier how Google can live-migrate VMs from one host to another for maintenance purposes and the default maintenance behaviour for VMs is to live-migrate. However that might not be what you want so you have the option to terminate your instance during maintenance events.

If your VM is terminated due to maintenance events, then your VM's default behaviour is to try and automatically restart. This is great when the VM has crashed but probably not what you want during a maintenance event so this behaviour can also be changed. These changes are made through the availability policies. Changes in behaviour can be configured both during the VM creation and also while an instance is running by configuring the automatic restart on host maintenance options.

When a VM is terminated, you do not pay for the use of memory and CPU resources, however, you are charged for any attached disks and external IP addresses.

In the terminated state, you can perform many of configuration tasks actions such as, changing the machine type, but you cannot change the image of a stopped VM.

Also, not all of the actions require you to stop a virtual machine. For example, VM availability policies can be changed while the VM is running.

Compute Engine Options for VM

When it comes to creating and configuring a VM through Compute Engine, there are three options; Web Console, Cloudshell, or the RESTful API.

There is no preferred method or one method being better than another as they all have their specific uses. For example, the Web Console is tremendous method for beginners or inexperienced admins as it is a graphical interface with check boxes and drop-down selection menus. This makes it very easy to build a VM as you have all the options available to you and are led through the build process in an intuitive manner. However, if you are building a few VMs the web console soon becomes tedious due to the manual repetition required when configuring each VM in turn. In that case Cloudshell may be the preferred method.

Cloudshell is the command line for the SDK which can be conveniently accessed through the web console or if you want you could install the SDK locally on your laptop. Regardless of how you access the SDK you will soon find that running commands to build VMs is far quicker and less tedious when building multiple VMs than using the web console. The advantage of Cloudshell is that you can run scripts or pre-configured multi-line configuration commands to build your VMs. These scripts can be readily edited and customised for example changing the VM name and then run with a simple cut and paste on the command line.

However, if you don't wanting to be manually running commands or the scripts are complex configurations then you would probably eventual want to automate the process. In this case you might want to use the RESTful API. The API will programmatically configure your VMs by defining all the different options for your environments and then run automatically will minimum intervention required.

A good tip for using either the Cloudshell command line or the RESTful API is to configure the first VM instance through the Web Console, and then ask Compute Engine for the equivalent REST request or command line code. Then you can copy and paste this into your own scripts or commands. This way, you not only avoid any typos but you can soon build up a library of scripts for each VM type that match your environment.

Regardless of the method you use to interface with the Compute Engine you are still going to first decide on the VM parameters that your application or service requires. The first step is to decide on which of the different machine types that are currently available fits your needs. These predefined machine types are managed by Compute Engine and come in four classes: standard, high memory, high CPU, and shared core memory machines.

Shared core machines or the micro VMs as they are often called are great in development environments especially when prototyping solutions because they are cost effective for running small non-resource intensive applications. However, these are unlikely to be sufficient for production environments for that you would need to look to the other three alternatives; standard, high memory and high CPU machine types.

The difference between the machines types listed is the ratio of number of virtual CPUs to the amount of memory.

The standard machine type is best suited to applications that have a good balance between CPU and memory usage. Specifically, standard machine types start out at 3.75 gigs of RAM per virtual CPU, but they can go all the way up to 64 virtual CPUs with 240 gigs of RAM.

In contrast the high memory machine types are best suited ideal for applications that are memory intensive so need more memory relative to the number of virtual CPUs. These machine types will start out at 6.5 gigabytes of RAM per virtual CPU. Nearly double the amount of ram per vCPU as the standard type.

On the other hand, the high CPU machine types are best suited for applications that are processor intensive and demand more virtual CPUs relative to memory. These machine types start out at 0.9 gigabytes of RAM per virtual CPU.

Now, these options are constantly being evaluated and some are going to change and in fact some of these configurations aren't available in all regions. So you need to check in the Web Console if the preconfigured type is available in your region.

If the predefined machine types don't fit your compute needs, you can always create a custom machine type where you can customize your CPU memory and GPU needs. In the vast amount of cases these general VM machine-types will suffice for your workloads.

However as more users are deploying in the cloud to use HPC (High Performance Computing) and ML (Machine Learning) infrastructures Google provides specialist machine types and CPUs to meet those requirements. The Compute Optimised and Memory Optimised CPUs meet the requirements of HPC and ML as they are able to provide the specific compute or memory requirements that matches your large workloads.

Compute Optimised VMs (C2) expose high per-thread performance and increased memory speeds that suite the requirements of most compute-intensive workloads. Compute-Optimized VMs are great for HPC and gaming but they are equally proficient serving single thread applications. The new Compute-Optimized VMs offer a greater than 40% performance improvement compared to current GCP VMs and you can choose Compute-Optimized VMs with up to 60 vCPUs, 240 GBs of memory, and up to 3TB of local storage.

On the other hand Memory Optimised VMs (M2) offer the highest memory configuration for a Compute Engine VM. They are well suited for memory-intensive workloads such as large in-memory databases, e.g., SAP HANA, as well as in-memory data analytics workloads. The M2 family offer up to 12 TB of memory and 416 vCPUs, enabling you to run scale-up workloads on GCP.

These custom and specialist VMs are generally more expensive than the predefined VMs, but they provide you with more flexibility and specialist configuration for heavy workloads.

But in case of custom VMs it has perhaps crossed your mind there is then a question as to how Google will give discounts on your custom machines?

The issue is that custom machines don't really fall into a category. Therefore they are not a fit with Google's standard machine type discount plan as we can't aggregate their resource use to get the best discount.

Instead Google's billing plan for custom machine types requires that Compute Engine calculates the virtual CPU and memory usage and then applies the discount described by the sustained user's discount.

For example, consider this scenario where you have two instances that have different custom configurations and run at different times of the month. In this scenario Compute Engine breaks down the number of virtual CPUs and amount of memory used across all the custom instances and then aggregates the resource usage to qualify for the biggest sustained usage discounts possible. More specifically, Compute Engine will aggregate all of the CPU and memory resources, multiplied by the amount of time that they were used and then apply the appropriate sustained used discounts.

Finally one last thing about machine types and that is you should be aware of the advantages of the pre-emptible VM. This is a VM instance that you can create and run at a much lower price – typically circa 80% discount- than normal VMs. Therefore you really should investigate whether your application can function completely on pre-emptible VMs or at least benefit because an 80 percent discount is a significant saving.

To make this point clear, these VMs have their draw backs after all you don't get a huge discount for nothing so a VM might be preempted or terminated at any time. This is something you should be aware off but it is still a cost effective way to use a VM as there's no charge if that happens within the first 10 minutes.

Nonetheless, you must realise that pre-emptible VMs are only going to live for up to maximum 24 hours and that you only get a 30 second notification before the machine is terminated. Hence, pre-emptive VMs are not for every use case but they are still hugely cost effective for most projects if deployed correctly.

There are also some operational caveats that you must keep in mind when contemplating pre-emptive VMs. For example, when you use pre-emptive VMs there are no live migrations possible nor are automatic restarts, as that would defeat the purpose. However, there are some techniques we can highlight, which are actually useful in re-spawning terminated pre-emptive VMs. These techniques typically require instance monitoring and the use of load balancers that can start up new pre-emptible VMs in case of failure.

One valuable use case for using pre-emptible VMs is when running a batch processing job.

In this scenario, some of those VM instances may well terminate during processing, but the analytical task may well slow down but it does not completely stop.

Therefore, you can economically deploy pre-emptible instances to complete your batch processing tasks. Not only does this save money but it doesn't place additional workload on your existing instances and doesn't require you to pay full price for additional normal instances.

Region and Zones

After you select the machine type the next question you will contemplate is where you want to host the VM. Therefore the first thing you need to consider when choosing a region and zone is the geographical location, which is closest to your customer base as that is where you want to run your resources for lowest latency and highest customer experience.

However, there may be some other considerations such as Google's proclivity for consistently deploying new hardware architectures and these new hardware architectures are not deployed to all zones simultaneously.

Therefore, you're going to find that there are different CPU architectures in different zones.

In fact, it has been noted that there can be a differential of up to three generations in those processor types. Of course this will only be a concern if you need the latest high end CPU or GPU for your processor intensive application. So you might want to check the GCP website to see where those high end processors have been deployed before choosing your region and zone.

In this scenario from a latency and customer experience perception hosting your resources in another region and zone would have no detrimental effect. Similarly from a billing perspective, you pay the exact same amount regardless of the type of individual CPU processor that you might be using.

Google is constantly increasing the number of regions and zones and updating the supported CPU architecture. For an up to date list, go to cloud.google.com and search for regions and zones.

Images

The next step after selecting the machine type and then the region/zone is to decide upon an OS image. When creating a virtual machine, just like when you commission server on-premises you will have the option of choosing the boot OS disk image.

This image just like any physical OS boot CD will include, the boot loader, the operating system, the file system structure, any preconfigured software, libraries, tools, and any other features and customizations for the specific version.

Furthermore, when you select an image from the drop-down menu in Compute Engine the Google Cloud is included. These OS images are stored as tar gzip'd files, and are stored in a private area of Cloud Storage. Thus, when choosing an image, you can select either a public or custom image. And you can select from a wide choice of both Linux and Windows Server images.

However some of these images, specifically Windows OS Server images will have a proprietary license so some of these images are premium images as indicated in parentheses with a 'p'. These images will have per second charges with the exception of SQL Server images, which are charged per minute. Premium image prices vary with the machine type. However, these prices are global and do not vary by region or zone. Furthermore you are advised – just like with any proprietary software - of the billing fees before you select and activate the OS image.

You can also use upload and activate on your VM a custom image. For example, if you have a licensed enterprise version of Windows Server that you have customized with preconfigured software that's been authorized for your particular organization for use in your data centre then you can upload and then create a VM using that custom image. You also have the option of importing images from another cloud provider.

Managing Disk Storage

So you have selected an OS image but that needs some kind of persistent disk where it can be stored and booted. You will also need to have somewhere to store your applications data and that needs to be durable and that means it can survive if the VM terminates.

Therefore you must select a persistent external disk type. What this means is that the disk is not part of the VM it is simply attached to it. The result is an interesting condition where you can terminate or delete the VM instance but retain its boot disk and data. To have a boot disk survive a VM deletion, the "Delete boot disk when instance is deleted" box needs to be cleared in the instances property.

There are different types of disks and you should understand the difference as some are persistent and some are not.

The first disk that we create is what we call an external persistent disk this is where we will store and boot the OS image. What 'external' means is it not integrated within the VM it is going to be attached to the VM through the network interface. Its 'persistent' because the drive is not physically attached to the VM and neither is its data they are independent of one another.

This separation of disk and VM allows the disk to survive if the VM terminates. But we must not confuse a disk with a physical object it is after all virtual storage. This delivers some handy features such as persistent disks are dynamically resizable even while they're running and attached to a VM. Also, you can attach and share a disk in read-only mode to multiple VMs. This lets you share static data between multiple instances which is much cheaper than replicating your data to unique disks for individual instances.

But, there is a drawback as persistent disks are bounded to their region and they can't be moved between regions. This is why if you move a VM across regions you need to first take a snapshot of the data and then copy it onto the new disk that you create in the destination region's zone.

The choice that you have of disk storage when building your VM is between persistent HDD and persistent SSD disk and this choice will be determined by cost or performance. By their nature persistent disks are durable network storage devices as the data is distributed across several physical disks. It is Compute Engine's responsibility to manage the data distribution and to ensure redundancy and optimize performance for you. Indeed you need not concern yourself with most disk management tasks such as disk partitioning, redundant disk arrays, or sub-volume management. However to get the best performance simply format your persistent disks with a single file system and no partition tables. However, if you need to separate your data into multiple unique volumes, then you should add more disks rather than create multiple partitions on the existing drives.

Standard persistent disks are basically standard spinning hard disk drives (HDD) whereas SSD persistent disks are solid-state drives (SSD). The differentiator between these two disk types is that the standard HDD persistent disks compared against the SSD are more efficient and cost effective when handling typical sequential read/write operations. However, SSD drives are designed to handle high rates of random input/output operations per second (IOPS). Thus, if your applications require very high rates of random IOPS, then you should use SSD persistent disks. This is also because SSD persistent disks are designed for extremely low millisecond latency in the single-digits.

Now there is another type of disk storage called local SSDs but these are fundamentally different from persistent disks in that they're physically attached to the virtual machine.

Therefore, these disks are ephemeral but provide very high IOPS offering 680,000 read input/output operations per second (IOPS) and 360,000 write IOPS. Local SSDs are suited to applications that need fast scratch pad storage but if you want to keep the data make sure to copy it to a persistent drive as it will not survive a VM termination.

Currently, you can attach up to eight local SSD disks with 375 gigabytes each resulting in a total of three terabytes. However, although the data on these disks will survive a reset it will but not survive a VM stop or terminate because these disks can't be reattached to a different VM.

A similar concept to the local SSD is a RAM disk where you store data in memory.

This is going to be the fastest type of performance available if you only are working with small data structures. If that is what your application requires then you should perhaps look to selecting a high-memory virtual machine along with a persistent disk to back up the RAM disk data.

In summary, when it comes to selecting a disk drive you've got a number of different disk options. Persistent disks, whether they are HDD or SDD can be rebooted and snapshotted and the data can survive even a VM deletion, but local SSD and RAM disks are ephemeral and volatile.

It is probably best to stick with a persistent HDD disk when you don't need performance but just need capacity. If you do have high-performance needs, start looking at the SSD options.

The persistent SSD disks offer data redundancy because the data on each persistent disk is distributed across several physical disks.

Local SSDs provide even higher performance but without the data redundancy or the persistence – they survive a reboot but not a VM termination.

Finally, RAM disks are the fastest of all of them but also the most volatile.

Now, just as there is a limit on how many local SSDs you can attach to VM, there is also limit on how many persistent disks you can attach to a VM. However remember that the persistent HDD and SDD connect to the VM through the network interface so it will compete with any network egress or ingress traffic throughput. There is a physical limit and it depends upon the number of CPUs that the VM supports. For example a VM with 8 CPUs can support up to 128 persistent drives and that is a colossal amount of storage.

In addition, you must be aware that there are some key differences between a physical hard disk in a computer and a persistent disk, which even though it is described as being either a standard type drive or an SSD is still essentially a virtual network device. Firstly, the most obvious difference with computer hardware disks is you will have to partition hard disk drives so that the operating system will get its own segregated share of the capacity. Partitioning though has always been problematic because if you want to expand the partition at a later date then you will most likely have to repartition or reformat the drive.

Secondly, if you want disk redundancy, then you might need to create a redundant disk array and if you want encryption, you will need to encrypt files before writing them to the disk. Failing to manage the encryption on a computers disk drive is a common way of users losing all their data.

On the other hand, with cloud-persistent disks all the management is handled for you on the backend. You can simply expand disks and resize the file system at will as the disks are virtual network devices. Also, redundancy and data encryption on disks are performed automatically and the keys managed by GCP. However if you want you can use your own keys. You then have the responsibility for managing the decryption keys that is risky but it will ensure that no party – even Google - can get to the data except you.

We briefly mentioned earlier that Compute Engine can help you automate the migration of VMs between zones within a region. This is a pretty common occurrence and if you move your VM instance between zones within the same region, you can simply use the gcloud, 'move' command for the specified VM instance.

However, if you should want to move your instance to a different zone in a different region, then this cannot be automated. In this scenario you will need to manually move the VM. This is not difficult but it does require carefully following the procedure as you need to be careful how you move the VMs persistent drive's data to the new drive in the destination zone.

This procedure involves some handy features with cloud persistent drives such as making a snapshot of all the attached persistent disks. You can then create some new disks in the destination region, and move the data across regions using that snapshot.

The next step is to create the new VM in the destination region and then attach the new persistent disks.

Snapshots are very handy features that have several other use cases. For example, they can be used to backup critical data into a durable storage solution to meet your organizations business continuity requirements. These snapshots can then be stored in cloud storage, for data recovery purposes.

Snapshots can also be used to simply transfer data from one zone to another.

For example, you might want to minimize latency by migrating data to a drive that can be locally attached in the zone where it is used. Another common snapshot use case is when transferring data to a different disk type.

For example, if you want to improve disk performance, by upgrading from standard HDD to faster persistent SSDs then you could simply transfer data from a standard HDD persistent disk to a SSD persistent disk using a snapshot of the data. A caveat that you should be aware of is that snapshots are available only to persistent disks and not to local SSDs.

Snapshots are also very useful for periodic backup of the data on your persistent disk as they are incremental and automatically compressed. This means they are perfect for doing traditional incremental backups of data on a persistent disk. As snapshots are incremental backups they are faster as they only backup data that has changed since the last snapshot. Also if used regularly backups by snapshots will be much quicker and cheaper than making a full image of the disk.

Another thing to understand is that snapshots are not the same thing as the public images and custom images, which are used primarily to create VM instances or configure VM instance templates. A snapshot contains all the drive's data, which could contain application and user data along with the OS image and applications.

Before taking a disk snapshot, you should freeze or unmounting the file system. This is not strictly necessary as you can take a snapshot of a persistent disk even while your applications write data to that disk. But it is the most reliable way to ensure snapshot consistency.

Another common compute action that you can perform is to resize your persistent disk to increase storage capacity and/or to improve I/O performance. This is another feature that can be performed while the disk is attached to a running VM. You can even safely do this without having to create a snapshot of the drive. But something to note is that while you can grow disks in size, you can never shrink them, so do keep this in mind.

Use Case – 13

You are required to move several VMs in Compute Engine to another region but they must retain their persistent data and drives. However persistent drives are regional so cannot be migrated between regions. How can we effectively and quickly move these VMs and their data and if you are not an admin what specific roles would we need? Secondly you are also required to import virtual disks running windows and RHE - so you need to keep the original licenses from an on-premises site into Compute Engine how can you do this?

Solution

The way we could do this is by using Snapshots and for this we would require at a minimum the roles/compute.storageAdmin privileges. However, you could also do this if you were an editor on the project. The way that using this method will work is that first of all you take a snapshot of each VM's persistent drive. Then you move the VMs or simply recreate them in the new region and then you will attach new persistent drives using the snapshots of the original drives.

With regards importing the virtual disks into Compute Engine using the on-premises images you will use the images import API. This can be accessed via the command line; gcloud compute images import. You should run the pre-check tool inside the VM first to check for any compatibility issues. Now in order to preserve the windows licences we need to over-ride the default condition, which is to import VM images as premier images. These premier images have additional charges such as licencing so we need to tell the process that we are bringing our own license by specifying a BYOL value such as windows-2016-byol for windows or rhel-7-byol for Red Hat Enterprise.

Chapter 14 - Identity Access Management a deep-dive

In this chapter, we took a deeper dive into some of the core services that we introduced in Part 1, which provided you with a high level introduction to Google Cloud Platform. The first core service that we examined in far more detail than previously was Compute Engine's VMs, now we will take a closer look at Identity and Access Management (IAM).

Hence, we will be introducing you to one module in the GCP covering the identification, authentication, and authorisation based upon a hierarchy of security entities such as roles, groups, organizations, folders, and service accounts.

We will look at some basic use cases to explain how and why we deploy IAM in practice. By doing so we will demonstrate the rich granularity of the IAM hierarchy and how we can use that to suit our own environments. For example, in your current IT project do you want to give access to the entire development project team? Perhaps you would prefer to handle IAM via individual roles and customize what individuals have access too?

Perhaps you need in your organization a higher centralised authority to control audits and billing, in order to control cost and prevent the uncontrolled proliferation of VMs in the cloud. In this case we will need to use groups and roles to assign some permission such as audit and billing to some groups or roles, while restricting access to other permissions, such as the ability to create, modify or delete VMs. Conversely, for senior project developers we might want them to have the permission to create, modify and delete VMs across all their projects, folders and resources but limit other developers to their own home folders and resources.

When we start to contemplate automation of processes there will be a need for a resource rather than a human to have access to another resource or service through IAM roles. In this case you might create a service account which will allow your applications to have the same credentials as/or act on behalf of a human to do some kind of automated function.

But IAM is not all we will cover as we will also revisit some other core services and examine the security features that are available to us.

We'll cover things like Google Cloud Storage, and its features such as lifecycle management, Object change notification, resource monitoring as well as resource management.

Identity and Access Management

So, what is Identity Access Management?
A simplistic way of understanding what IAM is to think of it as way to control who can do what, on which resource.
With IAM, who can be a person, group or an application, what refers to specific permissions to perform actions and the resources could in this context be any GCP service.

For example, you could give a person the role of Compute Engine viewer. This role provides them with the specific permissions to read only restricted access to list Compute Engine resources without them being able to read the data stored on them.

Cloud IAM is composed of different objects that form the Cloud IAM resource hierarchy.

GCP resources are organized hierarchically as shown in this tree structure.

Figure -13

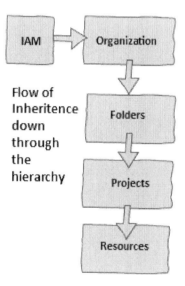

The organization node is the root node in this hierarchy, and is the parent to the folders node. Folders are the children of the organization and the parent to the project nodes. Projects are the children of the folders, and the parents to the individual resources node, which in turn are the children of the projects. Each resource has exactly one parent.

Cloud IAM allows you to set policies at all of these hierarchal levels, where a policy contains a set of roles and their enrolled members. Policies are inherited by children from their parents. Therefore the highest node, the organization resource, effectively represents your company. A Cloud IAM role granted at this level will be inherited by all resources under the organization. The folder resource being a child of the organization could therefore represent a department or business function – such as finance, marketing, manufacturing, etc. Cloud IAM roles granted at this level is inherited by all projects and subsequently the resources that the folder contains.

Projects are interesting as they provide a trust boundary within the organisation. This is because services within the same project have a default level of trust.

The Cloud IAM policy hierarchy always allows the same path as the GCP resource hierarchy.

Meaning, if you change the resource hierarchy, the policy hierarchy also changes.

For example, should you move a project from one organization to a different organization this will update the project's Cloud IAM policy. It will now inherit from the new organization's Cloud IAM policy.

Another thing to point out is that child policies can over-ride access granted at the parent level. For example, if you as an organisation admin where to grant a person the editor role for a specific project, and then a project managers grant that person only the more restrictive viewer role, then effectively the person will still have the editor role for that application.

However the reverse is also true, for example, if you an organisation admin where to grant a person the viewer role for projects at the organisational level, and then a project manager grants that person the more capable editor role for a specific project, then effectively the person will have the editor role permissions for that application in that project.

Therefore it is a best practice to follow the principle of least privilege as the most generous permissions are applied in the case of conflict. This principle applies to identities, roles and resources. So it is best practice to always select the smallest scope that's necessary to reduce your exposure to risk.

The Organisational Node

The organization resource is the highest-level node in the GCP resource hierarchy. This node has many roles, which have permissions and privileges that will be inherited throughout the organisation. This makes these roles suitable for performing centralised administration, auditing, and enforcing policy. An example of such a role is that of the organization admin role.

The organization admin provides a specific role or group the privileges necessary to access and administer all resources belonging to the organization, which is useful for auditing and applying organizational policy.

However there is also a role of project creator, which allows a specific user or group to be able to create projects throughout the entire organization as it will be inherited by all projects within the organization.

The organisational level roles are very suitable for providing centralised control and policy management through auditing. However these roles are extremely powerful as their privileges are inherited throughout the hierarchy. But this raises the question as to who then creates the organization and assign the organisational admin and project creator roles?

In short, the organization itself will be created by Google sales, which includes establishing the organization owners who can then assign the organization admin role.

Organization administrators on the other hand, will manage GCP from the Google cloud console. For security purposes, it's the best practice to always have more than one organization owner.

Folders

The next level in the hierarchy is the folders as they represent sub-organisations or departments within the organization. Therefore folders provide a mechanism for segmenting and segregating the entire organisation into semi-autonomous departments or business functions. In addition folders also provide a grouping mechanism and isolation boundary between individual projects. Hence, Folders can provide even greater granularity when it comes to modelling the organisation into different legal entities, business functions, and even teams within the company.

For example, a first level of folders could be used to present the main departments in your organization, like Finance and IT. But as folders can also contain projects and other sub-folders, each folder could then include projects to represent different teams. For example the IT folder could a sub-folder called DevOps which contains the projects for Team -Development and Team - Testing.

Each team folder could contain several additional sub folders to represent different applications, development areas, test-beds, or staging areas.

Folders also allow autonomy as they allow delegation of administration rights at the folder level. So, for example, each head of a department can be granted full viewer and auditing roles for all GCP resources that belong to their departments.

Similarly, access privileges can also be restricted to prevent access to resources in particular folders. So, users in one department can only gain access and create GCP resources within their own folder.

Resource Manager Roles

While we must keep in mind the best practice of applying the minimum access required to perform a role and that policies are inherited top to bottom. Indeed we have seen this applied in the top level organisational node. But, the folder node also has multiple roles that mimic the organizational roles, but are applied only to resources within a folder.

There is an admin role that provides full administrative control over all the folders. There is also a creator role, to browse the folder hierarchy, and also create folders, and there is a viewer role, which enables members to view folders and their projects and sub-folders.

Similarly, when we look at roles at the projects level, we see there is a creator role that allows a user to create new products, making that user automatically the owner.

There's also a project leader role that grants deletion privileges for projects.

Project Roles

Overall, we have seen that at each level of the hierarchy such as at the organization, folder, project, and resource- we have specific roles. Project roles mimic the primitive roles in that there is a viewer, editor, and owner role and all of these roles are concentric. A project owner can also invite others to become project owners. Extending an invitation is done by sending an email from the GCP console and having the prospective project owner accept the invitation. This type of email invitation is only available for project owner roles and not for other roles.

With regards to the many Product-specific roles, like the Compute Engine's, Instance Admin role, which provides the permissions to create, modify, and delete virtual machine instances and disks. These are resource and product specific so each product or service has several of these roles.

Cloud IAM Policy

Resource Manager policies can secure your projects and their resources but you also want more granular control as to how users will gain access to resources through the application of IAM policies and group memberships. Without strict control over policy changes and group memberships you tend towards permissions creep. This is what tends to happen in all environments and organisations when the users, typical due to changes in role, eventually and inadvertently gain more permissions than they need, which violates the principle of least privilege.

Therefore, it is a good idea to audit policy changes. The audit logs should record project level permissions changes, and any additional levels that are being added. Since managing permissions for individual users can be cumbersome and error prone. The best practice recommends using groups. For example, you should create a DevSecOps group for your development and security operations team that has multiple roles. For example, you could grant the security admin role to manage firewalls, and the log viewer role for auditing. If you follow this suggestion you can add new members that join the team, by simply adding them to the group. It is more convenient and less error prone to use groups rather than users. Nonetheless, for high risk areas, you can assign roles to individuals directly rather than using groups.

Types of IAM Roles

Roles are task related bundles of necessary permissions, which defines who can do what on which resource. There are three specific types of roles in Cloud IAM; primitive roles, curator roles, and custom roles.

Primitive Roles

The most basic are the primitive roles and these are the original roles that were available in the GCP console. Specifically, these are the owner, editor, and the viewer roles.
The owner has full administrative access and hence the ability to add and remove members and delete projects.

In contrast the editor role has the modify permission in conjunction with the read access permission. This role is suitable for a developer or operator that needs to deploy applications and modify or configure its resources.

The viewer role, on the other hand, has read-only access it cannot edit or modify any resource. This role might be suitable for a manager or project leader for audit purposes.

All of these roles are concentric. This means the higher role includes the permission of the lower roles. So for example, the owner role is inclusive of all the permissions of the editor role. Similarly, the editor role is inclusive of all the permissions of the viewer role. However, there is one other role, the billing administrator role, which is used to
manage billing and add or remove administrators. Again this role may be suitable for a manager or a project leader.

Finally, each project can have multiple owners, editors, viewers, and billing administrators.

Curated Roles

In addition to the primitive roles, Cloud IAM also provides additional more granular curated or pre-configured roles that give more refined access control to specific GCP resources. Granular roles also reduce the risk of inadvertently providing unwanted access to other resources.

These roles are a bundle of task related permissions because in order to do anything meaningful you typically require more than one or two permissions. However, most meaningful tasks, such as performing the system admin tasks will require many permissions. Roles therefore represent abstract functions and are customized to align with real jobs.

The permissions themselves are classes and methods in the APIs. For example, compute instances start, can be broken down into service, resource, and verb, meaning that this permission is used to start a stopped Compute Engine instance.

Bundling all the permissions together to perform this task and then present it as a pre-configured role makes life a lot easier for the admin and greatly reduces errors.

Custom Roles

IAM custom roles allow you to make your own roles if there is not a suitable preconfigured role. You can create a custom role and then bundle all the prerequisite permissions to fulfil that particular role. However, this is no easy task so you are advised to look for the closest preconfigured role and then edit it by adding or removing specific permissions in order to meet your requirements. Custom roles require a lot of testing and can be considered to be risky but sometimes there is no alternative. However when making up your custom roles you should keep in mind the principles of least privilege and separation of duties. After all it would be very easy to give permissions to an employee or a group that enabled them to both raise invoices as well as to authorise payment on invoices. Therefore you really need to think hard when creating custom permissions as to why they are required and whether what they are attempting to achieve is compliant with company policy and regulatory standards.

Members

Members define who can do what on which resource. There are different types of members. Basically there are users, and there are service accounts. We will look at both in turn.

Users can be members but they must have an identity that can be securely authenticated so GCP provides several ways - Google accounts, G Suite domains, Google Groups, or Cloud Identity domains;

- A Google account would be used by a user such as a developer, administrator, or any person who interacts with GCP. An email address that is associated with a Google account such as a gmail.com address, can serve as an identity.

- A G Suite domain represents a virtual group of all the members in an organization. G Suite customers can associate their email accounts with an Internet domain name. When you do this, each email account takes the form of username @ mydomain.com. You can specify an identity by using an Internet domain name that is associated with a G suite account.

- A Google Group is a named collection of Google account and service accounts. Every group has a unique email address that is associated with the group. Like groupname@mydomain.com. Google Groups are a convenient way to apply and access policy to a collection of users.

You can grant and change access controls for a whole group at once, instead of granting or changing access controls one at a time for individual users or service accounts.

You can also easily add members to and remove members from a Google group instead of updating a cloud IM policy to add or remove users.

Importantly, GCP does not create or manage users or groups as that is the task of the G Suite Admin, which manages users and groups for an organization in a separate product from GCP.

Service Account

As we mentioned earlier, another type of member that you can have in GCP is a service account. This is a type of account that belongs to your service or application, and is used in typically automation scenarios where you want the application to interact with a resource without any human intervention. Hence you will need the application or the service to have an identity instead of an end user.

A service account provides an identity for a service that is responsible for executing a server-to-server interaction within a project. The issue here is how service accounts manage this without supplying hardcoded user credentials. For example, if you write an application that reads and writes files on cloud storage, it must first authenticate to either the Google Cloud Storage, via an XML API or JSON API.

Now with GCP you can enable service accounts and grant read/write access to the account on the VM instance where you plan to run your application. Then, the next step will be to code the application to obtain credentials from the service account. In this way your application can then authenticate to the storage API without embedding any secrets or credentials with-in the VM instance, image, or application code.

There are three types of service accounts; user creator or custom, built-in, and Google APIs service accounts.

All projects have the built-in Compute Engine default service account. In addition, all projects come with a Google Cloud platform API service account, identifiable by the email, projectnumber@cloudservices.gserviceaccount.com. This service account is designed to run internal Google processes, and it is automatically granted the editor role on the project.

The default account is automatically created for every project. Also, this account is identifiable by the email, projectnumber-compute@developer.gserviceaccount.com, and it is automatically granted the editor role on the project.

Moreover, you can start an instance with a custom service account. This provides more flexibility than the default service account, but they do require more management. You can make as many custom service accounts as you require and assign them to any Cloud IAM role, arbitrary access scopes, or any virtual machine instance.

When you start a new instance using gcloud, the default service account is enabled on that instance. However you can prevent this by specifying another service account, or by disabling service accounts for that VM instance.

Access Scopes

Authorization is the process of determining what permissions and privileges an authenticated identity has on a set of specified resources. Scopes are the mechanisms used to determine, if an authenticated identity is authorized.

If we consider an example where applications A and B contain authenticated identities or service accounts now let's assume that when both applications want to use a Cloud Storage bucket they will request access from the Google authorization server, and in return, they receive an access token.

Application A receives an access token with 'read-only' scope, so it can only read from the Cloud Storage bucket.

Application B on the other hand, receives an access token with 'read-write' scope, so it can read and modify data in the Cloud Storage bucket.

These tokens can be short-term privileges so if you want to provide read access for only a limited time, say 24 hours, then you can create a 24 hour access token that your application service would use.

Scopes can be further customized when you create an instance using the default service account. These scopes can also be changed after an instance is created by stopping it.

However, access scopes cannot be customized for user-created service accounts, but you can always use the granular Cloud IAM roles instead.

This restriction is due to access scopes being the legacy method for specifying permissions on your instance. As before the development of the more advances IAM roles, access scopes were the only available mechanism for granting permissions to the service accounts.

Moreover, another distinction between service accounts is that default service accounts will support primitive, project, and curated, or Cloud IAM roles. While user-created service accounts only use Cloud IAM roles.

Nonetheless, the roles for service accounts can also be assigned to groups or users as a service account can be looked upon as being a resource. Thus, like any other resource you can assign IAM policies for access.

To achieve this you will first create a service account that has been assigned with an IAM role. In this example we will use a service account with the, instance admin role, which has the permissions to create, modify, and delete virtual machine instances, and disks.

Then, you treat this service account as you would any other resource and decide who can use it by providing users or group with the service account user role.

This allows those users to act as if they were that services account, to create, modify, and delete virtual machine instances, and disks. Users who are also service account users for a service account, can access all of the services for which the service account has access. Therefore, you need to show some caution when granting the service account user role to a user or group.

Now you might wonder how service accounts get authenticated as they obviously can't have passwords hard coded in APIs and when they are working autonomously with zero human interaction there is no way to provide credentials. After all, users require a username and password to authenticate so for a similar purpose service accounts use keys.

Authentication Keys

There are two types of service account keys; GCP-managed keys and user-managed keys.

GCP-managed keys are used by Google Cloud platform services, such as App Engine and Compute Engine.

These keys cannot be downloaded but Google will keep the keys and automatically rotate them daily.

User-managed keys are created, downloadable, and managed by users. When you create a new key pair, you download the private key, which is not retained by Google. With external keys, you are responsible for key privacy and secure storage of the private key and other management operational chores, such as key rotation. Each service account can support one or more keys and these are used to authenticate with Google Cloud APIs. The specific keys should be periodically rotated, which involves a process where you will generate a new version of the key. This is because the fact that you may well be distributing the key amongst users will make it susceptible to leakage so it is better to rotate the keys regularly and remove the old version of a key. This systematic rotation of the service account keys is done to limit the risk of them being used by a malicious third-party user in the event of keys being compromised. Regularly creating and distributing new keys limits the impact of leaked keys being used by malicious third parties to access publicly available GCP API endpoints.

IAM Best Practices

Before we close this chapter on IAM we will summarise some of the Cloud IAM best practices that we have discussed in order to assist you in designing your own IAM policies.

Initially, when designing your own IAM policy you must have a good understanding of the GCP IAM resource hierarchy. This is critical as it lets you leverage the concepts of inheritance and isolation, which can be established between the various tiers in the hierarchy. Specifically, you should be looking to establish projects in order to group and share resources that have the same trust boundary.

With regard to the concept of policy inheritance make sure you recognize the effects of inheritance and use the principle of least privilege when granting roles. This is especially important at the highest levels because a child tier cannot rescind permissions given at a parent tier. To minimise the risk of permission creep and enforce the policy of least privilege establish audit policies using Cloud audit logs and regularly audit the memberships of groups used in policies.

To make administration easier it is generally best to grant roles to groups instead of individuals. Doing this doesn't just ease the administration burden it also importantly reduces error. An exception to this is when allocating permissions for high-risk tasks in high security environments, in which case you should assign rights to the user rather than the group. Typically, it is preferable to update the group membership than change a Cloud IAM policy. Therefore, you can sub-divide specific roles into multiple groups so that you can assign privileges more granularly for finer control. Therefore look at groups as a method for assigning specific roles with the concept of least privileges to a more specialised group.

When it comes to using service accounts, here are some best practices. Diligence is required when granting the service account user role, as it provides access to all the resources for which the service account has access. Therefore, design the service accounts to be specific to a single task and give it an intuitive name that advertises its purpose. This shouldn't be done on a whim so there should be a coherent and common naming convention throughout the organisation.

Service Accounts authenticate through private keys and unless there is a real need to do otherwise let GCP manage the keys for you. If you a working in a high-security environment that dictates that you must manage the keys yourself, then you will have to secure the keys and store them in a safe place. You will also need to establish a key rotation policy as well as the methods. Key rotation may sound a simple concept, however, implementing a common process in a way that is user convenient while simultaneously guaranteeing the security of the keys is not a trivial task. Also you will have to regularly audit the keys using the serviceAccount.keys.list method.

It is a best practice is to rotate your service account keys regularly. You rotate a key by creating a new key and then forcing applications to use the new key before you depreciate and then delete the old key. Use the serviceAccount.keys.create() method and serviceAccount.keys.delete() method together to automate the rotation.

For applications accessed by HTTPS it is recommended to use Cloud Identity-Aware Proxy (Cloud IAP) to establish a central authorization layer. IAP give you access control at an application level rather than relying on network-level firewalls.

Cloud Identity-Aware Proxy (Cloud IAP) controls access to cloud applications and VMs running on Google Cloud Platform (GCP) by verifying the user identity and context of the request to determine if a user should be allowed to access an application or a VM. Cloud IAP is an enterprise security model that enables employees to work from untrusted networks without the use of a VPN. Instead end users simply point their web browser to an internet-accessible URL to access Cloud IAP-secured applications. As a result Cloud IAP provides a single point of control for managing user access to web applications that saves them and their administrators time and effort.

Cloud IAP protects applications and resources by enforcing IAM access policies as these can only be accessed through the proxy by users and groups with the correct credentials. With Cloud IAP you grant a user access to an application or resource based upon their IAM role. This means that they're subject to fine grained access control without the need of a VPN. This is because the Cloud IAP performs the authentication and authorization checks when a user connects to the proxy in order to access a secured resource.

Use Case – 14

You have an application running on Compute Engine VMs that are running a microservice called component-one and these are granted Editor access to project-A.
However, you also have VMs running a microservice component-two that are to be granted 'object viewer' access to bucket-one in project A. How can you isolate the permission and prevent unauthorised access using IAM?
Solution

The way to do this is to create two separate service accounts. For example service account 1 will have the Editor permissions for project A. Another service account, for example service account 2 will have the 'object viewer' permissions. By assigning a service account to the appropriate microservice we can control their individual access rights. In this way, you can scope permissions for VMs without having to recreate the VMs as Cloud IAM essentially lets you slice a project into different microservices, each with access permissions to different resources. You do this by creating service accounts to represent each one.

You can assign the service accounts to the VMs when they are created, and a big benefit is that you don't have to worry that the credentials are being managed as GCP handles the security for you.

Chapter 15 - Data Storage Services a deep-dive

Data is often characterised by the 3Vs; variety, which refers to its structural variability as to how similar or different the data can be; velocity, which is essentially how fast the data arrives; and finally, volatility, which refers to how long the data retains value and therefore how long it needs to be stored and made accessible. There is a 4V, which is veracity a measure of the correctness and integrity of the data but that isn't relevant to our topic regarding cloud data storage methods.

Nonetheless, when we contemplate the various data storage techniques it doesn't really matter from an application's point of view whether the storage technology is a database or an object store. What is important, from the application perspective is that the technology behaves like a service, which provides the efficient and reliable storing and retrieving of the data.

When you take a look at GCP's service offerings for data storage, there are a lot of services to choose from. In previous chapters we discussed all of these at a high functional level and compared their individual suitability for specific tasks. In this chapter we will take a deeper dive into the workings of each of them; Cloud storage, Cloud SQL, Cloud Spanner, Cloud Datastore/Filestore, and Cloud Bigtable.

Cloud Storage

Cloud storage is designed for storing unstructured data at scale - petabytes and even exabytes of capacity. There are four classes of Cloud Storage; regional, multi-region, nearline and Coldline. We have discussed all these types earlier along with their specific properties, characteristics and usability. Nonetheless in this chapter we want to look under the bonnet so to speak to see how they store and access data in their own specific ways. We will also see how we can control individual, group, or service accounts to protect the data and control the authorised access that they may require via IAM.

Cloud storage is perfect for unstructured data because conceptually it is simply a big bucket and you're going to store objects, which are unstructured blobs of variable size and type of data, in that bucket. This makes it the perfect staging point for ingress data into GCP. As a result when you upload data to GCP you will typically initially upload it into a cloud storage bucket before it is sent to its final storage destination, such as Cloud SQL for example.

This is because the concept of an unstructured data bucket where you simply dump your diverse data makes it very flexible and intuitive to use. Indeed you don't have to worry about schemas or the like you just dump the data as it is and Cloud storage provides you with a URL to access it. Conceptually it is just a lump of data – a blob - so it can be anything from raw text such as log files to video files it doesn't matter to cloud storage.

There is no easy way to index all of these files like you would in a file system as all you have is a specific URL to access each object in the bucket. You can create directories but that is just another object that points to the various objects in the bucket so it kind of defeats the purpose.

So let's look at how cloud storage works and to do so we have to break it down into a couple of different components. First, there are buckets, which are required to have a globally unique name, and they cannot be nested. The data that you point to in those buckets are objects that inherit the storage class of the bucket, and those objects could be text files, doc files, video files, etc. There's no minimum size to those objects, and you can scale this as much as you want as long as your code allows it.

To access the data, you can use the SDK tool commands in the console, or either the JSON or XML API's. We will look at how to access objects later in the chapter.

For now, let's consider that once you've created a bucket, you might want to change the storage class of that bucket. There are several caveats here that you should be aware of;

- The first is that you can change the default storage classes of a bucket, but you can't change a regional bucket to a multi-regional and vice-versa.
- Second, a regional or a multi-regional can be changed to coldline and nearline storage classes.
- Third, you are able to move objects from one bucket to another using the GCP console.
- However, moving objects to buckets of different storage classes, requires using the gsutil command-line tool in the console.

Securing the Data

Dumping your data objects into a bucket might sound convenient but security and convenience are rarely good bed partners, so how secure is it? To understand how the GCP provides convenience while preserving the object's security and privacy we need to consider how GCP controls access to your objects and buckets. When you create a Cloud storage bucket it automatically becomes just like any other resource in a project. Therefore we can use the Cloud IAM service to apply a policy for access control. Using the IAM service enables us to explicitly dictate what individual user, group or service account can access the bucket. Furthermore we can determine who can see the bucket, list the objects in the bucket, view the names of the objects in the bucket, or create new buckets.

IAM Cloud Storage Roles

You can grant roles at either the project level or at the bucket level. However, granting roles at the lower more specific bucket level does not affect any existing roles that you have already granted at the project level, and vice versa. Thus, this gives you some flexibility in the way that you can use these two levels of granularity to tailor your permissions. For example you might use a general set of permissions at the project level say to view all buckets and all their objects but only grant the permission to create objects to a specific bucket. Moreover, there are some roles that can be used at both the project level and the bucket level. In this case, to avoid conflict if the role is used at the project level, the permissions they contain apply to all buckets and objects in the project. When used at the bucket level, the permissions only apply to a specific bucket and the objects within it. Examples of IAM Cloud Storage roles that can be applied at both project and bucket level are; roles/storage.admin, roles/storage.objectViewer, and roles/storage.objectCreator. On the other hand there are also some roles that can only be applied at one level. For example, you can only apply the Viewer role only at the project level, while you can only apply only at the bucket level the roles/storage.legacyObjectOwner.

Deploying IAM as the method for access control for objects and buckets will for most purposes be sufficient as the IAM roles are inherited from project, to bucket, to object.

However there are more granular access controls techniques that you may wish to implement. One of these is an access control list or ACL and this offers even finer control. Project and Bucket level roles work sympathetically with ACLs in so much as they both work independently from the ACL. This provides a way to create more granular policies. For example you could grant permissions at the bucket level to grant access to all objects then at the ACL level block access to specific objects.

However, if you need even more detailed control, you can use signed URLs, which provide a cryptographic key, which gives the key holder highly-restricted access to a bucket or object. Finally, a signed access policy document further refines the control, by determining what kind of file can be uploaded by someone with a signed URL.

Access Control Lists

An ACL is a simple mechanism or technique that you can use to define who has access to your buckets and objects, as well as state what level of access they have.

An ACL consists of one or more entries hence the term list, and these entries consist of two pieces of information; a scope, and a permission. The scope defines who can perform the specified actions such as a specific user, group or service account. The permission stipulates what actions can be performed, for example, view or modify.

Signed URLs

Access lists are fine generally but for some applications there is a need to enforce time-based access control criteria. For example, if you are making available for anonymous download a video file for a predefined time then is will be easier and more efficient to grant limited time access tokens.

Access tokens can also be used by any user, instead of using account based authentication for controlling resource access. For example, if you wished to allow visitors to your site free access to a download or when you don't require users to have a registered account. If those are the criteria than instead of access lists you can use signed URLs, which lets you do this for anonymous access to cloud storage.

Signed URLs are also simple to set up and all you have to do is first create a URL that will grant a permission such as read or write access to a specific cloud storage resource.

Then you can optionally specify when the access permissions will expire. The URL is then signed using a private key associated with a service account.

When the request is received, cloud storage will verify that the signed access granting URL was issued by a trusted service account as it delegates its trust of that account to the holder of the URL. However there are some security concerns you should be aware of because once you give out the signed URL, it is out of your control. So, you want the signed URL to expire after some reasonable amount of time.

An example of a signed URL is shown below:
https://storage.googleapis.com/example-bucket/car.jpeg?X-Goog-Algorithm=GOOG4-RSA-SHA256&X-Goog-Credential=example%40example-project.iam.gserviceaccount.com%2F20181026%2Fus-central-1%2Fstorage%2Fgoog4_request&X-Goog-Date=20181026T181309Z&X-Goog-Expires=900&X-Goog-SignedHeaders=host&X-Goog-Signature=

This signed URL provided access to read the object car.jpeg in the bucket example-bucket. Your applications could call it, or you could make the URL available to individuals for download.

The query parameters that make this a signed URL are:

- X-Goog-Algorithm: The algorithm used to sign the URL.
- X-Goog-Credential: Information about the credentials used to create the signed URL.
- X-Goog-Date: The date and time the signed URL became usable, in the ISO 8601 basic format YYYYMMDD'T'HHMMSS'Z'.
- X-Goog-Expires: The length of time the signed URL remained valid, measured in seconds from the value in X-Goog-Date.
- X-Goog-SignedHeaders: Headers that had to be included as part of any request that used the signed URL.
- X-Goog-Signature: The authentication string that allowed requests using this signed URL to access car.jpeg.

Signed URLS are good way to ensure a predetermined expiration to the access of a file. This means you do not have to rely on life cycle management to delete older files. However, there are some considerations you should be aware of:

- Always transmit the link to your users using HTTPS
- When specifying credentials, identify your service account by using its email address; however, the use of the service account ID is also supported.

Cloud Storage Features

There are a variety of different object management features that come with Cloud Storage. For example you can use your own encryption keys, instead of the Google-managed keys which are available for Cloud Storage.

Cloud Storage also provides Object-Lifecycle Management, which lets you automatically delete or archive objects after a specified time period.

Another feature is Object Versioning which allows you to maintain multiple versions of objects in your bucket.

There are other features such as Object Change Notification, Data Import and Strong Consistency, but we will discuss these in more detail after discussing Object Versioning and Object Lifecycle Management.

Object Versioning

To provide a measure of protection for objects from being deleted or overwritten while in Cloud Storage, Google offers the Object Versioning feature. You can help with the retrieval of objects that have been accidently over-written by enabling Object Versioning for a bucket.

The way that Object Versioning works is that once it is enabled, Cloud Storage will track objects within a bucket. Now objects are immutable so they cannot be modified while in a Cloud Storage bucket but they can be over-written and deleted. To prevent accidental loss and to help in the subsequent retrieval of a deleted or over-written object the Object Versioning feature creates an archived version of an object each time the live version of the object is overwritten or deleted.

The archived version retains the name of the object, but is uniquely identified by a generation number, such as g1. However, you should be aware that this is considered from a billing perspective to be an additional object so you will be charged for the storage of the versions in the archives accordingly.

Nonetheless, once Object Versioning is enabled, you will be able to list archived versions of an object, restore the version of an object from an older state, or permanently delete an archived version as needed. You can turn versioning on or off for a bucket at any time. Turning versioning off leaves the existing object versions in place. However, it does stop any further versions being created so the bucket will stop accumulating new archived object versions.

Object Lifecycle Management

To support some of the use cases that are common place in the enterprise such as setting a time to live for objects, archiving older versions of objects, or migrating objects to longer term cold storage classes to help manage costs, Cloud Storage offers Object Lifecycle Management.

The way that lifecycle management works is that you assign a set of rules to a bucket. The rules will apply to all the objects in the bucket. So when an object meets the criteria of one of those rules, Cloud Storage automatically performs a specified action on the object.

Here are some use cases where you could use lifecycle management to your benefit;

- You could set a time to live for downloadable objects that you wish to make available during a promotion
- you could downgrade the storage class of objects older than two years to Coldline Storage
- You can archive or delete objects created before a specific date for example January the 1st 2018
- If you have versioning enabled, you could decide to keep only the three most recent versions of an object and archive/delete the others

When you change the lifecycle configuration it doesn't take effect immediately and it may take up to 24 hours to come into effect. So be aware that when you change your lifecycle configuration, the Object Lifecycle Management service may still perform actions based on the old configuration for up to 24 hours.

Object Change Notification

Object Change Notification can be used to notify an application when an object is updated or added to a bucket through a watch request. Completing a watch request creates a new notification channel. This is the channel over which a notification message is sent to an application watching a bucket.
After a notification channel is initiated, Cloud Storage will send a notification to the application any time an object is added, updated, or removed from the bucket.

Storage Transfer

The GCP Cloud Storage browser allows you to conveniently upload individual files to your bucket. However, in real world scenarios you may have to upload terabytes or even petabytes of data so you are going to need a more robust transfer mechanism.
The GCP provides three services that address this issue; Storage Transfer Service, Google Transfer Appliance, and Offline Media Import.
The Storage Transfer Service enables high performance imports of online data. That data source can be another Cloud Storage Bucket, an Amazon S3 Bucket or an HTTP or HTTPS location.

Transfer Appliance on the other hand, is a specialist solution consisting of a high capacity storage server that you lease from Google. However it is not available in all regions. If you are lucky enough to be in a region that does offer this service then all you have to do is simply connect it to your network. Then load it with data and ship it to an upload facility where the data is uploaded to Cloud Storage. This service enables you to securely transfer up to petabytes of data on a single appliance.

Finally, Offline Media Import is a third party service where physical media such as storage arrays, hard disk drives, tapes and USB flash drives is sent to a provider who uploads the data.

When you upload an object to Cloud Storage and you receive a success response, the object is immediately available for download and operations from any location where Google offer the service. This is true whether you create a new object or override an existing object. This is because when you perform an upload the data will be now strongly consistent, so you will never be likely to receive a '404 Not Found' response. Moreover you are also unlikely to experience stale data after a Read-after-write or Read-after-meditate-update operation.

Strong global consistency also extends to deleting objects. If a deletion request succeeds, an immediate attempt to download the object or its metadata will result in a 404 Not Found status code. You get the 404 error because the object no longer exists after the delete operation succeeds.

Also Bucket listing is strongly consistent. For example, if you create a Bucket, then you immediately perform a list Bucket's operation; the new Bucket appears in the return list of Buckets without any lag or delay.

Finally, object listing is also strongly consistent. For example, if you upload an object to a bucket and then immediately perform a list object's operation, the new object appears in the returned list of objects again without delay.

Structured data services

In the previous section we dealt only with unstructured data in the Cloud Storage core service. But many transactional type operations do need to store data within a structured schema or a relational data storage service.

Cloud SQL

If you do need a structured data storage service then there are several options. From a customer experience and convenience perspective Cloud SQL is a fully managed, no ops, database service. This makes it easy for you to implement as Google will set up, maintain, manage, and administer your relational databases on the Google Cloud Platform.

Alternatively, if you want you could install your own SQL database application image, such as MySQL on a VM using Compute Engine. In this case you would have to build the schema, set up, maintain, manage and administer the database yourself. This method gives you all the freedom and flexibility to run your own database as you perhaps are used to doing on-premises. But there are certain benefits to be had when using Cloud SQL as a managed service instead of running your own instance of a database engine.

For example, Cloud SQL can scale to a high capacity database, which is capable of handling terabytes of storage. Accessing and using the databases will be exactly the same as they are relational, which means that you can simply run SQL type queries such as SELECT statements to read a field's data or INSERT statements to write a field's data.

In addition since Cloud SQL is a fully managed service, you can choose either MySQL, SQL Server or PostgreSQL database engines, the security patches and updates are automatically applied for you. Now, if we consider MySQL as an example we can see that Cloud SQL is not a simulation it is a real MySQL instance. This means that there will be no compatibility issues and you should be able to easily lift and shift the on-premise to the cloud without any issues. After that Google will manage the MySQL cloud instance for you. However, you will still have to administer the database users but you can also do this through the native authentication tools that come with these databases.

 However, Cloud SQL also supports other applications and tools that you might be familiar with, such as, SQL Workbench, Toad, and other external applications that use the standard SQL drivers.

Cloud SQL is available in two different generations. It is recommended to use the second generation unless you have some legacy constraints because it provides up to seven times the throughput and 20 times the storage capacity of the first generation. As a result the 2nd Generation provides up to 208 gigabytes of RAM and 10 terabytes of data storage.

Also, the 2nd generation version works with either MySQL 5.6 or 5.7, but be aware that it will only supports InnoDB as the storage engine.

On the other hand, the 1st generation version provides considerably lower memory and storage capacity and only works with MySQL 5.5. However, this generation does support the MyISAM storage engine as well as connections over both IPv4 and IPv6 addresses. In addition it also supports the on-demand activation policy.

On-premises MySQL vs. Cloud SQL

Regardless of the generation, the MySQL functionality provided by a Cloud SQL Instance is exactly the same as the functionality provided by a locally hosted MySQL Instance.

However, there are a few differences between a Standard MySQL Instance and a Cloud SQL Instance. For example, user-defined functions are not supported in Cloud SQL and some additional services that are required to be enabled and configured in standard MySQL are automatically provided by Cloud SQL as part of the managed service.

For example, The MySQL replication feature, which requires considerable thought to the design and configuration in an on-premise standard MySQL deployment, can be enabled as part of the Cloud SQL managed service by just ticking a few checkboxes. The replication service will replicate data between multiple zones and provide automatic failover without loss of service if a service outage should occur in one of the regions.

In a similar vein Cloud SQL also provides automated and on demand backups with point in time recovery.

Just as you can with an on-premises MySQL instance you can easily import and export databases using MySQL dump or import and export CSV files. However, another feature of Cloud SQL that is difficult to reproduce on-premises is its ability to scale up, albeit it does require a machine restart, or scale out by using read replicas. Essentially, choosing between a standard MySQL instance and Cloud SQL managed service comes down to a few basic questions. If you have specific OS requirements, custom database configuration requirements, or special backup requirements. If that is the case then you perhaps want to consider hosting your own database on a VM using Compute Engine. Otherwise, it is strongly recommended to use Cloud SQL as a fully managed service for your relational databases.

SQL IAM

You can control permissions and access to Cloud SQL resources via primitive roles (owner, editor, and viewer) or through the predefined roles. The difference between them is down to the level of granularity that is available when working with the predefined roles. You can of course also create your own custom IAM roles. Primitive Roles:

- roles/owner - Full access and control for all Google Cloud Platform resources; manage user access
- roles/writer – (Editor) Read-write access to all Google Cloud Platform and Cloud SQL resources (full control except for the ability to modify permissions)
- roles/reader – (Viewer) Read-only access to all Google Cloud Platform resources, including Cloud SQL resources

Predefined Roles:

- roles/cloudsql.admin - Full control for all Cloud SQL resources.
- roles/cloudsql.editor - Manage specific instances. No ability to neither see or modify permissions, nor modify users or SSL Certs. No ability to import data or restore from a backup, nor clone, delete, or promote instances. No ability to start or stop replicas. No ability to delete databases, replicas, or backups.
- roles/cloudsql.viewer - Read-only access to all Cloud SQL resources.
- roles/cloudsql.client - Connectivity access to Cloud SQL instances from App Engine and the Cloud SQL Proxy. Not required for accessing an instance using IP addresses.

Cloud SQL Connections

When it comes to configuring connections between applications and the database there are a couple of options you should be aware off. A very popular method of connection favoured in development environments uses a basic connection. This is where you simply grant any application access to a Cloud SQL instance by authorizing the applications host IP address.

This is the fastest, easiest, but least secure method to make a connection, hence its popularity in non-production development environments but it is certainly not recommended for production instances.

Instead, for a more secure access, but only suitable for temporarily access you can use whitelist IP addresses to easily connect from the GCP Console. These are fast and secure enough for quick administration tasks requiring the MySQL command line tool. But for regular client connections you should configure SSL certificate management for a Cloud SQL Instance and connect to the MySQL client using TLS/SSL.

Cloud SQL also provides instance level access to authorize access to your Cloud SQL Instance from an application or client that could be running on Google App Engine or on another GCP service such as Compute Engine or even running externally.

Cloud SQL Proxy

For production or robust development environments there is an alternative method of connecting a MySQL client to your Google Cloud SQL instances over IP and that is using the Cloud SQL Proxy. The Cloud SQL Proxy provides you with a method for secure access to your Cloud SQL second generation instances without having to whitelist IP addresses or having to configure TLS/SSL. Cloud SQL Proxy works by having a local client called eth-proxy running in the local environment. Your application will directly communicate with the SQL proxy not through IP but by using the standard database protocol that is used by your database. To accomplish this task the Proxy will establish and use a secure tunnel to communicate with its companion process running on the server.

Cloud Spanner

If Cloud SQL does not fit your capacity criteria because you need large scale horizontal scalability, then you might consider using Cloud Spanner. This is the specialist fully-managed storage service built by Google to scale for the Cloud. Cloud Spanner is designed specifically to combine the benefits of relational database structures with non-relational horizontal scale. This means that the Spanner SQL service can provide petabytes of capacity, support over 4,000 concurrent connections and offer transactional consistency at global scale. Just like Cloud SQL it supports schemas, SQL, as well as automatic synchronous replication for high availability and business continuity.

In addition to its design-criteria for scalability the Cloud Spanner service is also designed to deliver strong consistency including strongly consistent secondary indexes. It also natively provides SQL support with alter statements for schema changes. Moreover, Cloud Spanner also offers managed instances with inherent high availability through transparent synchronous built-in data replication. These features make large transactional intensive operations such as financial trading systems and inventory management applications traditionally served by a relational database technology the most suitable use cases for Cloud Spanner.

Cloud Spanner use cases

In order to better understand the concept behind Cloud Spanner and how we can benefit from its vast scale yet high consistency it is often beneficial to compare it with both relational and non-relational databases. After all Cloud Spanner is designed to be like a relational database, as it has schema, SQL and strong data consistency. But, it is designed to resemble a non-relational database as Cloud Spanner offers high availability, horizontal scalability and configurable replication. Cloud Spanner is essentially a hybrid that offers the best features of the relational and non-relational worlds. These features deliver the performance that match mission critical use cases, such as building consistent systems for financial trading, ecommerce transactions and inventory management in the financial services and retail industries.

Cloud Spanner supports many open standards. It also supports many workloads like transactional workloads where companies that have outgrown their single instance relational database management system and have already moved to a NoSQL solution but need transactional consistency or are looking to move to a scalable solution.

Cloud Spanner also allows for database consolidation where companies that store their business data in multiple database products with variable maintenance overheads and capabilities need consolidation of their data.

To a better understand how all of this works, let's look at the architecture of Cloud Spanner.

Cloud Spanner Architecture

A Cloud Spanner instance will replicate data in 'n' cloud zones which can be contained within one region or spread across several regions. This feature of configurable database placement means you can not only choose which region to put your database in for performance, politics or legal constraints. You can also use this choice of placement to design an architecture, which allows for high-performance, high-availability and global reachability.
This is due to the high-speed replication of data being synchronized across zones over Google's global fibre network. This high speed, SDN network uses atomic clocks that ensure atomicity when you're updating your data. This ensures the high levels of data consistency demanded by large global transactional systems.

IAM Roles

Cloud Spanner has its own set of IAM access roles. This allows you to have the same security mechanisms without having to create something separate for your database. These IAM permissions can be granted to a database, instance or GCP project.
The predefined roles that you will use at either a project or database level are:

- roles/spanner.admin – This is recommended at the project level and it provides for; Grant and revoke permissions to other principals for all Cloud Spanner resources in the project; Allocate and delete chargeable Cloud Spanner resources; Issue get/list/modify operations on Cloud Spanner resources; Read from and write to all Cloud Spanner databases in the project; Fetch project metadata.

- roles/spanner.databaseAdmin - This is recommended at the project level and it provides for; Get/list all Cloud Spanner instances in project; Create/list/drop databases in the instance on which it is granted; Grant/revoke access to databases in the project; Read from and write to all Cloud Spanner databases in the project.
- roles/spanner.databaseReader – This is a machine role so it is applied at the database level. It provides for; Read from the Cloud Spanner database; Execute SQL queries on the database; View schema for the database.
- roles/spanner.viewer – This is a person role applied at the project level and provides for; View all Cloud Spanner instances (but cannot modify instances); View all Cloud Spanner databases (but cannot modify databases and cannot read from databases).

Like all predefined roles in IAM you can combine roles for added flexibility. For example you could combine the roles/spanner.viewer so that they can have view only access to all instances and databases with the roles/spanner.databaseUser to grant a user access to a specific database.

Additional features in Cloud Spanner

Cloud Spanner offers many features such as tables, primary and secondary keys, database splits, transactions and timestamp bounds. However to understand what features are essential to you and under what circumstances you would use Cloud Spanner, you need to consider a few salient points.

If you have outgrown your existing relational database or are sharding your databases for high performance throughput. Then you are probably looking for transactional consolidation for global data with strong consistency in your databases, then you should consider using Cloud Spanner.

If you however you feel that these features are not essential and you don't need many of these relational focused capabilities, consider a NoSQL server such as Cloud Datastore which we will cover next.

Cloud Datastore

If you're looking for a highly scalable database, but do not need relational properties then a NoSQL database might be the answer. A NoSQL database will allow you to store structured data for your web and mobile applications if these are your typical use cases then you should consider using Cloud Datastore. A key benefit of using the Cloud Datastore service is its ability to scale seamlessly as your application's data storage needs grow. This allows you to concentrate on developing your applications rather than concerning yourself with capacity planning and trying to forecast for anticipated loads.

Another key feature is that Datastore is schema-less, which provides you with a much more flexible data structure. This is also important as it again means that you can concentrate on writing the application rather than struggling with modelling the database schema.

Furthermore, you can think of Cloud Datastore as a persistent hash map that can scale to terabytes of capacity. Cloud Datastore is a managed service and that means it handles all regional and multi-regional replication and sharding on your behalf, while maintaining a good balance of strong and eventual consistency. This is because Cloud Datastore will strive to find the entities that match the lookup key and in the case of ancestor queries they will always receive strongly consistent data. All other queries are deemed to be eventually consistent. This consistency model facilitates the delivery of strong query consistency while handling large amounts of multi-regional data and a global user base.

Yet this is a simple and flexible database, which is easy to provision and integrate making it a perfect point of connection for web and mobile apps that span across App Engine and Compute Engine.

Datastore use cases

Indeed, one of Cloud Datastore's original purpose and its main use cases is to store structured data from App Engine apps. You can think of Cloud Datastore as a persistent hash map that can scale to terabytes of capacity yet it can perform at the highest levels despite its scale. A hash map can be thought of as a collection of key and value pairs where each key maps to a value. Cloud Datastore's performance though comes about because it is paired with a Memcache service to increase performance for repeatedly read data. Typically in development, the App Engine application will try Memcache first, and then on a cache miss, access Cloud Datastore. This strategy radically improves performance and reduces costs.

In addition, Cloud Datastore provides a myriad of capabilities, such as ACID transactions, SQL-like queries, indexes, and much more.

Datastore structure

Despite the Cloud Datastore interface sharing many of the same features as a traditional database it is actually a No-SQL database. As such it differs from traditional relational databases in the way that it describes relationships between data objects. We can see this in this table;

In Cloud Datastore, a category of object is known as a kind, an object is an entity, individual data for an object is a property, and a unique ID for an object is a key, whereas in a relational database these would be table, row, field, and primary key respectively.

Also, built-in to Datastore is synchronous replication over a wide geographic area. When you first create a Cloud Datastore you must choose a location where the projects data is stored. To reduce latency and increase availability store your data close to the users and services that need it.

GQL

Cloud Datastore does not use SQL as there is no concept of tables, rows and columns. However, it does have a way to make similar type queries and that is by using an API called GQL.
Here is an example of a GQL query:
// List Google companies with less than 400 employees.
var companies = query.filter('name =', 'Google').filter('size <', 400);
Cloud Datastore actually originated from Google's internal-use database, Megastore, and it is believed to be going to be superseded by Google Firestore, which is part of the Google mobile platform suite.

IAM Roles

With IAM, every API method in Datastore mode requires that the account making the API request has the appropriate permissions to use the resource. Permissions are granted by setting policies that grant roles to a user, group, or service account. In addition to the primitive roles, owner, editor, and viewer, you can grant Datastore mode roles to the users of your project. The following list shows the Datastore mode IAM roles:

- roles/datastore.owner with roles/appengine.appAdmin – Gives full Datastore admin
- roles/datastore.owner without roles/appengine.appAdmin - Full access to Datastore mode except the user, group, or service account cannot: enable Admin access; see if Datastore mode Admin is enabled; disable Datastore mode writes; see if Datastore mode writes are disabled
- roles/datastore.user - Read/write access to data in a Datastore mode database. Intended for application developers and service accounts.
- roles/datastore.viewer - Read access to all Datastore mode resources.
- roles/datastore.importExportAdmin - Full access to manage imports and exports.
- roles/datastore.indexAdmin - Full access to manage index definitions.

You can grant multiple roles to a user, group, or service account. However something that you should be aware of is that an entity that is assigned the App Engine owner, editor, and viewer primitive roles and the App Engine Admin predefined role have complete access to the Datastore mode Admin page.

Geographical Database Placement

There are two types of geographical placement where you can store data using Cloud Datastore, multi-regional locations and regional locations. Both of these options have trade-offs you will need to consider when evaluating the best placement for your apps. Multi-regional locations provide multi-region redundancy with higher availability. On the other hand Regional locations provide lower write latency and the opportunity to co-locate within the same region/zone as your other GCP resources that your application may use.

Both of these options provide high availability but with slightly different SLAs for monthly uptime percentage.

Cloud Firestore

Cloud Firestore is a cloud-native database, which has been introduced as an upgrade to Cloud Datastore to deliver a more scalable solution. Indeed Firestore is built from the ground up to take advantage of Google Cloud Platform's powerful infrastructure. It is designed to provide a great developer experience and simplify app development with live synchronization, offline support, and ACID transactions across hundreds of documents and collections. Cloud Firestore is integrated with both Google Cloud Platform (GCP) and Firebase, Google's mobile development platform.

Cloud Firestore is a flexible, NoSQL, scalable database for mobile, web, and server development on the Google Cloud Platform. Firestore is the successor or next generation of Cloud Datastore as it has a few key advantages. Although for backwards compatibility Cloud Firestore can operate in Datastore mode, making it fully compatible with Cloud Datastore. To do this you can create a Cloud Firestore database in Datastore mode, which makes it compatible so that you can access Cloud Firestore's improved storage layer while also maintaining your business logic and query behaviour. Cloud Firestore in Datastore mode removes the following Cloud Datastore limitations:

• Queries are no longer eventually consistent; instead, they are all strongly consistent.

• Transactions are no longer limited to 25 entity groups.

• Writes to an entity group are no longer limited to 1 per second.

Datastore and Firestore are both NoSQL databases but they are designed for different purposes, with the latter targeted at web and mobile applications. Both Datastore and Firestore scale from zero upwards but, if you require NoSQL flexibility and efficiency but also need vast scale but importantly, you don't require transactional consistency, you might want to consider Cloud Bigtable.

Cloud Bigtable

Cloud Bigtable is Google's NoSQL Big Data database service. Cloud Bigtable is a sparsely populated table that can scale to billions of rows and thousands of columns allowing you to store terabytes or even petabytes of data.

Cloud Bigtable is ideal for storing very large amounts of single key data with very low latency. A single value in each row is indexed and this value is known as the row key.

Cloud Bigtable also supports higher read and write throughput at low latency, which makes it suitable for both operational and analytical applications including IoT, user analytics and financial data analysis.

Cloud Bigtable is actually the same database that powers many of Google's core services including search, analytics, maps, and Gmail. Nonetheless, despite its pedigree Cloud Bigtable is simple to deploy and use as it is a fully managed NoSQL database with petabyte-scale and very low latency. Further, Bigtable can seamlessly scale for throughput and it also learns to adjust for specific access patterns.

There are different ways for applications to interact with Cloud Bigtable such as through multiple client libraries including a supported extension to Apache HBase library. Also, Cloud Bigtable also excels as a storage engine for batch Map Reduce operations, steam processing/analytics, and machine learning applications.

Cloud Bigtable's powerful backend servers offer several key advantages over a self-managed HBase installation. From a scalability perspective, a self-managed HBase installation has a design bottleneck that limits the performance after a certain query per second rate is reached. Cloud Bigtable does not have this bottleneck and so you can scale your cluster up to handle more queries by increasing your machine count.

Also, Cloud Bigtable handles administration tasks like upgrades and restarts transparently and can resize clusters without downtime.

Cloud Bigtable Structure

Cloud Bigtable stores data in massively scalable tables each of which is a sorted key value map. The table is composed of rows, each of which typically describes a single entity, and columns, which contain individual values for each row.

Each row is indexed by a single row key and columns that are related to one another are typically grouped together into a column family. Also, the tables within Cloud Bigtable are sparse, as every cell does not need to contain any data, hence it does not take up any space.

What is interesting about the Bigtable architecture is that processing is done through a front end server pool consisting of nodes, but this is handled separately from the storage. A table is sliced into a shard of blocks of contiguous rows called tablets which helps to balance the workload of queries. Tablets are stored on Colossus, which is Google's file system in SS table format. An SS table provides a persistent ordered immutable map from keys to values where both keys and values are arbitrary byte strings.

As mentioned earlier, Cloud Bigtable learns to adjust to specific access patterns. If a certain big table node is frequently accessing a certain subset of data, Cloud Bigtable will update the indexes so that the other nodes can distribute that workload more evenly. That throughput scales linearly. So, for every single node that you add, you're going to see a linear scale of throughput performance up to hundreds of nodes.

Cloud Bigtable use cases

In short, if you need to store more than one terabyte of structured data, have very high volumes of writes, need read-write latency of less than 10 milliseconds along with strong consistency, or need a storage service that is compatible with the HBase API, then you should consider using Cloud Bigtable.

However, the smallest Cloud Bigtable cluster you can create has three nodes and can handle 30,000 operations per second, but do you need that scale? Keep in mind that you pay for those nodes while they are operational whether your application is using them or not.

If you don't need any of these and are looking for a simple to use starter service that scales both up and down well, then consider using Cloud Datastore.

IAM Roles

Cloud Bigtable uses Google Cloud Identity and Access Management (IAM) for access control. However when using IAM for controlling access to Cloud Bigtable, you can configure access control at the project level and the instance level. You can use primitive roles (owner, editor and viewer) or predefined roles such as:

- roles/Bigtable.admin - Administers all instances within a project, including the data stored within tables. Can create new instances. Intended for project administrators.
- roles/Bigtable.user - Provides read-write access to the data stored within tables. Intended for application developers or service accounts.

- roles/Bigtable.reader - Provides read-only access to the data stored within tables. Intended for data scientists, dashboard generators, and other data-analysis scenarios.
- roles/Bigtable.viewer - Provides no data access. Intended as a minimal set of permissions to access the GCP Console for Cloud Bigtable.

If these predefined roles are not sufficient even in combination you can roll your own custom roles.

Comparing Data Storage Options

The problem that having a wide spectrum for data storage options is it can be confusing as to which option is the best choice. For example, Cloud data storage options on GCP range from the unstructured Cloud Storage to the structured relational options like Cloud SQL, to NoSQL Cloud Datastore, and then to options such as Cloud Bigtable, Cloud BigQuery, and Google Spanner. The last three however, as their names suggest, are focused on scalability and handling large volumes of data.

Use Case Summary
Cloud SQL

To summarise what we covered earlier Cloud SQL is a relational database that supports customized table views, stored procedures, tons of indexes and ACID compliance. If this is what you need then Cloud SQL is definitely your choice. However, it is not quite that simple as Google Cloud SQL database service supports three popular types of databases: MySQL , SQL Server and PostgreSQL. Both these options support High Availability (HA) and Pay per Use without Lock-in. In addition Cloud SQL can scale up to 32 processor cores and more than 200GB RAM. This option is popular as it does make moving your data from on-premises to the cloud easier. However you do miss out on some of the key advantages of the cloud as it does have all the limitations inbuilt in MySQL, SQL Server and PostgreSQL that they do not scale well for huge data volume.

Cloud Datastore

Google Cloud Datastore is the GCP NoSQL database for web and mobile applications. It is a scalable NoSQL database as it automates sharding and replication but interestingly it also supports ACID transaction, SQL-like queries and REST API. Datastore is optimized for smaller set of data, which for most general purposes this is what you will be looking for rather than its sibling, Bigtable. Although Cloud Datastore is a NoSQL data storage so there is no need to define a schema before storing data, it actually uses more capacity when having to do ad-hoc storage of structured data.

Cloud Firestore

Essentially, Cloud Firestore's is GCP's next generation NoSQL database but with Cloud Firestore you store data in structures called documents, which contain fields mapping to values. These documents are then stored in collections, which are containers for your documents, which are used to organize your data and make it easier to build queries. Documents support many different data types, from simple strings and numbers, to complex, nested objects and you can create sub-collections within documents and build hierarchical data structures that scale as your database grows. Additionally, the way that you make a query in Cloud Firestore is efficient and flexible as you can create queries to retrieve data targeted at the document level. This means you do not need to retrieve the entire collection, or for that matter any nested sub-collections. Furthermore you can also add sorting, filtering, and limits to your queries to make them more expressive and to paginate the results. The Cloud Firestore data model supports whatever data structure works best for your app and to keep data in your apps current, without retrieving your entire database each time an update happens, you can also add realtime listeners. This feature also keeps your data in sync across client apps, which makes it popular for mobile apps and offers offline support for mobile and web so you can build responsive apps that work regardless of network latency or Internet connectivity. Finally, we can consider that Cloud Firestore also offers you the opportunity for seamless integration with other Firebase Platform and Google Cloud Platform products.

Pricing

When you use Cloud Firestore, you are charged for the following:

- The number of reads, writes, and deletes that you perform.

- The amount of storage that your database uses, including overhead for metadata and indexes.
- The amount of network bandwidth that you use.
- Storage and bandwidth usage are calculated in gigabytes (GiB), where 1 GiB = 230 bytes. All charges accrue daily.

However you get 1GB of free storage per month and 50,000 document reads per day as well as 20,000 document writes and deletes per day. After that quota has been exceeded the price is $0.06 per read, $0.18 per write and $0.02 per delete. Storage is charged at $0.18 per Gigabyte per month.

Bigtable

Google Bigtable is Google's cloud storage solution for high-performance and low latency data access. It is widely used in many Google's core services like Google Search, Google Maps, and Gmail. Big Table, like Cloud Datastore is designed in NoSQL architecture, but it can still use row-based data format. Where Big Table comes into its own is in throughput as it can handle data read/write under 10 milliseconds, which means it is perfect for those applications that have frequent and large amounts of data ingestion. Furthermore, unlike Datastore, which is similar in purpose, it is designed to scale to hundreds of petabytes and handle millions of operations per second (IOPS).

What makes Bigtable popular is its compatibility with HBase 1.0 API via extensions as this simplifies any migration from HBase. Bigtable, like Cloud Datastore, has no SQL interface and you can only use the API to use Put/Get/Delete commands on individual rows or run scan operations. Bigtable can also be readily integrated with other GCP tools, like Cloud Dataflow and Dataproc.

Pricing

Unlike other cloud providers, GCP prices the compute and storage separately therefore you will need to consider the following three billable items when calculating the overall cost.

1. The type of Cloud instance, and the number of nodes in the instance.
2. The total amount of storage you use.
3. The amount of network bandwidth used by egress traffic.

The problem here is that although it is good that you are billed only for active instances and you pay only for the storage used it is not easy to forecast if you have a large datasets. Moreover, the compute cost becomes less important as it is the same no matter if you choose an SSD or an HDD storage type. For example the difference in performance between SSD and HDD are not comparable. For example, although the timing to perform writes is the same for both cases, the timing for reads is about 20 times faster with SSD. Of course there is a case for going with HDD as scans for HDD lags behind SSD by just 20%. Hence, if you know your access pattern is mostly going to be scans, then HDD option might be a good option as HDD storage is only 15% of the cost of SSD.

BigQuery

Finally we will address BigQuery as it is Google's Cloud-based version of a data warehouse. But, unlike Bigtable, it targets data as a big picture and can run a query against vast volumes of data in a short time. This is because in BigQuery the data is stored in columnar data format so it is much faster in scanning large amounts of data compared with Bigtable. In addition, BigQuery allows you to scale to petabyte and is targeted at the enterprise data warehouse for analytics market space. BigQuery is serverless, which means it is a fully managed service. Serverless computing also benefits from scamless scalability as computing resource can be spun up on-demand without involving administrators managing any infrastructure. As a result of this transparent scalability BigQuery can scan Terabytes of data in seconds and Petabytes of data in minutes. On the other hand with regards data ingestion, BigQuery integrates to load or stream data from/to Google Cloud Storage, or Google Cloud Datastore.

However, we must remember that BigQuery is designed as a data warehouse so is best for analytical (OLAP) type of query and scanning large amount of data and is not designed for transaction type queries (OLTP). For example, for small read/writes, it takes about 2 seconds while Bigtable takes about 9 milliseconds for the same amount of data. Bigtable is much better off for OLTP type of queries. Although BigQuery support atomic single-row operations, it lacks cross-row transaction support.

For pricing, there are two major components in the cost of using BigQuery: Storage Cost and Query Cost.

For storage cost, it is $0.02 per GB/month. However, Google has a long term storage pricing, which is 50% off to $0.01 per GB/month. The definition that Google uses is that long term storage is defined as a table that is not edited for 90 days. Each partition in the table is considered separate storage. So you could have standard pricing for some recent partitions while have long term storage pricing for some historical partitions. Even the data is in long term storage, there is no degradation of performance, durability and availability. For query cost, the first 1 TB of data processed in a month is free, and then it is $5 per TB. No charge for cached queries. As BigQuery is stored in columnar data format, the query cost is based on the columns selected. For enterprise with large amount of data and tons of applications, although the bill for data storage is predictable, the bill for query cost is not. The good news is that Google does offer a flat rate monthly cost model instead of on-demand pricing. For example, you could decide to pay $5,000 for 100 BigQuery Slots and then BigQuery will automatically manage the quota.

Cloud Spanner

Cloud Spanner is a globally distributed database and it is a versioned key-value store. From this perspective, it is similar to Bigtable. However, it supports general-purpose transactions and also provides SQL-based query language.
Two stands out features of Cloud Spanner are:
1. Replication Configuration

Data replication is handled automatically and transparently. But user application can control the way how data is stored. For example, if user data has the requirement to stay in USA only, you could specify to store data in US data centres only. If you want to improve the read performance and availability, you could increase the number of replicas used and geographic placement of replicas to make the data is close to the users as much as possible. If you want to have fast write throughput, you could decide how far replicas are from each other.

2. A globally-distributed database does allow consistent reads and writes. This feature is critical if you want to have a consistent backup, or have consistent reads at global scale. The implementation of this feature is using Google's TrueTime. Instead of using only one source for the time reference, TrueTime is based on the time references from both GPS and atomic clocks. Google indicates the reason to use two different kinds of time reference because they have different failure models. The use of atomic clocks is essential as you need precision as standard clocks can fail over long periods of time or drift significantly.

Spanner is organized in a set of zones. Each zone has one zone master and 100 to 1000 spanserver. Each table is split into multiple tablets. A table's state is stored in set of B-tree like structure files and Write-Ahead Log on a file system called Colossus. Colossus is a global distributed file system and the successor to Google File System (GFS). Spanner's data model is a hybrid so not relational instead it can be considered to be semi-relational. Each row must have a unique name, and each table must have an ordered set of one or more primary-key columns. Google publishes a Best Practice for Spanner Schema Design.

The following shows the option to create a Spanner instance with 10 nodes.

The storage cost is $0.30 per GB/month and $9 per hour per node. Each Spanner node can provide up to 10,000 QPS of reads or 2000 QPS of writes (writing single rows at 1KB data per row), and 2 TB disk storage. Google also recommend provision more spanner nodes to keep CPU utilization below 75%.

Among these five database storage options in GCP, deciding the best option can be problematic so Google has provided a decision tree to help you to determine the best option for you.

Figure 15

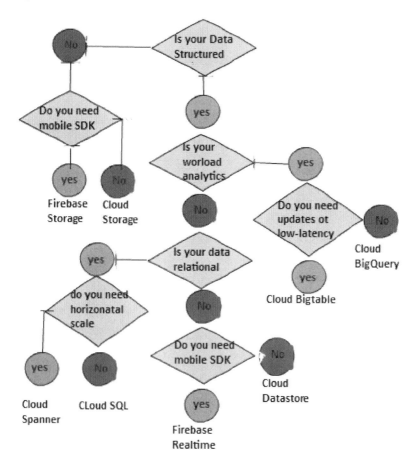

Summary

In this chapter, we covered the different data storage services that GCP offers. Specifically, you learned about cloud storage, a fully managed object store. Cloud SQL, a fully managed MySQL, SQL Server or PostgreSQL database service. Cloud spanner, which is a relational database service with transactional consistency, global scale, and high availability features. Also we considered Cloud Datastore, a fully managed NoSQL document database, and introduced its successor in many ways, Cloud Firestore. Finally, we contemplated Cloud Bigtable, which is a fully managed NoSQL wide column database.

From an infrastructure perspective, the goal was to understand what services are available, and how they're used in different circumstances.

Use Case – 15

You are required to accomplish the following tasks, 1) transfer data from Cloud Storage in project A into project B. 2) transfer data from Cloud Storage to BigQuery, How can you go about this?

Solution

Moving data between projects involves the following steps:

1. Create a Cloud Storage bucket to hold the data from your source project A.
2. Export the data from your source project to the bucket you have just created.
3. Give your destination project B the required permissions to read from the new bucket.
4. Import the data from the new bucket into your destination project B.

With regards the transfer of data from Cloud Storage to BigQuery you must provide the Cloud Storage URI. The Cloud Storage URI comprises your bucket name and your object (filename). For example, if the Cloud Storage bucket is named projectabucket and the data file is named projecta.csv, the bucket URI would be gs://proctectabucket/projecta.csv. You can also use a wildcard in the URI if you a multiple objects.

1. Browse the list of buckets and objects using the 'gsutil ls', command to view all the buckets and objects.
2. Compose the URI, by replacing the URL parameters, i.e. gs://bucket/file with the appropriate path, for example, gs://projectabucket/projecta.json. Where the bucket is the Cloud Storage bucket name and file is the name of the object (file) containing the data.
3. To import the data into BigQuery you will have to have the relevant permission these roles have them; bigquery.dataEditor, bigquery.dataOwner, bigquery.admin
4. You can then use the console or the bq load command to update a table and load the data in a single step.

Chapter 16 – Resource and Cost Management

In this chapter we will introduce the concept behind diligent resource management and asset organisation. This practice is also called resource management but that can be confusing as it is quite ambiguous due to the heavy usage of the term resource to mean different things within GCP. For example Resource Manager is the way we organize and secure access to our resources throughout the organisational hierarchy but that is only a part of what we are dealing with here. As in addition we are contemplating how to manage our resources or assets in both the most productive and the most cost effective manner.

Resources in GCP are not free they are billable, so you will need to diligently manage them for cost control purpose. There are several methods that you can use for controlling access to your projects resources and there are also fixed quotas that are set to limit the risks of runaway consumption. In most cases, the default quotas will be sufficient but if you do start to find them a constraint they can be raised on request. But be aware those quotas are there to provide a check-point to prevent runaway costs. Also quotas provide an opportunity for you to evaluate if this is the correct resource for the purpose and that its escalating consumption is explainable and that it is desirable to consume it in greater quantity.

In this chapter, we will build on what we learned earlier about the Cloud Resource Manager. Then we will go into quotas, labels and names. Next, we will cover billing to help you set budgets, alerts and set notifications. Finally we will look to resource monitoring so that we can be confident our resources and assets are working optimally and we are being billed correctly.

Cloud Resource Manager

The Cloud Resource Manager lets you manage resources by project, folder, and organization. Resource management policies contain a set of rules and members. However, these policies are also a set of resources so they can inherit policies from their parent. Therefore, we can consider resource policies to be a union of parent and resource.

Also, keep in mind that if a parent policy is more generous with its permissions, so less restrictive, it will by default take precedence over the less generous and more restrictive resource policy.

However, where resource manager has a significant difference to IAM is when we consider policies. As we saw earlier IAM policies are inherited top to bottom, but resource manager's billing policy is accumulated from the bottom up.

This is because resource consumption for the purpose of billing is measured in quantities, such as rate-of-use or features- used. But as a resource belongs to only one project, then a project accumulates all the consumption of all of its resources. Further, each project is associated with only one billing account, meaning that the highest entity, the organization node, contains all the billing accounts.

Just to reiterate, an organization node is the root node for all Google Cloud platform resources. Now, since a project accumulates the consumption of all of its own resources, and a resource can only be in one project, then a project can be used to track resources and quota usage. So to interact with cloud platform resources, you must provide the unique identifying project information for every request.

A project can be identified in three ways, first there is the project name, which is a human readable way to identify your projects but it isn't used by any Google API. Second there is also a project number, which is automatically generated by the server and assigned to your project, and third, there is a project ID, which is a globally unique ID that is generated from your project name.

You can find these three identifying attributes on the dashboard of your GCP console or by querying the cloud Resource Manager API.

GCP Resource Hierarchy

From a physical organization perspective, resources are categorized as global, regional, or zonal. For example, images, snapshots, and networks are global resources, external IP addresses are regional resources, and VM instances and disks are resources contained within a zone.

Remember, no matter the resource type, each resource is organized into a single project. It is this rule that enables each project to have its own billing and reporting based on resource usage.

All resources in GCP are subject to project quotas or limits. These typically fall into one of these three categories;

- How many resources you can create per project, for example, you can only have five networks per project.

- The rate that you can make API requests in a project, for example, by default it rate limits you to 300 administrative requests per minute when using Cloud Spanner API.
- There are also regional quotas, for example, by default you can only have 24 CPUs per region.

As you make more use of Google cloud platform over time, and GCP becomes more familiar with your typical usage behaviour then your quotas may increase accordingly. However, if you do foresee a requirement for a notable increase in usage, you can proactively request quota adjustments from the quotas page in the GCP console. This page will also show you your current allocated quotas and rate limits.

Why do we need Quotas?

Project quotas are there for your financial safety as they prevent runaway consumption in case of an error, or malicious attack. For example, it is quite easy for you to make a typo and create 100 instead of 10 Compute Engine instances using a gcloud command. Quotas provide a consumption ceiling on a resource and that helps prevent any billing spikes, or nasty surprises should your application under development or testing malfunction. Of course not all peaks in consumption are a malfunction far from it as it might be down to the runaway success of your newly launched application. If that is the case then you will need to request an increase in your relevant quotas through GCP.

Finally, quotas force sizing consideration and periodic review. For example, do you really need all those High CPU VM instances, or can you go with a shared, standard and cheaper alternative?

It is also important to mention that quotas are not guarantees of availability they are the maximum amount of resource you can create for that resource type, as long as those resources are available. For example, if a region is out of local SSDs, you cannot create local
SSDs in that region, even if you still have a quota for local SSDs.

Labels and Names

Projects and folders provide a level of isolation for their own resources. But often you will want to audit the billing at a more granular level, such as to report on what team used what resource or audit the total resources consumed per team?
That's where labels and names come in to play. In this context we use labels as a utility for organizing GCP resources into smaller categories.
Labels are key/value pairs that you can attach to your resources like VMs, disks, snapshots, and images, in order to categorise them. For example, you could create a label to define the environment of your virtual machines. Then you define a label for each of your instances to be for example, production, development or test. Using this label, you could search and list all of your production resources for inventory purposes.
Labels can also be used in scripts to analyse costs or to run bulk operations on multiple resources. The labels applied to a resource must meet the requirements listed here;

- Each label must be a key-value pair.
- Label keys and label values can contain lowercase letters, digits, hyphens, but they must start with a letter and they must end with a letter or digit.

- Keys must have a minimum length of one character and a maximum length of 63 characters and they cannot be empty.
- Values can be empty and have a maximum length of 63 characters.
- Finally, each resource can have multiple labels up to a maximum of 64.

Besides naming requirements, there are also some best practices and common use cases for labels. It is considered to be a best practice to add labels based on the team or cost center to distinguish instances owned by different teams;

- You can use this type of label for cost accounting or budgeting. For example, team:development and team:testing.
- Use labels to distinguish individual components, for example, component:redis, component:frontend.
- Use labels based on the owner or a primary contact for instance. For example, owner: smith, owner:rka.
- Finally, add labels to your resources to define their state. For example, state:live, state:readyfordeletion.

Labels, we just learned, are user-defined strings in key-value format that are used to organize resources and they can propagate through billing. So we mustn't go confusing them with tags as these are user defined strings that are applied to instances only and are mainly used for networking, such as when applying firewall rules.

Billing and Budgets

The Billing Account Overview page in the GCP Console provides you with a summary of your charges to date, estimated end-of-month charges, and any credit balances. To view the Complete Billing Record you can configure your Cloud Billing reports to view your billing charges by invoice, including invoice-level charges (for example, taxes, contractual credits, or surcharges) and any rounding errors. You can then use this view of the billing account to reconcile your Cloud Billing reports to your invoice, to the penny. There are also additional detailed Cost Breakdown Reports: these billing reports are now available for a quick overview of how usage-based discounts and credits could save you money on your GCP invoice.

Since the consumption of all resources under a project accumulates into one billing account, and an important part of project planning is controlling costs, it would be handy if we could set a budget. Well, in resource management you can set a budget that lets you track how much you are spending relative to your target. This will allows you to monitor your spending throughout the month and you can either set a budget on a billing account or your project.

You can set the budget at a specific amount or compare it against a historical record such as the previous months spend.

First of all you need to determine your budget amount, and then you can set budget alerts.

These alerts send emails to billing admins after spend exceeds a percent of the budget or a specified amount. For example you could set alerts to be sent by email when spending reaches 50 percent, 90 percent and 100 percent of the budget amount.

Alerts are based on estimated expenses so actual expenses may be greater. An email notification contains the project name, the percent of the budget that was exceeded, along with the budget amount.

Another way to provide billing visibility is to export billing. A billing export would include its corresponding JSON field, CSV field, data type and description. You can then export this to a file, or import it into a larger dataset for analysis. For example you could export it to BigQuery, the GCP data warehouse, which will allow you to run complex queries to gain insight into your billing and resource consumption.

Use case – 16

A concerned client contacts you regards some unexpectedly large monthly billing for their GCP environment. They have subsequently been forced to put any further development or migration to the cloud specifically of a SQL Server Cluster on hold until they can get reasonable estimates of the monthly charges. They are very concerned regards the billing of their MySQL servers and would like you to assist them in verifying the charges and finding out what they can do to lessen these recurring monthly costs.

Solution

This problem is unfortunately all too common as many customers will try out GCP using either a free trial or just on a pay-as-you-use basis. The problem is that those VM charges look miniscule at first glance but they do mount up if constantly used over a one month period. This is because you will be billed for every hour 24/7. Therefore it is critical that the client understands the need for resource management and diligent audit of resources in use. The issue being is GCP like other cloud providers makes it easy to provision resources and that makes developers sometimes spin them up off the cuff and then forget about them. So you can advise the client to use Stackdriver to audit for running, sleeping, and zombie instances and then terminate any they do not use.

As for verifying the monthly cost the client can use the Billing Account Overview page on GCP along with the Google GCP calculator to get estimates of the monthly costs. The Billing Overview will provide cost forecasts for both the client's long term cost trend as well as any consistent monthly cycles such as sustained use discounts, which makes it easier to see at a glance how much they are projected to spend by the end of the month. However as the client is concerned regards the monthly charges for deploying a SQL Server cluster running 24/7. They should be using the Google calculator so that they can get an estimate – excluding network charges – of the approximate billing. For example:

Estimated costs

Windows Server 2016 Datacenter Edition Usage Fee = $262.80/month

SQL Server 2014 Enterprise Usage Fee = $2,330.16/month

Google Compute Engine Costs

VM instance: 1 vCPU + 3.75 GB memory (n1-standard-1) + 100-GB Boot Disk =$39.47/month

2 x VM instance: 4 vCPUs + 15 GB memory (n1-standard-4) + 200-GB Boot Disk = $296.60/month

Sustained-use discount (30%) = $93.62/month

Total $2,835.41/month

The important thing to convey to the client is that cloud computing is a trade-off between low to negligible capital investment, which facilitates rapid development and high or rather higher than on-premises operational costs incurred through cloud resource usage. Cloud computing is not cheap and certainly not free so they should use the calculator to determine estimating resource charges before they deploy them.

Part 3 – Elastic Cloud Infrastructure: Scaling and Automation

Chapter 17 – Network Interconnects and VPC Sharing

In the following few chapters we're going to address network connectivity and a very compelling feature of the cloud, which is elastic cloud infrastructure through scaling and automation. In the previous chapters you've learned the foundations of the Google Cloud Platform and you know where your applications are going to live and the optimum place to store your data. You will also now have a good idea whether you're going to be deploying it through App Engine, or through Compute Engine, virtual machines, maybe even using containers in Kubernetes engine. Regardless, you will need to start to think about scaling for growth. This is essential as hopefully you are going to be very successful and your application is going to be going viral. In which case, you are going to have to learn about interconnecting with the Google network and then leveraging its elasticity to grow and automate at logarithmic scale. You should keep a few factors in mind when choosing a method to interconnect networks.

First, how much bandwidth does your application require? Second, what is your application's tolerance for connection downtime? Perhaps this can be described in a number of minutes per year. Finally, does your application require a service level agreement?

The content in this chapter should assist in helping you make the right decision, for your infrastructure.

Interconnecting Networks

There are three general ways to interconnect your on-premises or other cloud provider's network to Google's cloud network. You can connect through an intermediary, which is a network service provider that also offers interconnect services. Or you can use a technology like virtual private networking, also referred to as VPN, to create one or more private and secure tunnels through the public internet and connect that way. Or you can connect via the internet using cloud router. In this chapter, we will discuss in more detail than before the implementation of cloud VPN, cloud router, cloud interconnect, direct peering, and the Google cloud DNS.

The Google Network

Google Cloud's well-provisioned global SDN network is composed of hundreds of thousands of miles of fibre optic cable and seven submarine cables. It spans a large majority of the most popular destinations across the world, with multiple redundant links. From a global perspective, Google's global fibre backbone runs networking services including HTTPS, TCP, UDP Load Balancing, Cloud CDN, and Cloud DNS. Networking services support IP addressing for global, private, as well as regional segmentation. The scope of Google's networking services includes Google's Software Network Virtualization, Global Networks, and Granular Subnetworks.

As well as networking services there are other GCP services that enable you to control access permissions such as through Resource Manager, network IAM roles for identity and access management, as well as firewall rules and bastion hosts for security. However it is notable that when you connect to GCP you are actually connecting into Google's own global network and the very same infrastructure that YouTube, Gmail, Maps, Drive, and Android development run on. So you are in effect inheriting many of Google's own access, security and privacy controls.

There are several ways that you can connect and benefit from Google's robust and secure network infrastructure. You can use a VPN or Cloud Router, which will be sufficient for most organizations but for large scale deployments with heavy ingress and egress traffic you might consider Cloud Interconnect or even connecting through Direct Peering.

Cloud VPN

Google Cloud VPN provides a secure communication channel over the internet, which will securely connect your on-premises network to your GCP VPC network through an IPsec VPN connection. Traffic travelling over the VPN between the two networks is protected by the IPsec protocol, which creates a secure encrypted tunnel between the end-points to provide data; confidentiality, integrity and availability. The IPsec protocol ensures that all packets are encrypted by one VPN gateway at the tunnel ingress and then decrypted by the other VPN gateway at the tunnel egress. This ensures that all your data is encrypted as it travels over the Internet. Importantly, as the VPN is constructed using private IP ranges this ensures that traffic can only flow between networks when the VPN tunnel is established and secure.

To establish a VPN does not require any hardware devices in the Google Cloud as there is no actual VPN device on the Google side as it is purely software defined. Therefore, you should not experience any compatibility issues running your VPN between your existing on-premise hardware and the GCP as it supports standard versions of IKE (Internet key Exchange) protocol. The IKE protocol is used, between gateways, to establish the tunnel via the exchange of secret keys for encryption. Hence IKE is crucial for building the secure encrypted tunnel between the parties.

Using a VPN to interconnect your on-premises network with your GCP virtual private cloud is ideal for small organisations or those starting out perhaps with just a development VPC to test the waters. After all it is secure and as it connects over the network it can be configured and setup anywhere in the world where there is internet access.

A VPN is a good starting point for a secure interconnect as it is very convenient or at least to start with. There are some significant issues however that may arise when you start to grow your GCP network and then interconnect it with your on-premises network. As we said earlier a VPN is ideal for creating a research and development area or a DevOps lab in GCP where there is going to be limited access from other departments or areas within the on-premises network. The issues arise when you start to grow and move more organisational functions onto the GCP. The issues will arise when your VCP becomes effectively part of the on-premises network.

The thorny issue here is that of network routing. For traffic to flow between subnets on both sides of the VPN they need to know about one another's existence. This is easy to start off with as you will only need to exchange subnet information for a few subnets on either side of the VPN tunnel. This is typically done through configuring a few static routes to let the routing process know that anything for those specific subnets are to be sent over the VPN tunnel.

However as the two networks gradually merge then static routes to subnets become unwieldy and do not scale well. This is because with static routing, updating the tunnel requires the addition of adding all the static routes for each on-premises subnet to GCP. It also requires adding routes for every existing subnet in GCP for the on-premises network. That is bad enough but any new subnet will also need to be added before it can interconnect and the VPN tunnel restarted to include the new subnet. This is not really sustainable.

Classic and High Availability VPN

Google Cloud Platform offers two types of Cloud VPN gateways, HA VPN and Classic VPN. The legacy type is called a classic VPN gateway and it has a single interface, a single external IP address, and it supports tunnels using static routing. The second type of VPN that you can create is called a High-Availability VPN (HA VPN) and it lets you securely connect your on-premises network to your GCP Virtual Private Cloud network through an IPsec VPN connection in a single region.

When you create a HA VPN gateway, GCP automatically chooses two public IP addresses, one for each of its two interfaces. Each IP address is automatically chosen from a unique address pool to support high availability and multiple tunnels on each interface. In addition you can create multiple HA VPN gateways. Both types of VPN, classic and HA VPN, support dynamic routing using BGP, which we will look at next.

Managing static routing soon becomes untenable after a point and this is why large networks use routing protocols even within their own networks. A routing protocol manages the exchange of subnet information dynamically, discovering new subnets and changes to the network topology and then advertising those changes to its routing peer.

Eventually, you may find that you will also require a dynamic solution as you outgrow your VPN interconnect as the burden of updating the static routing becomes just too great.

Then it might be time you considered the Cloud Routing service.

Cloud Routing Service

Administration of static routes in networking is just too slow, tedious and error prone for managing any large network. How don't let that stop you using a VPN if your network will have only limited access to the cloud VPC. For example if only a few key and identified departments (subnets) need to interconnect with the VPC networks then static routing is fine. It is when your network admin becomes more holistic and the cloud and on-premises networks merge that you will need dynamic routing using either the HA VPN or Cloud Router. In order to accommodate this common requirement Google has delivered the Cloud Router managed service.

To explore the concepts around the Cloud Router Service we need a basic understanding of the issue with static routing and what benefits a dynamic routing protocol brings us. It is those administrative issues - that we discussed earlier - that Cloud Router service addresses. This is because the Cloud Router as its name suggests is basically a virtual router that runs in the cloud. The purpose is to provide the same dynamic routing and advertising of new networks and topology changes through a routing protocol as on a physical router in the on-premises network. However, the GCP's cloud router is only a virtual router as it is part of Google's SDN (Software Defined network) running the BGP routing protocol. The Border Gateway Protocol (BGP) allows you to dynamically discover and advertise new route changes that might be in your network. However, the advertising of routing information and updates only occurs through neighbours, which are preconfigured peers running the BGP routing protocol.

Thus, when you use the cloud router service you're peering with Google. This means that you are exchanging dynamic routing information and BGP is auto-discovering the network topology and exchanging information about any existing or new subnets within your VPC. This is especially beneficial if you're peering with GCP from multiple locations. After all BGP is the protocol that makes it possible for the largest network of them all to run – the Internet. But BGP is daunting and hugely complex but thankfully you don't need to concern yourself about that as Cloud Router is a managed service so GCP does all the heavy lifting for you. Therefore, if you want a simple, hands-free and dynamic solution to static routing you can utilize Cloud Router for that purpose.

We can demonstrate the benefit of using Cloud Router with subnetworks through a use case. If you are a developer working within your organisations VPC and you want to spin up a new environment for the purpose of analytics. When you create the resources within that environment they will interconnect over a network that will use a new subnet range. Now you can connect to it fine as you are connecting through GCP but how will others in your organisation connect to your new dashboards as it on a newly created subnet.

Well you could update every router in the on-premise network with a static route to the new subnet or you could use cloud router to advertise the subnet for you.

Cloud router will advertise the subnet through its peering arrangement with a remote neighbour on the on-premise peering network.

Cloud router's BGP protocol will announce to its neighbour that the new subnet is now available. Then the neighbour BGP router on-premise, will update its routing tables and any of its peer's so that all internal on-premises routers will now know how to get to this new allocated subnet. Now any departments that want to access your new analytics dashboards can do so.

Importantly this process works in both directions so if your data centre adds a new physical rack and it goes online with a new range of subnets, the VPC resources will need to know about them. This is because any hosts on this new range of subnets will be able to reach your new analytics dashboard okay but the VPC network will not know how to return the traffic as it knows nothing about the new range of subnets. However with cloud router the on-premises BGP process will discover the new range of subnets and it will tell the BGP neighbour on the cloud side that a new network exists. Now they will have a route to return traffic from that new range of subnets.

As Cloud Router uses the Border Gateway Protocol (BGP) to dynamically exchange routes between your Virtual Private Cloud network and your on-premises network you will need to configure an interface and a BGP peer for your on-premises router. The interface and BGP peer configuration together form a BGP session. However, when configuring BGP you must stipulate an autonomous system number; this is a unique BGP identifier for the organization. There are two types of ASN there is a public and a private ASN. A public ASN is unique like IP addresses and are registered to your organization so if you already have a public ASN you are likely running BGP on your routers already. Nonetheless, if you do not have one you can use a private ASN, which like private IP addresses are only unique within the organization and so are not valid on the internet. Fortunately, you can use a private ASN within private networks such as when operation a VPN connection.

Within GCP, a Cloud Router interface connects to exactly one of the following GCP resources:

- A traditional VPN tunnel that is using dynamic routing (you use a private ASN)
- A HA (High Availability) VPN tunnel that will be using dynamic routing (you use a private ASN)

- An interconnect attachment (VLAN) for a Dedicated Interconnect (you use a private ASN)
- An interconnect attachment (VLAN) for a Partner Interconnect over the internet (You must use a public ASN)

However, Cloud Router does support multiple interfaces so you will not need to create a separate Cloud Router for each VPN tunnel or interconnect attachment (VLAN). However, each Cloud Router uses the same Autonomous System Number (ASN) for all of its BGP sessions. Because, the Google option of Partner Interconnect does require that you have your own public ASN and that all the other types of interface require private ASNs. This means that a Cloud Router that manages the BGP sessions for an interconnect attachment (VLAN) on a Partner Interconnect cannot manage BGP sessions for any other type of interface.

When you create a Cloud Router service so that you can dynamically exchange routes between your cloud VPC network and your on-premises network you effectively establish BGP sessions between it and your on-premises router. By default, Cloud Router will advertise only the subnets within its own region for regional dynamic routing or for all subnets in a VPC network for global dynamic routing.

You can also create your own custom route advertisement; this is where you tell BGP specifically which routes that you want Cloud Router to advertise, such as external static IP addresses or specific CIDR ranges.

Classic VPN and HA VPNs supporting dynamic routing via the Cloud Router enables you to connect reliably and securely over the internet from your location to the GCP. However if you are transferring lots of data or require high data speeds with low latency then a VPN might be too restrictive for your needs. In that case you may want to consider the Google Cloud Interconnect service, which provides direct physical connections and RFC1918 communication between your on-premises network and Google's network.

Cloud Interconnect

Cloud Interconnect will enable you to transfer large amounts of data quickly and securely between directly connected networks. This method of interconnection can be more cost-effective than purchasing additional large amounts of internet bandwidth when using VPN tunnels. It will also be much faster and latency more predictable as you are no longer subject to the vagaries of the Internet.

This is because the traffic flowing between your on-premises network and your VPC network doesn't traverse the public internet. Instead the traffic flows over a dedicated connection with fewer hops, meaning there are less points of failure where network traffic might get delayed, dropped or lost.

Furthermore, you do not need to use a VPN tunnel as your VPC network's internal IP addresses are directly accessible from your on-premises network. This is because they are now directly connected as an extension of your on-premises local area network. Therefore you don't need to use a network routing protocol to reach the VPC's internal IP addresses.

However, to reach Google's external IP addresses, you must still go out your existing internet gateway using a separate connection. The choice of Direct Connection is determined by your data capacity requirements and it is delivered over one or more 10 Gigabits per second Ethernet connections. There is a minimum of one connection with a maximum of eight connections.

That's a capacity on offer of between 10 and 80 Gigabits per second total per interconnect.

 However as the minimum deployment per location is 10 Gigabits per second, and the capacity scales by 10Gbs with each additional connection up to a maximum of 8 connections or 80Gbs this provides a range of capacity to suit most large organisations.

If your traffic doesn't require that minimum level of capacity of 10Gbs, then you should consider using a Cloud VPN.

From a billing perspective, you will find that the cost of egress traffic from your VPC network to your on-premises network is reduced. This means that having a dedicated connection is generally the least expensive method if you have a high volume of traffic travelling to and from Google's network.

However, there is one important caveat and that is the circuit between your network and Google's network is not encrypted. This means that your data will be travelling over a dedicated circuit in plain view so you might need to provide your own encryption such as application level encryption or use your own VPN.

Currently, you aren't able to configure and use the Google Cloud VPN in combination with a dedicated connection, but you are able to configure and use your own VPN solution.

Direct connections are the fastest, reliable, lowest latency, and maintenance free method for interconnectivity. But before you commit to a dedicated interconnect you should consider a few other points;

- You must be familiar with basic network interconnections as you'll be ordering and configuring circuits.
- Your network must physically have a point of presence that can meet Google's network in a colocation facility.
- You must provide your own routing equipment.

What happens is you will be required to order and configure circuits to bring your network to meet Google's within the colocation facility. In order to do this requires that you host your own on-premises network devices within the co-location facility as this is the termination point for your network. The network equipment must support the following technical requirements and support for; Ethernet 10Gbs single-mode fibre, IPv4 link local addressing, LACP for bonding multiple links, EBGP-4 with multihop, and 802.1q VLANs.

Deciding on a direct connection is not a trivial task as it can take a lot of time and expense initially setting up the pairing in the co-location facility. However let us take a look at some practical use cases to see where it can be highly advantageous.

If you want to transfer large amounts of data back and forth with Google Cloud Storage, you would also want to invest the time to setup a direct pairing arrangement to enable you to do so efficiently, reliably and cost effectively. An added bonus would be that you could take advantage of the on-site backup of the data. Another example is if you have a data-intensive production network that requires high data transfer rates for daily backup, you probably would want to take advantage of using Cloud Interconnect. This method would not just simply save on bandwidth connection cost, it would also cut-down data transfer times, and perform far more reliably. In addition it would also free other circuits for high-performance, low-latency, and operationally critical traffic.

In another use case, we can see the benefits of a direct connection in the hosting of high-performance, latency-sensitive applications. For example, you might have VPC webservers that benefit from GCP load balancers, but they may still be pulling data from on-premise database servers. This could be because the data is highly sensitive and you are not permitted to store it in the cloud. However, by peering with Google across a direct connection will ensure that you have the lowest latency possible between the two locations. Finally, Cloud Interconnect allows you to take full advantage of your own, your partners, or Google's, Content Delivery Network (CDN).

How that we know some basics about why you may want to use the GCP services to achieve external peering let's look into how it can be done in practice.

Direct peering is a private connection between your network and Google's network, where you will exchange BGP autonomous system numbers. An autonomous system number is your registered identity on the internet that represents your block of public IP addresses. Your co-located router and Google's edge router will form a BGP session as peers. With this established connection, you can exchange routing updates and pass internet traffic between your network and Google.

After a direct peering connection is in place, you can use it to reach all of Google's services including the full suite of Google Cloud platform products.

Direct Connection through a Partner

In some locations it might not be technically feasible to meet at a Google edge point-of-presence. In that case you can go through one of Google's partner's locations. It's a similar setup, but you have a service provider, a so-called middleman hosting the co-location on your and Google's behalf.

Carrier peering allows you to obtain the same benefits of enterprise-grade network services that connect your infrastructure to Google. You can also make connections with higher availability and lower latency using one or more links.

Shared & Network VPC

In large organizations, you may need to put different departments or different applications into different projects for purposes of separating budgeting, access control, or for privacy.

However it is often not the desire to strictly isolate these departments it is only to control access and manage resources. Sometimes it is likely that you will want to share some information or services with other departments. Indeed sharing resources would actually be highly beneficial to the organization as it prevents them being duplicated unnecessarily in every project. Also it would reduce resource spread and reduce costs if projects could share common resources.

However, with GCP you can share a VPC networks across projects in your cloud organization using shared VPC. With shared VPC, cloud organization administrators can give multiple projects permission to use a single shared VPC network and corresponding networking resources.

Shared VPC allows for the creation of a shared VPC that is named the host VPC, which can share its network of private IP subnets and their attached resources with all the associated projects called service projects. VMs and their application and users can then share the use of the resources in the host VPC, which means that a service project will not even require its own network let alone any dedicated resources.

With shared VPC, you can allow project admins to create VMs in the shared VPC networks spaces and allow network and security admins to create VPNs and firewall rules that are usable by the service projects in the host VPC network.

In addition any security policy applied to the host VPC will automatically be inherited by all the service projects, which makes it easy to apply and enforce consistent policies across a cloud organization.

The diagram shows a host project sharing its VPC network with two service projects.

It is sharing Subnet_1 with one project and Subnet_2 with another project.

Figure -16

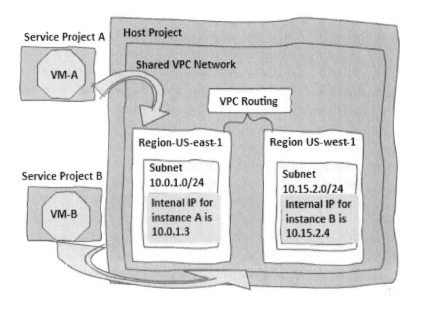

However, there is another way you can connect two VPC networks regardless of shared projects or organizations using VPC network peering. It allows you to build software as service ecosystems in GCP by making services available privately across different VPC networks in and across organizations.

VPC Network Peering

It's useful for organizations with several network administrative domains that want to peer with other organizations. VPC network peering gives you several advantages over using external IP addresses or VPNs to connect networks including;

- Reduced network latency - Public IP networking suffers higher latency than private networking.
- Network security - Service owners do not need to have their services exposed to the public internet and deal with its associated risks.

- Network cost - GCP charges egress bandwidth pricing for networks that use external IPs to communicate even if the traffic is within the same zone. However, if the networks are peered, they can use internal IPs to communicate and save on those egress costs. Regular network pricing still applies to all traffic.

Internal Load Balancing

Internal load balancing services are available to clients and directly peered networks only.

That is, in the case that network B peers with network C, the internal load balance backends in network A will not be reachable from clients in network C. If you have peering between your VPC network and another VPC network, you want to block traffic to a given set of VM instances or internal load balancing endpoints. You must use firewall rules to do this because there is no way to exclude certain VM instances or internal load balancers from the peering arrangement.

If you want to disallow communication with certain VM instances or internal load balancers, you can install ingress firewall rules on the network you want to block the communication to.

The diagram shows you how you could create a firewall rule to allow all traffic

from Subnets 1 and 2 in network A to Subnet 4 in network B and deny traffic from Subnets 1 and 2 in network A to Subnet 3 in network B.

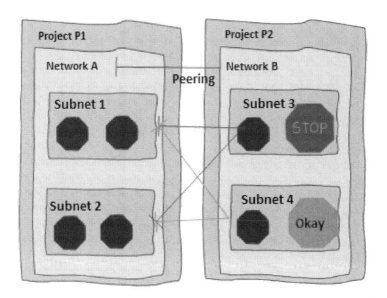

Figure 17: VPC network peering allows peering with a shared VPC. Firewall drops traffic from subnets 1 & 2 for subnet 3 but allows traffic to subnet 4.

As discussed earlier, a shared VPC host project allows other projects to use one of its networks. In the shared VPC diagram right here, network-SVPC, is in a shared VPC network and host project P1.

Service projects P3 and P4 are able to attach VM instances to network SVPC peers with network A.

Figure-18

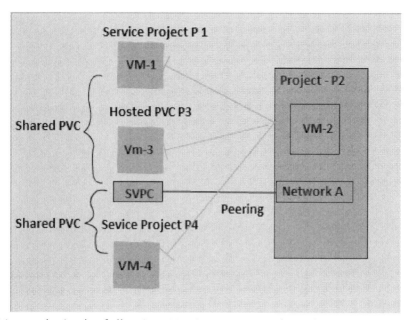

This results in the following. VM instances in shared VPC service projects that are using the network SVPC have private internal IP connectivity with any endpoints associated to network A. VM instances associated to network A will have private internal IP connectivity with any endpoints associated to network SVPC regardless of whether they live in the host project or a service project.

You can set up VPC network peering between two shared VPC networks. An instance can have multiple network interfaces, one each in different VPC networks, which is shown here on the diagram that follows:

Figure-19

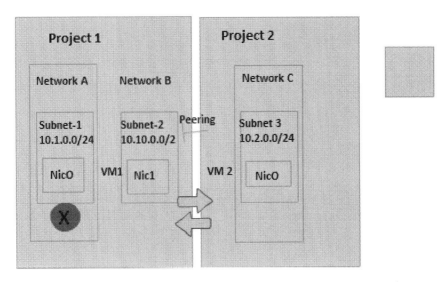

In the diagram, VM1 has a network interface in both network A and network B.

Network B is peered with another network C. VM2 in network C can send traffic across to network B to VM1 because nic0 is peered with network B, and network B routes are automatically propagated to network C when the two networks are peered. However, for VM2, to send traffic to network A, which is also on VM1, you'd have to configure policy routing for the nic1 interface. This is because addresses and flows for subnet A and interface nic0 are not installed in network C, so network C knows nothing about network A's nic0 so it cannot access network A. Similarly network A knows nothing about network C as it is not privy to the peering arrangement so does not get the routes forwarded even though it is on the same VM1 as network B.

Private Google Access

Private Google Access enables virtual machine instances on a subnetwork to reach

Google APIs and services using an internal IP address instead of an external IP address.

External IP addresses are routable and reachable over the internet whereas internal or private IP addresses are internal to Google Cloud platform and are not routable or reachable over the internet. As an alternative you can use private Google access to allow VMs without internet access to reach external Google services.

The services that can be made reachable include but are not limited to the following: Cloud Spanner, Cloud Big Query, Cloud Bigtable, Cloud Dataproc, Cloud Datastore, Cloud Pub/Sub and Cloud Storage. One notable exception, however, is that private Google access does not apply to Google Cloud SQL. In addition although a VPC is required both auto and custom mode networks are supported but only on networks with only private addresses. Private Google Access, is ignored if an instance has an existing external IP address configured.

Google Cloud DNS

The last topic we'll cover in this chapter is Cloud DNS. Google Cloud DNS is the only Google service that offers a 100% SLA. That is a 100% uptime guarantee. In fact, because nothing runs unless your DNS can resolve you to an IP address, there may be small application issues, small availability issues, but if you can't look up a domain name, the internet might as well be down. So, that's why you have never gone into google.com and it says sorry I can't find this IP address. This is very important to note.

You can actually host all of your authoritative DNS records directly through Cloud DNS.

You can call those through an API or through the Web Console. Cloud DNS managed-zones are an abstraction that manages all DNS records for a single domain name.

One project may have multiple managed-zones. You must enable the Cloud DNS API in the GCP Console first by running the command; gcloud dns managed-zones.

Managed-zones provide permission controls at project level and allow you to monitor propagation of changes to DNS name servers.

Use Case -17

A client contacts you to say that they are having difficulty interconnecting across the on-premises and cloud network. The problem appears to be that some subnets on-premise cannot intercommunicate with others in the cloud. The problem has persisted even though they have added static routes. So there still doesn't appear to be any way to connect from on-premises departments to the cloud and vice versa.

Solution

This is a very common problem as routes have to be known by both parties if you are to be able to communicate. This means that even if you are using static routes that every router in the network needs to know where to send that traffic. Therefore if you should create a new subnetwork in the cloud then the on-premises network must know about it and how to direct traffic to it. Similarly, any new subnetworks created on-premises must be known to the cloud network if you wish them to communicate. The simple solution is to use static routes on both sides. However that is not scalable as it would mean static configuration on every on-premise router. The next solution is to use an on-premises internal routing protocol such as OSPF, EIGRP or RIP to redistribute the static routes throughout the internal network so that all internal routers would have those routes. This is possible. However, GCP uses BGP an external routing protocol to distribute routes between the cloud and the on-premises router and that is not automatically redistributed. Instead you will have to redistribute routes between BGP and your internal routing protocol and vice versa to maintain the interconnectivity. This is not a trivial thing as two ways redistribution requires complex configuration except in the most trivial cases. Therefore be aware that although the cloud router seems like an ideal solution it may indeed be a complex task to deploy.

Chapter 18 – Automation, Elasticity and Auto-Scaling

In this chapter we are going to look at architecting the infrastructure for elasticity and scaling via load balancing and the in-built options that GCP provides. Understanding load balancing is critical in designing high performance architectures. You will need to understand the different types of load balancers and how and why they are deployed within the infrastructure. You will also need to understand how to deploy and configure the load balancer to provide consistent performance across state and stateless server farms both at the front-end and at the backend.

Types of Load Balancing

The purpose of a hardware load balancer is to receive data on a single published IP address and redirect it - using some traffic distribution technique such as round robin - to one of multiple servers. In practice however it is more complex than that as the hardware must track each IP session flow and redirect it consistently to the same server. Also modern hardware load balancers are feature rich and switch traffic based upon advanced algorithms that redirect ingress traffic not only on load, protocol, port or session but by content type, URLs and even the URL parameters – such as the source's geo-location and/or the closest available web service. This gold-plating of the feature-sets comes at a cost, not just financially but in user configuration complexity.

Load balancing in GCP, on the other hand, is a managed service and is software defined and although less flexible than a hardware load balancer it is easy to configure. For example, Global load balancing in GCP performs the same geo-location feature not by URL and HTTP header analysis but by capturing the request at a location closest to the requestor. It can do this by using Anycast – a method of using the same public IP address on replicated load balancers across all the regions. This means the requestor will always connect to the closest load balancer typically with their region. It also provides for high availability for should that be unavailable they will be redirected – without any human intervention - to the next closest service. On the other hand GCP regional load balancing can be configured to distribute traffic across an array of backend servers based on the TCO and UDP protocols and ports. So for example, a regional loan balancer will send HTTP traffic to a pool of web servers with some of the servers in the pool acting as overflow capacity to others.

This kind of flexibility and behaviour comes with some additional configuration complexity, but this can all be easily configured using the GCP console.

In this chapter, we will also cover managed instanced groups and different types of load balancing that you can configure using GCP.

We've already discussed how to configure networking between different virtual machines. Further we have discussed the concept of horizontal scaling where we can replicate a VM to provide additional capacity to scale to match a growing demand. But how are we going to route incoming traffic between multiple virtual machines on different IPs that are offering the same service? This is where the concept of load balancing comes into play.

There are five types of load balancing covered in this chapter. We will discuss each in turn but it's important to note that three of the five types; HTTP(S), SSL Proxy, and TCP Proxy load balancing are global services, whereas the other two types; network and internal load balancing are regional.

Managed Instance Groups

However before we dive into discussing the types of Load Balancers available in GCP we need to take some time to discuss Managed Instance Groups as these ease the burden of configuration when replicating the setup of several VMs within a shared environment. Managed Instance Groups provide several administrative benefits. They allow you a method to create several VMs simultaneously using an instance template, which define the properties for every VM instance in the group. The VMs do not need to be identical in their properties as the template can be made to hold the specific common properties for each instance. Therefore, you can initially configure your environment using a template. Then just as easily update all of the instances' properties within the Managed Instance Group by specifying new parameters for each instance with an edited template in a rolling update. The instance group updater feature provides you with a method for deploying staggered releases with zero downtime; this makes it useful in applying canary updates with rollback.
It is also useful when your applications require additional compute resources as Managed Instance Groups can then use the edited template to scale the number of instances in the group.

The relevance of Managed Instance Groups in this chapter is that they can work with load balancing services to distribute network traffic to all of the instances in the group.

Furthermore, using Managed Instance Groups provides a robust automated system for maintaining service availability. For example, if a VM instance in the group should stop, crash, or be accidentally deleted, then the manage instance group will automatically restart or recreate the VM so it can resume its place in the group and continue processing tasks.

A notable feature is that the recreated VM instance uses the same name and the same instance template as the previous instance, even if the group references a different instance template. Another caveat is that restarting and recreating an instance does not occur if the instance was stopped or deleted via the instance group's commands.

Additionally, Managed Instance Groups are useful in identifying and recreating unhealthy instances in a group and this will ensure that all the instances in a group are running optimally. Also, you are not restricted to working with instance groups that belong only in single zones, as you can create regional Managed Instance Groups which distribute instances across multiple zones in the same region. Regional Managed Instant Groups are also used to support autoscaling, network load balancing, and HTTPS load balancing.

Creating Managed Instance Groups

You create instance templates using the console. The instance template dialogue follows the same steps you use when manually creating an instance, the difference being that the properties you select are recorded so that they can be repeated.

The steps to create Manage Instant Groups are as follows;

The first step is to create an instance template, and then using this template you're going to create a managed instance group of 'n' specified instances, and then the instance group manager will automatically populate the instance group based on the instance template.

However, during the creation of an instance group you can also define specific rules to apply to the instance group.

For example the additional rules you may want to stipulate could be;

- Is it to be single or multi zoned?
- Where will the instances be located?
- What ports are allowed and load balanced?
- Will they auto scale?
- What criteria to use to maintain a minimum number of instances?
- What criteria to use to maintain a maximum number of instances?
- And what criteria we want to use for the health check?

Essentially, you're still creating basic virtual machines, but you're now able to apply more rules for that instance group.

When you define the criteria for a health check, you are able to define periodicity and the method used by the health check. A health check can be configured with complex criteria and thresholds to determine under what conditions we want to declare an instance as unhealthy.

The health check capabilities are built-in for managing instance groups, load balancing, and autoscaling. GCP health checks support HTTP, HTTPS, TCP, and SSL or TLS.

The way the health check works is that it polls instances at specified intervals. Instances that do not respond successfully to a specified number of consecutive probes are marked as unhealthy. In that scenario, no new connections are sent to unhealthy instances although to prevent unnecessary disruption existing connections are maintained.

The health checker will continue to poll unhealthy instances so if an instance should later start to respond successfully to a specified number of consecutive probes, it is then marked as healthy. In this case it can resume normal operation and will receive new connections.

Auto healing is another useful feature that works closely with Health Checks as it allows for automated server monitoring and restarts. So for example, should an HTTP health check detect that a service has failed on an instance, the instance can be automatically recreated where the service failed.

To mitigate the risk of a single point of failure and also to ensure high availability through redundancy, GCP replicates each health checker. These redundant health checkers also probe your instances. So, if a health checker should fail, there is another one instantly available that can take over. These redundant health checkers are created automatically and are not separately user configurable.

Autoscaling

Managed Instance Groups also provides you with another benefit as it allow you to automatically add or remove instances from a managed instance group based on increases or decreases in load. This capability is called autoscaling.

Autoscaling is extremely useful as it allows your applications to gracefully handle increases in traffic load. It can scale up by adding instances when more resources are required under heavy load and scales down when traffic is lower and this reduces costs. What's more, the autoscaler performs all this automatically based on your policy and the current measured load.

In short, this means you don't need to go into in-depth capacity planning or over-provisioning of resources as the autoscaling works by adding more instances to your instance group when there is higher than expected load, upscaling, and also removes instances when the load is lowered, downscaling.

Connection Draining

The concept of automatic upscaling and downscaling of instances in reaction to fluctuations in traffic load raises some interesting questions. In the case of the former the autoscaler will determine that the threshold of the number of connections per VM in the group has been reached so will spin up another instance to lessen the load across the group. The introduction of a new instance will mean that it will receive new connections until the load once again balances across the group as a whole. However, with downscaling, it a bit more problematic because if the load balancer is doing its job and distributing the number of connections across the group there is unlikely to be one VM conveniently doing nothing. Therefore when it comes to downscaling there will have to be a way to close down one of the instances gracefully without any interruption to users. The way this is achieved is through a technique called connection draining.

The purpose of connection draining is to prevent disruption to active connections and user sessions. So it works by delaying the termination of an instance until all existing connections are closed. Thus, during the connection draining process no new connection are sent to the instance, but importantly the VM instance preserves existing sessions until they end or a designated timeout is reached. This process minimizes any interruptions to your users' active sessions.

HTTP(S) Load Balancing

As we mentioned earlier there are three types of Global load balancing in the GCP. The first type or service is the HTTP(S) load balancer, which provides global load balancing for HTTP(S) requests destined for your web instances.

With the HHTP(S) load balancer you can configure some URL rules that will route traffic targeting that specific URL to one set of web instances and route other URLs to other instances.

Requests are always received by the closest point-of-presence to the user and this is done via Anycast IP addressing this to minimize latency and increase efficiency. Thereafter the request will be routed to the closest relevant instance group provided that the group has enough capacity to handle the request. If the closest appropriate group does not have enough capacity, the user' request will be redirected to the next closest group that does have sufficient capacity.

A notable aspect is that the HTTP(S) load balancers do support both IPv4 and IPv6 addressing for your client traffic, however the client IPv6 traffic have their requests terminated at the global load balancer. Downstream the traffic is sent as requests over IPv4 to the backend services.

In addition, HTTP requests are load balanced based on the traditional ports 80 or 8080. HTTP(S) requests on the other hand are load balanced on port 443.

It is not just IPv6 to IPv4 that the load balancer proxies as it must also handle diverse versions of HTTP. To accomplish this the load balancer acts as an HTTP/2 to HTTP/1.1 translation layer, which means that the load balancers may receive requests in HTTP/1.0, 1.1 or 2.0 but the web servers always receive and respond to HTTP/1.1 requests.

To get a better understanding how the global HTTP(S) load balancing operates in practice we need to consider a use case scenario. In this example, we will consider the situation where we have users in say three different geographical locations, such as the US, Europe and Asia who are simultaneously sending a request for the same web page URL. Now we know that the user's machine will try to resolve the URLs domain name to an IP address. The global DNS server will return all three users with the same public IP address. This so far is perfectly normal behaviour however the difference soon becomes apparent. In our scenario we have three users in diverse geographical regions all trying to simultaneous request the same service using the same public IP. However GCP uses Anycast addressing on points-of-presence locations in each of the three regions. Consequently, our users in the US, Europe and Asia will connect to their own regional mirror thereby getting the lowest latency service.

Now we will have to apply some forwarding rules based on IP address, protocol and port, but we also have a target proxy that's going to be a URL map. With this we can get a little bit more granular as it gives us something more specific to differentiate between the requests in the form of URLs that are being passed through to us.

For example, if the URL is for a specific content page then we can send the user to the relevant web server, if it is for a download we can redirect the user directly to the download service page. If it is for an upload we can similarly redirect the user to the appropriate service page they require. Therefore, we will typically want to refine which backend services can best handle which target URL. A backend service is conceptually similar to a target pool, the difference being that here we're going to configure some additional health checks to determine the conditions under which we will send traffic to that pool.

After all this is the global internet and the cloud so we don't just want to be sending all traffic to one region by default. For example, we don't want to just send all traffic to Seoul, on the basis that most of the users are in Asia. We need to have some regional redundancy so that if the Korean instance group is overloaded and we've maxed out the number of servers that we're going to scale too, we have an alternative region to redirect requests to that can service our requests.

Now let us consider the different health checks that we might want to deploy that would ensure we were able to continue forwarding traffic for our application. Since we have the option to route traffic to completely different regions, we might even want out health check to instigate a fail-over mechanism. So for example, if we are experiencing high latency in Korea, we could route traffic to another region within Southeast Asia.

Regardless of the region or backends we choose to send our traffic too we must ensure it is handled in a consistent manner. To accomplish this we use Session Affinity, which we can configure so that requests from the same client go to the same instance and thereby maintain their current session.

With basic client IP affinity this directs requests from the same origin IP address to the same server. However, there are issues with IP Affinity due to Network Proxies and Network Address Translation (NAT), which can cause requests from multiple different users to look like they come from the same address. This confuses some IP affinity methods and so many users will get routed to the same instance.

On the other hand, there is the other extreme whereby a user who moves between networks may be seen as two completely different users and not be directed to the same instance all of the time.

To solve these issues you can use within GCP a technique called, Generated Cookie Affinity. This method causes the load balancer to issue a cookie named GCLB on the user's first visit or request, and then it directs subsequent requests with the same cookie to the same instance.

Despite all of these good intentions to maintain session affinity we have to be realistic and accept that session affinity can break. If for example an instance group runs out of capacity and traffic is routed to another zone, or if auto scaling changes the resource capacity and load is reallocated, or if the target instance fails health checks. Consequently, we will need to understand the conditions and criteria that would determine the need to divert traffic to another backend.

The load balancer and the capacity-scaler will track and react to the designated maximum utilization thresholds set for a backend. The balancer-mode is a setting that lets you select one of the following metrics to determine whether the backend instance group is at capacity; CPU utilization, maximum request per second per instance, maximum request per second per group and CPU utilization and rate. Which one you choose will be down to how best they match the operational dynamics of your application.

The capacity scaler is an additional setting that directs the load balancer to only direct requests to a given backend instance group as long as utilization is below a percentage of the balancing mode maximum. For example, if balancing mode is set to track utilization and the max CPU utilization is 80%. Then by setting the capacity scaler to 50% would mean the load balancer would see the backend as being at capacity, when CPU utilization is at 40% average across the entire instance group.

Ok let's summarise what we have covered here with another use case.

In this use case we have users coming from North America and some coming from Europe.

Now you have one single IP Anycast address representing the globe, but they're entering the Google cloud network from different locations.

A GCP cloud load balancer is not a physical device it is purely a software concept. But it does have a list of rules that we can apply to any ingress traffic no matter where in the world it comes from. That's why they are called global load balancers. But in reality they are just a set of rules that Google apply to ingress traffic that enters into Google's software defined network (SDN).

In our scenario we have users in North America and Europe who will due to Anycast connect to their own region where we will need to determine what to do with the traffic. This is where we configure what is known as a URL map as it lets us define where, or rather to which, backend service we will send the traffic.

We could for example send the user to a backend based upon the individual user's location, IP address, protocol, or port towards a managed instance group in the US or to one in Europe.

Therefore, URL maps are essentially the place where you can actually route traffic on criteria other than the protocol, IP address, or port, but specifically by what is in the URL header.

So let's just say you're processing videos and you're expecting those to be uploaded.

In that case you would need a global forwarding rule which sends all that type of traffic to your HTTP proxy. But you may want to handle HD videos differently from standard definition videos and so you may map those to a different backend service.

By segregating the application into two distinct services, one for a high definition video and one for standard video, we will then use a URL match to apply different rules. So we're going to look at that rule and determine from the incoming URL whether it is going to be directed to the high definition or to the standard video backend application.

In this example we have only two but you could have 50 or more different backend services running, so you can see you can get a lot of flexibility depending on the incoming rule-set that you create in your URL map.

Traffic allocation for backend services is going to be determined based on the zone, region or by multiple regions. These are all things that you can define as well. So again, it's going to be based on health checks, URL rewrites and whatever other protocols you choose to take advantage of.

HTTP(S) load balancing does handle the termination of TLS/SSL sessions but you can also use SSL load balancing, which is when the balancer acts as the target proxy and the VMs actually terminate the SSL session. To use HTTP(S) or SSL load balancing, you have to create at least one SSL certificate to be used by the target proxy for the load balancer. Each target proxy can be configured with up to 10 SSL certificates and each SSL certificate has a created SSL certificate resource.

Cross Regional Load Balancing

Now let's learn a little more about cross-regional load balancing. Cross region load balancing is particularly useful if you have users spread out all around the world. By default, Google will route those requests to the closest regions, unless of course you have URL maps and different URL rewrites to determine otherwise.

Having Google determine the location of the user is beneficial in a number of ways but one is that it eliminates the need for a DNS load balancer because utilizing Global Server Load Balancing or GLSB lookups for DNS locations is not always reliable. In direct comparison, with this global load balancer, we don't need to rely on DNS to determine the destination because we can identify where they actually entered the Google network in order to handle that HTTPS load balancing.

In this example, we will see how we can use an HTTP load balancer to route traffic between multiple regions and multiple zones. Again, you will use that Anycast single global static IP address to represent your entire frontend application.

Earlier we saw how hardware load balancers were adept at handling the balancing or redirection of traffic based on content-type. The Google load balancer can also support content-based load balancing but it only applies to HTTP and HTTPS and it will involve configuring multiple backend services to handle each of the different content types.

Basically, it is really more like URL rule matching as it compares the parameters within a URL to pre-configured path rules to each backend service. For example, within a URL it might match against a parameter /video to filter traffic destined for the backend video services and then /static for determining any static content.

Now that you have a way to identify, filter and redirect traffic based upon content-type albeit only in the URL you can go ahead and configure different instance types for different content types in the backend.

However, to return to the original example, let's say that user traffic is entering through that global HTTP load balancer. Then we are splitting traffic based on the URL header to determine location and content-type.

So if they're going to the directory '/video', we can send that to the specific backend video service or if they're just going to the website, we can send them to a general purpose frontend web cluster.

The other types of Global load balancers that we have available to us are the SSL proxy and TCP proxy load balancing services. As you might expect the SSL proxy load balancing performs global load balancing of SSL traffic, routing clients to the closest instance with sufficient capacity.

Some advantages of SSL proxy include intelligent routing, better utilization of the virtual machine instances, certificate management, and security patching.

The main feature of a SSL proxy is that it terminates the incoming TLS/SSL session, which is the incoming connections arriving at the load balancer from the users. So for example, SSL traffic from users in Iowa and Boston will be terminated at the global load balancing layer and a separate SSL connection is then established between the proxy and the selected backend instance.

TCP proxy load balancing also allows you to use a single IP address to present to all users around the world and automatically routes traffic to the instances that are geographically closest to the user. The advantage of using TCP proxy load balancing include, intelligent routing and security patching.

Regional Load Balancing

In this chapter so far we have considered the options for global load balancing, specifically the HTTP(S), TCP Proxy and the SSL Proxy. However there are also regional load balancers that you can deploy and they come in two flavours; network load balancers and internal load balancers.

Network Load Balancing

Network load balancing allows you to balance the load of your systems based on incoming IP protocol data such as the address port and protocol type and distribute the traffic across a pool of servers.

In order to achieve this the network load balancing will use traffic forwarding rules that are applied to the incoming traffic flows to determine which of the servers to connect to within the target pool. Each of the target pools contains the server instances that are setup for load balancing purposes and they also define which type of health check should be performed on these instances.

In contrast to the HTTP(S), TCP proxy and SSL Proxy load balancers, which have global scope the network load balancing is a regional and non-proxy load balancer. When we say that the network load balancer is regional it means that it is regionally available across multiple zones. Non-proxy means that the network load balancer is effectively a pass-through load balancer as it does not terminate and then proxy connections from its clients. Therefore the load balancer plays no part in the return path.

However, it does provide a way to load balance UDP traffic as well as TCP and SSL traffic on non-standard ports as these are not supported by the global SSL proxy and TCP proxy load balancers.

In practice the networking load balancer receives TCP/IP traffic coming in through the internet at the regional level and can redirect the traffic across multiple zones via forwarding rule protocols. For example you may choose to forward ingress traffic based upon IP address, port or protocol to a pre-configured target pool of VM instances.

Now where this is useful is that pool of VM instances could actually be different applications running on different Compute Engine instances. It could be you are replicating a 3-tier application on the cloud. One instance might then be an Apache webserver, another a web based PHP application server and the other could be a MySQL back-end.

Before the traffic is forwarded by the load balancer it will need to check against the firewall rules. Now, remember that the load balancers and firewalls are not physical devices so this doesn't add latency or a change in subnet as they are all part of the SDN. Therefore the checks to see if the traffic matches any firewall rule that deny its forwarding is performed almost simultaneously and near instantaneously.

Once the firewall rules have been checked it is either dropped or the traffic is forwarded to the designated target pool and its appropriate VM instance.

This is a simple use case example but we could add some added features such as a fail over mechanism, as well as set up a health check and then have a fail over target pool which could exist elsewhere in another zone for redundancy and business continuity purposes.

Of course we don't have to just use that redundant environment just for fail-over it could equally also apply to a continuous deployment model.

Internal Load balancing

The other type off load balancer that we can consider is the Internal HTTP(S) Load Balancer, which is a proxy-based, regional Layer 7 system. The Internal load balancer enables you to run and scale your services behind a private IP address in your VPC network. The internal load balancer distributes traffic to backend VM instances or endpoints in network endpoint groups (NEGs) in a single region of your VPC network using a URL map, but clients and backend VMs or endpoints must all be in the same region.

Network Load Balancing with Managed Instance Groups

So far we have discussed network load balancing in relation to a target pool of resources. But how does that differ when you're running a managed instance group?

The first point to note is that a target pool will often have different types of VM instances. This is particularly pertinent when using a network load balancer as you can maximise the opportunities of filtering and forwarding traffic to different applications based on protocols and ports. However, a managed instance group is going to be all the same exact type of virtual machines. What this means is that you will be effectively distributing the same type of traffic across identical VM instances and using the same forwarding and firewall rules.

Consequently the reason for load balancing is now primarily to evenly distribute traffic across all the instances within the group and thus balance the load.

In this scenario we will need to consider how to monitor the load and perhaps deploy the auto-scaler. The benefit of running a managed instance group is then clear as it does inform the load balancer of the load and the Managed Instance Group configuration. And the benefit is that a Managed Instance Group tells a load balancer when that group has changed, so it can adjust the routing for the target pool accordingly.

Forwarding Rules

A target pool resource defines how a group of VM instances should receive ingress traffic flows from the pre-defined forwarding rules. When you configure forwarding rules to apply to ingress traffic these will direct traffic to a target pool, but how does it select a specific instance? The way this works is that the Compute Engine will pick one instance from the target pool by performing a mathematical hash of the source IP and port and the destination IP and port. Therefore target pools can only be used with forwarding rules that can handle TCP and UDP traffic. If you are using other protocols then you must create a specific target instance instead. There are also a few caveats that we need to be familiar with when it comes to forwarding rules. For example;

- You must create a target pool before you can use it with a forwarding rule.
- Each project has a max quota of 50 target pools.
- A target pool can have only one health check.
- Network load balancing only supports HTTP health checks.
- Network load balancing supports Compute Engine auto-scaler which also allows users to perform auto scaling on the instance groups in a target pool based on CPU utilization or custom Stackdriver monitoring metrics.

Session Affinity

When the forwarding rules filter traffic and direct it to a target group it is then up to Google Compute Engine to select an instance from the target pool to send the traffic to. We discussed briefly that in making the selection the Compute Engine performs a mathematical hash of the source IP and port and the destination IP and port.

The interesting thing about the hash process is that every combination of the source and destination parameters no matter how small the difference will always result in a unique result. However a single combination will always result in the same hash result.

This means that we have a method for enforcing session affinity, which is where we can ensure that an individual user is always directed to an individual VM instance so long as his network properties do not change. This is generally a good thing but we should be aware that session affinity also influences load distribution.

The hash method is used to select a backend instance based on a subset of the source and destination IP, the source and destination port, or the network or transport layer protocols whether it's TCP or UDP.

Possible hashes are as follows;

- There is the hash of NONE in the five tuple hashing model, which uses the source and destination IP source and destination ports and the protocol. Each new connection can end up on any instance, but all traffic for a given connection will stay on the same instance if the instance stays healthy.
- There is also the CLIENT IP PROTO, which is a three tuple hashing model and it uses the source and destination IPs

and the protocol. Again, all new connections can go to any instance but all traffic for an existing client will end up on the same instance, as long as they use the same protocol and the instance stays healthy.

- Then we have CLIENT IP, which is a two tuple hashing model, which uses the source and destination IPs. Once more, all new connections can go to any instance but all existing connections from a client will end up on the same instance regardless of protocol as long as the instance stays healthy.

In order to decide which hashing model to use we have to look more deeply into the parameters that they use in their hash function. This is not initially very intuitive and requires a trade-off between traffic load distribution against session affinity.

For example, while the five tuple hashing provides very good distribution of traffic across many virtual machines as it takes five parameters into the mix when running the hash function it can provide poor affinity. This is due to the issue where not all the parameters are fixed over time. For example should a client establish a second session from the same network then they will probably arrive on a different instance. This is because the source ports will most likely change as it is picked at random when the initial connection is established so does not persist across sessions. This is fine if you want good distribution and only per session affinity, but if want session affinity to persist across sessions you will need to consider another way.

Indeed if you want all sessions that are established from a returning client to reach the same backend instance, then you have a choice of using CLIENT IP PROTO or CLIENT IP methods.

Typically, selecting a three tuple or two tuple method will provide for better session affinity than the default five tuple methods. But the trade-off is that the distribution of all traffic across the instances may not be as evenly spread.

Load Balancing Best Practices

In this section we will take a look at some established load balancing best practices. It is important to contemplate these as often they are not necessarily intuitive and so it is easy to make design mistakes. So let us look at each in turn;

- When load balancing it is best to spread and balance load across multiple zones in a region. This being the cloud there are no restrictions and the back-end can be chosen at random as they share the same network anyway. But importantly it protects against any type of individual zone failure.

- When load balancing across zones for mutual redundancy remember to over provision. This is in case there's a zone failure, which means that you will failover to another zone's backend and it will now have to handle the combined traffic. So you want to avoid suffering latency and performance issues because you only set the capacity split to 50 percent. So provision at 100 percent for two-thirds of an outage, or 150 percent for a full service outage.

- Load balancing multi zone is a case of the more the better so if you can go across three zones then do it.

- You need to test out your fail-over mechanisms and see how lost instances affect performance.

- To simulate failure scenarios you can use the Managed Instance Group commands to stop an instance to simulate a VM failure without it restarting automatically.

- A better way to simulate a VM instance failure is to use metadata tags. What you can do is tag a virtual machine with a special name called failure_zone and that will automatically remove it from the load balancer's

calculations. Using tags is an elegant way to test to see how upscaling and downscaling work for VM failures.
Remember that load balancing is often unpredictable and unintuitive, at least at first, as there are so many features such as health checks, firewall rules and many other configuration tweaks that you can inadvertently apply, so test out your configuration in a separate lab environment first.

Instance Groups

Please keep the following best practices regards restrictions and guidance in mind when creating instance groups for use with load balancing;

- Do not put a virtual machine instance in more than one instance group.
- Do not delete an instance group if it is still being used by a backend.
- It is advisable to not add the same instance group to two different backends, it just adds complexity.
- If you must add the same instance group to two backends, then ensure that both backends have the same balancing mode, this could be either the utilization or rate mode.
- You can use maxRate per instance and maxRate per group together.
- It is acceptable to set one backend to use maxRate per instance, and the other to use maxRate per group.
- If your instance group serves two or more ports for several backends respectively, you have to specify different port names in the instance group.

- All instances in a managed or unmanaged instance group must be in the same VPC network, and if applicable, the same subnet.
- If you are using a managed instance group with autoscaling, do not use the maxRate balancing mode in the backend service.
- You may use either the max utilization, or maxRate per instance mode.
- Do not make an autoscale managed instance group the target of two different load balancers.
- When resizing a managed instance group, the maximum size of the group should be smaller than or equal to the size of the subnet.

Securing load balancers

It is very important to not overlook securing the load balancers themselves. Therefore you will want to create firewall rules that only allow traffic from the GCP load balancer networks. You might also want to further secure your load balancer instances by disabling their external IP addresses, as then the load balancers can only communicate using their internal IP addresses.

Another, security measure you may want to consider is in deploying a bastion host for remote management purposes. For example, you can then use a bastion host to manage the instances via an SSH session.

GCP offers several kinds of load balancing services so before you choose a specific load balancing configuration, it is best to give your requirements some serious consideration. After all you need to contemplate not only your applications requirements today but also where your requirements might be in the near future, as your applications demand will hopefully increase.

Use Case -18

How can we combine the various types of load balancers available to us in a typical use case that demonstrates their unique purpose?
Solution
3-tier web services
You can use Internal HTTP(S) Load Balancing to support traditional 3-tier web services as three different types of load balancers scale the three tiers: for example, at the web tier the traffic enters from the internet and is load balanced by a global, external HTTP(S) load balancer. Then at the application tier the traffic is further scaled using the regional internal HTTP(S) load balancer. Finally at the database tier the traffic is scaled using the internal TCP/UDP load balancer.
In more detail the design would be to have:

- A global, external HTTP(S) load balancer at the front-end, which distributes traffic from the Internet to a set of Web frontend instance groups in various regions.
- These frontends send the HTTP(S) traffic to a set of regional, internal HTTP(S) load balancers
- The HTTP(S) load balancers distribute the traffic to middleware instance groups.

- These middleware instances send the traffic to internal TCP/UDP load balancers, which load balance the traffic to data storage clusters

Chapter 19 – Automating infrastructure with GCP APIs.

In this chapter we are going to turn our attention away from manual configurations and look at ways you can automate infrastructure provisioning and configuration. These techniques are critical to any production system because they make the generation of the infrastructure documentable, accountable and repeatable. Thus, we will discuss infrastructure automation, images, metadata, scripts and the Google Cloud platform API.
Thus the first thing that we need to contemplate is why would you want to automate infrastructure?

Automating Infrastructure

Manual configuration through the web console is fine for small on-the-fly configuration changes and even when setting up new environments for testing a prototype or a proof –of-concept. But it quickly becomes tedious especially when you are creating lots of near identical VMs. That is when you can see the initial benefit of automated provisioning.
 In this scenario we also want to automate the provisioning of our environment, as many of the resource building-blocks are very similar across project designs. So we want to make it repeatable, so you don't have to rebuild all over again from square one, because now you have a repeatable documented process.

Automation allows you to scale and ensure there is consistency across the organisation.

Hence it is of great benefit that you spend a little extra time creating a consistent, repeatable automated process for resource provisioning. Now when we speak of automation we don't necessarily mean high-tech autonomous processes it can just as easily mean simply running predetermined scripts to build infrastructure.

If you will be designing and building large complex systems, you will really need a way to ensure that there's a repeatable process that prevents and corrects any of the inevitable human error. Fortunately there are many tools both built-in to GCP and from third party vendors that are available to assist you in this task. Indeed there are tools available that cover the entire spectrum of automation from provisioning to operations and maintenance processes, and often you will start off using simple tools such as a base image.

When you are provisioning a VM instance you have several choices of base image. Google makes available a wide selection of base images, which are maintained, updated, and patched. But you can also if you want use imported images as this can be useful should you need to integrate your VPC environment with an on-premises network. It is also cost effective if you already have enterprise licenses for the OS and/or any applications stored within the image.

You can automate the provisioning of a VM by uploading and then selecting a custom image to be installed when you create a running VM. This custom image could be just a core OS or more likely it could be a fully configured production copy of an on-premise server. In the latter the OS image will be production ready with all its configuration, licence, policies and hardening. If that is the case then all that is required is for you to connect to the VM and change its basic network configuration and then install any additional software, and so on.

After the VM is customised to your liking, you can create a snapshot of its boot disk. Snapshots are global resources, so you can use them to reconstitute a boot disk in any region and in any network in your project.

A baked image, on the other hand is a custom image that comes with pre-installed and pre-configured software. It is fully ready to go with just minimal if any configuration required. A good reason to bake an application into an image is to prevent unauthorised changes from being made so you effectively lock the application preventing editing of its configuration.

Also, Baked images are typically much faster to provision as they are operational-ready as soon as the VM spins up. You may hear the term, golden image, but it is simply one step up from a baked image as it is enhanced with all the environment settings pre-configured, and is ready on launch for production.

However not all pre-configuration or customisation needs to be done proactively. Instead you can make use of startup scripts to fetch and install software. The use of metadata is another method used to implement boot time customization in software installation. Regardless of the method, the benefit is being able to change configurations including which software to install on the fly. Startup scripts are an ideal way for passing parameters within the metadata that can only be known when the VM is being created and not beforehand.

Using metadata provides a persistent environment that survives the termination of any individual VM. This means that you can use metadata to maintain not just system level infrastructure data but also store persistent state information.

We discussed earlier instance templates and how we use them. But in the context of automation we can include any type of image, startup scripts and metadata within an instance template. Thus, instance templates give you a method of automation that is system documented and is a repeatable way to make identical VMs or recreate development environments instantly. In addition, when used with a managed instance group and with auto scaler, they provide automated horizontal scaling in reaction to variations in system load.

All of these tools and methods will get you consistent, reliable, and automatic provisioning of VM instances. But what they don't do is allow you a way to automate provisioning of the other resources within the GCP infrastructure. For example they don't allow you to create load balancers, VPN connections or networks.

However, there is a solution and that is to programmatically interact with the GCP via the APIs. After all every method that we use to interact with GCP regardless if it is through the web console, gsutil commands or Cloud Shell is effectively only a way to pass parameters to the relevant Cloud API as they ultimately perform the implementation. Thus, anything we can accomplish using any of the other methods can ultimately be done programmatically though calling the correct API. Thus the goal should be to write programs that call the cloud API to create and manage infrastructure using the SDK.

In order to accomplish this though we will need to install the Cloud SDK on its own VM instance. Then we can authorize the VM to interact with the Google Cloud APIs, and this will allow us to write programs that automate provisioning of all the resources within GCP.

We will explore the possibilities of API programming later but for now we will return our attention to importing, customising and running boot disk images.

Importing a boot image

Earlier in the chapter we said that you could import your own custom boot images. However we didn't go into any detail of how you actually can do this. In this section we will give you a step by step run through of importing, customising and managing your own custom boot images.

The first thing to note is that you can import a boot disk image a wide range of locations such as your on-premises data centre, from a VM on our local workstation, or from virtual machines that run on another Cloud platform.

The image import process though is limited to importing only one disk at a time. However, there are other methods such as importing a boot disk image into Compute Engine, by using the following process:

- Plan your import path. The first step will be to specify where you are going to store and prepare your boot disk image prior to uploading it.
- Prepare your boot disk so it can boot within the Compute Engine environment so you can access it after it boots.
- Create and compress the boot disk image file.
- Upload the image file to Google Cloud Storage and import the image to Compute Engine as a new custom image.
- The imported image is now available to create a Virtual Machine instance
- Ensure the custom boot image boot correctly. If the image does not successfully boot, you can troubleshoot the issue by attaching the boot disk image to another instance and reconfiguring it.

You can then optimize the image and install any software that you require so that your imported operating system image can communicate with the metadata server and use additional Compute Engine features.

Creating a VM using a persistent disk snapshot

Another way to create a VM with a custom image is to migrate one from a snapshot backup of a persistent boot disk attached to an existing customised VM. To do this you will need to first create a new disk using the snapshot backup. Then you can connect that new boot disk to a new VM instance in another region.

You might wonder why we don't just move the VM along with its persistent disks and we can do this if we are only moving within zones. This is because persistent disks can migrate across zones just by copying the VM as they are zone resources, however, they cannot migrate across regions. But you can effectively move them using snapshot backups. We can do this because snapshots are global resources. Therefore, you can use a snapshot backup to create a copy of the boot disk in any region and also in any network in your project.

There are several benefits to creating an image from a VM's persistent boot disk. A VM can be generated directly from the custom image and it can be used in instance templates shared across projects.

Managing custom images

We can share custom images across projects and even across regions but you should be aware that when you create a new disk in a different region or network that egress charges apply to the data transfers. Nonetheless, you can also share your custom images and control access by utilizing cloud IAM.

There are also some other neat tricks that are available to you such as you can set image families so that, for example, you can always point to the latest version of the image. Using image families, means that people will not inadvertently select older versions of the custom image.

Similarly, you can also define a deprecation schedule to delete old versions or simply to warn users that version is soon to become obsolete.

Using metadata for infrastructure automation

Metadata plays an important role in VM provisioning and throughout each of the individual lifecycle phases. Indeed metadata in this context are in fact custom key value pairs that we have reserved so that we can use to pass or later obtain specific information about the virtual machine.

Metadata tags allow you to create your own custom metadata. This enables you to store important information that you want to pass to the VM instance during start up or shut down. For example, this is commonly done using specific shut down and startup scripts in the metadata tags.

There are different types of metadata tags available. For example there are project wide metadata tags, which are accessible by default to all of the VMs inside of your project.

On the other hand we have private metadata tags that are Virtual Machine specific metadata, which is only accessible from within that VM. So for instance you can run a query and discover its instance hostname, the SHH keys, its project IDs, and additional details.

Many forms of metadata are not tags but all metadata are simple key value pairs. So you can search for and have returned individual values for the key. You can also probe an entire directory tree or a list of recursive keys as well. You can query this metadata in a number of different ways such as by using the Web Console, Cloudshell, or using the Google cloud platform, API.

Interestingly you can also use the curl command to repetitively identify if there are any metadata changes. For example; with a pre-emptible VM, that preempt API notification is actually going to come as a metadata update. Another example is that if your server is going to be migrated live or if it has to go down for emergency host maintenance, those actions will all be done by updating the metadata tag. So it would be advisable to monitor any change in the metadata updates so that you are pre-warned. This obviously is not feasible for manual intervention so it will be your applications job to monitor metadata notifications and take the appropriate pre-determined action.

Using Scripts in Infrastructure automation

VMs can be configured to automatically run startup and shutdown scripts. A start up script is guaranteed to be run however the shutdown script is only a best effort endeavour. This is because there is no way to guarantee a graceful shut down of the VM. After all there are a multitude of reasons why a VM might shut down or crash suddenly so there is no guarantee it will be able to complete running the shutdown script. You can update and edit these startup and shutdown scripts at any time, even after the virtual machine has been created and is running.

Windows utilizes Sysprep as its startup process and a major difference is that these startup scripts are going to be hosted in Google Cloud storage. Furthermore the scripts will need to be publicly available, although the VM tags will be private.

Startup scripts can be run immediately after the boot process has finished and common use cases includes software installation, operating system updates, checking security patches and switching on services. Because starts up scripts are guaranteed to run they are a great way to update a system or enforce policy.

Shutdown scripts on the other hand are based on best effort, which means they may not always finish running if the shutdown isn't graceful so tend to be less useful. Common use cases for shutdown scripts are for general housekeeping, releasing resources and closing down services.

However, using system images allow you to bake configuration into an image, increasing consistency and decreasing the time until the system is fully functional. This method makes it more difficult to implement undocumented changes.

Metadata and scripts enable boot time configuration, adding flexibility and allowing a consistent way to install and configure software. They also provide a straightforward method to change the configuration in code.

The cloud API is extremely versatile and gives you complete control over your cloud resources directly from code.

The concepts covered in this chapter should get you well on your way to automating the provisioning and configuration of your infrastructure.

Infrastructure Deployment Automation

As we learned in the previous section every interaction that we do when provisioning a VM or any other resource ultimately is implemented through the GCP API.

To interact directly with the API you can download the cloud SDK and it is very easy to install and run. Once you have the SDK you will be able to leverage its functions to create your own automation tools. Moreover you can do most of this without any coding as Google provides the necessary client Libraries and they are available for many popular languages.

When you login to the SDK you can authorize as a user or as a service account and use the SDK utilities to list, add, update and remove components from the command line.

There are two other command line utilities that take advantage of the cloud SDK, and one is called BQ, which is a Python-based tool that accesses BigQuery from the command line. The other is Kubectl tool, which allows you to manage Kubernetes from the command line.

Using a VM to leverage the APIs to create infrastructure can be a powerful tool for automation. You can accomplish this by authorizing a VM with a service account to use the Google cloud API and then leverage the SDK software in the VM to interact with the API to create infrastructure on your behalf.

Calling the cloud API from your application code is a powerful way to interact with GCP, but be aware that writing code to create infrastructure also has some pitfalls. One such issue is that that the reliability and the subsequent maintainability of the infrastructure depend critically on the quality of the underpinning software.

For example, a program could have many locations in the code that call the Cloud API to create infrastructure resources. This can make discovering and fixing a problem in the code very difficult if there should be an issue with say a flaw in the definition of a VM as it would require first identifying which of the API calls actually created it.

Needless to say that standard software development best practice should apply even if it is only a development project. It is crucial to know that leveraging APIs via code does lead to rapid development and creation of infrastructure but it is just as important to realise that things can go wrong rapidly, requiring emergency maintenance on code.

Another issue is the difficulty in understanding the often hidden complexities of the infrastructure that we're building from the code. The more complex the infrastructure becomes, the more complicated the code and the less likely that anyone actual understands all of it so the more likely it is that errors would occur. Clearly, we are going to need another level of organization. That's the purpose of Deployment Manager.

Deployment Manager

In short, Deployment Manager uses highly structured templates and configuration files to document the infrastructure in an easily human readable and understandable format.

Deployment Manager does a good job of abstracting the complexity of the actual Cloud API calls. Therefore, there is no need for you to write code, which leaves you free to focus on the architecture of the infrastructure.

In this section, we will discuss concepts around Deployment Manager, configuration and introduce Cloud Launcher.

Deployment Manager is an infrastructure automation tool, which allows you to automate the creation of GCP resources. In concept the Deployment Manager uses highly structured templates and configuration files to document the infrastructure. You can create these Deployment Manager templates within a cloud API enabled environment such as Cloud Shell, and then view the results and manage your deployments in the web console. Deployment Manager is not just a tool for documentation as it is a fully fledged declarative deployment orchestration tool specifically for Google Cloud platform. Indeed Deployment Manager is tightly coupled with the GCP so it allows you to integrate with other GCP core services such as Identity Access Management.

Deployment Configurations

Before we can start using Deployment Manager, we have to create a deployment configuration. A yaml file defines the basic configuration, and you can include an import in the yaml file to expand to full-featured templates written in Python or Jinja2. Program configuration is bidirectional and interactive. Meaning that the configuration receives data like machine type and returns data like IP address.

You can also use the preview tag when creating a deployment configuration to validate it without actually launching it.

All configurations are expanded on the server side within a controlled environment that Deployment Manager maintains. In order to prevent abuse, the environment is closely managed by Google's Deployment Manager team, so it does have some limitations.

Neither your original configuration nor your expanded configuration can exceed 10 megabytes. In addition you must bear in mind that any configurations that you upload into Deployment Manager will be limited. The constraints are based upon the amount of time the configuration will take to run and the resources used i.e. the amount of processing power used during the operation.

An important caveat to be aware of is that if you use Python templates then you must not make any system or network calls, if you try to, then these templates will automatically be rejected.

Deployment Templates

Some of the basic features of Deployment Manager's templates are that;

- Templates can be nested so you can create a set of reusable assets. For example, you could use different templates for firewall rules than you would for virtual machines.
- Segregating the different components that you might want to set up allows you to update them independently without having to use one single master file.
- Templates have properties and can use environment variables.
- Templates support startup scripts and metadata capabilities.
- Deployments can be updated using the GCP API, and you can add resources or remove resources.

Cloud Launcher

Cloud Launcher is basically a marketplace for third party vendors to sell their cloud ready products. The vendors on GCP have already created, tested and verified their own deployment scripts for their application, software stacks and cloud tools, based on Deployment Manager.

It is essentially a marketplace to quickly deploy common solutions such as complete open source LAMP (Linux, Apache, MySQL and PHP) stacks or licenced versions of proprietary software such as SAP, Salesforce or Oracle DB.

Not all the vendor software within Cloud Launcher is open source and some have separate fees for software licensing and image use, however all estimated monthly fees are all available in the pricing details for each solution. But beware as these are only estimates of the vendor's monthly fees you will still have Google's data and resource charges to factor in to the billing.

The image fee versus licensing fees are up to the vendor of the solution but Google does update the images to the latest versions in the repository, and will apply any update patches but not on the running instances.

Cloud launcher is very easy to use to deploy software packages and stacks and it literally is don't with two clicks, one to select the software package and launch on Compute Engine, another to select the zone. At it will be done in around 30 seconds. It is that painless.

Summary

This high-level overview to Deployment Manager does not by any means do it justice. There is a vast amount more to learn before you become skilled in using Deployment Manager's configurations and templates.

However in the Google GCP website and in the code repository there are many example configurations and templates for you to examine and edit to meet your requirements.

Remember, that the other infrastructure automation methods you've learned in this chapter can be used with Deployment Manager.

If you don't see the option you want in a template, you have alternatives, including building images, using startup scripts, and directly calling the Cloud API.

But if you don't want to have to reinvent the wheel then there is always Cloud Launcher, which is a great place to look, for both production ready open source and proprietary solutions published by third-party vendors.

Use case – 19

A member of the operations support team has come to ask you if there is a way of receiving notifications of a change in status of a pre-emptive VM. They would like to understand when a VM was about to be pre-empted so that they could trigger a script to spin up a replacement.

Solution

There are many cases where we would want to know about either pre-emptive VMs being terminated or of standard VMs being migrated by Google for maintenance purposes. Now, you can use curl to watch for the metadata tag change and as we have just learned all maintenance events involve updating the instances metadata attributes.

Now, in practical terms you're only going to get an update about 60 to 90 seconds before the event actually occurs and even less perhaps only 30 seconds for a pre-emptive VM event. That provides no time for human intervention so we have to automate this if we are realistically expecting to make any effective response.

We can first examine the instance metadata to see what is in there by running this command within Cloud Shell:

```
gcloud compute instances \
describe pre-emptive_VM \
--zone $CPO200_ZONE
```

Where 'preemptive_VM' is the instance name.

You can also obtain the metadata through the guest OS for example by using the URL:

```
curl \
"http://metadata/computeMetadata/v1/instance/\
?recursive=true&alt=text" \
-H "Metadata-Flavor: Google"
```

The output from this command will list all the metadata associated with the VM instance such as it configuration and status.

To find out when the VM is preempted you need to run the following Curl command.

```
curl "http://metadata.google.internal/computeMetadata

/v1/instance/preempted" -H "Metadata-Flavor: Google"
```

```
?wait_for_change=true
```

The code appended in blue is used to trigger the request only when the status has changed. This hanging GET request can be used to trigger a shutdown script, which can be used to copy data to cloud storage and then shut down gracefully. Managing a pre-emptive shutdown using metadata preemption notices in combination with a shutdown script can save a job's progress so that it can pick up where it left off, rather than start over from scratch.

Chapter 20 - Elastic Cloud: Containers and Services

Essentially, containerization is something that Google has been developing over the last decade or so. It conceptually falls somewhere between a virtual machine and a platform as a service solution. The idea being is that you can deploy your code in a small package with its dependencies but abstracted from an attached OS. This makes the code reusable and portable. Therefore a container can run on-premise, it can run in other cloud providers and it runs really well in Google Cloud platform.

In this chapter we will introduce the concept of containerization in general. Also we're going to introduce something called Kubernetes, which helps you to automate and orchestrate where your containers live.

 Since Kubernetes has to be portable and able to run anywhere, it can't really integrate tightly with many cloud provider functions and features. Hence, GCP has a managed service version called Google Kubernetes Engine to help integrate all those container and provider features.

Kubernetes can set up amongst other thing; firewall rules, load balancing, auto scaling rules, as you're also doing all these things with containers.

We will also take a look into some of the other application infrastructure services such as PaaS (platform as a service). This is where you're deploying your own code Java, Python, Go, PHP, etc. on Google's managed infrastructure and development platform.

However you may want to go further and take advantage of deploying just micro services. In which case GCP has their cloud functions platform. There is also Cloud Endpoints, in which you can publish your own APIs.

Plus, there are a number of other managed services, which we will consider such as

Google Cloud Pub/Sub for messaging services between your applications.

Application Infrastructure Services

The concept behind Application Infrastructure is that it is a set of technologies that are commonly needed by any distributed Cloud-based and globally-scalable application. Rather than requiring you to create this part of your application yourself, GCP offers it as an integrated service.

For example, every distributed application needs a method for the separate parts to communicate with each other. To this end, GCP offers Cloud Pub/Sub to provide that communication without requiring you to install, configure, and maintain other messaging software.

In this section, we will cover Cloud Pub/Sub, API Management, Cloud Functions, Cloud Source Repositories, and Specialty APIs.

Cloud Pub/Sub

GCP addresses the issue with scalable and reliable messaging via their Cloud Pub/Sub fully-managed real-time messaging service. Pub/Sub allows you to efficiently send and receive messages between independent applications. Also the Cloud Pub/Sub service is a highly scalable messaging queuing service that guarantees – if it is feasible - the delivery of all messages. In order to do this the Pub/Sub service will store undelivered messages for up to seven days. However, despite is efficient delivery method there are a few caveats such as; it does not guarantee first in first out. So, you're not guaranteed to get messages delivered in order. More importantly it does not guarantee only a single delivery of a message; you may get several duplicate deliveries.

Where Cloud Pub/Sub becomes of interest to the cloud architect is that it can act as a single ingest for all of the different data points. This can be a very significant design building-block in many modern cloud architectures. If for example, a network was built to support hundreds of different IoT devices then the design issue would be how to interconnect and service all these data sources efficiently? With Pub/Sub all those IoT devices could all publish data to the Cloud Pub/Sub service, and then applications that need that data could proactively subscribe to and pull down these messages as they become available to the subscription service.

Here are some of the benefits of cloud Pub/Sub;

- It is a globally managed service with extremely low latency.
- You can dynamically rate limit, so you can throttle exactly how often or how much Pub/Sub will push those messages.
- Pub/Sub provides end-to-end reliability because we're going to acknowledge at least one guaranteed delivery and receipt of each individual message.
- Everything is completely encrypted,

- it's maintenance is free and,
- you simply just pay for exactly what you use.

The way that Cloud Pub/Sub works is that it uses two levels of abstraction between the publisher and the subscriber. This deliberately de-couples the sender's transmission of the message from the receiver's receipt of the message.

Let's take a look at how publishers and subscribers interact in theory.

- A publisher in our example an IoT device wishes to publish a message.
- A message consists of a payload and optional attributes that describe the payload.
- The Pub/Sub service that receives the message from the publisher on behalf of the topic is called the publishing forwarder. A topic is a feed of messages.
- The topic stores the message ensuring availability and reliability. The message is transmitted to one or more subscriptions.
- The Pub/Sub service that receives the message from the publishing forwarder and ensures delivery to subscribers is the subscribing forwarder.
- A subscription is an entity that represents interests in receiving messages.
- The Pub/Sub subscribing forwarder determines which subscribers are registered to receive the message and queues up the messages to be sent.
- Subscribers can either receive the message through pull or push.
- The subscribers either receive messages by Pub/Sub pushing them to the subscriber's endpoint or by pulling them from the service. Pull subscribers use HTTPS requests to Google

APIs. Push subscribers use web hook endpoints that can accept post requests over HTTPS.

- The message arrives at the subscriber where it is consumed and an acknowledgment sent back to the subscribing forwarding service.
- The Pub/Sub subscribing forwarding service receives the acknowledgement and registers each delivery. When all of the deliveries are complete, it removes the message from the queue.

There are many common cloud Pub/Sub use cases, such as in deploying IoT or in balancing workloads in network clusters, for example, a large queue of tasks can be efficiently distributed among multiple workers such as Google Compute Engine instances. But there are myriad other use case;

- Implementing asynchronous workflows, for example, an order processing application can place an order on a topic from which it can be processed by one or more workers.
- Distributing event notifications, for example, a service that accepts user sign-ups can send notifications whenever a new user registers and a downstream service can subscribe to receive notifications of the event.
- Refreshing distributed caches, for example, an application can publish invalidation invents to update the ID's of objects that have changed.
- Logging into multiple systems, for example, a Google Compute Engine instance can write logs to the monitoring system, to a database for later querying and so on.
- Data streaming from various processes or devices, for example, a residential sensor can stream data to back-end services hosted in the cloud. Also

- Reliability improvement, for example, a single-zone Compute Engine service can operate in additional zones by subscribing to a common topic to recover from failures in a zone or region.

API Management

Applications rarely work alone and so will need to communicate with others. But they have to interact efficiently with low latency or there will be a poor user experience. Many of the issues related to slow communication between tiers in a multi-tier application are down to low latency. Most of these delays are down to network issues but another major cause is that of authentication with active directory or other strong means of authentication.

But if we look at the issue from another perspective we can see that the application wants to consume or provide a service. So if we make that service only available through an endpoint we can expose an API.

Google Endpoints

Google Cloud Endpoints fulfils this requirement as it enables you to create, deploy, protect, monitor, analyse and serve your APIs. It does this using the same advanced infrastructure, which Google uses for its own APIs.

You can actually use any language and framework to write the API, just add an open API specification or gRPC API configuration, and Cloud Endpoints will monitor and protect your API.

Let us take a look at a very common application for this style of architecture which is deployed often for a mobile backend. For example, if the application's users need to do very small but frequent synchronous interactions between their device and the backend mobile application. If that is the design criteria then that can be accomplished using Cloud Endpoints. Essentially the user's device can publish/subscribe or communicate directly with that Cloud Endpoint.

Cloud Endpoints can be though off as the demarcation point where your communications will transmit or receive communications on behalf of the application. The Cloud Endpoints can subsequently publish any received communications to other backend application servers. The advantage here is that now you have a mobile backend API, so you don't need to set up an entire environment just to handle all of the incoming connections.

Cloud Endpoints is a managed service, which means it is serverless and maintenance free. This way you have a backend service constantly running with your Cloud Endpoints that will automatically scale up or down to handle traffic load for you. After all, do you really want to depend on creating auto scaling engines every time a couple of hundred mobile phones came online? Instead consider using Cloud Endpoints as they can be a nice suitable environment for setting that up.

Furthermore, Cloud Endpoints are only made available whenever users are trying to interact with it so you are only billed for the connections that you use.

GCP Cloud Functions (Serverless)

At the far end of the continuum that is service offerings there is Cloud Functions, which is a fully managed infrastructure and software platform designed to host micro-services architecture. You can think of Cloud Functions as a zero-touch managed platform where you can host lightweight code, which are no more than single functions triggered by event driven actions. Instead of having to design and provision a complete environment with plethora of dedicated resources you just publish code such as a few lines of JavaScript to do something specific based upon an event trigger. You might be wondering then what the difference between Cloud Endpoints is and Cloud Functions as they both seem to serve the same purpose.

A simple comparison between Cloud Functions and Cloud Endpoints;

- Cloud Endpoints exposes an array of endpoints or API functions, whereas Cloud Functions exposes a single specific endpoint
- The Cloud Endpoints function has as an App Engine backend so you have tightly coupled programming environment where you will have full access to other complementary data, and storage services
- In Cloud Functions, you are executing a single snippet of code typically for a single function that accepts a limited input, executes and passes the limited output to another service and then exits.

Cloud Source Repositories

For developers Google provides another useful service with its Cloud Source Repository, which provides a Git version control service. This service is provided to support collaborative development of any application or service, including those that run on App Engine and Compute Engine.

For example, if your development team are using Stackdriver debugger, you can use Cloud Source Repositories and related tools to view debugging information alongside your code during application run-time.

Google Cloud Source Repositories also provides a source browser that you can use to view your repository files from within the GCP console. You can easily create a repository using the listed gcloud commands.

Repositories can be a mirror of a hosted GitHub or Bitbucket repository. When you push a change to the connected repository, it automatically syncs to the Cloud Platform repository. You can easily get amazing functionality into your applications by leveraging the services and APIs already supported in the larger Google Cloud, beyond the Google Cloud platform APIs. Using very little coding you can add cool features to your application by leveraging the machine learning API and/or the many other specialty APIs. Specifically, the cloud speech API provides speech text functionality, and supports over 80 languages and variants in real-time streaming or batch modes.

The application infrastructure services we've covered can help you grow your application in directions you might not have considered. For example, if you have a successful application, wrapping the API with security, monitoring, and documentation can enable third-party development on top of your solution turning it from an isolated application into an extensible platform and enabling business partnerships.

App Engine Managed Service

The Google App Engine is a Platform as a Service (PaaS) offering, which handles all the front end and back end infrastructure provisioning, management and scaling transparently on your behalf. So you do not need to concern yourself with building infrastructure all you need to do is focus on the application code. Google App Engine gives you infinite autoscaling as the standard environment is a fully managed environment, and it allows you to scale from nothing to thousands of different modules and instances running concurrently.

There are two flavours of App Engine; standard environment and Flexible environment.

Google App Engine's flexible environment is as the name suggests more flexible because it's based on Docker containers. It gives your VMs better exposure so you can access and configure it directly, as a result you can install whatever language you want because it's now your container. So remember, in App Engine's flexible environment, you are managing containers instead of the underlying development environment.

With App Engine services are a modular abstraction hence they provide a method to decompose the application into separate functional parts. So, instead of architecting your entire application inside a single App Engine service you could implement your application in multiple modular services.

You can have more than one service in a project. You can also use multiple projects to further isolate services. Splitting traffic to different versions enables incremental roll outs and AB testing. Each service can have multiple versions deployed simultaneously.

In App Engine the code is isolated by, versions, services, and projects. Services in a single project share some resources for example, Datastore, Memcache, and Task Queues. When services are in the same project, they are isolated in some ways, but they can share certain resources. For example, code in one service can't directly call code in another service.

However, services in separate projects are completely isolated. On the IAM level, you can assign different roles at the project, but not at the service level.

Code is deployed independently so each service can be written in a different language. Then with built-in autoscaling, and load balancing, the machine instance types are all independent per service.

App Engine makes it easier and faster to get an application up and running; since it handles the infrastructure, and lets you worry about your application instead.

GKE and Containers

Google Kubernetes Engine, which is actually a managed version of Kubernetes, is an open source container management system. Google Kubernetes Engine is really that blend of both infrastructure as a service and platform as a service. The benefits include automatic scaling of the cluster with a lot of the flexibility of being able to deploy pre-configured containers. Your developers can package up their applications and dependencies, and you as the administrator can publish or push those, or even delegate that control to them.

Kubernetes Engine has a lot more built-in capabilities that we will discuss in this chapter.

Indeed GKE provides you with a lot of control as you have less restrictions than you might have with other configurations.

Working with Containers

A container can be considered to be a mini-virtual machine. It is intentionally designed to be small, independent as well as hardware and OS agnostic. This means that unlike a VM a container does not need an OS or any host hardware drivers. This makes a container highly reusable and deployable on any host system that supports containers.

For example, if you want to install Apache Spark with Jupyter notebooks on a Linux server. There are several ways to do that. You could install it directly on the physical server's OS or more likely today install it via a VM. But setting up a VM requires installing an OS image and machines will be underutilized if dedicated for just one task. However, a virtual machine is simply a means to run an application but that application needs only some skeleton operating system to run. So the logic went; why not make a stripped down version of an OS, put Apache Spark with Jupyter notebooks (iPython) inside, and run that?

But making the container small is not the only advantage. The container can be deployed just like a VM template, so you can spin up an application and all its dependencies contained in one self-contained package - a container. Then you have a self-contained, machine-agnostic unit that can be installed anywhere and consequently there are now thousands of preconfigured Docker images for all sorts of applications at the Dockerhub public repository.

For example, to install Apache Spark with Jupyter notebooks (iPython) you would simply run this one line command, which will download, install, and start Apache Spark with Jupyter notebooks (iPython):

docker run -d -p 8888:8888 jupyter/all-spark-notebook

Essentially, a container lets you package your preloaded applications and all their dependencies so they can run in any environment that supports containerized workloads. Hence, you can write the code once, and run it anywhere.

However, there are some issues. When technology makes deploying applications too easy we tend to find that the natural barriers to VM and container proliferation vanish. Now, that uncontrolled spread and the resultant increase in orphaned containers and their applications is an inherent problem with containers. As a result, there is a need to keep track of them. Orchestration tackles these problems and this is where Kubernetes comes in.

Kubernetes Engine

Google made Kubernetes an open source project back in 2014. Kubernetes was designed to run anywhere and be hardware and vendor agnostic. Within GCP there is the Google Kubernetes Engine, which allows you to run all of your Docker format containers, but like most managed services Google will handle most of the complexity for you.

For example Kubernetes Engine will manage autoscaling as it is already tightly integrated with Stackdriver. So you can benefit from having native logging and monitoring. Moreover if you are already running open source Kubernetes on-premise, Google Kubernetes Engine can manage the on-premises Kubernetes for you over a VPN.

Integration with other Google services is a big advantage of Kubernetes Engine for example it can integrate with identity access management. Indeed, Google Kubernetes Engine can make it much easier to manage container clusters because it throws in all of those additional GCP services that aren't natively part of Kubernetes.

Kubernetes at work

At its core, Kubernetes is about organising and managing containers, so it creates what are called a container cluster. The cluster consists of physical hardware resources so in GCP the cluster is going to be made up off Compute Engine's virtual machines. Kubernetes engine automates the setup and deployment of the entire Kubernetes cluster. You can choose between a standard minimum cluster, which is going to have exactly one master to start with and your choice of the number of cluster nodes. Or there is a high availability cluster for production environments that supports multi-master configurations.

Regardless, that master is going to be the orchestrator as it will be conducting the API access to communicate with the individual nodes. Each of these individual nodes is going to be running a docker runtime. In addition there will be a kubelet agent running, which is there to handle the managing and scheduling.

The Kubernetes cluster will also include a network proxy so that they can communicate internally with each other and with other containers inside of the virtual machines.

Kubernetes master

The Kubernetes master is the cloud endpoint fronting the Kubernetes cluster and it runs the Kubernetes API server and it handles all of the scheduling.

The master is responsible for managing the cluster so it runs the health checks to ensure everything is running correctly and it provides all the cloud service integration that you need.

In your own on-premises Kubernetes environment you will set up your own Kubernetes master and all the individual nodes and be responsible for their administration and management. But in the GCP, the Kubernetes Engine is a fully managed service so it is going to be running this master node on a VM for you. Google takes over the management node for you, integrates that with Stackdriver, IAM, and other automated processes. Indeed you do not see the master VM let alone get to manage it.

How are containers organized?

Containers are organized inside of what we call a pod, which is similar to a target group in load balancers. In Kubernetes, you create a pod where you can bundle multiple containers together that might be tightly coupled.

However in Kubernetes engine it is recommend that you only run one container per pod. The reason for this difference between Kubernetes and Kubernetes engine is that the latter is not distributing containers it is distributing pods across multiple physical nodes.

A pod acts like a target group as it exposes these container applications through a single public IP address. Containers in the pod share a single internal IP address and a single namespace so they can communicate with the other nodes in the cluster.

A pod also gives containers access to centralized storage. This is useful if there is information that needs to be shared such as SSL certificate keys.

When it comes to load balancing across pods you use labels. A label is an arbitrary key value pair that you apply to pods to identify them. They're used by Kubernetes Engine to configure orchestration. For example, if you wanted to restart all the development pods, you'd look up those labels and shut down the appropriate matching pods.

In addition, you have the ability to base your queries on labels, which provides a method for getting full command and control over any pods that match those query labels.

Kubernetes Pods though are mortal in so much as they are created but when they die they are not resurrected. This can cause an issue because each Pod gets its own IP address, however the set of Pods running one moment could be different from the set of Pods running that application a few minutes later. The problem arises when we have the scenario where a set of Pods provides functionality to other Pods inside your cluster. How then do those pods initially discover and track the IP address to connect to? This is where Services come into play.

Kubernetes Engine Services

Here's a basic example to explain the Kubernetes Engine service concept the problem scenario is as follows; an application needs to communicate with a group of pods. But what will happen if a pod has to be restarted as it will be dynamically assigned a new internal IP?

One solution would be that the service would be given a static IP, which can be either an internal IP or an external IP just so long as it is persistent across restarts.

In which case, the application will communicate with the group of pods through this persistent service IP address. Moreover, the service is also connected to the pods by a label, so if a pod has the correct group label, it will be connected to the service automatically at restart.

Services can expose internally, externally, and they can load balance incoming requests to the pods in the group. Indeed services combine the functions of a group and a load balancer.

Kubernetes Deployment

In Kubernetes a set of pods is called a deployment. A deployment has a controller that ensures that a sufficient number of pods are running to service the app and it can automatically upscale or downscale, whichever is appropriate. It can do this by monitoring, for example, CPU utilization. A deployment also gives you a place to set the rules for determining the conditions for autoscaling those individual nodes towards the ideal state of the number of pods that we want to be running.

In this example, we have a service that will create the target pool of VM instances. Then a deployment group defines the rules that determine the conditions under which we can automatically spin up additional pods based on health checks or load balancing requirements.

Once you have a deployment, a group of pods, you can specify a particular service that you want to deploy, which consists of pods and individual containers.

You can install a deployment onto individual nodes. The master node is going to be responsible for equally distributing the number of pods across these nodes depending on what your container cluster looks like.

Remember, a container cluster is going to consist of actual virtual machines, compute instances that you can go into your console and see.

Deployments provide you with built-in resilience. For example, if you have a physical node failure that has running pods, all of these pods will become unavailable. However, the deployment will have specific rules stating it must have a minimum of two pods running at all times.

So, if there is only one physical node left running, then deployment controller must move the containers from the unhealthy node – if it can – or spin up new ones onto the remaining node. So for example, in a deployment of nodes A and B should physical node B fail, the deployment will automatically redeploy pods from node B to node A.

Another built-in administrative feature is rolling updates, which is based upon the same deployment concept, and it allows you to safely and with zero downtime upgrade systems to a new version. In this scenario, we can consider that a version 1.0 of the application is running on three separate nodes in a deployment. Moreover the deployment rules determine that at all times there must be three running pods available to service the application. What we can do here is launch a fourth pod onto node three with the new version of the application, 2.0.

Once the pod is operational, the service picks up the pod based on the label and now we have four pods, but we only need three. So, deployment manager will shut down the older pod with version 1.0 on node three. This process is continued until all three nodes have a pod with the updated version 2.0 of the application.

Another benefit of running Google Kubernetes Engine is the built-in IAM support for controlling access to the containerized environment. Using IAM service you can set the Kubernetes engine's command and control to the same level of security that you give to an administrator.

Deployment Manager with IAM gives you central axis control when it comes to managing the rest of the platform objects. You can design container clusters so that they are spread across multiple zones for resiliency.

When you enable multi-zone container clusters, the container resources are replicated in the additional zones and work is scheduled across all of them. If one zone fails, the others can pick up the slack.

For example, we would want to ensure a design so that any single zone is capable of running the entire application. In the design, node pools are instance groups in the Kubernetes cluster and very similar to a managed instance group. All of the VMs in a pool are going to be exactly the same. However, Pools can contain different virtual machines in other designs. Pools can also be located in different zones and Google Kubernetes Engine is node pool-aware via labels.

So, based on the pool specific labels that you designated Kubernetes engine can manage those accordingly. Consequently, the Kubernetes Engine will replicate all node pools and multi-zone container clusters.

When running across multi-regions it is always advisable to check any quotas or limits associated with those specific regions.

Cluster Federations

Cluster federation is useful when you want to deploy resources across more than one cluster, region, or cloud provider.
Cluster federation applies to multi-region cluster containers. You may want to use federations to enable high availability, offer greater geographic coverage for your app, to use more than one cloud provider, combined cloud providers and on-premise solutions, or for ultra-high scalability.
Cluster federation is also helpful when you want resources to be contactable in a consistent manner from both inside and outside your clusters without incurring unnecessary latency or bandwidth costs penalties or being susceptible to individual cluster outages.
As an example of how you'd use cluster federation in practice, let's consider that you're going to be running environments in Asia, Europe, and the Pacific, or even through other cloud providers. In this scenario, cluster federation will allow you to manage and deploy this in a multi-cloud solution.
Federations also integrate with network load balancing and of course, Google's cluster autoscaler.

Container Registry

Container Registry provides secure, private, docker image storage on GCP. While Docker provides a central registry to store public images, you may not want your images to be accessible to the world.

In this case, you must use a private registry. The Container Registry runs on GCP, so it can be relied upon for consistent uptime and security. The registry can be accessed through an HTTPS end point, so you can pull images from any machine, whether that machine is a Google Compute Engine instance or your own hardware.

GKE Scalability

One of Kubernetes Engine's most notable features is its ability to scale from small and medium sized clusters to a truly vast size. This makes Kubernetes Engine extremely flexible as it can support single cluster web application just as proficiently as HPA (High Performance Computing) and HTA (High Throughput Computing) where vast scale is a prerequisite to operations.

The way that Kubernetes handles scaling is important because when we initially deploy our clusters we can declare how many replicas that we want. We then scale by increasing or reducing the number of clusters as we desire to suit a specific criteria. The fastest way to scale an application is to use the following command:

kubectl scale *[CONTROLLER]* my-app --replicas 4

Where you would substitute (Controller) with the controller type such as deployment or statefullset

The output from this command will look something like this:

Name	Desired	Current	Up-to-date	Available	Age
Test-scaler	4	4	4	4	5min

Where Desired is the number of replicas that you configured; Current is the number presently active and healthy; Up-to-date is the number of replicas that have been updated so far in order to achieve this desired state; Available is the number of currently available replicas; and Age is a measure of the time that the application has been running in the cluster.

Autoscaling

Manually configuring and scaling our cluster has of course certain limitations so ideally we would want to autoscale the cluster to meet some preconfigured criteria. We can do this using a simple command:

```
kubectl autoscale deployment test-scale  --max=6 --min=4 --cpu
percent=50
```

Alternatively we can use the GKE Workloads menu in the console to achieve the same thing. Regardless, what the autoscale command does is to create a scaling device known as an HPA (HorizontalPodAutoscaler) object that targets a specified resource (called the scale target) and scales it to meet the desired objectives. Therefore in practice what the HPA does is to periodically check and adjust the number of replicas of the scale target to match the average CPU utilization that you specified. In the example above we set the desired level at a CPU utilisation level of 50% and with the constraints of a maximum of 6 replicas and a minimum of 4 replicas.

Custom Metrics

We can also extend the metrics that we use for autoscaling by integration of Kubernetes Engine with Stackdriver. In this scenario we can use metrics identified in Stackdriver to trigger the autoscale events.

There are two ways to autoscale with custom metrics:

1. You can export a custom metric from every Pod in the Deployment and target the average value per Pod.
2. You can export a custom metric from a single Pod outside of the Deployment and target the total value.

The metrics that you use can have unexpected results so you must be aware as to how they work in practice. This is important because the metrics are not always intuitive. For example the purpose of the custom metric is to get a Deployment to scale its replicated Pods based on the given metric value. However, metrics with a *total target value* should always be defined only when the effects of the scaling will bring the updated value of the metric closer to the target value. We can see this better is we consider how we might go about scaling a frontend application. We could do this by choosing a custom metric based on the queries-per-second metric. Thus we are expecting that when the metric value increases, the number of Pods should scale up, with each Pod serving a similar amount of traffic as before. Now we could go about his by exporting from each pod the queries-per-second value and setting a desired target average value results. This results in the desired behaviour that we are looking for. However, if we had exported from each pod the total number of queries-per-second and then set instead of an average but a total target value for this metric it will not work as we hoped. This is because increasing the number of Pods doesn't have any effect on the total traffic value so the HPA will not scale the deployment based upon that metric.

Use Case – 20a

A University comes to you seeking your advice as how to run an
High Performance Computing analytics project on a vast internet
based dataset. It is a collaborative project and the application is
being shared across several participating Universities. They do not
have the on-premises infrastructure to host such a project so would
like to host in in the cloud as then they could share the access and
the costs. The application that they have developed in-house and a
processing and an analytical function but it has already been ported
to Docker containers for portability between partner Universities.
The problem is that they have a limited grant so funds are tight but
they also don't know where to start? How can you help them?
Solution
The place to start is if their application is in container technology
already then they could look for a highly scalable architecture based
upon Kubernetes Engine clusters with auto scale and pre-emptive
VMs.

The advantages are the Kubernetes Engine clusters can scale automatically to meet demand so that you don't need to pay for nodes that are sitting doing nothing you only pay for the nodes that you are using. This can save a lot of waste but using pre-emptive VMs (PVM) can provide some major cost savings. Pre-emptible VMs are affordable, short-lived compute instances suitable for batch jobs and fault-tolerant workloads. In addition they offer the same machine types and options as regular compute instances but the catch is they only last for up to 24 hours. However some workloads are not suitable or do not benefit from PVMs so the design is usually to build two pools of node into the cluster for each function so that pool-a consists of standard VMs and pool-b of PVMs. This ensures that there will always be nodes available to meet the workload. The advantage is that PMVs with GPUs can then become affordable as you will benefit from large discounts (approx. 50%). Autoscaler works well with PVMs as they can spin up replacements if they are available failing that they will spin up a standard VM node. By using PMVs you can also choose CPU or Memory optimised machine-types as these are now affordable and you can use whichever best suites your workloads. An important caveat though that they should be aware off is that PVMs only last 24 hours maximum so if they are provisioned in a pool at the same time then they are going to terminate at the same time. The way we work around this is by using an open-source solution: Estafette GKE Pre-emptible Killer, which can spread out the termination of our PVMs so they don't all get deleted simultaneously. A basic architect would look like this:

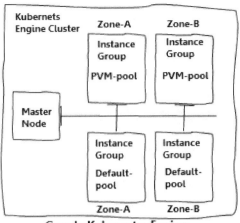

Google Kubernetes Engine

Use Case – 20b

The developers in your company have been tasked with deploying a containerised application but they are unsure on which Cloud Platform they should deploy the containers, how can you advise them?

Solution

The issue here is in deciding which is the preferred platform for the deployment of containers and this comes down to:

Kubernetes Engine Vs. App Engine-Flex Vs. Compute Engine

You should make them aware of some considerations and a few differentiators which they need to bear in mind when deciding where to deploy their proposed containerized applications. This is because running containers on Compute Engine is a good choice when you absolutely want control over the VM resources while also benefiting from Docker image development.

However, if the developers don't need to use Docker containers in their application, App Engine standard environment might be a better option. In this case they would simply deploy the code and App Engine will handle the infrastructure for them.

On the other hand there is also App Engine –Flexible environment which is a developer focused, no ops, compute infrastructure platform that abstracts the underlying infrastructure to a large extent in favour of developer friendliness.

App Engine Flex does not run on standard run-times but instead it runs Docker containers in VMs, which makes it easy to deploy. Further, App Engine- Flex handles much of the ops for you as it handles things such as capturing logs, scaling, versioned upgrades, and traffic splitting.

Nonetheless, if the developers are familiar with Docker, containers, configuration, and settings and they do want to run containerized workloads then Kubernetes Engine will be a better option.

GKE provides for more control but also requires an understanding of the underlying infrastructure and of container orchestration concepts. Kubernetes Engine is also a better choice if you are already running Kubernetes on premises as it can work across a VPN to manage both on-premises and cloud environments.

This should be sufficient to give the developers a better understanding of the best platform for deploying their containerised applications.

Part 4 – GCP architecture design and process

Chapter 21 – Cloud Service Design

This chapter will describe the layered and iterative approach to cloud service design and process. In order to better understand the design process we will undertake an architecture design challenge that is iterative and will expand to address particular issues that will be introduced with each subsequent chapter. By taking this iterative approach to the design we will encounter issues that force us to take a new perspective, so that over time it will evolve from its humble origins as a prototype into a scalable, reliable, stable, and secure design.

After introducing you to the concept of using a layered model for cloud service design, the chapter discusses the three concepts that are critical to design and to cloud architecture in particular: these are state, measurement and requirements. It is by using these three key concepts along with our iterative approach that will let you start to design a solution.

Importantly in the beginning we do not need to understand the exact process of how our design is going to evolve into a stabilized production environment. Indeed we accept that we are not going to get it right first time. Thus, we just need to know that applying the three concepts iteratively within the design process will get us there eventually. What we do need to have confidence in is the knowledge that following design thinking principles will lead us to a solution.

Design Thinking

Design thinking is an iterative approach to problem solving that intentionally seeks out people with different perspectives, knowledge, skills and experience and has them work together to create a practical solution for a real-world problem.

Design thinking uses a process-based approach to solve problems and like any process, it involves a series of steps that are carried out in a particular order to achieve a goal. In this case, the goal is to identify a solution that is capable of succeeding, can be carried out in a timely manner, is cost effective, fit for purpose, and is likely to be accepted by all stakeholders.

The 5 Steps of Design Thinking

The five steps in design thinking are empathize, define, ideate, prototype and test. Therefore, as we are using the iterative design process we are going to start by defining the service. If you are creating a new service its recommend you just start out with something rough, a prototype or proof of concept model. What this means is that we will not initial concern ourselves with making it scalable or highly available as we will just concentrate on getting its core functionality working.

Once we have our proof of concept, and can demonstrate it working then we can take a more structure design approach. So, in the beginning get a good grounding of the use case and what you are trying to achieve by asking yourself, the team and the stakeholders some questions about how the design is this going to handle specific scenarios.

Once you have a good understanding of the use case you can then start identifying the system's specifications and requirements as well as the deliverables, such as the service objectives (SLO) and setting measurable metrics, known as service level indicators (SLI) that will allow us to define the project goals.

Four-Tier Design Methodology

When we start working on our design we're going to move through our four-tier architecture. The first tier we visit is going to be addressing the presentation layer, and that's the underlying infrastructure and networking. Later we progress to contemplate the business logic. It is at this business logic tier that we will plan exactly how our service is going to work. This is where we will decide which components will provide the features and functions that comprise all those little bits of logic that we will need to occur to drive our design. It is then that we begin to understand the different attributes that should be applied to those components. Fortunately though modern design is less about reinventing the wheel and much more about reimagining and assembling tried and tested functional building blocks.

Of course there is always going to be data that needs to persist so we have to store our data somewhere. This is the purpose of the 3rd tier, the data layer. When we visit this tier we will need to understand what our data is going to look like. Will it be structured or unstructured?

Will it be a relational database or will just be static storage?

Maybe it's going to be a mix of both, perhaps it's going to be NoSQL or global relational databases we won't know until we have an understanding of our business logic and what the requirements of that may be. For the business logic will also define exactly what our storage data layer is going to look like.

The fourth and final tier is the security layer and no design or prototype should go online without thorough scrutiny of its security controls and its threat surface. Security should be encouraged at every stage of the design process from prototype to development through to production and should never be bolted on as an after-thought at the end.

Indeed security along with identity and access management (IAM) should be contemplated throughout the design process and IAM integrated into the design where appropriate. You may also consider bastion hosts, service accounts, access-lists and firewall rules to bolster some vulnerable areas in the design.

Once you have designed your logic, you understand what services you need, what components are going to make it work, the type of data storage you need, as well as the security controls that you need, and you have a working proof of concept, only then will it be time to start to expand the design.

Reliability and Availability

Once we have modelled the business logic and designed the underpinning network that connects all our functional components together we can start thinking about resiliency and capacity planning. For example it is at this stage that we might contemplate how resilient can the design be made in case of failures? What about the designs ability to scale above forecasted loads? What if this becomes a popular application, how will the design cope?

We have forecast capacity and load and even overprovisioned for optimistic use-cases but are we prepared in case things fail or succeed well beyond expectations?

In order to answer that question sufficiently we need to understand the concepts and realities of business continuity and disaster recovery. This might mean a complete redesign, but that's why you begin with a proof of concept, which addresses the logic. Only then are you going to see if it can expand to deliver resiliency, scalability and DR.

Project Design Constraints

In this chapter we are focusing on cloud service design and process but that discipline doesn't exist in a vacuum. Indeed you will have all the other tiresome constraints that every other IT project has to rail against. And as ever, and it has always been so, there's going to be a compromise on how much budget you have, versus the best most optimal design that you envisage that meets all of the service objectives that you're trying to achieve. Despite this we still need to forecast and plan for load and capacity regardless of what the budget might be. Eventually, though we will have to face the harsh economic reality and compromise through making design changes and tweaks to bring that price costing down.

Cloud Deployment and CI/CD

Then of course, we're going to have to move eventually from development and testing to staging and live production. So what is the deployment process and strategy that we will use? Will it be a continuous improvement and continuous deployment? Perhaps we might want to do some market research using blue green deployments? Gradually upgrade an application through rolling and zero downtime deployments? Or even use Canary tactical deployments?

Regardless of which strategy we use how are we going to monitor and measure our service indicators?

Nonetheless, when we set tactically service thresholds are we going to alert a human every time a metric breaches a threshold? Probably not as it would only bring on alarm fatigue and these spurious false alarms can lead to future genuine alerts going unanswered.

To summarize and close this design specific section, we're going to learn some of the expectations on how we should approach the design and what to expect during the design challenges. These are best practices from the Google SRI project. So again, we're going to take you step by step through from something small to something at full enterprise scale.

So something to keep in mind, ideals will evolve iteratively. So take small steps, fail first and fast, try to create something, try to find out whether it's going to work or not, then adopt or rule it out.

Your first design may work but continuously improving on an original design within an iterative process is the more likely way to succeed. You'll be surprised at how much you can actually do just through the design and thought process without ever publishing anything to production.

Don't skip design layers - take those iterative steps as you might be able to discover something that didn't occur to you before.

Don't search for the universal solutions where one fancy trick will promise to fix it all. Instead, be aware that there's no universal solution, so try to eliminate that bias. Indeed you might be better to consider some of the new and very quickly evolving technologies that others in similar fields are developing as you might be able to utilize them in your design.

However, you must also try to be aware of recency bias when contemplating new technologies and solutions. Just because it's a new idea and works in one scenario or use case doesn't mean it will work for you. So always try to assess it by its worth to your design and use case and not because it is new and fashionable.

On the other hand don't always try reusing what has worked in the past. Recycling and reusing code is good but you definitely might want to look at refreshing processes and trying new versus old methods and tactics.

So focusing on the design process itself, let's summarize.

- Begin simply and iterate,
- always plan for the future,
- Avoid bottlenecks and any single points of failure.
- Understand that this application is possibly going to grow. There are very few services that shrink with most growing as they gain popularity; otherwise you really have no problem if it does not grow you just start turning resources off and save money.
- Measure, and make sure you identify what to measure. Measurement and analysis is where we have the capability nowadays as we have Big Data analytics to measure and really get granular and use data for a lot of our insights.

- Understand exactly what are the constraints, quotas and limitations, and benchmark things ahead of time, as references.
- Manage things in production to identify where potential failures might occur. This way, you can quickly analyse potential cascading effects.
- Identify and then measure the symptoms, but don't jump to conclusions as you want to try to understand the root cause rather than treat the effects.

Understanding State

In cloud service design we refer to an entities current condition as being its state. Being aware of an entities state is often important to applications that perform an action that depends on the memory of a preceding state. When that memory of state persists it is called state information.

Protocols

The protocol of choice for internet communications is HTTP(S) which is a stateless protocol though several techniques have been developed to make it appear to be stateful such as using cookies and session IDs that enable browser or server side storage of stateful information.

To complicate matters, network protocols can be layered so although HTTP(S) is stateless the TCP/IP protocol its sits on top of is stateful. Yet the underpinning IP or Ethernet layer is stateless. Therefore, understanding whether a system is stateful or stateless will influence the design as you will have to decide how to process the state information, where to store it, and how to efficiently retrieve it.

It's fair to say that state is the cornerstone of any cloud-based design, so the first steps to focus on in designing cloud apps is in handling persisting state and the potential design solutions available to us.

Many design discussions in this chapter will contemplate where state information is located in the system, and how it's going to be maintained. Taking this approach leads to a general solution for the design of large-scale cloud-based services.

Stateful versus Stateless

If we consider the features of a stateless application you will see that they have several common traits. For example they are typically designed and built to perform just one function or service; an example would be an IoT device. Because of this highly specialised behaviour the client sends all the information required to the service with each individual request. Therefore the service is designed to rely on only the information relayed with each request — this means that the service doesn't need to rely on any historical data so there is no need to hold onto state information between requests.

This situation is very flexible with regards to scale as it doesn't matter what physical server processes a request from a client, which makes horizontal scaling a perfect solution for managing growth. Indeed, because a service instance can retrieve all the application state it might require from elsewhere enables resiliency, elasticity, and flexibility. This makes it feasible for any available service instance to process any task;

In cloud networks stateless applications are most commonly deployed as containerized microservices apps. However, this is not without its own drawback as containerisation at scale leads to a need for orchestration. In GCP there is the Kubernetes Engine managed service that serves this function for managing and conducting stateless apps. Orchestration determines the best location to run the containers from the perspective of its resources, including maintaining high availability.

Stateful applications on the other hand mean stateful applications are typically transactional by nature so require somewhere to store state information. They will involve users logging into an account or the user's activity being tracked via a session cookie. Stateful applications are most commonly deployed in the cloud for ecommerce, CRM, ERP, on-line banking and other such applications that need to track and maintain transactional real-time data.

With Stateful applications the service will process inbound requests based on the information relayed with each request and also key information stored from earlier requests – this means that the server must access and hold onto state information generated during the processing of the earlier request.

This can cause an issue with horizontal scaling as the same server must be used to process all subsequent requests linked to the same state information, otherwise the state information must be shared with all servers in the pool. The trick here is to either maintain session affinity at the load balancer so that it always sends a returning client to the same server or to store all state information in a shared database that is accessible by all servers in the pool. Orchestration for stateful applications is still required and it involves determining the best location to run the containers from the perspective of the of the applications' overall needs. Orchestration for stateful applications also manages high availability – moving containers and remounting volumes with no application or code changes.

In the latter scenario of using a shared backend database, then you can certainly handle scale and you can handle distribution as well. But here lies a problem; if you have a shared backend database your data is centrally located. However, a central database can be a choke point and a single point of failure, and latency in retrieving the client state information can slow down the application.

But there is a bigger issue than that. This state information is your customer data; this could well be the data on active sessions that a client was going through on an e-commerce website. So, it had better not get lost or corrupted as it is now the single source of truth for all the transactional data in the billing system.

Hence, we have to really contemplate and take into our design where we're going to be storing stateful information. There are several ways in which the load distribution facilities in the product can maintain state information between client requests, including:

- Transaction affinity – in which the load distribution facility acknowledges a transaction's existence and tries to direct all requests within that transaction's scope to the same server;

- Session affinity – in which the load distribution facility acknowledges a client session's existence and tries to direct all requests within that transaction's scope to the same server;
- Server affinity – in which the load distribution facility acknowledges that while multiple servers might be acceptable for a specific client request, a specific server is best suited for processing that particular request;

In the case of distributed operating systems, the session manager (part of the application server) stores information about each client session and considers session affinity and server affinity while directing client requests to an application server's cluster members; The workload management service takes into account both server affinity and transaction affinity when deciding how to direct client requests between the cluster members of an application server.

So, how do we deal with state?

State information can take many forms from just basic key-value pairs contained in a tracking cookie to extensive SQL transactional data in a backend database. Google's SRI team's best practices are to distribute state information across the servers rather than store it in a central database.

However, distributing state across the frontend servers also has its issues. The scenarios we really want to try to avoid here is in creating hotspots in the database. For example, if you have distributed state across multiple different servers as per SRI best practices then you have stored the state with the actual front-end servers that are handling its associated client. Well, the problem with that design is that a particular server could become a hotspot.

This is because load balancing may distribute a larger number of stateful transactions to a single front-end server and that may become overloaded. What is now recommended is that you push state off of the actual services that are handling and relying on state information, and that you push the state information onto a back-end server.

Measurement

In all stages of the design process from early prototyping through to commissioning and deployment we need to set performance goals and metrics so that we can measure the designs performance. Hence, measurement is considered to be the key to creating a stable and manageable system.

However the evaluation of a design does not end with commissioning and sign off. The Cloud Architect will usually still be involved after the implementation to hand over the knowledge, maintenance tasks and administration routines to the local support team. This will ensure that the system is stabilized and that it can be operated and maintained properly.

Therefore it is critical to design from the onset as to how you will identify key performance indicators. These will be the metrics that you will use to benchmark system performance.

As the architect it will be up to you to define how your service should look and feel. It's also equally important to address customer experience and expectation so we will need to establish metrics that lets your users' feel that they are benefiting from your service in terms of reliability and performance. This is generally termed the service level.

Service Level

In order to define a service level, you must first identify what your customer expects from the service and what features and functions that they care about. Hence the first step in designing a good customer experience is to identify the Service Level Indicators or SLIs that deliver the vest customer solution. This of course should mean benchmarking each process and following through a function from start to finish. This can mean measuring the time to execute for every process and how many CPU threads it might consume. These benchmarks will give us performance metrics and the thresholds for each of these SLIs.

What this means is that the users will have a real-world benchmark to decide whether the service is working properly. Having this fixed indicator or target of system performance and a set threshold to measure against allows us to determine the Service Level Objective or SLO. The designer can use the SLO to finesse their architecture and meet customer expectations by addressing and controlling the service level indicators. Typically though the SLO is only used within in-house operations and applications. The SLO provides a major metric for application design as it sets the level for application performance and customer experience when internal to the organisation.

Nonetheless, some cloud services will be so critical to an organisation that a formal business contract will be needed. When you have a requirement for a formal legal agreement to exist between the provider and the consumers to guarantee a service level and perhaps even to compensate the consumers if the service fails to meet this expectation, then things become more complex.

This is where we have Service Level Agreement or SLA and when they come into the picture. Service levels agreements (SLA) will define how a given service or product should behave and be fit for purpose under normal production environments. There are a number of factors that might be contemplated within service levels agreements, which will be dependent on the critically of the service. For example, the SLI's might be determined on availability. In this scenario the SLA specifications night guarantee 99.99 percent up time or perhaps other performance specification such as a minimum latency.

Regardless, service levels, whether they are SLO or SLA, will determine the user's expectation and they manage customer expectations.

Service Level Indicators

When we select service level indicators we should ensure that they are directly observable and measurable by the users. This means that the SLIs should not be internal system metrics such as CPU utilization or other internal metrics such as network bandwidth utilization. The reason for this is that the user must be able to relate to the indicator and be able to directly measure them and that is not something they can do with those internal system metrics. Another reason is that measuring utilization isn't actually an effective measure of the usability of a system. Rather, utilization is best deployed as a metric by auto-scalars to maintain a consistent user experience. Service Level Indicators should be a quantitative measure of an attribute of the service. SLIs could represent things such as error-rate, latency, or availability.

Finally, the user experience will be determined by application performance, which will be determined to be poor more commonly when there is excessive delay, the application hanging or the failure to complete a process. Therefore we should make sure you are measuring the correct pain points when setting your SLIs.

However this raises an interesting question. If you so not know your customers, how do you know what they care about? The answer comes from the marketing concept used when developing user interfaces - the user persona.

A user persona is an abstract representation of how a certain set of users will use your service. For instance, a user persona could be described as the power user, business user, casual user, and the impatient user.

User personas can help you determine the SLIs and the SLOs for your service by understanding how each group will actually use your service.

Also, once you've identified what the users' care about, we will need to quantify the individual SLI thresholds and then group them to form one overall service metric that is a reliable indication of system performance. This is represented as the Service Level Objective or SLO.

The SLO is an internal measurement that has threshold values for individual SLI set at the lowest acceptable level of service. The Service Level Objectives are thresholds that represent the point at which action must be taken to improve the reliability or performance of the service. Sometimes, the thing you need to do isn't just fixing a component or a process. It might mean delaying an update or fast-tracking an upgrade or even a full engineering review. The SLO threshold is at the point where any further deterioration in service would be both detrimental to the service and an obvious degradation of the service from the customer's point of view.

The SLO is an internal metric used to monitor system performance but sometimes a service is so critical we need to provide service level guarantees to the customer. This is often the case where a loss of the service could represent financial loss for the customer or even loss of life in extreme situations such as medical or emergency services.

These contracts are Service Level Agreements (SLA) that is legally binding agreements that are defined at an even more restrictive level of service than in the SLO.

The key difference here is that the SLO is a soft target used internally by the support teams to measure the level of the service. The SLA, on the other hand, is a business contract that grants a customer some compensation should the contracted level of service fall below a certain threshold.

Therefore, SLAs are set at a less restrictive and demanding level than the SLOs this is so that the operations team can strive to achieve the more demanding SLO, which will inherently meet the SLA target. To provide an accurate measurement of the latency a user would experience, we will sometimes need to monitor additional systems. For example, if we need to know the true latency of our application from the customer perspective we must account for the additional latency of all the system components that are in the customer path, such as the load balancer and the data server.

Therefore, our SLIs will be based upon the total end-to-end latency from the front-end web load balancer through our service and then through to the data server.

SLOs differ from SLAs as an SLO defines the thresholds of the user's pain tolerance to performance or availability issues but from an internal operations team's perspective, whereas an SLA is a legal contract. SLAs are known to the consumers of the service, and are measurable and verifiable.

Contrary to popular belief, SLOs aren't set at the maximum performance a service can achieve. Rather, the business will determine an appropriate and achievable level of the performance or reliability that the provider can realistically deliver. After all the service must be financially viable so we can't make it too responsive or too available because then it would be too expensive.

One important thing is that your SLOs are not immutable and they might change as you continually improve and upgrade your service. Also, keep in mind the four golden monitoring signals when creating your SLOs: latency, traffic, errors, and resource saturation. When designing your SLOs, it's important to be realistic and not over optimistic. While we would all like to think we have designed a service that is 100 percent reliable and available, that is sadly rarely the case. This is why many organisations use an error budget methodology when it comes to maintenance and managing service windows.

Error Budget

By taking a realistic approach to maintenance it is assumed that every service will not run perfectly. Hence, services are given acceptable error limits for the SLOs that operate a bit like any financial budget. With an error budget, each service will be given a set level of credit which is a set amount of errors, which are measured in downtime, that are considered acceptable, i.e. normal and expected maintenance and service downtime. However, any errors in excess of this budget are considered to be service outages. You will commonly see error budgets displayed as SLAs such as 99.9% and the like. Therefore, the goal with an error budget is to perform all the system maintenance and updates within this budget. The error budget in effect provides a strict window of opportunity for unscheduled maintenance and servicing. Each month there will be opportunities for implement changes and applying updates but as the days go by the error budget is replenished.

Service Requirements

A key design focus is on the requirements that are important to the stakeholders, for example the business goals. Requirements are also measurable for example; one operational requirement might be that the service must be highly responsive to users. That requirement is now contained in an objective, such as; the system must respond to customer requests in no more than 400 milliseconds latency.
The design objective can then be mapped to a corresponding measurable service indicator, such as; measuring round trip time between receiving a user request and delivery of a result to the gateway.

An initial step in all project or design methodologies place importance into diligently gathering requirements. This is so that we understand what our design objectives might be.

Therefore we can consider that a design always starts by simply identifying the stakeholders and asking them questions.

By asking stakeholders questions you can define the key service level objectives that are important to them and this will be helpful in thinking through the design decisions later.

For example you might start out asking some basic questions that will provide you with some qualitative requirements; why is the system needed? Or, what problem does it solve? Or, what are the priorities?

Once we have our answers as qualitative requirements it is now time to define them quantitatively, with relation to time, data, and users.

In effect we will be defining how much time we will allow this system to be down. But this is quantitative so there must be logic backing up our decision. So we have to consider things such as; what is the cost of data?

What this means is that how you handle data will come with related costs. For example, data replication for redundancy and data backups for business continuity and DR do not come cheap.

You will also have to contemplate how fast will the data grow? This might mean that you will need a dedicated 10 Gb Ethernet link. Another important design requirement will be where are the users located? Are they going to be close to the data? Or are they going to be all over the world? If it's the latter you will now have to starting to thinking about distributed caching, or about data replication across regions.

The user's locations will define data storage requirements, and it also defines the time element. The inherent delay in accessing data storage around the world will determine where you replicate your data storage. Of course this duplication of resources has a financial impact on the design. So you need to determine what level of latency is acceptable for the production design and any fail-over scenarios.

So there is a lot to think about with storage alone let alone start contemplating capacity planning and; what happens if we had an unexpected growth?

Then we would need some method of automatic scaling. In this case we will have to start worrying about what resource constraints are going to be important to the design stability?

You will also need to think about handling state, and where you need the resources to scale.

So, what we have to try and understand is how do we create sufficient dimensions around this forecasted requirement without massive over-provisioning of resources?

We also need to consider horizontal or vertical scaling and can our design handle these methods. A good example is with MySQL as it doesn't scale horizontally it needs to scale vertically. In this scenario where you want incremental horizontal scaling then a NoSQL, data storage solution would be preferable.

Business Logic

In computer science, business logic is the code that implements business rules, which in turn determines how the data is processed.

The business logic determines how the application process works in fulfilling its purpose. An example would be in banking, as the business logic would determine how the application handled a financial transaction and which accounts would be debited or credited and in which order.

By definition, business logic operates on data, which means processing some code. Essentially, the business logic layer design is where you'll consider all of the cloud processing options in order to determine what services the business logic code will need to use.

Microservices

In computer software, business logic or domain logic is part of the program that encodes the real-world business rules that determine how data can be created, stored, and changed.

Microservices design is a popular approach to applications design in the cloud as they leverage small, stateless processing code to provide scalability and resiliency. Microservices architecture can be thought of as independently deployable, small modular single purpose functions. As such microservices can be used like tiny building blocks of single function micro-applications.

Building application using these functional building blocks is very efficient and well suited for the cloud. This is due to each modular service running as a unique process that is going to contribute to some individual business goal. Also microservices can communicates effectively through a lightweight mechanism such as Cloud Pub/Sub, which is GCP message queuing service.

There are a number of benefits to using microservices rather than large monolith applications. The first is that they are single-purpose modules, which makes it very easy to develop and maintain. Microservices are also specialist code that does one thing and it does it very well and this makes it highly reusable and portable. For example in a monolith application you can write an entire function that would be called within the application. But, if you use that code as an independent microservice it can actually exist as a separate service that can be called upon and used by other services that it may not even be intended for.

Just think of how APIs work and you can see the benefit of calling specialist modular functions. They also provide for redundancy and resiliency because we can make as many clones as we need to match the requirements.

With microservices you can quickly swap a particular functional component without having to recompile a big and complex application. Microservices also makes troubleshooting much easier as they aid in things like fault isolation and debugging. But, they can also make it harder to understand how they interoperate. This is because all these different independent services means that integration testing can be a challenge because you can have a chain of events and you have to understand where the source cause is. In practice, one little hitch in the system can also have a huge chain of event effects on the entire system.

Microservice vs. business logic design

In general microservice can make development in the cloud much easier and faster, for example, unit testing is going to be easier because they're individual small functional modules. Nonetheless, microservices can still complicate the business logic. If we look at an example, such as a simple unified banking service where you have a machine that's going to accept deposits and withdrawals. If a customer deposits money into the machine the bank needs to be able to determine within the centralised system, that the transaction is accepted and the relevant customer account has been updated.

On the other hand if the customer withdraws cash, then the bank will have to deprecate the amount from the user's account.

Now, in most banking apps the two functions of withdrawal and deposit will be tightly coupled within the code. But what happens if you have microservices in which you actually have segregated deposits and withdrawal functions?

Well, if you deposit money into the bank, you need to somehow be able to update the withdrawal service so it knows that it can now give out that money that was just deposited. Now with the monolith application that is okay as both services are tightly integrated. So should the application fail then the entire service fails. However, in a microservices design if a particular microservice was to fail or communication was interrupted between the segregated microservices. There is the possibility that somebody could actually fail to withdraw their money because an earlier deposit was never recorded against their account?

So, understanding the integration and importantly the communication protocol between microservices is an important aspect in business logic design. With microservices it can be a little bit complicated, but fortunately GCP have a number of mechanisms to actually monitor and help troubleshoot integration and business logic issues.

So, when designing business logic you may want to use microservices where they make sense in the design. This is typically when many consumers are going to be performing the same single function all the time then deploying microservices makes sense. Of course many times these single functions are closely related and despite being independent are highly dependent on one another.

If for example you have an application where your customers are uploading images all the time then you may think this an ideal case for a microservice. But these images have to be processed so that would mean deploying another microservice for the process of accepting and storing uploads, and then a further microservice at least will be needed to actually process the uploads.

In this case, when there's a popular process consisting of tightly coupled functionality, then using the microservices architecture can actually add overhead without much benefit. So, if you can encapsulate these multi functions all into one consolidated service, you may not need to decompose and segregate the functions down to the microservices level.

This scenario of having tightly couples functions cooperating via a number of microservices requires some overarching logic to actually perform an aggregated and grander function. And this is where Cloud Functions comes into play.

Cloud functions

This is a lightweight computes solution for the GCP that Google offers as a managed service.

It allows developers the freedom to create the single-purpose standalone functions that respond to Cloud events without having to worry about infrastructure or platforms. They can get on with their application without concerning themselves with managing servers or runtime environments.

Cloud Functions runs on JavaScript on node.js, so it can deliver the capability to do both front-end and back-end functions.

Cloud Functions are designed for a microservices business logic integration issues as you're solving the integration problems of having one specific service, whether it's a front-end or back-end service make calls to other services and when it's done to pass along the business logic.

There are unfortunately performance limitations when using Cloud Function as it is not designed to be low latency service even though it's written in very lightweight JavaScript. So as Cloud Functions is a fully managed service, this means you can't really adjust anything within the environment to counteract the latency.

If the latency is a design constraint and you are still committed to using microservices then there are alternatives. You could use the Kubernetes engine, for example, or even Compute Engine as there you can tune and optimized your own environment.

Nonetheless, hopefully latency isn't such an issue that it prevents you from using Cloud Functions for deploying microservices.

What we will explain in the following use case is how to best utilize Cloud Functions when deploying a real-world application. What we're going to do is we're going to be uploading a video file and then we want to transcribe the audio into text and store that as a file.

So, the first thing is that we accept the file upload, and then we have a Cloud Function which is going to perform the transcribing service. Now, Cloud Functions doesn't have this inbuilt logic to perform this task so we are going to use the Google Audio-to-Text API. After processing it's going to accept back whatever text is discovered, and then it's going to pass it on to the next function. However as these are independent single function microservices it will not know what that downstream function is. Therefore, it publishes the output, in this case, transcribed text, to a Cloud Pub/Sub topic.

Essentially, this absolves it of any responsibility for the message, after all it has now done its task. It processed the file, transcribed the audio to text, and then put it onto a queue, and now, that message will to be pulled from the queue by another downstream function.

In the Cloud Pub/Sub vernacular we call these topics, queues and subscriptions. In this case another microservice tasked with writing a file, such as into Word or in PDF format, will have a subscription to that topic. It will simply read from that topic and then create a Word or PDF file before sending the output to Google Cloud Storage and thus completing the process in full.

So, you can see here that for these independent microservice functions to interact there must be additional mechanisms for the transference of the business logic downstream via automation or orchestration. In most cases this coordination between microservices will be triggered by events that are going to be occurring as a matter of course during the execution of the process.

There are several places we can create your event driven triggers such as in your video storage bucket. You can actually publish notification events which we can use to call functions and then of course we have Cloud Pub/Sub, which can be our message queuing service. This allows for inter-process or inter-function communication without them having to know anything about each other.

App Engine

The core benefit of App Engine is often realized through having full code isolation, which enables you to forget about infrastructure and software and just publish your code. Further, the code can be in many languages as all the code is going to be executed through HTTP or RESTful API calls. Within App Engine you already have this isolation of code so you can have multiple versions running simultaneously. However you can also share services amongst them if you like so that despite the code isolation they will be able to communicate with one another. You have the options of using shared Memcache, Cloud Datastore for storage, task queues, or even cron jobs. However as you are limited in effect to running one master applications in production per project this will inevitably incur some overhead.

Mapping Functions and Services

When you consider mapping functions and services you need to consider ensuring that you have a single codebase that is tracking and managing version control. This allows you to do multiple deployments.

To do this you could develop your application inside of Google Cloud Shell as it's managed, this means it is automatically patched and updated. GCS is deployed as a microservice or a micro virtual machine that has five gigs of storage and it acts as a bastion host, which also supports any of the APIs within the Google Cloud infrastructure. In addition, its secure as it is authenticated using Google IAM for authentication and access control and hidden from view.

You will require somewhere secure to store your development source code and you could use Cloud Source Repositories. This private code repository integrates with GitHub but importantly it is segregated in a private location.

Another consideration is that you must ensure separation between the production and development environments in order to isolate different versions of code. This was exactly what the Google App Engine was designed to do. Hence, after writing your build code you can simply upload it directly up to Google App Engine. This type of manual deployment is a feature of App Engine as it allows you to simulate a resource performance such as a data store on your laptop, and then push the code directly up to App Engine.

However in production environments you will want to be automating the process through deployment manager. In this way you can control automation through spate but similar production and development templates. Using templates will ensure that there is a consistent build process. This is a goal of good development as it will allow you to deploy, frequent, consistent, and error free applications.

Custom Images

However sometime we might want to deploy resources with different properties that may explicitly declare some isolated dependency, and we do this by creating custom images.

With custom images you not only stipulate your own separate source code repositories for storing different versions of the code, but now, you can also have separate compute images.

So, if we have certain versions of code and you do not want them all deployed within this standard set of libraries and applications, you can create custom images which can be stored in your own pre-defined source repository.

Now, storing the configuration in the environment will make microservices more difficult to administer and if you try to create it in your own environment you may have external dependencies that are missing. Hence, you may not necessarily want to publish to GitHub sensitive data such as your private SQL database password. In this scenario what you might do is that you store these sensitive configuration properties in an external environment that's dynamic and accessible to the VM upon boot up, such as, from the metadata server, or from a storage area, which can be called externally.

Therefore, you can use a startup scripts to pass attributes to your function code which can dynamically configure the code itself and these scripts will also provide a method to externalize those separately. Similarly, there should be a way for you to control features such as fast startup and graceful shutdown and instance templates are one way that allow you to replicate the same instances every time. There are also managed instance groups, which are another method which will allow us to dynamically upscale and downscale using the same configuration, the same hardware components, and startup scripts and of course, there is also auto-scaling.

With these techniques we have the ability to grow our environment dynamically utilizing preconfigured templates. This provides the opportunity to store the state information within the environment. However, storing state information in the metadata is always going to be localized and that brings us back to horizontal scaling issues. The same is true if you store it on local memory such as in SSD. You may be able to store half a megabyte of state information, whether it is object data, cache data, and you're going to get very low latency and terrific performance but the same scalability issues arise.

 Now if you were to store state information in the network such as in Google Cloud Storage you would have a shared resource available to other instances. However, if you only have a single core virtual machine with only about two gigs worth of throughput, then that could in comparison to SSD increase your applications latency dramatically.

When you start to think about scale and persisting state information you need to contemplate more than just offloading the state as that's part of the design process. But you must understand the ramifications and just how dependent you can be on underlying resource performance. So, measure your service level indicators of state as you start to think where that state is stored, and that is something that is crucial when we think about our process design. When we're mapping our applications compute requirements to the different GCP platform products such as Compute Engine, Apps engine, Kubernetes or Service Functions and in this case, it was our business logic in the application which is reliant on CPU cycles that we need to find a best match. Well, you could run our application using the CPU on a virtual machine, or you could run it in containers on Kubernetes Engine or even App Engine. So, what we like to recommend is, when you're thinking of which platform service can offer exactly what your service needs, first of all think about App Engine this is because it's the quickest to deployment.

After all there are internet-scale companies that have already built their applications on App Engine, like Snapchat for example, they have built a billion-dollar businesses exclusively on the App Engine platform.

App Engine provides you with the ability to get up and running quickly. You're not going to bother with having to tune the run-time environment. Instead you just have to understand the ramifications and if that doesn't work you can always go down the containerization path. Containers can be used on Kubernetes engine and also with App Engine, and of course even the Compute Engine for those unique one-off use cases. Nonetheless, the reason why Google App Engine is often recommended is because it's been around for a while and was specifically developed to be code first.

Once you've chosen a platform or designed an infrastructure, it's now about deploying your applications. If you're not writing your own code and you are going with third party software then you are likely to be going with VMs or docker containers and there's a different architectural design for that. But if you are going with your own microservices or third party functions and APIs then you should look for a platform that allows you to focus on your programming, minimizing your work overhead and gives you dynamic scale and reliability - after all it all built-in to the platform. Choosing the right platform also allows you to autoscale, support different versions, do AB testing, and continuous integration/continuous deployment and also performs canary deployments.

Google also supports containers natively in the Google App Engine Flex Edition, which gives you more flexibility and more time to run your processes before they're killed off. The Google App Engine standard edition would kill an HTTP session after 60 seconds, but now with the Flex edition you can run processes up one hour. So, there is a lot of flexibility with App Engine Flexible Edition so at least look at that in your design process before you go with that old virtual machine route.

Next in line comes the Google Kubernetes engine. The benefit here is there is complete platform independence. You can pick up containers, and run these anywhere even on another cloud provider. With Google Kubernetes Engine there are no operating system dependencies, or infrastructure to worry about as you're still just deploying code and dependencies. However, if you're already using Kubernetes on-premises, this would allow you to integrate and scale, and Google will manage this for you.

Then perhaps not as a last resort we can turn to Compute Engine. This platform is when you need the utmost granular control over the infrastructure and its processing efficiency. It is also a good choice when you need to choose the exact hardware components or the platform instruction set. In this case you may have a dependency on the specific operating system version or perhaps you need direct hardware access, you need local SSDs, GPUs, specific drivers and/or hardware performance has to be tune and optimized.

That's what Compute Engine is designed for, in application development it's usually a one-off case for most projects, but there are situations where the infrastructure must be very specific and meet tight guidelines and that's why Google has this IaaS offering.

So, what about compute system provisioning?

So, now we're going to consider provisioning. We have to decide how the system is going to acquire new resources, and adapt to changing requirements. Remember, App Engine is an auto-scaling platform, Container Engine also autoscales but it is based on distributing and scaling containers and pods within the cluster. But in this case, we will concentrate on Compute Engine and VM's.

So how do we autoscale in Compute Engine where it's not automatic?

Well in Compute Engine you will have to do a little bit more configurations but you should be comfortable with that if you have chosen the compute platform . So, let's think about this, we have our initial Video transcribing Service and as it grows it needs more resources.

We could scale vertically by upgrading the CPU and memory but we started out with a prototype two-core machine. Also one larger box only makes the risk of a single-point-of failure greater so you might want to start considering horizontal scaling. Indeed, horizontal scaling solves many issues especially if you design ahead of time for this kind of flexibility.

Horizontal scaling makes upgrading easy because now you can do rolling deployments. This means you don't have to take the service offline as you would have to do if you were running on one larger server.

The problem is with the horizontal scaling that you should be aware of is that the end-to-end latencies are going to creep up. You are also going to have a lot more networked induced latency and chatter, so we need a different design process. But none of those concerns matter when it comes to scaling.

The limits of horizontal scaling?

We should be careful to not consider horizontal scaling as just being about duplicating servers, as it simply doesn't scale. For example if you having two servers you will certainly have some level of fault tolerance, so if one machine fails then the other one takes over. However that means that you operate both servers at around 40% utilisation for if one server fails the other server will now have to take on 100 percent of the workload. Best practices typically recommend an 'n plus three' model because for example, with an N plus 3 configuration it allows you to spread the load of a failed server across the other surviving servers while maintaining a healthy workload without wasting too many resources.

Furthermore, this model is designed and deployed in the full expectation of failures so the best practice with the n plus 3 configuration is to deploy small stateless servers. In an on-premises setup these would be typically commodity-off-the-shelf servers but with Compute Engine we are not so constrained by choice. We may decide that we can get more efficiency with slightly larger machines, but when you're getting into the hundreds, a quad-core versus a dual-core could make a significant difference. Of course that will be something we actually contemplate when we get around to our budgeting and cost management.

So, now we have to consider the trade-offs. In our Compute Engine design we're going to try and balance latency, capacity, scaling and costs. So, if we start with small stateless servers, then we need to increase reliability and scalability so we may have to have extra boxes. But then we have to worry about coordination, separation and isolation. This would not be an issue with a large powerful server as its all one big box, therefore it's simple to consolidate everything on one machine, and it might even make automated deployments easier.

In order to achieve this balance of design requirements we need to really understand what the stakeholders care about. We also need to write that into our SLO so that we can optimise the design to meet the objectives.

Thus, you will need to be able to plan on adjusting and making trade-offs but so long as you are monitoring and measuring the service indicators as you grow, you will not go far wrong. Just remember not everything in our design is linear in scale. There are going to be at some point potential bottlenecks that we may not know about which is why you should always benchmark and test your scale. If possible work out some estimates as to where the bottlenecks may occur as they can crop up anywhere inside of the actual application or perhaps within the infrastructure and that's why best practices say design first and dimension later.

As a result it is best to start with the fundaments such as with the basic infrastructure. Here you will be looking at whether you need lots of high speed memory, local SSD and what kind of caching and storage. That is all you really need to know to get started but remember all of this can be dynamically changed later. These are important questions as you start to scale, but to begin with just start using a general guideline, and understand the attributes of your business logic. Remember, that the best thing about the cloud is you can always switch and delete a virtual machine and switch out all of its underlying hardware at a later date. Moreover you will not lose any information as the data can easily be saved and attached to a new instance that you can spin up in seconds.

We will cover provisioning of Compute Engine resources in the next section when we consider the design for our video application.

Chapter 22 - Use Case: Cloud Service Design

This use case concerns cloud service design and it is used to introduce the approach to developing a new Video Transcribe Service. This will be a cloud-native application that will evolve and develop throughout the remaining chapters of the book as we further tune the design.

The applications design focuses on applying the principles that were learned in the previous chapters. In this use case, we're going to introduce a very basic video transcribing service.

Proof of Concept

The first step in our product design will be to make a proof-of-concept model in order to give us confidence that it will actually work. This doesn't require any infrastructure as it's a very simple process so we can walk through the process manually. We do this simply by loading a few videos onto a local computer and then manually inputting them into a video transcribing API and capturing the resultant text output as a file. We can also time the process and measure the CPU and memory load. However, as all the application heavy lifting is done via a third party API running on another Google cloud service so our system resource utilization shouldn't be a major issue.

Now that we have a demonstrable proof-of-concept the next stage will to automate and design the physical infrastructure for a prototype. Hence, we will start with the task of gathering the design requirements. Initially this raises some issues as it's a brand new service so we don't really know how popular it will be. This means that some of our requirements will be simply guesswork. A second concern is that our potential users are going to be on the internet, so that means they could be anywhere in the world.

What we do know, however, is the users are going to access the application via a web browser from their computer or mobile device. Essentially, the user will upload a video and our service is going to generate a transcribed text file of the audio. The resulting Word or PDF file will then be sent back to the user.

Design Specification & Requirements

As for application performance; speed will be an issue but that is largely out with our control as it is an API hosted by a third party. But as we don't want the whole user experience to take too long we need to improve the upload and file write processes which are under our direct control. So, we would like to keep the entire user experience to under a minute for a 5min video, this beats the estimated transcribing time on our proof of concept computer. Forecasting the resources we might need is problematic as we don't know how popular the service is going to be or the traffic it is likely to generate so we will start small and have the capability to scale quickly. With regards, scale, we will start off with a single virtual machine with a couple of cores. The VM will be hosted in just one location to begin with until we see where our users are coming from. Hence, we will go for some central location in the US.

With regards availability, as this is a new service having high-availability is not an immediate design criteria as no-one is reliant on its services. But, we will design for future redundancy to be easily accomplished via an upgrade at a later stage.

Business Logic

Next we will examine the application's business logic, in order to clarify how this video transcribing service is going to work in practice. To understand this clearly we need to comprehend and be able to visualise the process path. Basically, we want to take a video and then run it through a transcribe API to get a text file of the audio track. Therefore, to start with we will have some kind of user interface as our front end presentation perhaps it's a website, perhaps it's an application on a mobile platform. It doesn't really matter, the point is that there will be some logic on a user device, which will decide where and how the video is coming in to the application. The actual upload process is then going to ingest the uploaded videos and we're going to store them somewhere. Whether we store them temporarily, or store them on disc or in memory, it doesn't matter.

Then we're going to have to process the video file and send it via the API where a third party service provides the transcription process on the video file and outputs a text file back out to some kind of storage, then we're going to serve it back to the user, through that same user interface as before.

Building a Prototype

Now that we understand the logic and the basic process path for our simple application, we can go ahead and start to create some design to build our prototype. So, here is how we build our prototype service. Remember we start small and rough so here is our basic prototype 'back of a beermat' design.

Specifications and Requirements

We initially define a service level objective (SLO), which states our intention is to run the service for 23 hours a day and that gave us an hour each day as a maintenance window and that comes out to about 95.83% availability. We set this SLO because we want our system to be robust and available but we are also well aware that in the early days there will be much tuning and upgrading to be done so we will need a daily service window. But we're going to measure this by simply measuring whether the server is up or down.

With regards the infrastructure specifications we're going to provision a single VM with dual cores and 7.5 GB of memory and it's going to run on a single Compute Engine instance. However we also need some persistent-storage to upload our video files and we're also going to store the process log files as well so we will need a storage location for them. That will become important as the application grows, so we need to keep the application separate from the log data it's generating.

The basic design is now going to look like this:

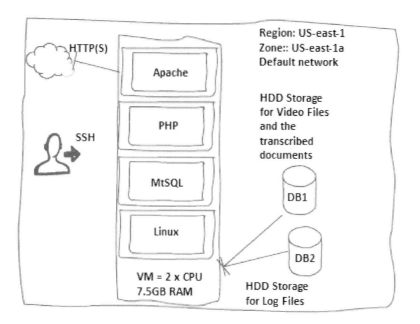

Prior to launching we might want to consider stress testing the system so we can see it can work to the scale that we anticipated. Further, stress testing at various loads can quickly surface any bottlenecks in the process.

Once you are satisfied that the system will perform under anticipated load you will have to continue testing in production. Moving a system from development into production can be done in several ways. One way is to perform a rolling launch. This is where you can roll out the service to a small number of users. For example, the service could be made available internally first of all. If it goes well then you can make it available to a subset of customers, and just start to deploy to more and more customers over time. When it comes to testing and upgrades then you can also do AB testing, roll out upgrades or canary deployments, whichever minimizes user disruption. There are a number of different ways depending on the scale and the amount of interruption that would be tolerated by your users.

Use case - 22

Now that we have the application up and running we are beginning to get some feedback that the service started to perform okay but declined over time. Now we have to troubleshoot this problem and try to find out why the application is not performing as expected. We will need to determine what is the actual root cause of the deterioration of service?

We will also have to have to check our measurements to obtain quantifiable data in order to determine the extent of the slow-down and what we can do about it.

However in this case our NOC team are informed that the application is lagging and users are reporting that the application is performing very slowly. So, you now have confirmation that the video transcription service is working very slowly and not meeting your SLO. This of course raises a few questions such as; what's causing the service to run slowly? And what weakness can you find in your earlier design that you can fix?

Therefore it is necessary to take a systematic and logical approach to troubleshooting so that you are addressing the root causes as to why these symptoms are occurring.

This is where collaboration and communication is important because it's often not one system, team or person involved. Instead we tend to use as a team the 'Five Why's' iterative interrogation technique to explore possible root cause and the effect on processes and relationships.

So, now that we have our Video Transcription Service under the scrutiny of a design team let's break down the business logic behind the process flow:

- First you have a User Interface (UI), something presented to the user that allows you to present you service and offer the user an interface to upload their video.

- The next process will require that you accept the video and that you store it using some kind of processing logic in the local file-system.
- The true processing comes when the application reacts to a notification of a new video, which triggers a processes that executes the Google Audio-to-Text API.
- On completion the API posts the text output and the downstream process that writes the file will pick it up and convert the raw text into Word or PDF format
- Finally the application will handle local storage and returning the text file to the user.

If we measure all these individual processes we will be likely to identify where the process flow may be experiencing a bottleneck that is causing a poor user experience. After all it appears that something is going wrong internally with one of these independent processes. Consequently, the first possible cause that comes to mind is usually based on your own past experience, but if it is a new service we will often not really fully understand the different behaviours of the service.

However if we take a deeper dive into the behaviour of each modular process we can often get a better view of what is going on. For example to start with if we focus on the User Interface, this is where the user interacts with a standard web server. If the unit testing of the web service appears to be okay then we move on to the file upload process.

The upload of the video file is going to be done through the HTTP protocol. Also the stream is going to be handled by high-throughput writes to disk so the disk I/O transactions shouldn't be a problem.

Next we have the transcribe process from the video's audio channel to text conversion. This is actually handled by a third party API so this shouldn't cause problems unless there are delays in continually having to make and authenticate connections because all you really are doing is preparing the API parameters and sending it to the external transcription service. The final stage is generating a text file as output that will be stored on disk. On the other hand there are our log files that we will be generating and you are storing these locally, so that could potentially use up some disk I/O cycles. Now we have to consider the video file storage capacity and process. After all this amounts to a potentially a lot of files both large and small so you might have to worry about the file system's capacity. The application could grow to being a disk I/O intensive process and that could be a potential performance issue too. Then you have to take into consideration the file writing process and how the transcribed text file will be delivered back to the user.

So now when you unit test each process and you discover that the slow user experience is being impacted primarily by the API transcription process. So what do you do?

One thing you can do is to separate the user-interface web service from the back-end high utilisation CPU process? By doing this you will reduce the memory allocations on the web servers so now you can support more active sessions. Also you can now combine all the logic into the one app server application. This means that the underpinning business logic is still being handled by the web server which is handling the user experience in both ingesting and serving the videos. But now the video storage, the processing, and the output of the text file storage, is going to be handled by a separate process on a separate VM instance.

So this is what we come up with:

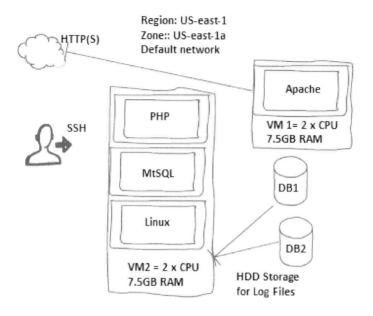

However by separating our design we bring about another design challenge and that is that in doing so we have split the process logging across the frontend and the backend. This means processing the logs is more difficult as they are now stored on different servers. Fortunately, they do share a common session ID field so we need to have a process that will join those logs together for analysis during troubleshooting.

Hence, the new design challenge is to address log aggregation. What we now have to do is have a service that will match the session IDs and stitch them together into a single log file. In this case, we have logs on two different servers and the goal is to aggregate them into a single log file. Hence, what we need here is a logging server that's sole purpose will be to accept logs using something like a daily cron job that's going to take all these log files and it's going to aggregate them.

This isn't a particularly good design but it is simple and sufficient for our needs and meets the design specifications for scale. Thus our revised design looks like this:

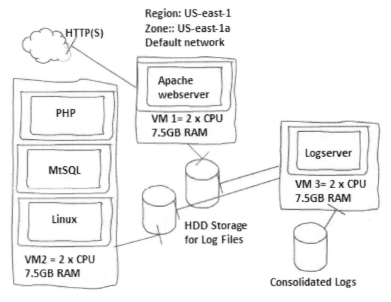

The way it will do this will be to ingest log files from both sources then combine them in a single log file. But we also need to transform the file so that all the data is sorted by the unique session ID, so we need to join the log files together based on that session ID.

 Fortunately the logs are simply a Session ID, a Timestamp and a Payload of maximum 256 bytes. Hence, we want to match on the session IDs on both the web server and apps server logs and then append them together via a simple transform process. The logging service output will then be the aggregated log files we require. Then the cron job will go ahead and run every 24 hours.

Chapter 23 – Cloud Architecture Layers

The data layer covers the storage and retrieval of data, including the mechanisms of storage and retrieval, such as databases and file systems, including the access methods that use the services, such as SQL and API's.

Data layer design

The data layer includes; the data persistent mechanisms, such as the database services and storage services, and the data access layer, which encapsulates the persistent mechanisms that exposes the data.

There are many ways to characterize data such as structured or unstructured, persistent or ephemeral but our chief concern should be in characterizing data based on what the user cares about. Typically, the user is pretty much neutral about the underlying technology as they are concerned far more about whether the data is accessible when they need it. And whether the data they retrieve is the same data they stored and not modified or deleted in other words they care about data integrity.

Users can't really distinguish the difference between data access, data corruption, extended unavailability or other engineering terms as they just want their data to be available when they request it. For example if you change a user's privileges on some data denying them access to say read or even list a file then from their perspective the file is lost. Therefore, our data storage design methods should aim at persistence, proactive detection and rapid recovery from the users' perspective.

Furthermore, should there be a case where data is somehow accidentally lost we want to be able to get it back, recover it through available methods or techniques such as using version controls or replicated data stores or some kind of live streaming backup mechanism.

So when you're contemplating data storage, you need to think about the data transaction properties and if maintaining state is going to be required. Then of course there is the CAP Theorem, which makes designers aware of the trade-offs required when making networked shared data systems.

CAP Theorem

Basically, you have to choose a balance or trade-off between having consistency, availability, or partition tolerance as you can't have all three.

Thus, if you want availability and partition tolerance, you can go over to BASE, which is reassuring called basically available storage. Now, what that means is, you may make an update but it may not show immediately but it will eventually. This is due in part to data being distributed across many tables or cubes and even across servers so it takes time for updates to propagate over all instances of the data. The advantages with that type of availability are that it allows you to write data very quickly and eventually everything will all be consistent. This makes BASE suitable for Big Data soft state applications.

Now if you were demanding pure data consistency, then you would need ACID transactions which stand for atomicity, consistency, isolation, and durability. That means if you write some data to your data storage system, it is guaranteed to be there and be consistent as soon as you get an acknowledgement. This makes ACID highly suited to transactional systems.

When designing data storage solutions we have to understand the user data consistency requirements and the properties and nuances of the potential solutions.

For example, what if we consider Google Cloud Storage?

Cloud Storage Properties

With Google Cloud Storage, you definitely will get a lot of data consistency capabilities, such as its inherent mechanisms of read after write, read after metadata update, read after delete. Therefore, if you've uploaded data, you'll instantly get it listed and have access to it, similarly, if you delete something it will be gone instantly. Any time you list the actual items in the bucket, those are guaranteed, and that is the exact list as of the time of that request. However consistency can be sometimes ambiguous under certain circumstances and actually sometimes GCS can display the properties of an eventual consistency nature. This is apparent if you use versioning as that will depend on how often you run the update to overwrite the data.

We also see this eventual consistency behaviour when we apply access controls to data in GCS. For example if you wanted to decline access to data by changing the privileges.

However that security update requires a wide distribution mechanism throughout Google. This mechanism ensures that all Google's security tables are updated, but that can take time. Therefore security privileges may not show up instantly they may be inconsistent for several hours.

There is also another use case where GCS displays eventual consistency and this is when caching an object. Caching does not show strong consistency as you could have an older version in cache until the next refresh. That's a well-known trade-off with cache, consistency versus performance, as you can only get that high consistency with low cache performance.

So when you look at the properties that you're trying to optimize. You want to be able to choose a specific service, which meets the requirements of the data. For example, if you are concerned about uptime, which is essentially, how often the data is going to be available and accessible to the user. Then the ideal solution is going to make the data immediately available.

But that will also require that you contemplate the latency. This is how quick your data can be made available to your users. For example, early web designers didn't often appreciate this fully and they used large images and slow downloading static data on a website, which took ages to appear. Therefore latency is something you must consider because it doesn't take long for a user to abort a task if it appears to have hung. But if the task is unavoidable slow at least warn the user that it may take a few minutes as user patience is very limited.

Another property that we need to consider with data storage is scale, how large will it grow? And there is another closely related property, velocity, how fast will it potentially grow?

What you need to be considering here is whether once you hit certain thresholds you can really keep scaling the solution out on the fly, or is it really going to need some serious re-architecting?

Data Regulatory Compliance

In May 2018 and in early 2019, we saw regulation such as the GDPR and the CCPA introduced respectively that set strict controls on user data privacy. These are just two of the regulations that are appearing worldwide that set penalties for the loss or the inappropriate use of customers' personal data. One of the key controls is deleting users' personal data once it is no longer required.

So we need to ensure that personal data is destroyed and cannot be recovered and this must be done after a reasonable amount of time. But of course there also has to be conflicting safety mechanisms. For example we will want at different times a mechanism that will allow us to recover accidentally deleted data if required, but will also need to ensure that once deliberately deleted that data is gone and it never comes back.

Navigating Storage and DB options

Google Cloud Platform offers a wide variety of storage and database services.

This section will show you a general method you can use to narrow down the list of potential data storage solutions.

To simplify the choice we can use a decision tree to narrow down the choices.

The first branch on the decision tree is;

- Is your data structured or unstructured,
- If it is unstructured then Cloud storage is perfect as this is going to be globally available, replicated, it uses APIs, which makes it a lot more available than the unstructured alternative of using a persistent disk attached to a VM.

- Are you doing analytics on the data?
- If you're going to be performing analytics, then you want to contemplate using either Cloud Bigtable if you need very low latency, you want to do frequent updates, or BigQuery for large data warehouses, just storing petabytes of data either streamed or in batch or being able to query very massive datasets.
- Is your data relational?
- Do you need to draw insights from that data?
- You can even do that from Cloud BigQuery, but if you need frequent updates and very tight schemas and you've got a lot of data that's going to be coming in and updated often, you'll be looking at one of these two relational choices, either Cloud SQL, which is MySQL, SQL Server or PostgreSQL, or the newly released global relational database called Cloud Spanner. Now, this gives us the utmost in scalability, also partition tolerance across zones. It is the panacea of cloud offerings when it comes to relational databases.
- Then finally, if nothing else fits, do you need mobile SDKs? Are you going to be plugging this into something like an App Engine or Kubernetes? Well, Firebase for mobile SDKs and Cloud Datastore for high transactions.

Use case – 23: Data Layer

It seems that something is wrong with the video transcribe application. We are getting reports that the service fails to product a transcription file every time. This failure to return the transcribed text file has become more frequent and is resulting in a poor customer experience.

The issue appears to be random so how can you change the design to address this intermittent problem?

Solution

The first stage is for you to try and ascertain the root cause of the problem so we use the Five Whys analysis technique once again.

Defining the Problem

What we know so far is that the video transcription service is growing and the number of users is increasing rapidly. However, there are increasing reports that sometimes the service fails to produce a transcribed text file and the issue appears to be intermittent and so difficult to replicate.

However after some prolonged systematic and logical troubleshooting by the team they've answered the five why's. Consequently, the team has determined that the root problem is the persistent disk on the application server. Their belief is that the Disk I/O performance cannot meet the demands being placed on it as there is not enough virtual machine disc I/O performance. Therefore as demand increases the disk I/O can't keep up so it randomly starts dropping transactions.

Here is our business logic;

- We are ingesting videos for transcription into a front-end web service

- The webservers directly upload the video files into block storage on the local HHD persistent storage drives
- Video processing is handled by a separate application VM that downloads the video file from the upload servers for processing via the API.
- The application server combines both the storage processing, the video transcription API handling, and the additional text file storage processing, as well as a final file writing process before it sends it back to the user via the web server.

The team's belief is that because the persistent disc I/O was increasing it was causing scaling issues and had become the bottleneck. But there was another issue and that was that now the service was handling up to one thousand video uploads per day and that was a bit much for our local file system, which wasn't able to handle the demand. This is because we are relying on the operating system's file system to perform all off the required disk I/O and indexing. So we have two issues both related to data storage, one, the poor disk I/O performance, and two, the VM OS file system performance.

The solution

What we can do to resolve these issues is to replace the persistent disk storage with Google Cloud Storage as this will decouple our storage and provide unlimited scale. However it will require that we rewrite our application code as we will need to use API calls to the Cloud Storage bucket instead directly accessing our original file system lookups. What we have to take into consideration is that making this change is not going to induce unacceptable additional latency that will affect overall system performance.

The potential performance issue comes about due to both the transcribe and rewrite processes are now handling files that are no longer on connected persistent drives, instead they will have to be retrieved across the network, so the actual processing time will be longer.

So, how does this affect our business logic?

Well, the business logic is the same, but the logic steps are different as the video storage will now start on the data storage service and the processing and rewrite services will pick up the videos from the GCS. When finished the written file will then be output back to GCS before being picked up for delivery to the user by the front-end webserver.

Presentation Layer Design

The presentation layer concerns itself with the flow of data across the network and through the system so for example between the user, business logic, and the data storage. Thus the presentation layer design means configuring the network for data transfer within the service and also the network edge for integration with other environments.

In general, with presentation layer design there will be a direct trade-off as the more that you distributed elements through your design the more tolerant the system will be of outages. On the other hand this increased fault tolerance comes at a cost as there are real performance limitations because the round trip time is much longer and unpredictable between distant elements in a distributed design. Furthermore, in GCP, there are those egress data traffic charges to consider.

Intelligent Traffic Management

In a good presentation layer design we need to consider implementing Intelligent Traffic Management (ITM) into the design. ITM is based on three factors, location, load balancing and caching. Fortunately, as we covered earlier the Google Cloud platform offers a robust set of load balancing and caching services that are optimized for different use cases.

Location

Distributed networks offer greater reliance to outages and are more available but they suffer from introduced latency. In networking latency – delay - and jitter – variations in latency – are hugely important as they have a very large effect on application and system performance and also ultimately the user's experience. A clear example is when you witness a developer proudly demonstrating their application on their laptop and then compare its almost instant and seamless flow against the same application when hosted on the network. This is because, inter-process flows within an application or host machine are much faster that communications between external hosts. These inter-system interactions might only be measured in milliseconds, but that in network terms can be considered a lifetime. Therefore, network design and the placement and locations of interacting entities must be carefully thought out.

For example, if you are sending a two kilobyte packet over one gig network connection you can do this in 2000th of a second. However when it comes to a round-trip time (RTT) across the same network and within the same data center then the RTT will be around 5000th of a second, sometimes even faster, depending on the design.

However, if you try to send that same packet across the internet, from say California to the Seoul and back again then you will be lucky if the RTT are around 200 milliseconds and they may also have considerable jitter.

Fortunately with GCP, any regional and inter-continental RTT is considerably faster and more deterministic thanks due to Google's global fibre network. However, even with Google's fibre there are design considerations you will need to put in place to reduce latency and increase user experience.

As a rule of thumb you can consider that only around five to seven round trips between continents are possible per second but within a data center approximately 2000 RTT per second can be achieved. These are generalizations but you must understand the underlying principle to locate data closer to the user or better still actually locate your application in multiple data centres around the region or the world depending upon your customer location footprint.

Load Balancing

One we have considered the importance of location we now need to look at the technology that allows you to control the location of the network resources used by your service. This technology is called Load balancing.

We covered the load balancing offers from GCP earlier but there are a few tips that we can add here. First of all, when you need to communicate over the internet you have to have a public external IP addresses. Google does supply external IPs that you can assign to virtual machines, but you're only allowed seven static IP addresses per project. Hence the best practice is to recommend you use those external IPs on a load balancer.

Now, if you're doing a network or an internal load balancer, you're going to get any external IP that you can use as part of the managed service. Nonetheless, Google does have a reserve set of global IP addresses available to you should you require them.

The caveat is though that these external IPs are available only for GCP global load balancers and that's because they are Google configured and advertised BGP routes that are announced at every single pop in the world. The BGP routing protocol is what makes the Internet work so that your customers will enter the Google network as close, within say 250 to 500 miles, to any major location or any major city in the world. Furthermore, Google's networks are far faster than the Internets in general so this will be a major boost from your customer's perspective of application performance and responsiveness.

Caching

There are other ways to increase the user experience when it comes to application responsiveness and performance. Indeed one highly effective way is to distribute your applications or data around the world and this is how cloud Content Delivery Network provides. The idea behind CDN is that the cloud service can push and cache content closer to your customers in order to dramatically improve the performance and reduce latency when using your applications. To use the CDN, all you have to do is turn on HTTP(S) load balancing or any other network load balancing so from the network layer, you can automatically start to cache any data that goes through the HTTP(S) load balancer. But you can also push and publish content directly from Google Cloud stores to the CDN.

Moreover, CDN is very affordable as any egress data charges from cloud CDN or even one of our cloud CDN providers, is reduced by 50 percent.

Use Case – 23 – Presentation Layer

The transcription service is now working reliably with no further recorded issues with application failures or unfulfilled requests. Nonetheless, there have recently been reported some intermittent slowdowns of the service. In the reported cases it appears that users are experiencing delays and when this is the case then it's taking an increasingly long time for the system to respond with a transcribed file. Again, as the issue is intermittent it is not easily reproducible and per the users reports it does not persist for very long. Therefore, we start by defining the problem, collecting operational data and logs and then applying the 5Y technique. Hence, our problem definition is that our video transcription service seems to suffer from periodic slowdowns, which means that under certain unexplained conditions the service is for a short period very slow, but normally it's fast.

From our logs we can see clearly that the transcription service is growing in popularity and this can be seen through the number of transcriptions files being generated. But the logs also confirm that there is a slowdown during peak periods and it can take up to several minutes after submitting a video for the transcription file to be returned to the user.

Now if we consider the business logic we can see that:

- The Video Transcription Service has a front-end web server, which is responsible for uploading the videos
- We then store the videos as an object in a Google Cloud Storage bucket,

- Then the Transcription Server will extract the video and process it.

The issue is that sometimes it's taking minutes to generate transcriptions. The team's conclusion is that the issue is definitely tied to the capacity of the system to generate transcriptions. It's also been established that it isn't the front-end web server that is causing the delays, but the back-end transcription generating service, which is failing to keep up with demand.

This could be because our application server is overloaded at peak times and running out of CPU. Indeed we can see that the CPU utilization isn't linear and during peak traffic it is going to 100%.

Solution

It was determined that if our application was to be able to keep up with demand in a timely fashion then it would have to scale. So instead of scaling vertically by upping the CPU and Memory we decided to scale horizontally by adding a load balancer and increasing the number of transcription servers.

This is quite easy to do as all we have to do is distribute identical code across each VM in the instance group of application servers. The cluster of application servers will help reduce the CPU by distributing the workload across the cluster.

However, this solution brings a new issue as it now means that instead of a single app server log, you now have logs coming from each server in the pool. This requires that we revisit the design of the backend logging service to accommodate the new scalable application cluster logging design.

There is another potential issue and that is the new multi-application layer design will mean that the application logs will be growing and a single logging server may not be sufficient to process and aggregate all the logs.

The simplest solution is to put an internal load balancer in front of multiple instances of our logging server. So again we can adopt an auto scaling instance group that will collect the logs as they're ingested and feed them directly to Big Table. In this scenario, we can run our queries, get our session IDs, and it scales well.
So now are design is beginning to take shape:

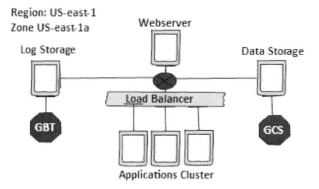

Chapter 24 - Resilient or High-Availability Design

This chapter deals with resiliency, which is the ability of a system to stay available and to automatically recover from problems. As such we can say that resiliency is the quality of a design that accounts for and handles failure.

One principle of design is that sometimes a quality you want in the system isn't readily available and you need to take a radically different approach in design to accommodate it.

In this case, the elusive quality that we are looking for is availability. Now to build that quality into our design we must contemplate the potential causes and sources of failure.

So a highly available or resilient web application is one that continues to function despite expected or unexpected failures of components in the system. So if a single instance fails or an entire zone experiences a problem, a resilient application remains fault tolerant, continuing to function and repairing itself automatically if necessary.

So we have to redesign our application so that is highly resilient to failure and highly available.

Causes of failure

First of all we have to define the causes of failure as typically it's due to a loss of a dependency or due to overload. And this is where business continuity becomes so important, i.e., How does the business continue to run if there is a failure or in the worst scenario in disaster recovery? The solution is through developing a scalable and resilient design as it is necessary to mitigate all the potential risks associated with failure.

So to demonstrate this we're going to have an out-of-service issue with our video transcription service, and then we're going to have to redesign our logging system.

Unfortunately there is no way to eliminate the threat of errors and loss as they are going to happen and that is inevitable. So the challenge isn't to avoid the threat, but to accept and mitigate risk. Hence, the need to design systems, which are resilient to failures caused by the unexpected loss of resources. Of course loss could be through a single point of failure or by correlated loss so we need to cover all the potential risk surfaces.

This is why Google came up with their own processes and best practices to try to mitigate some risk of loss, such as;

- Don't depend on hardware.
- Design and build modular software that you monitor.
- Use canary testing to minimize the risk your customers from the pain of any bugs or issues.
- Understand that people are a major source of loss so review procedures and understand a proper escalation path.
- Finally, communication you have to have a design process that communicates with your customers, other team members and stakeholders.

So why don't you design your applications along the lines of the Internet that is designed to work around expected loss. Hence;

Anticipate failure, design for failure, and fail gracefully.

Now if we consider the risk of loss in our design we should start with identifying any single points of failure. As a single point of failure could be anything, within the design, for example it could be hardware, software, power sources and network links. Unfortunately this means expensive replication of just about everything and this is why we have disaster recovery hot sites. Fortunately replication is much easier and a lot cheaper in the cloud so it is feasible for even non-critical applications. But if we have designed to avoid single points of failure this becomes even easier. Some best practices when it comes to designing to avoid single points of failure are;

- Design for existing maintenance, i.e. a spare for the spare, so N+2.
- So don't make any single unit too large.
- Focus where you can on microservices.
- Don't concentrate responsibility onto a single process's server.
- Plan where you're going to maintain a single source of state
- Try to make units interchangeable clones. Microservices, Containers and the modules in Google App Engine are the way to do this that you can simply clone your applications and then just throw them onto any piece of hardware so that you can even fail over easily and rapidly, even to another cloud provider if required.

Correlated Failures

Correlated failures are when something fails and this directly causes a huge chain of events, for example if a zone or region is lost, all the resources in it will inevitably fail. This is what we call a failure domain. So you need to identify during the design process any potential failure domain that could create a correlated set of failures. The best practices around this are dividing business logic into services based on failure domains. In which case you are not just contemplating resiliency for individual components but entire failure domains.

It does make this easier to look at it from a high level perspective for example identifying failure domains at the zone or regional level. The goal is to separate and isolate the risk of correlated failures and at the same time design independent but collaborative services.

Failure due to Overload

When a system is overloaded the system eventual will exhibit nonlinear behaviour, such as local or even adjacent applications may hang, crash, disks start thrashing or just stop responding altogether.

Now overloading occurs for several reasons but a common reason is due to a very specific relationship between failure due to loss and failure due to overload. For example, if a system goes offline due to the loss of a downstream resource then that system is also lost to upstream systems that depend upon it so they in turn have to queue up the work. However, when the system suddenly comes back online then that queued backlog of work is sent across and it will need to be processed before any new work can be handled. This may well be too much for the system to handle and it then goes from being totally unavailable due to resource loss, to totally unavailable due to overload.

Here are some common behaviours of failure due to overload that you should recognize as these occur when a resource crosses into a nonlinear behaviour by running out of memory,

running out of disk which causes thrashing of the disk. It can stop responding, perhaps there's no network available or the CPU is too high.

Regardless of the symptoms, what will likely happen is its unavailability creates this huge chain of effect and all dependent services will fail. In identifying potential points of overload we need to take an overall look at the networking service architecture. This because once you have overload on a resource for example and overloaded frontend there is a huge list of cascading failures that will more than likely occur. But it can be very difficult to try to troubleshoot when you have all of these independent alarms being triggered.

This is why you have to identify in the design process what are the important first things that can happens, which indicate an overload.

This is why measuring and logging data is so important as it will enable you to determine what was the first thing to alarm. Therefore we must plan for monitoring the individual services but from the user experience as well, which might help give us additional clues.

When designing to prevent cascading failures; prevention is the best strategy as it can be very difficult to roll back once it occurs. To do this we really want to monitor a resource's threshold and set safe limits. For example, we want to make sure our CPUs utilisation don't exceed a safe threshold and if they do then we want to autoscale a little bit earlier to prevent overload. Setting the trigger threshold lower allows us to be proactive and keep one step ahead. The cost of adding VM resources as additional servers to absorb the short-term or even longer-term traffic load should not be an issue because what is the alternative cost of downtime.

So for example if we started to experience overload in the frontend we would want to auto-scale in order to increase the size of our clusters for failover, not just for operating capacity.

Also remember the best practice of n+2 in order to handle for failover under routine maintenance conditions, but also adding additional resources so you can handle growth.

Nonetheless, adding clusters by themselves may also lead to overload if we are not careful. This is because if one server is distributing to a clustered backend it can become a bottleneck. This is because it alone has to handle the requests from each cluster node. Therefore we need to cluster in pairs and keep redistributing two clusters of nodes through different tiers. This solves a lot of issues as it limits the single server fan-in issue because you no longer have exactly one node distributing to every single node in the cluster. Another issue it mitigates is the queries of death overload failure caused by feedback loops.

This occurs when failed requests are continuously resent causing further overload of an already stressed resource. The design problem though is that although you are trying to make the system more reliable by adding retries it also creates the potential for an overload.

There is a trade-off required when considering retries between how often you retry and how much you back-off. With a back-off you set a penalty each time to discourage being swamped by retries. This is the same concept that you see in Gmail when it retries after a connection is lost. It is also the way that BGP handles all those flapping links on the Internet by ignoring them via a back-off process called route dampening. Using a back-off algorithm is a really good concept that you can apply to a lot of health checks and retries.

Use case - 24

The popular video transcription services suddenly crashed. Therefore like before we need to define the issue and then develop a process to rectify the problem and then try to ensure that this will not happen again.

This time the troubleshooting to determine the root cause is easier as an entire zone failed in GCP. Unfortunately, all the backend transcription services were in that single region and zone. So our goal will be to design controls that protect against a future zone outage.

This was designed that way as the app was not considered to be business critical but its growing popularity and use now makes it so.

In this case, a decision has been made to replicate the entire architecture between region: US-east1 and region: US-west-1. This will also give us better geographical diversity across the US in addition to region/zone redundancy.

However, by introducing scalability and redundancy into our primitive design we can't help noticing one glaring issue. The issue is that we now have only one front end webserver which is not only a single point of failure it is also vulnerable to a feedback loop coming from the app cluster that will cause overload. So what we need to do now is add a webserver cluster to distribute the load and provide redundancy.

Now the webserver cluster will need to be fronted by the global HTTP(S) load balancer. Deploying a cluster of webservers resolves the fanning and feedback loop issues but raises a bigger issue as how to handles state as our cluster will need to be stateless. This was the reason we were reluctant to move away from the one webserver design for it was a prime location for handling stored user experience, and the state information.

The issue with maintaining state is that we now have multiple webservers handling user connections and passing the user's session state back through to the transcription servers. Furthermore, when the webservers actually retrieve data from the data storage server they need to know the correct user session ID.

Therefore the new design problem is how to maintain user session state throughout the entire business logic process or isolate state by breaking it out into many different microservices.

If we consider the business logic we can see that our webservers need to become stateless – if they are to scale and not be a single-point of failure. However the applications servers don't really care about session state but the strorage does need to track state to identify the correct objects for each specific user. Therefore we need to define some kind of state storage. We can do this because the transcription servers don't really need to handle state. In this case, we could use Google Cloud Storage as it must maintain state in order to pass the correct transcription files back to the webserver.

But that isn't our only issue as we still have a problem with aggregated logs as working on day old logs is not good in a production environment. Furthermore, having day old logs not only prevents us quickly resolving issues it prevents us have better SLOs. Indeed the way to resolve this issue also points towards deploying a microservice architecture design.

The idea here is that if we were to refactor the application into separate microservices we could get much more granular control over messaging and queuing. By controlling queuing we can be assured that we will not overload any other service but to do that we need to deploy Google Cloud Pub/Sub as it does allow for real time if we can process the messages quickly enough. Nonetheless, if we cannot Pub/Sub will store the message as a topic subscription. However. now that we are refactoring for microservices we need not only Pub/Sub but a method for event triggering of specific microservices and for that we can use Cloud Functions.

With regards to aggregate logging we can now use Cloud functions to trigger events and as it is tightly integrated with Pub/Sub it will create published topics that will be ingested inside of Bigtable.

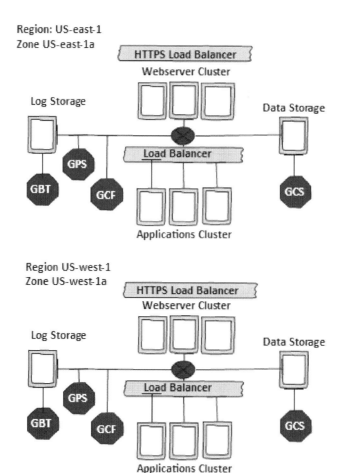

With this design we now have Pub/Sub as a scalable messaging queuing processing services, as well as Cloud Function for scalable microservices so we don't need the log clusters or the crone job anymore as we can do streaming log processing.

Chapter 25 – Security by Design and by Default

There are three kinds of security services built into the Google Cloud platform.

The first kind are services that are transparent and automatic, such as encryption of data that occurs automatically when data is transported and when it's at rest.

The second kind are services that have defaults but that offer methods for customizations,

such as using your own encryption keys rather than those provided.

And the third kind are services that can be used as part of your security design, but only contribute to security if you choose to use them in your design.

Google takes a multi-layered approach, and their security team do not assume that they can keep everything secure and everybody out as that isn't feasible in a multi-tenant customer accessible cloud. Instead Google takes a shared responsibility approach, where they expect the customer to play their part in responsibly managing the security of certain aspects and Google will takes responsibility for the rest.

When it comes to areas that fall under Google's responsibility they take a defence in depth approach. This security model uses different layers of security controls to restrict unauthorised access. But should an intruder get through the policy is to try to isolate and discourage them by ensuring that it's very difficult for them to do anything meaningful.

Therefore in this chapter we will contemplate cloud security and all that entails such as; network access control, firewalls, denial of service, resource sharing and isolation, data encryption and key management, as well as identity access management and auditing. As these are all part of the security stack.

In order to demonstrate these techniques being applied during the design process we will also apply this to our video transcription service. So we will create a scenario where our application is under an intentional attack. Then we will consider the options available for designing our defences in depth strategy.

Pervasive Defence in Depth

One major advantage to the migration of applications to a cloud environment is that you benefit from the inherent security controls. An example is with Google Cloud Platform where your application inherit all of the existing security controls already in place protecting Google's own applications and environment. Therefore you need to know about them so you don't go duplicating them or leaving gaps in your own security position. So Google's strategy for cloud security is what they call pervasive defence in depth and it starts with transparency.

The importance of transparency is that you need to know which parts of security is Google's responsibility and which parts are yours, which is achieved via a segregation of duties. However Google does provide you with the tools to access and monitor your service as they want you to leverage the Google Cloud Platform security controls when designing your own security model. Nonetheless, depending on the technology there are different approaches and areas of responsibility.

Cloud Networking

A prime example of the concept of defence in depth being implemented in practice is with cloud networking security. A fundamental concept is that of the virtual private cloud (VPC) as they can be completely isolated networks. The idea being that the least exposure to the internet the better.

However, the customer must be able to connect securely from the internet to provision their VPC applications and services. Hence, there are secure cloud interconnect methods that allows you to connect on-premises networks to either VPN or private interconnect to third-party cloud providers.

Another layer of defence is that GCP supports third-party virtual appliances, which are virtual machines running security audited applications that you can install.

Finally, there are the Google load balancers and the Google network with all its battle-hardened security controls and vast operational experience in protecting Google's own applications and assets.

Customer Security Controls

The security level where the customer can have a significant impact is on network level access control. For example, in locking down access to reduce the potential attack surface.

This can be done via the GCP network access control and firewalls.

The Customer can set up their own rules for firewalls and it really is their first line of defence. By doing so they are trying to prevent any unauthorized access to ports, protocols,

and communications. Firewall rules are applied to the ingress and egress traffic so we can actually isolate the virtual machines in both directions. This means that the virtual servers can actually talk privately to the other virtual machines on the same network but remain isolated from other networks. However the firewall rules consist of permit and deny statements so you can then permit (allow) traffic from authorised hosts and networks.

A firewall rule is also distributed because when you set up a Google Cloud firewall it is a virtual entity that contains a distributed set of rules that are applied to traffic as soon as it enters the Google network. Hence, based upon the destination IP it will be matched against all relevant firewall rules, both internal or external, to ensure security is enforced throughout the entire connection. Firewall rules should ideally be put on a virtual Firewall placed logically behind a Google network load balancer, that way your firewall rules will only permit traffic to the VMs. This keeps everything very simple and you effectively can block everything from the outside Internet and only allow internal hosts or networks that you have explicitly allowed via your firewall rules to communicate to your VMs.

Now this method prevents any of your VMs being accidentally exposed to the internet but should you or other clients need to access those VMS, set up a Bastion host and access that using the Google Cloud Shell. This way, you can allow SSL access only to specifically identified hosts and clients and effectively block access to all other networks.

So, the first step in security is to protect your VPC with GCE firewalls placed behind a load balancer. And, of course, if you have VMs without external IP addresses, then they are effectively isolated from the Internet anyway so that's another case where a Bastion host is perfect.

Another security level where customer input can have significant impact is in API access control when using cloud endpoints. Often there will be times when want to expose an application or service to the Internet through a protected API endpoint. Well, with GCP you now can control who has access. By applying API access control you stipulate who is allowed to use the service by authorizing every API call with a JSON Web Token and Google API keys. So this way, we can do dual authentication to identify users and/or actual other applications and services that may need to communicate with our web endpoint.

Denial of Service

Part of the protections against denial of service attacks are built into the cloud infrastructure. The network, for example, is software defined networking (SDN) so there are no physical routers and no physical load balancers, which effectively means that there are no actual hardware interfaces that could be overloaded. In addition, there are also services that adapt to demand in intelligent ways such as in autoscaling. These can be added to your design to provide additional resiliency against overload attacks.

So how does Google protect against distributed denial-of-service?

As we have already seen there are a lot of denial-of-service protection actually built in to the Google network but there are others that Google have available to you if you are behind a global load balancer. These denial of service controls are not published so are against the ethos of transparency but that is deemed to be necessary in blocking these types of denial-of-services attacks. Often denial of service attacks may sometimes may be indistinguishable from actual production traffic so it requires careful monitoring and this is why Google takes responsibility for this type of attack using round the clock monitoring, quotas and limits

Another interesting way that Google protects against DDoS at the edge is to provide Cloud CDN as it protects and maximises available bandwidth. This is done through caching content at many points-of-present locations at the edge using Google Cloud CDN. However once more you have to have a global load balancer to gain the benefit. This is because it's the load balancer that's automatically detects and terminates inbound connections. Typically the load balancers will drop all UDP floods and also SYN floods which can exhaust the TCP connections pool.

So, as we have seen the network already protects against distributed denial-of-service attack through its scale, SDN, CDN and its global load balancers. So put your VPC behind a load balancer protected by firewall rules so that you can filter any known bad traffic or certain countries you know won't be using your service. You can of course also block on different ports and protocols.

In addition there is a technique available called VM traffic throttling. This only allows about 10 gigs of throughput per VM for ingress. You can do up to 16 gigs worth of throughput from a VM, but there's also built in protections using quota and limits. So the Google network protects VMs against large scale and sustained attack.

So that is something of a benefit but as we said earlier sometimes it is hard to determine natural production traffic from a denial of service attack especially if the increase in connections, CPU or memory usage and bandwidth consumption is gradual.

Defending the Infrastructure

Should a denial of service attack not be detected by the network security controls the infrastructure is still protected by the cloud load balancers and auto scaling.

At some point, you may need to absorb the attack and it may be for a brief period of time,

but in this case you can scale up by adding more resources but that might if it's a sustained attack expensive.

An alternative technique is to split traffic between different regions and you can do this if you're using a global load balancer. For example, if you are subjected to a denial-of-service attack which is originating from Asia and you're based in the US, you could literally spin up a region in Asia, this way you could absorb that traffic and that might help in thwarting that particular attack.

Sharing and Isolation

As we demonstrated earlier the least secure and the least resilient design is where everything is hosted within a single failure domain. This is because all the components in the design must directly interact, collaborate and communicate in order to fulfil the design goals, which makes them fully dependent on one another.

There are many methods or techniques we can use to separate those inter-related parts. By decoupling their dependencies on one another we produce more private, or fault tolerant communication channels between them. One method is to redesign using multiple failure domains, which inherently provides better isolation and resiliency. However, distribution of resources leads to increased latency so we must also be aware of the need to share and collaborate on resources. Thankfully, Google Cloud Platform provides many network topology features you can use in your designs to provide different blends of resource sharing and isolation.

In the next section we will take a deeper dive into resource sharing and isolation. First of all we need to define the terms in the context of cloud networking. For cloud architects we define sharing as an enabler for collaboration between components of the architecture. On the other hand architects can define isolation as a control that prevents the compromise of one part from spreading to the other. And one very effective way to provide isolation is using a microservice architecture.

Microservices do not really communicating with other services as they have no concept of downstream or upstream services they simply accept an input and hand off an output. Therefore there is no effective communication with which to compromise another service. For example, should an exploiter gain access to one machine they can't get into the others.

One way to achieve this type of isolation is through leveraging the natural separation techniques built-in to the virtual private cloud. For example, if you have two different projects under different administrative control but they need to talk to each other, in this case you can isolate the two networks from each other. Using a VPC means that they will have their own private IP space and their own IAM. So any user, even though they're capable of communicating over the network, may not have authentication capabilities to do so.

Then there is a more traditional networking technique of IP address isolation using VPN tunnelling. In this scenario, we now can have an encrypted link between two or more projects. This is not a feature exclusive to the cloud it is used regularly in on-premises networks. Nonetheless, if we want projects to talk to each other privately then they can use another private IP address subnet space to increase the privacy and even if you want encrypted communications between each party.

Regardless, GCP will encrypt your communications between all services by default. But in some use cases there may be a requirement for more granular control over the encryption policy. Then we have a new feature called cross-project Virtual Private Cloud network peering or as it used to be known, cross-project networking. In this case, network peering allows us to directly connect two projects together using a private IP address.

And then in this case, we can have two different companies, two different organizations sharing and collaborating on resources and in projects. Hence if you need to collaborate with an external partner and you want to be able to communicate then you can set identity access controls. This gives you the ability to control what kind of communication can occur between these two particular domains.

And then of course there's the shared private cloud.

In this scenario, you may have different Virtual Private Clouds with their own projects that need to collaborate or share resources. Again you can use that cross-project networking technique, which will allow them to communicate. However in this case you need to establish a separate project as this new project is responsible for allowing all of this inter-project communication to exist.

So this can have several use cases for example; If you have multiple partners collaborating on a development project. The issue is that you still want to isolate them but at the same time want to allow them to communicate. Well you can do this by letting them communicate on a private subnet network isolated from the public internet.

There are many more isolation techniques available to the architect, such as you can isolate based on the virtual NIC and each virtual machines can now handle up to eight private NICs.

Now, every time you have another NIC, you can actually have a private subnet that's connected to them.

So some applications may retrieve data incoming on one subnet, but actually communicate with another application on another. However you are going to need some sort of routing or a proxy to be able to communicate with that other network. This is also good for software-defined security applications whereby you install a third party security application that will examine and inspect all incoming traffic, and perhaps it will do some intrusion detection before passing it through to the other network. This common when applications require multiple virtual NICs to represent their on-premises appliances.

So what if we want to access the GPC services over an internal IP? Well, that's now available.

But you need to select the option for private Google access when creating the VPC. The purpose of this feature is that you can isolate your VPC completely from the Internet and communicate only over the internal private address.

Encryption

Google automatically encrypts data in motion and data at rest, but you can use Google's built-in key management, or you can provide your own keys. Also for particularly sensitive data, you can add your own encryption methods in addition to those provided. However using your own methods for data encryption this means you have to manage the keys yourself. But when it comes to standard encryption, GCP already provides the server side encryption that will meet most requirements. Indeed the remote web connection is already going to be connected over HTTPS. Now if you then use an HTTPS load balancer you will also get encryption that's communicating between any cloud services and any applications. All of that is done on the fly, in fact, Google will store keys in memory, so nothing is actually being stored on the applications that can be compromised. Furthermore the keys are automatically periodically rotated.

However many customers want have full control over encryption and the key management process. This is common in high-security environments where customer want no one – including Google – to be able to decrypt their data. Thus, they don't want Google to hold the keys. That's why GCP now offer Customer Managed Encryption Keys.

And in this case, when you supply and manage your own keys the GCP does use those keys in memory but does not write it to storage this way, your data is still stored safely with Google, but you hold the decryption keys.

Now if you need more control over your encryption, there are lots of other tools you can use. A common method is to use your own client side encryption. Here you would encrypt the data before you send it over to Google Cloud Storage, and then you could also encrypt the storage bucket.

You can also do disk encryption, or even file system encryption using third party tools and techniques. TrueCrypt for example is a very popular one as it's an open source project.

So there are many different levels you can go to when encrypting and protecting your data.

Blending Security Controls

We saw earlier how to blend IAM and Resource Manager to provide better separation, maintainability and simplicity when defining our security policies. Here, we are going to add some tips on how to get the best out of blending the security controls that are available to you. The principle we follow here are based on Control, Visibility, and Security Solutions. To get started we will begin with the principle of control.

IAM is the foundation of all GCP security but it can get complex very quickly if you work at the user level rather than using groups. Therefore you should always create groups and then place users into the groups as this greatly simplifies the administration and maintainability of the security policy. Similarly when working with folders in resource manager it is always best to mimic the organisational structure and to use the same naming convention. This is because folders are then easier to identify when looked at out of context. For example calling a folder 'development' might look okay when viewed in its hierarchal structure as we can see the context but it is not very informative if we view the folder name in a log entry. Thus, we should be more verbose with folder names so as to relate their structure i.e. instead of just using the name 'development' we could use, 'ABC - IT- Development', which follows the organisational naming convention so we can see at a glance the owner of the folder. The importance of following a naming convention becomes very apparent when you are looking through logs and trying to identify folders or other resources.

Service accounts are another resource and identity – as it is both – that requires to have verbose identifiers so that they can be readily recognised and their function understood. Indeed with service accounts it is a good practice to incorporate the role it performs into the name. This makes it easier to understand during troubleshooting but also cuts down on potential errors when assigning service accounts to a group. Sometimes this may not be possible as the service account serves many roles but that really is a concentration problem and you should look to making the service accounts role more specific. The problem with having too many roles or permissions assigned to a service account is that when it is assigned to a group then all group members may then inherit all the service accounts permissions. They cannot use the permissions directly but they can access all the resources available to the service account by connecting through it even though they have no need or reason to. This is a significant security hole that you do need to audit regularly. You will be perhaps surprised to discover just how many permissions you are granting indirectly to users via poorly defined service accounts. Some ways to mitigate the risk is to use a strong naming convention that stipulates that it is a service account as in logs and reports it just shows up as an email address. So add a prefix to identify it as a service account. Secondly, if you can include its function or role into the name so you can clearly define its appropriate usage. Limit the service accounts own roles and permissions to specific resources and tasks. It is better to create more specific service accounts that to continually keep empowering an existing account with more functions and roles. This begs the question, how many service accounts do we need?

The answer to this depends on your architecture but as a rule of thumb each resource or application should have its own service account. The roles assigned to the service account will vary some may have 10 – 20 roles assigned but that is a clear sign that your application needs to be decomposed into smaller modules as that is known as a concentration risk. If you consider the risk you will see that if a user is granted permission to use that service account they will now indirectly have access way beyond the user's own role as they can access everything that the service account can. For example if you try to consider who can access a resource and with what permissions it starts to become a very difficult question to answer. This is why GCP uses an open source product they developed themselves called Forseti Security to answer these questions. The way Forseti works is that you simply give it your list of users, groups and their roles and Forseti then builds a model from your access policy and provides a query interface. You can then ask it questions such as , 'who can delete this VM?'. Or you could ask, 'what resources can this user access?'.

A final point before we conclude our discussion on control and move on to visibility, is don't rely on default service accounts. The issue is don't rely on just having the projects own default service account. Every project in GCP gets a default service account upon creation but they are not immutable and the roles and permissions are not guaranteed as they can be depreciated at any time so only use them for initial testing do not use them in production.

When we consider visibility we are going to be using tools such as logs, Stackdriver and Forseti, which we introduced earlier. These are the tools that we need to discover who or what service accounts can access resources and with what permissions. We need to be able to have visibility into the underlying permissions matrix in order to understand what is going on and who is doing what.

Typically we will use Stackdriver for logging and monitoring as it is inherent within GCP but when we are using containers and microservices we may use Istio integrated with Stackdriver, Istio for monitoring and Stackdriver for logging and visualisation. When we consider logs we need to be aware that there are two distinct types log logged data. First there are the admin data logs, which record every action done through the admin user account. These are immutable and cannot be switched off. The second type of logs are the private data logs, which are logged changes within your applications and resources. You need to configure these and have a higher permission level to access them as they hold more sensitive information about your apps and resources. However the data private logged output can be huge so be warned and be careful what you log. For example as you are in effect logging every data read and every data write you probably will not want to include Cloud SQL service in your logs. Fortunately you can exclude services that you don't wish to monitor, which makes the process feasible as you only monitor the services that you are interested in.

Another interesting aspect regards logging is that in GCP logging remains within the projects that they are created in. This can be problematic for large organisations that have perhaps 100s of projects as it means flipping back and fore between projects to access the logs. Fortunately Stackdriver has a log aggregation export feature that allows you to collate logs from many projects across the organisation into a single log. Further, you can filter and transform the logs into a common format before sending them to either, BigQuery for analysis, Cloud Storage for long term archiving or to Pub/Sub for integration with other third party services.

If you choose to archive the logs perhaps due to regulation compliance then be careful to configure object versioning on the Cloud Storage bucket as this will prevent the archive's bucket from ever being accidentally deleted. Similarly you should do the same and prevent deletion of the project where the bucket resides although you should have this protection in place for all your production projects. You can do this by using the Lien command which acts as a defence against a projects accidental deletion. It is simple to implement on a per project basis using resource-manager: Gcloud resource-manager liens create – restrictions=resourcemanager.projects.delete –reason="Important Compliance Archive"

In practice this command will prevent the project from being deleted either by a malicious third party or by accident. It will inform the user that the request has been denied and give them the reason- you supplied in the command - as to why it cannot be deleted.

The third principle that we want to cover is Security Solutions which are really the types of blended solutions we discussed earlier. These security solutions are made up of components from the GCP security stack and applied to compound their effectiveness in certain scenarios or conditions.

One of the most common security related questions that Google receives from customers regards how they can access their remote applications securely without having to use VPNs.

This is a common problem for large organisations whereby they have applications located in some but not all of the geographical areas where they have an office or presence. Typically, the solution required the use of VPNs but that is an admin overhead and is not scalable. The solution to this dilemma is to use a compound security solution comprising of three security elements:

- Cloud Armor for edge protection

- Identity-Aware Proxy – for identity management
- VPC – for global reach using Google's Private Network

The way it works is Cloud Armor at the edge of the network intercepts all the incoming connection requests from remote users to internal Google hosted applications and using a simple whitelist/blacklist it determines IP addresses which are accepted onto the network. The second step is that the connection is established with the global HTTPS load balancer that will forward your request to the application. At this step the load balancer checks the user's identity using the Identity-Aware Proxy and it considers the users profile such as the groups, roles and permissions that they are entitled too. But it also checks whether the user's job function is compatible with the application or resource that they are requesting access too. For example if your job function is an IT Developer then it will likely reject your request to connect to a Finance system. The Identity-Aware Proxy is not confined to using IAM it can also check network identity through Active Directory Federations, LDAP or two-factor methods as these can all be integrated with the Identity-Manager. Once the identity and authorisation checks have been successfully completed the user request is passed over the Google private network using private IP addressing to the closest location of the application or resource. On-premises hosts can reach Google APIs and other services over a Cloud VPN or Cloud Interconnect connection to GCP as they don't need an external IP address; instead, they can communicate using their private IP addresses. To enable Private Google Access for on-premises hosts, you have to first configure DNS, firewall rules, and routes in your on-premises and VPC networks. You don't need to enable Private Google Access for any subnets in your VPC network as you would for Private Google Access for GCP VM instances.

Cloud Security Scanner

Cloud Security Scanner is a web security scanner that comes with GCP at no additional cost and is used to detect common vulnerabilities in App Engine, Compute Engine, and Google Kubernetes Engine applications. CSS will automatically scan and detect the most common system vulnerabilities, such as cross-site-scripting (XSS), Flash injection, mixed content (HTTP in HTTPS), and insecure libraries. As a result Cloud Security Scanner enables you to set up, run, schedule, and manage security scans quickly to identify and remediate well-known vulnerabilities with low false-positive rates.

Use Case - 25

You need to conduct a security audit of the video transcription service to identify any potential vulnerabilities as well as define the protections already in place. You also need to lock down access by applying IAM and Resource Management techniques such as folders and projects to limit access to the infrastructure. In short the production and staging internal teams need access as do third party partners but the external partners should not have access to the other internal project teams. How can you achieve these security goals?

Solution

There are many risk mitigation controls provided by GCP by default, so you should identify them before considering any additional security design changes.

When trying to identify any security vulnerabilities you start by auditing your existing architecture. To do this you could use the Cloud Security Scanner to surface known vulnerabilities and then work through those identified to remediate any issues. However some security vulnerabilities may be due to design flaws so we need to address them as well.

Now we never addressed security as part of the initial design because there are several important GCP vulnerability controls in-place. For example, GCP built-in security within the network, with HTTP Global Load Balancing, in Cloud Load Balancing, and default VPC configurations. Nonetheless, we really haven't specified any internal IP addresses,

private networks, firewall rules, or any other security controls. The first pass of the security audit surfaces an issue with the front-end security so we need to lock-down the external facing webservers.

Nonetheless, there are some security techniques already deployed for us such as the default firewall and its rules when we created our webserver VMs. We also have built-in network protections because of those Global Load Balancers as they protect against major denial-of-service attacks. We could bolster DoS security further by adding Cloud CDN and Cloud DNS to the design but what we do need to consider is implementing auto scaling for the front-end cluster to absorb the attack by adding additional servers.

The other major risk is hackers gaining access and potentially gaining unauthorised access to sensitive user information. However we already have a Virtual Private Cloud, and so we are using private IP subnet range, this prevents a hacker getting directly inside from the internet. Therefore the first layer of defence must be to prevent hackers gaining a foothold on the public facing webservers. After all we don't want them using the webservers as a launching pad for attacks on the internal application servers.

Therefore the first step is to isolate the upload web servers by using private IP addressing on their internal interfaces. By giving them private IPs means that if these web servers are going to talk to the back end, they are going to need a secondary NIC in the same private network as the back end servers. We can use the same strategy of private addressing and the same subnet to lockdown the backend storage. So we will be accessing the GCS and the CBT over the private network as well.

Working through our security checklist based upon the original design we have added firewalls and firewall rules to restrict access to only certain ports. We have also addressed the denial of service risk by making the design more scalable and reliable by adding auto-scaling to the front-end group. We have also restricted access the backend servers by giving them private addresses which are inaccessible from the internet. Hence they can only be accessed via the frontend servers secondary interface that resides in the private address space. Also as the design is now in separate zones we can isolate against fault tolerances.

However, there is also assumed implicit trust between all components on the network so we should consider utilizing security accounts via IAM.

Our objective is to allow access to the production development project team as well as the Staging project. Now we can do this by making our VPC a shared VPC and a designated host project and sharing its subnets with the Production and Staging project teams as service projects along with the DevOps that is in another folder. We can further lock down access by placing both the production and staging service projects in a common folder and assigning IAM permissions to that folder. This will allow both the production and staging projects teams to communicate with all the resources in the host VPC. The DevOps project team we want to keep in its own folder so that we have better granular control of the IAM permissions.

However when it comes to the external partner network we cannot share the VPC instead we will need to peer with the partner network to establish a connection so that they can communicate without a VPN using private addressing. Using a peered VPC will ensure that the partner project have access but only to the peered VPC and not access to our internal Production, DevOps or the Staging projects.

To further bolster the security we could lock down remote administration access so we could consider implementing a bastion host to limit administrative access, or even going strictly to serial console. Some additional considerations are that we could start to encrypt our data using our customer supplied encryption keys but that just adds additional complexity.

The security measures that we have considering implementing in the video transcription service will make the system much more secure. However we still haven't addressed the logging system. It's critical that logging is not overlooked as it is a prime target for hackers. This is because typically the logging server will have access by necessity to every server in the network and it also has all the user information and event information that will be contained in the logs.

 As securing the logging system is so critical we will want to consider more advanced methods to isolate and secure the service. To start with all we have to go on is a workflow of business logic but maybe we haven't explicitly introduced different security mechanisms into each of these different services. After all if we think about it we can see that these logs are application-driven, so we could restrict access to those allowed to send data to our logging server by creating service accounts. We'll also create service accounts that will allow us to communicate on behalf of these applications directly to Bigtable.

Furthermore we can deploy the same network tactics as we used for the backend servers of implementing both internal firewall rules and create the logging infrastructure on its own virtual private network.

The private networks will be a bit more complex in this situation as the logging server will have three virtual private NICS. These will all be on private networks. Furthermore there is no need for these individual servers or services to talk to each other as they only have to communicate with the logging service.

So, they will all exist on their own isolated network, but they will also exist on the back end network for the machines that they have to capture logging data from. But the logging server is going to be the most unique because it's going to reside on multiple networks to ingest all of the log data from the other private networks.

Finally after our security tweaks we have a design that looks like this:

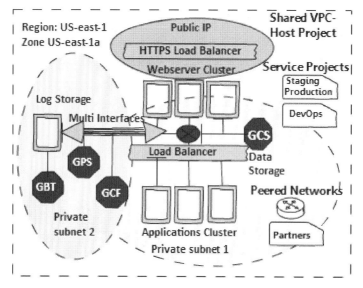

Chapter 26 – Building an Architecture for IoT

An Introduction to IOT on Google Cloud Platform

When it comes to demonstrating the power and utility of GCP a very good use case is when building IoT architecture. The Internet of Things is not just about connecting sensors and manageable devices to the cloud in a scalable fashion although that in itself is challenging. It is also about ingesting, processing and analysing sometimes vast amounts of realtime data. To do this effectively requires a robust IoT cloud architecture. So in this chapter we will describe how to build such an architecture s using many of the services we have already learned about that we will use to make up the physical aspects of an IoT network.

In the Industrial Internet of Things as well as in Industry 4.0 interconnectivity between sensors, devices and systems are fundamental to extracting and ingesting data for further processing and analysis. Data can come in many forms and it is being created and captured constantly from machine, systems and processes. Some data can be ingested and stored for processing at a later time using batch processing whereas other types need real time data streaming and processing. An example of data that can be batched processed is quality control data as it can be analysed at leisure to improve the process. Data that needs instant processing would be machine control data for example the signals that monitor and control the speed of a motor.

There's plenty of valuable data that is produced everyday using devices that can capture, convert, and process data to get actionable information. Capturing and processing this data at scale however creates a real problem that requires specialist architecture.

Google Cloud Platform offers the small business the powerful tools and services to enable us to capture, process, and analyse these massive volumes of data using Big Data tools and zero infrastructure management.

High Level IoT Architecture

Basically an IoT architecture consists of devices, gateways and the cloud. Devices interact with their environment and collect or generate data; the gateway collects and aggregates data from all the devices and then communicates with the cloud; and the cloud provides the capabilities for processing, storing, and analysing the data.

A device can be anything that can interact with its environment from a passive temperature sensor with zero intelligence to embedded devices with fully computerised capabilities. The gateway is required to interface the devices to the cloud. This is because many devices will not have the capability to communicate directly. However gateways also provide local intelligence where it may be needed for example to process time-dependent data and this is called edge computing. The cloud will handle all other computation and data storage, real-time and batch analytics, and machine learning and visualization.

However when we dig a little deeper into the architecture we soon discover that in an IoT network, devices are often added, removed, or modified all the time. Therefore, for security and scalability the cloud must be able to recognise, authenticate and connect the device quickly to meet the operational demands. Also, we will need communication protocols and data pipelines that are designed to handle large-scale message traffic and storage.

When we design the IoT architecture we must also cater for IoT solutions that require machine learning capabilities locally on the device or at the edge as well as in the cloud. This type of machine and edge processing is particularly commonplace now in Industry. The architecture also needs to support bi-direction communications and control as you will need to manage and control the devices connected to the cloud. For example to perform remote firmware updates. Therefore, to meet that requirement GCP supports a wide variety of embedded operating systems and you can trigger automatic changes based on real-time events this can be achieved using Cloud Functions_workflows.

Designing the IoT Network

When you are designing an IoT network, you should take the time to address the following issues:

Connectivity: The IoT is all about connecting things. However, IoT networks often still rely on a server/client model to authenticate, authorize, and connect devices to nodes in the network. This isn't very scalable and without proper throughput design considerations, bottlenecks may occur during the information exchange at the server. Hence, many IoT architectures are focused on moving the intelligence to the gateways or even the devices at the edge.

Security and compliance: When you have hundreds or thousands of remote sensors or devices connecting you need to have a way to identify and authenticate them.

Dealing with non-standard communication protocol: Networks need to support protocols that are lightweight as many IoT devices do not have the capability to support full protocols like HTTP. They will also need to support more efficient messaging systems to handle ever-increasing amounts of data from sensors.

Surface actionable intelligence from data: When we build the IoT network we will increase our capability to capture data but the volume, variety and the value of data also increases. This means that in IoT analysis we will need to be able to handle various volumes and types of data such as structured and unstructured data, as well as real-time data streams.

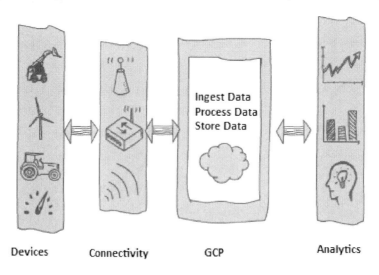

Devices   Connectivity   GCP   Analytics

Figure 20 – IOT Architecture

In summary, the IoT architectures will have to have the capability of scaling connectivity of devices, data ingestion, data processing, and data storage. The architecture must handle these tasks rapidly while not compromising the veracity of the real-time data insights. Traditionally this was a problem as sending ever-increasing amounts of data to the cloud will slow CPU, consume memory, overload I/O cycles and it requires ever increasing bandwidth to transfer and store data.

To mitigate this demand, edge computing is gaining popularity. Scaling also means that the architecture has the capability to monitor and handle thousands of device connections. Hence an asynchronous, scalable communication stack is crucial in bidirectional communication with devices. An asynchronous messaging protocol that decouples the sending and receiving functions, such as MQTT, is a critical requirement in IoT architecture. On the other hand, there are use cases when the response to alerts and commands sent to a device must be done immediately. This requires near real-time responsiveness and that necessitates synchronous (or near synchronous) deterministic behaviour.

To accomplish these IoT design goals, Google's IoT architecture can be divided into four stages: data gathering, data ingest, data processing, and data analysis.

Data Gathering

The first stage, data gathering, occurs at the sensors and devices. Sensors and devices gather data from the environment and pass it directly or via a gateway to the cloud.

Cloud IoT Edge

Sometimes the IoT architecture needs to respond in real time so we need to move some of the intelligence close to the edge. This can be embedded in devices or gateways. In Google Cloud IoT architecture the data gathering stage can be done using the Cloud IoT Edge service. In this scenario, we would use a collection of devices capable of doing real-time analytics and ML. This feature permits Google Cloud's data processing and ML to move close to the edge and subsequently extend its scalability to billions of edge devices. Cloud IoT Edge can run on the Android Things OS or a Linux-based OS. There are two components of Cloud IoT Edge: Edge IoT Core and Edge ML.

Ingest and process data

Once we have designed or contemplated the existing IoT network we need to consider how we are going to ingest and process the data we receive from it. Google IoT Cloud processing data encompasses several services that we can utilise; Cloud IoT Core, Cloud Functions, Cloud Pub/Sub, and Cloud Dataflow.
Cloud IoT Core is a fully managed solution for ingesting and processing IoT data whereby the IoT devices are securely connected to the cloud. Cloud Pub/Sub receives messages from devices and publishes them for subscribers to read. Cloud Dataflow on the other hand is used to create a data pipeline from the device to its destination, which can be BigQuery, Cloud Storage, or Bigtable. You can use either Google templates to create your pipelines or build custom pipeline using Cloud Functions.

Data Analytics and ML

As we have seen previously we can do data analysis and ML on the Edge or on the cloud. Regardless, Google's Cloud IoT Core Data Analytics and ML are fully integrated with Cloud IoT.

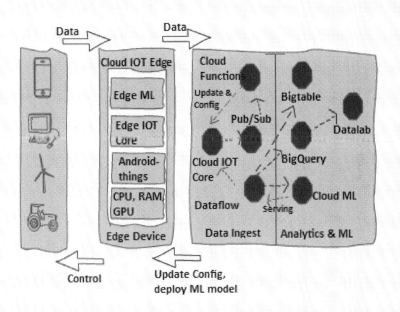

Figure -20

Google Cloud IoT platform has three stages that are necessary for an IoT pipeline: data ingestion, data processing, and data analysis. **Ingesting** IoT device data is collected through secure device connections authorized through Cloud IoT Core. Then the data is uploaded to the cloud through Cloud Pub/Sub.

Processing includes cleaning and storing the data using a Cloud Dataflow pipeline to direct data to Cloud Storage or BigQuery.

Analysis includes using BigQuery, Cloud DataProc, and Cloud Machine Learning Engine to analyse data and gain valuable insights.

Ingest

Cloud IoT Core is a fully managed service designed to:

- Help connect, manage, and ingest data from globally dispersed devices.
- Easily and securely ingest event streams from anywhere, at any scale, for simple, reliable, real-time stream analytics.
- Seamlessly move IoT data across Google Cloud services.
- Ingest data with Cloud IoT Core and distribute data with Cloud Pub/Sub.

Cloud IoT Core, using Cloud Pub/Sub, can combine device data that is widely distributed into a single global system. This single system integrates seamlessly with Google Cloud data analytics services. There are two main components of Cloud IoT Core:

- A device manager for registering devices with the service, so you can then monitor and configure them.
- Two protocol bridges (MQTT and HTTP) that devices can use to connect to Google Cloud Platform.

Cloud IoT provisioning service is an add-on service for Cloud IoT Core that simplifies device creation and monitoring. It allows you to securely add devices to your network by using hardware-based security this enables you to provision millions of devices to the right Cloud IoT Core without human intervention.

Process

This is the stage where we will have to clean and store data for on-demand solutions that scale.

You apply data extract transform and load (ETL) data with Cloud Dataflow. This is a simplified stream or batch data processing service.

Cloud Functions is a serverless solution for developers to create single-purpose independent functions that respond to specified Cloud events.

Cloud Bigtable is ideal for storing very large amounts of single-keyed data with very low latency. It supports terrabytes of data and very high read/write throughput it is ideal for MapReduce type operations.

Cloud Storage is used for storing and accessing unstructured data objects on Google Cloud Platform.

Analyse

With Google cloud IoT platform we can analyse, predict outcomes and generate insightful actionable intelligence. The key service modules deployed here are:

BigQuery is a highly scalable enterprise data warehouse that enables you to perform OLAP style queries on large data sets.

Cloud Machine Learning (ML) Engine is a managed service, which enable you to build and access machine learning models.

There are several other tools that GCP IoT provides that allow you to focus on data analysis. These integrated tools allow you to generating insights faster, by rapidly identifying patterns in the data, and by surfacing and sharing trends across the business.

For example, there is Cloud Datalab, which is based on open source Jupyter data notebook. Datalab is an interactive tool that is used in large-scale data analysis, and visualization. IoT data can be explored then combined with other data sources from outside the IoT within Cloud Datalab to generate valuable data insights.

Google Data Studio, on the other hand, is used to transform the data into dashboards and reports.

Cloud Dataprep is used to explore, clean, and prepare structured and unstructured data for analysis. Cloud Dataprep is serverless so there is no infrastructure to worry about and it works at any scale. Further, Cloud Dataprep requires no code and it uses powerful algorithms to analyse your data choices to suggest or predict ideal data transformations, which it displays in a ranked list. As it is tightly integrated with Cloud Dataflow you can process transformations of structured or unstructured data with just a few clicks.

Chapter 27 – Cloud Migration

Migration from an on-premises data center to the Google cloud might not make sense for everyone and for successful migration you will really need to get everyone onside. This typically requires an in-depth sales pitch that covers all the business areas such as; costs, security, governance, regulatory compliance, data privacy and lack of talent, among other considerations. This means that to be successful in getting your colleagues backing you will have to sell them on the benefits behind Google cloud migration, be open and address the challenges, and stress Google cloud's major selling points.

It is unlikely there will be a consistent response to a proposed cloud migration across all the business units. Typically, the business orientated departments will have a focus in terms of costs where as others may have governance and regulatory compliance as their area of priority. There will also be application developers and traditional support teams that feel a move to the cloud would be both detrimental to operational performance and maintenance efficiency. However, what most people will not pick up on is its more about digital transformation of the business and modernizing the workflows and processes that are the major business drivers. However modernization of the business is only one of the major drivers behind cloud migration. Hence, you should be aware of the other key business drivers and cloud benefits that will have appeal across the business.

1. **Scalability and agility**

The ability to scale up and down as required is very appealing to nearly all teams across the organisation at it eliminates the burden of carrying surplus capacity, as well as overprovisioning resources and provides more agility.

2. Visibility and governance

Despite existing concerns with governance in the cloud in general, GCP's features and tools can offer even more visibility, and thus provide better governance into the IT ecosystem. Indeed increased visibility saves on the proliferation of storage buckets and unnecessary running instances.

3. Cost effectiveness

The major cost benefits that a cloud migration could bring a company, particularly start-ups is well understood as it can significantly reduce capital expenditure on hardware but so can virtualisation however it is the operation expenditure that is not so easily understood. Virtualisation does not reduce the operational, maintenance, management and provisioning cost overheads. Cloud environments does significantly reduce these sometimes significantly if you opt for a fully managed service. Google cloud also provides you with the visibility into billing and offers tools and advise via reports on how to reduce unnecessary expenditure due to over-sizing.

4. Talent and innovation

Google cloud managed services allow IT pros to be less burdened by tedious tasks and housekeeping, which allowed them more time for involvement in projects that produced real business value.

5. Modernisation

The migration of systems and data to the cloud is a major project that gives you the chance to re-evaluate applications and their databases. Perhaps some of these are now legacy or even if they still are mission critical systems they could perhaps be due a modernisation. During any system migration project there will be some systems that will require to be re-architected or re-factored to make them suitable for the cloud. This is a tremendous opportunity to address some long term issues with existing systems whether you decide to move them to the cloud or not.

Planning the Workload Migration

The task of moving enterprise data and applications from inside the secure data center outside into the cloud can be particularly daunting. That is why it must be entered into iteratively in manageable steps following a fully prepared migration strategy. The strategy will differ from organisations in other industry but the core steps should be much the same.

1. Consider the applications suitability for the cloud

Unfortunately not every application is suitable for the cloud and it might require refactoring. It's also important to consider the amount of resources each application uses. The public cloud is a multi-tenant environment, which means applications share resources. And while autoscaling in the public cloud scales resources up or down based on demand, noisy neighbours can be an issue. High spikes in demand can also run up bandwidth costs and hinder an app's performance.

2. Evaluate costs

Many organizations move to the cloud on the basis that it's more cost efficient. However, cloud migrations are not cheap and although they may eventually reduce hardware and some IT overheads they actually increase operational expenses. Moreover, the increase in application OpEx will differ for each application. This is why it is critical to evaluate an applications suitability for the cloud not just on architecture but on cost efficiency. Some modern applications with volatile demand such as mobile applications, will tend to be very cost efficient if you move them to the cloud. But some older monolithic applications or earlier versions of an Oracle database may well be more expensive to run in the cloud. To assist you with this Google has a cloud calculator but you must still factor in network and bandwidth costs.

4. Rethink governance and security

As organizations move data to the cloud, IT's control diminishes as more responsibility is passed onto Google. Therefore, organizations must shape their governance strategies to rely less on internal security and control, and more on Google.

5. Prepare for cloud-to-cloud migration challenges

Cloud migrations aren't just a transition from on-premises technology to the cloud; they can also migrate data from one cloud to another. Additionally, cloud-to-cloud migrations involve considerable manual labour. To prepare for migration from one provider to another, enterprises need to test their applications and make all necessary configurations for virtual machines, networks, operating systems and more.

6. Define your cloud migration strategy

Once you've considered your data, costs, security and the challenges of cloud-to-cloud migrations, it's time to come up with a migration game plan. Organizations also need to determine migration timeframes for their data and applications. While some choose to migrate everything to the cloud all at once, this can be a challenging -- and risky -- proposition. It's often more effective to break the migration down by workload, starting with less critical applications.

Developing a Migration Strategy

Some suggestions for a viable migration strategy are:
1 - Leverage cloud resources for legacy applications when there is opportunity for cost savings for example, Backup, DR, Business Continuity, or for global reach.
2 - Focus your cloud strategy on new applications that will drive greater agility for the business and contribute to the bottom-line.
3 – Leverage cloud resources to fill gaps in your on-premises technologies and skills, for example machine learning.

Building a Cloud Migration Plan

When we come to build our cloud migration plan there are three key factors that should guide you through the process. These factors will help determine whether to move on-premises workloads to the public cloud or leave them where they are.
1. Evaluate current infrastructure

When it comes to evaluating an application for suitability for the cloud one must consider the existing investment. There is likely to be significant costs associated with servers and support infrastructure. The migration of a server's functionality to the cloud may leave it defunct and a wasted business investment unless the business can somehow repurpose the servers.

Servers are likely to be on a hardware lifecycle roadmap whereby they are refreshed every 3-5 years so that may be the ideal time to migrate on-premises resources to the cloud.

2. Consider application performance and portability

In the case of application servers, we must consider whether the application can function in the cloud. Compatibility and application performance are not likely to be a problem in the GCP environment but you must consider two important aspects.

The first is latency or delay because even though you can provision the virtual instance for the application server with nearly unlimited compute and memory resources if there is limited internet bandwidth then that may well be detrimental to the application performance.

The second aspect to consider will be the applications portability. In this case migrate a virtualized application server to the cloud will not be a problem but the application might have some important external dependencies. For example, a MySQL database may have several partner data source connections that are co-located or rely on direct connections.

3. Assess the network

When building a cloud migration plan you must consider the on-premises network and how it will integrate with the cloud. If an organization wants their users to be able to access applications in the cloud or if they wish to keep some of their resources on premises and some in the cloud, the cloud network must function as an extension of the on-premises network and vice versa.

This is even more complex if you are using windows as you will typically have to deploy cloud-based AD domain controllers, DNS servers as well as maintaining a secure communications path between the cloud and the on-premises network.

It is important to understand that when you build your migration plan that you do not usually need to move everything at the same time. Therefore you should strive for a lift and shift of easy applications and like for like databases early on. This is the low hanging fruit. Then as you build experience and confidence you can start to use Compute Engine VMs to migrate virtualisation of other legacy application or databases that aren't directly supported in GCP. For example MYSQL and PostgreSQL can be considered straightforward as GCP supports these databases natively. This is what would be described as a homogenous migration however if you need to later move a Microsoft SQL Server cluster or an Oracle server to the cloud you could run it within a VM on Compute Engine or a container in Kubernetes. The point being you don't need to lift and shift everything at once so take you time and look for the best deployment methods on an application to application basis.

Lift-and-Shift Vs. Refactoring

Unfortunately in many cases IT teams will often face time or budget constraints, so they believe they have no other option but to go for a lift and shift approach. But refactoring can often be the better path as it has significant benefits to basic lift-and-shift migration. One issue is that although it may be easier and seemingly cheaper to virtualise your applications and their stacks in the cloud as-built on-premises as you are basically just replicating the on-premises set-up. However this approach could ultimately cost more than it would to run a cloud-native app. Indeed there may well be an inability to properly utilize Google's services for monitoring, security and governance.

Therefore many believe that it is a better option to refactor an application as part of a migration. This is because they have had to do so many times retrospectively due to an applications performance failing to meet benchmarks after a lift and shift migration. There are also issues when migrated applications because they are not cloud-native so they cannot integrate with some of Google's security systems, such as the identity and access management (IAM) service.

However most IT departments don't want to go through unnecessary refactoring because it adds delays and expense so how do you know when to refactor an application? Application developers need to contemplate several factors when evaluating their apps and most important is cost. This is simple business logic - do not spend more money refactoring an app than will be saved in running costs. Therefore you must consider the cost as well as enhanced performance and security benefits when you evaluate the return on your investment (ROI). Remember the ROI isn't all about money.

There's a wide variety of refactoring tools available, and an application's needs will vary depending on what programming languages and databases that it uses. Today the categories of tools lean towards refactoring in building microservices that are designed to consume cloud-native APIs. On the other hand, lately there is a shift towards container development and Kubernetes engine deployment so these tools are also becoming a very popular way to refactor an application for the cloud.

Refactoring Strategies

There are two ways to go about refactoring. There is the complete refactor of the application and this is where over 50% of the code is edited and the database is also updated so it can benefit from many cloud-native features. This is a high risk and reward strategy as it can significantly enhance performance and features to meet the evolving requirements of the business. However, the draw-back is that the refactor process can be expensive or just too complex. On the other hand we have the option of a minimum viable refactoring process. In this case we prioritize speed and efficiency. A minimal refactor only requires minor code changes to the application. This approach to refactoring often results in integrating the app with cloud-native security and a cloud database into the migrated workload.

However, there is another method and that is to use a technique called containerization refactoring. This method is followed by moving the applications into containers with minimal modification. The concept behind this is that the applications execute within the containers. The container however also enables developers to insert cloud-native features and it also improves the portability. The costs and refactoring times also go down due to the wide acceptance of containers within IT.

There is another modern trend towards serverless application refactor but this has similar issues to containerization such as in having to learn new tools and technologies. However, with serverless refactoring there will be some code modifications required to make the application work. This is because although the serverless platforms support most languages and databases they don't yet support all of them.

In summary, you should be aware that in migration to the cloud most applications and data sets will require at least some refactoring if they are to reap the clouds benefits. However, this should be economically viable with some firm deadlines in place to ensure that most of the refactoring work will have a faster return on the investment.

Technical Issues

Now that we have covered the business and project details regards on-premises to cloud migration we will need to address some of the typical technical tasks that we will be expected to achieve.

The first technical challenge is going to be in migrating applications and webservers. Many open source applications will work on the LAMP stack, which we can readily deploy using a preconfigured image in Cloud Launcher. Similarly we can do the same with Windows Server instances so deploying applications and services directly into VM instances is straightforward. But what about workflows and the database?

Workflow Migration

When first planning workflow migration you need to prioritize the machines you want to move. In order to do this with confidence you will need to understand your application's dependencies. Then, you need to batch these dependencies within the same migration stage. For example: If an application depends on multiple VMs, migrate all of those VMs at the same time. However if that is not feasible then move the components logically. For example; if an application requires a database and a web server, then you can move the database before the web server.

In order to verify your migration strategy and tactics you could clone an on-premises workload and run it in Google Cloud Platform (GCP). This enables you to test the migration process without disrupting production.

Nonetheless, the points you must consider when migrating workflows are:

- Move the VM to GCP and once this is done perform validation testing and resolve any issues.
- Migrate the application storage to GCP
- After determining that you can rely on the VMs in the cloud, schedule downtime to cut over your application to GCP. This happens in two stages:

1. Detach the VM.
2. Test the application to verify that it functions accurately post-migration.

Migrate for Compute Engine

Cloud migration can be complex especially if you are to be moving 100s of applications and their VMs to the GCP. Consequently, Google provides a migration service called Migrate for Compute Engine (formerly Velostrata) to assist you in a seamless transition. Some of the features that Migrate for Compute Engine (MCE) provides are that as an agentless service there is no impact to the workload indeed you don't need to have your source instances running to migrate them to GCP. As for access to the application as its agentless you do not need to change or reconfigure your apps, VMs or network. In addition there are extensive pre-migration checklists and pre-migration testing to ensure your instances are validated before you move them to GCP

Many enterprises find MCE valuable due to its speed and scale. This is because MCE can rapidly migrate single applications saving potentially hours of time and labour yet scale to 100s of apps using several migration waves that have your stateful workloads running in the cloud within minutes rather than days. While your application starts running in Google Cloud very quickly, its remaining data will continue to synchronise and upload in the background. This means apps are live up to 100x faster, and migrations complete up to 10x quicker, as compared with traditional migration strategies.

How MCE works

The migration strategy that you use when deploying Migrate for Compute Engine is that you follow a typical workflow such as:

1. Validate and perform in-cloud testing on clones so that live applications are unaffected
2. Build your migration waves – these are pre-planned migration jobs that typically contain an application and all its dependencies so they are migrated all at once
3. Deploy the workloads to GCP
4. Background data synchronisation and transfer to GCP, which is transparent to end-users and results in near zero downtime
5. Detach and verify but if something goes wrong you can roll back with no loss of data or project time.

Migrate for Compute engine provides for automatic and seamless transitions between on-premises and the GCP for VMs and physical servers. To assist you further MCE also provides a right-sizing analytical tool so that you can provision and deploy the most optimal cloud instances for cost and performance.

Manually Migrating Databases

The task of moving databases to the cloud without incurring downtime is a tricky business as there are several problems to be overcome. The first is in physically transporting the schema and data into the cloud. Another is in keeping the databases synchronised as you do this. The following sections provide some suggestions as to how you can accomplish these tasks.

Migrating MySQL and PostgreSQL

Google Cloud Platform natively supports MySQL and PostgreSQL within its Cloud SQL service. Moreover, these are not just compatible versions they are the actual databases that you would deploy on-premises. This means that migrating either of MySQL or PostgreSQL to the cloud is going to be reasonably straightforward. Typically, all that is going to be required is that you build your database engine instance in GCP, copy across the on-premises schema and data and then switch over. In more detail these are the steps you would take for moving an on-premises MySQL or PostgreSQL DB instance to the cloud SQL.

1. Select the project you wish to use.
2. From the navigation menu, select the "Storage -> SQL" menu item.
3. click the "Create instance" button.
4. Choose between a "First Generation" or "Second Generation" instance. (2nd is advisable as it has better performance at a lower cost but doesn't support Mysql version older than 5.6)
5. Create a DB instance ID
6. Choose a location where you was your database to reside
7. Choose a VM type
8. Choose the storage capacity
9. Click create
10. From the instance page click on the DB instance ID
11. click the "Access control" tab and the "Authorization" sub-tab. Click the "Add network" button and enter the public IP address of the server
12. On the same page, select the "Users" sub-tab. Click the "Change root password" button and enter a new password for the MySQL root user.

13. You can now migrate your application database to Google Cloud SQL. However, before you do this, you must disable write access to the application so that the original and new databases stay in sync.

The way that you copy over your data schema and data is to do a sqldump and then copy that up to a storage bucket in Cloud Storage. Then you can reference that bucket as the source for the data schema.

However, if you cannot take the on-premises SQL server offline during the SQLdump transfer then you will need to create a replication session on the master on-premises SQL server and make the cloud SQL server the slave. This will ensure that eventually the two will synchronise. You then can stop the replication session or simply promote the cloud slave to a stand-alone instance.

This procedure requires you to complete the following high-level steps:

1. Configure your source on-premises database server for replication to Cloud SQL.
2. Make the on-premises SQL server the master and the cloud SQL the slave (replica)
3. When the cloud based slave is fully synchronized with the source database server, take your applications offline, and update the applications to point to the cloud SQL database instance.
4. Disconnect the replication from master to slave.
5. Restart your applications, which should now be pointing to the Cloud SQL instance.

Migrating Database Clusters

In this section we will look at a more challenging issue with database migration than moving clusters or high availability configurations to the cloud.

Migrating a PostgreSQL Cluster to the Cloud

To begin, you perform the following tasks:

1. Set up PostgreSQL in GCP.
2. Set up replication on Compute Engine.
3. Then, you'll seed the data to a new instance before you start replicating the master.

Set up PostgreSQL in GCP

1. You configure PostgreSQL on an Ubuntu virtual machine instance on Compute Engine.
2. Set up replication on Compute Engine
3. Configure PostgreSQL to run in Hot Standby mode on Compute Engine by using two Compute Engine instances. One instance will run the primary PostgreSQL server and the other instance will run the standby server.

Seed the data

Because the master database contains a capped transaction log, most PostgreSQL migrations require the data to be seeded to a new instance before you can start replicating the master. You can seed the data in one of the following ways:

1. Dump a single database into a script or archive file using Pg_dump.
2. Take a binary copy of a running database cluster using Pg_basebackup.
3. Replicate the data folder to the replica using rsync.
4. Restore a previous backup to the replica.

After the initial seeding of the database, you can use the rsync command to feed changes to the replica that have occurred since the backup; the command syncs the data directories between the two instances. This step is important if the backup has fallen too far behind the master to catch up through normal replication.

Setting up the PostgreSQL cluster on GCP

You can create the PostgreSQL cluster using cascade replication.

1. Take a full data backup from the running master server
2. Transfer the backup to the bucket you just created:
3. Transfer the backup file to the GCP master:
4. Restore the backup file into the GCP master:
5. Create a recovery.conf file in the $PG_DATA directory
6. Start the PostgreSQL service:
7. Wait until the GCP master server syncs with the running master.
8. Create a subordinate database
9. Shut down the database and the server:
10. In the GCP Console, go to the Snapshots page.
11. From the PostgreSQL disk, create a new snapshot.
12. Start the GCP master server.
13. Go to the VM instances page, click master-instance-name, and then click Start.
14. Start the new server and mount the disk:
15. Configure data directory and replication values. Copy the PostgreSQL.conf file and the pg_hba.conf file from the GCP master, and edit the recovery.conf file

Migrating a Microsoft SQL Server Cluster

When you decide to move a SQL Server DB instance you can for the time being either use Cloud Launcher to build a pre-provisioned image or build it yourself. Support for SQL Server in Cloud SQL is expected in late 2019 but until then we have to run it in a VM. Deploying and instance or a high availability cluster using Cloud Launcher is by far the easiest route as all you need to do is use Google Cloud Launcher to provision a SQL Server Enterprise AlwaysOn Cluster. Cloud Launcher will automate the creation of multiple Windows virtual machines,
one Windows Server and two SQL Server instances. It will also configure Active Directory and Google's virtual private cloud network with a topology that's optimized for rapid fail over of the SQL Server AlwaysOn Cluster. The build uses premium images and comes with licences for both server and SQL.

 However, if you decide to build the cluster yourself and use your own licenses then moving a SQL Server DB instance or a cluster to the cloud will mean you will have to use Compute Engine VMs. Therefore the first step is to provision a Windows Virtual Machine in Google Compute Engine then will access it using window's Remote Desktop Protocol (RDP). Creating a Windows Server 2016 VM is just like any other VM except we have to create a Windows administrator password. When building a cluster aim for a VM of 2 CPU, 7.5Gb of memory and around 50 GB of disk storage. You can then connect to the VM using an RDP client such as Chrome to log on. That is how easy it is to provision and run Windows virtual machines on Google's global infrastructure.

Google supplies pre-configured Compute Engine images for the Express, Web, Standard, and Enterprise 2012, 2014, and 2016 versions.

Each SQL Server edition can be deployed on a variety of versions of Windows Server and the licence for both the server and SQL comes with the build. However in the case of SQL you can use your existing licence. Once your virtual machines are up and running, you will want to connect to them to perform General Systems Operations tasks, such as installing and configuring Windows features and your own applications.

When you provision your Windows virtual machines, the default network configuration is to

have a private IP address visible to the instance and a public IP address that's maintained by Compute Engine.

When a machine doesn't have a public IP address, then it's not able to connect to the Internet without configuring a separate machine as the network addressed translation (NAT) gateway.

This is important for Windows virtual machines, as they need to be able to connect to the Internet to contact the Windows license server when the machine is first provisioned, and subsequently at regular intervals.

So you'll need to ensure that your network configuration has a public IP address or it supports NAT.

It's likely that you will need to load large amounts of data into your SQL cluster and this is a resource-intensive operation. Therefore you might want to use an easier way to reduce the disk IO and CPU cycles. A higher performance way of doing bulk data uploads is to create a separate database that will be used solely as a staging and transforming point for the bulk dataset before you insert it into your production database. You could also put this new database on a local SSD drive, if you have enough space. This will reduce the resource consumption of your bulk operations, as well as the time to complete the jobs.

Oracle to Cloud Spanner

There will be times when we have to migrate heterogeneous databases, for example Oracle to PostgreSQL or to Cloud Spanner. This may be to release the business from expensive licences or simply to make the database cloud native and benefit from scale and flexibility. Regardless, the migration is going to be more challenging as you have many more factors to take into account. The first formidable obstacle to overcome is the dissimilar schema, data types, queries and features that each support. Hence you are going to at a minimum have to convert the Oracle schema and data model to suit Cloud Spanner as well as translate queries. This will in all likelihood require some application changes so you have to be diligent in finding out what applications are using the Oracle database. This might seem trivial but todays databases can have many data connections to applications, partner system, and even ad-hoc connections to user spreadsheets.

Once you have performed the conversion of the data model and the translation of queries it will be time to contemplate how to export the data from Oracle to Cloud Spanner. For this task we can take advantage of Google's Dataflow ETL service.

Then when we have achieved data consistency between the databases it will be time to switch over and point the applications to the new Cloud Spanner database.

Converting your database and schema

When you start the conversion process you should be trying to match the existing Oracle schema as closely as possible to Cloud Spanner as this will make application changes simpler. However, changes are unavoidable due to differences in features, data types and SQL.

One such issue is the sequencing of primary keys that is inbuilt into Oracle but will be problematic in Cloud Spanner. This is because of potential hot spots arising from too many queries focusing on the same server. In addition to primary keys you should also look to benefit from using table interleafing and the creation of secondary keys to extract the most benefit from Cloud Spanners scalability.

Translate any SQL queries

You must convert any SQL queries that use Oracle-specific syntax, functions, and types to be compatible with Cloud Spanner. While Cloud Spanner does not support structured data as column definitions, structured data can be used in SQL queries using ARRAY and STRUCT types.

SQL queries can be profiled using the Cloud Spanner Query interface in the GCP Console to execute the query. In general, queries that perform full table scans on large tables are very expensive, and should be used sparingly.

Modifying the application to use Cloud Spanner

As part of the migration process, features not available in Cloud Spanner must be implemented in the application. You may want to look at using Cloud Spanner's client libraries for making read and write queries. These use Cloud Spanner-specific API calls. Using API calls may be faster as the SQL statement does not have to be translated.

Transferring your data from Oracle to Cloud Spanner

To transfer your data from Oracle to Cloud Spanner, you will need to export your Oracle database to a portable file format, for example CSV, then upload the file into a Cloud Storage bucket. From there it can be imported into Cloud Spanner using the extract, transform, and load (ETL) process in Cloud Dataflow.
Cloud Dataflow provides a service for running data pipelines in order to read and process large amounts of data in parallel over several servers. Dataflow is based upon Apache Beam and uses the Beam SDK connectors for Cloud Storage and Cloud Spanner so there is no coding necessary. You will only have to code the actual ETL process.

The next issue that you have to address is maintaining consistency between both databases during the migration process. The problem with data uploads is that we cannot, in most cases, keep the applications offline for the length of time the data import/export will take. Unfortunately, when you are transferring the data it may already be stale as the applications continue to write new data to update the existing on-premises Oracle database. Nonetheless, you need to keep the databases synchronised and there are several ways to do this, such as by using the Oracle Change Data Capture feature, or by programmatically implementing simultaneous updates in your applications.

The final step in the migration will be switching to Cloud Spanner as your application's source of truth. When you have verified the data consistency and synchronisation of the data, you can then switch your application to point to Cloud Spanner. You should continue to keep the Oracle database up to date as this provides a rollback path should there be issues.

Migrate for Compute Engine

Chapter 28 – Cloud Dimensioning

Designing optimal systems requires both forecasting for future demand and planning the resources for a system to meet that requirement, this is called dimensioning.

What makes dimensioning difficult is that optimizing for one factor by changing a resource properties can have other unforeseen consequences. For example, if you reconfigure the VM to optimize CPU capacity this can have a negative effect on network throughput and even memory and disk capacity.

As a result dimensioning requires a lot of careful planning and calculations to ensure there's sufficient capacity to meet your design goals. A common error made by designers is to be too ambitious when trying to dimension the system and they tend to optimize away resiliency. Remember that overcapacity or overprovisioning of a system is sometimes necessary and thus included by design to handle volatile periods, growth, or absorb the short term effects of an intentional attack.

This failure to recognize and accept the purpose of overprovisioning and subsequently reducing excess capacity in order to save money can create a perfect environment for cascade failures. On the other hand we must be aware of the price/performance balance but something to keep in mind is that cost optimization is built in to many GCP services. For example, in Google Compute Engine, it has a recommendation engine, which monitors your resource utilization over a 30-day period and makes recommendations on instance sizing. For example it will inform you that using a smaller configuration might save you money.

So the agenda in this chapter is to discuss the relationship between capacity planning and pricing, and then we will revisit our video transcription service and optimize it for cost and capacity. Then finally, we'll add some additional dimensioning for our logging service.

Capacity Planning

Capacity planning is an iterative process and by that we mean it is cyclical and seemingly perpetual. There are various common measures of sufficient capacity depending on the perspective and workload estimations. But these are all load and demand dependent, which will likely fluctuate. Therefore we can only design for sufficient capacity based upon forecasting and then monitor and adjust as the system goes into production and faces up to real world demand. We will need to monitor and measure for VM instance capacity, disk performance, network throughput, and workload demand. Regardless, capacity planning all comes down to answering; are there sufficient resources with reasonable certainty?

A key design principle in capacity planning is to allow other factors to influence your design and then come back and dimension later. This is because forecasting is never going to be perfect so you will likely have to change some of the design for capacity or for better pricing, at a later date. However at least then they will be informed decisions based on environmental measurements so you can make these adjustments knowing what benefits you may well be trading in return for reduced cost.

So let us start with taking a look at the capacity planning cycle. First, you will have to start with a forecast. This will likely be based on the project plan, marketing data or previous industry or product knowledge. Then you have to decide what resources are going to be necessary, and then try to go and get approval for that. But since cloud deployments are much more influenced by operation expense (OpEx) than upfront capital expense (CapEx), this is likely to be forthcoming and then you can go ahead and deploy.

The next stage is the monitor and measure. This would have started during testing and commissioning but it is only once you move into production that it starts to have real value. This is because you can now monitor the indicators in production. Now you will know the real world conditions rather than on pre-production forecasts so you can adjust and predict future trends and optimise accordingly. Then simply repeat that process and each time your forecasts should become more accurate.

So when it comes to these iterative forecasts the purpose is you want to monitor and predict future demand, and plan for future growth. Therefore once in production we compare the actual measured conditions against the forecasts, to see whether they were high or low, and we will try to make a more accurate prediction next time.

So this way, forecasting converges on a practical value by learning from previous errors.

Then consider what other values should you potentially include in your forecasting estimate and give yourself some over provisioning to cater for unforeseen happenings this is called an error budget.

Forecasting

So in forecasting estimation and measuring simply beats guessing. Advanced analytics and machine learning have taken a lot of the guess work out of predicting trends mitigating the risk of over-provisioning. Nonetheless, as we said earlier cloud deployments is about managing on-going operational expense rather than the upfront capital expense so overprovisioning is not such a large risk. Indeed we actually need to overprovision for instance when building resiliency so we use a n+2 model to cope with aggregated traffic in the case of a node failure. There is also a requirement for meeting non-linear demand such as peak hour traffic or volatile spikes in system load.

So the dilemma is when dealing with instance overhead estimation is; how do you overestimate without overestimating too much? Well, we know we have to provide some overhead for such things as spikes in demand and the like. There is also the requirements of fail-over in the case where a VM is acting in a redundancy configuration such as in a managed instance. So we must take all these known production overheads into consideration. However, we must also not forget the inherent capacity overheads within a VM, such as in running the OS. This means that if the VM is already consuming 30% of its CPU capacity just to run itself, then you're only going to get another 30%, to run the application. This is because you will need the remaining 40% to cater for fail-over in a managed instance design where it will have to accept the load of a failed instance. We allocate a generous 30% of capacity for the partial load for this burden and any unknown overheads that may occur in production. This leaves us with 10% spare capacity because it is not a good idea to plan to run at 100% due to the very real risk of introducing potential cascading failures.

Of course we will need to monitor and measure these failure scenarios and its recommended to perform some load testing especially if you're comparing on-premise to the cloud. AN important aspect to bear in mind when migrating systems from an on-premise network to the cloud is that replacing a physical CPU with, say, eight cores, actually will require a CPU with 16 virtual cores inside of the Google cloud platform. This is because every virtual CPU is a single hyper thread.

Understanding hardware architecture is essential and something to bear in mind is that different zones often have different hardware components available. This is due to the diversity of Google's data centres' hardware across the many different technologies.

If you go to Compute Engine and click on create VM and then Customize, you can actually choose a CPU platform type. It is important to give this some considerations as your application may actually benefit from running on a newer instruction set. So you may want to benchmark your application running on each one of these different processor types, to determine which may or may not benefit. You're going to pay the same price but you may well see a surprising difference in your performance benchmarking.

Another thing to consider benchmarking is the OS image that you are running. Google has done a lot of research into this for you and typically Ubuntu runs better over the GCP than other OS versions. But you should either compare Google's published benchmarks or run your own to determine the most optimal for your design. Regardless of your choice of OS image you can certainly turn off the OS firewall as Google's firewalls come with the VM instance, and that alone will realize a considerable difference.

Also, if you're running something like Windows, which is well known for swapping data to a page file, consider using a local SSD if you can afford it. This is simply because local SSD is much faster than standard persistent disk storage.

When considering which persistent disk to use its worth remembering that the IOPS are constrained by potential CPU. This means that although you can scale storage it may have an effect on disk IOPS. But the interesting thing with Google cloud persistent disk is that the disk IOPS grows as the storage scales.

You can see this by looking under Disks in the console and if you choose a standard persistent disk, you get a choice of 10 gigs, and you get a fixed performance. But if you then increase the capacity to 100 gigs, you'll notice that the performance will continue to increase.

Now this is of interest as its not magic its simply because Google has used quotas to enable that larger capacity disk to perform to that higher level. Do keep in mind if you don't have enough CPU to drive the disk I/O, well, then that could potentially be a bottleneck. A rule of thumb when capacity planning is that a higher amount of CPU is necessary to drive larger storage capacity and reap higher disk IOPS.

So also consider I/O bursts, because although the Google network is very, very consistent and almost deterministic in nature you can still get big spikes, especially if you're flushing data to disk for a database. So remember, if you're trading up for performance over capacity, you need to determine whether you're going to choose the faster SSD over the standard HDs.

Network Capacity

When considering network capacity you need to remember that network throughput for VMs, is limited by the number of CPU cores. So you get 2 gigs of throughput for every CPU core, this quota is capped at 16 gigs maximum, which requires 8 cores. However that 16gigs is not simply the sum of egress and ingress traffic flow as there is another limit on ingress traffic set at 10 gigs. Now, you can go up to 64 cores but the 16 gig throughput is still the ceiling so you need to get Google to open up the quotas for you. Another point of interest when capacity planning networks is that all VMs come with both internal and external IPs. Internal IPs are on a much faster network as they don't have a lot of the external overhead and inspection. If you benchmark the two, you will see a large difference in latency between them as the internal networks are always faster.

Then there is a need for workload estimation in order to get a firm understanding of the potential network throughput. In practice this can vary quite dramatically due to request types as some types are very verbose, others are small but very chatty, and of course the size of the payload.

Resource Allocation

After forecasting, the next step is to allocate sufficient resources. Forecasting will tell us basically how much capacity we're going to potentially allocate. For its part allocation is going to tell us how much resource is necessary to provide that capacity. For example, forecasting tell you that you will need 1.5 terabytes of physical persistent disk but allocation will tell you that you will need 2 terrabytes in order to realise the 1.5 terabytes usable capacity.

Now in some cases it might not be so clear and we will need to validate those estimates with load testing. By research or through testing and measuring we can calculate the resources required, based on the capacity/resource ratio.

As an example, if we determine that the demand for storage throughput in our video transcription service is going to increase by 30%. Now we have a figure for our Queries per Second (QPS) as we've already measured it. But now we are planning on adding a further 30% to that, so we now have a new number for QPS.

So we have determined that the new throughput capacity is going to be 327,600 qps and now we have to determine how many Bigtable nodes do we require.

Well, Google documentation on Bigtable and benchmarking reveals that you get about 10,000 QPS per Bigtable node - a 10,000 to 1 ratio; so for every Bigtable node, we can do 10,000 QPS.

So in our case, we just simply divide our QPS of 327.600 by 10,000 to come up with about 33 Bigtable nodes.

And we can benchmark that and kind of test it out, but it's a good rough estimate.

One sensible tip to try before you just simply add more hardware at the problem is to see if there's another way. For example, could you start enabling caching, could you cache data in Memcache or local SSD or something else that might be as beneficial but cheaper?

We should always consider the possibility of tuning our applications and processes to make them more efficient. You could also explore using better algorithms or alternative services.

So, for example in our video transcription application we're running this home grown ETL processing script that we made, for the sake of expediency as we didn't want to change languages. However, throughout the evolution of the video transcription service there was a better ETL service available to us, Dataflow. It's a fully managed service, it scales better, and the algorithms are tuned, so perhaps we should stop procrastinating and switch over to Dataflow.

Resource Deployment

After the forecast and allocate stages comes deploy, and if you've been using your service level objectives and indicators, you will now have data to drive these numbers to support your forecasts. So it should be a lot easier to get approval, you have the data, you have forecasting, and you can calculate and justify what the subsequent costs will be to meet the design.

So now, you're going to go to the deploy phase and then start your testing. We want to make the testing realistic but easy to run, but it should also be customizable. After all we want to be able to catch obvious errors and handle simple use cases. But we also need to surface some of those stubborn intermittent issues that are more difficult to find. Therefore, we want to try to build in some kind of unit testing for reproducible or hard issues.

You should always first surface and then work through any issues before serving it up to your users. By striving to maintain the integrity of our application to the users we want to identify any bottlenecks or other user pain points and make the user experience as good as possible.

If you can do dark launches then do so as this way you are going to be doing testing in an isolated launch. Then of course, you can start a slow stage and iterative process with canary deployments slowly rolling out. So if we do adversely affect our customer base it will be a very small percentage.

Pricing & Billing

A significant factor when designing for cloud deployments is that the method, techniques and perspective of pricing do vary tremendously between on-premises and cloud initiatives. Pricing is commonly used in on-premises for vendor evaluation and budget approval as it is typically very capital expense orientated i.e. you are pricing physical hardware for purchase or lease. What is more, most of the projects pricing will be on capital expenditure with operational expenses such as power and communications shared across the data centre. Pricing however in the cloud is much different because here you are pricing for the operational usage of resources with no capital outlay so it is more nuanced. But do not mistake this as being an opportunity to dispense with diligent pricing as it is still crucial to cost optimization, reducing cost, and for project budgeting.

When we said that pricing could be nuanced one example is that in Google Cloud Platform there is bulk-use discounting, which is built-in and automatic for many services. Conversely there are discounts for resources that are rarely used such as with cold storage or pre-emptive VMs.

In this chapter, you will find out some of the ways and the design choices, which can influence price.

For example, you may have distributed an element of your solution over multiple regions to improve reliability. However, that distribution design might result in additional network charges for egress traffic.
Is the cost of the additional reliability worthy of the additional network charges?
Pricing following diligent capacity planning can perhaps help you decide.

Why cloud pricing is important?

Google cloud platform has a number of built mechanisms to help you in keeping on top of costs, one of the most notable is virtual machine dimensioning. We have already mentioned the standard machine type discount, but GCP also have inferred type discounts, sustained-use discounts, and there are inferred instance discounts. Typically users will pick a standard template for a VM but you can use custom VM that you optimize for high memory or for more CPUs. But some special purpose VM may need things like GPUs or TPUs for machine learning purposes. Hence VMs may be customized to match your workload but of course then they would not match any standard machine type discount. Google though has provided a work around for this anomaly via the inferred type discount.
The way this work is that Google will calculate how often and for how many hours you've used a particular type of VM. Then they will try to match it to a similar standard lower cost configurations and give you a discount at the end of the year.

There is also committed use discounts, which are a pre-pay model where you commit use a stipulated amount of CPU cores over this period. Therefore you can use any configuration it doesn't matter so long as you meet your obligations on core use you will get a fixed discount for anywhere from one year to three years depending on how much you'll commit to. Unfortunately this discount doesn't apply to Google managed services such as; App Engine, App Engine Flex, Dataproc, so on and so forth.

Another interesting way to lower costs is to use pre-emptible VMs. In case you don't know a pre-emptible VM is one that you allow GCP to terminate if they require the resources during peak demand and they are shutdown with 30 second notification. Furthermore, the VM is guaranteed to be terminated within 24 hours if you're not preempted. That doesn't sound very attractive so they give you an 80% discount to encourage you to use them. The thing is though sometimes pre-emptive VMs are very attractive because they can fit in nicely into your design and save you money. For example if you are building a highly available environment you've already built in the ability for fault-tolerance and failover. In this case you might as well use the pre-emptive VMs as not only will you get the 80% discount but you will also have an inbuilt continuous fail-over test environment.

So, what about optimizing disk costs?

When it comes to pricing for storage it is really driven by whether you are chasing performance or capacity. This is another trade-off, as high performance SSD is certainly more expensive as it costs more per gig (capacity), but it's a much lower price for IOPS (performance). Trying to find a balance that matches your budget is typically driven more by the technical capacity/performance demands of the design and the system properties more than the pricing but you can make savings here when neither is critical.

Don't forget the network?

In optimizing the network for pricing, you have to really understand how traffic flows across your network and where you're placing your data. For instance if you going for resiliency and availability and have a multi zone design, which is best practices, there are charges on the egress traffic between the multiple zones within the same region.

You can save money on that multi-zone design by deploying Google's or a partners CDN service. Alternatively you could get a dedicated network interconnect to Google, either through a partner interconnect or private interconnect, which will save you also 50 percent on your cost.

Now if you're egressing between regions, that's going to have the same standard egress charges as well as intercontinental egress charges. In fact, intercontinental can sometimes be a little bit more expensive.

In this chapter, you learned about capacity planning, including the planning cycle,
and you learned about GCP discounts. The two of them together, capacity and pricing, provide another perspective on design options. You can modify the design for cost optimization or to limit resource usage. One important point is to apply dimensioning to your design after you've considered other functional aspects of the design.

Use Case – 28a Cost & Sizing Scenario

In this scenario we will consider that the annual capacity planning for the coming year's budgets have been completed. The report details the growing VM capacity requirements. Now you need to determine would it be better to choose a bigger capacity VM, or is sticking with the current size VM the most cost-effective?

However, before you submit the capacity planning report, you want to see if you can actually do some cost optimization. This means taking a closer look at the VM options and performing some cost optimization analysis.

Hence we will try and optimized for cost and capacity on our video transcription application. The focus is on VM sizing and performance. So we want to try and determine if moving the current upload instances which are n1-standard-1 to n1-standard-4, will provide the required capacity and at what cost.

So what we have to consider is can we optimize these upload servers by reducing the quantity and increasing the number of cores. So for the sake of argument, let us say that the current upload VMs are n1-standard-1, they have one vCPU and they run Debian 9 OS. Our Perfkit Benchmark indicates that current performance of an n1-standard-1 comes in at 1.4 Gbps, while in n1-standard-4 is 6.1 Gbps. Furthermore, our monitoring of the upload VMs show that the highest number used was about 576 machine so we use that as our standard.

Now thanks to our benchmarking we can see right away that there's some network throughput efficiency delivered by upgrading to four CPUs. Now from a network perspective that sounds great but is it cost effective, will we actually utilize this performance boost?

Therefore we need to check for the cost effectiveness of the VM upgrade of our peak of 576 servers.

We've already established our throughput for those servers with Perfkit, so that basically comes out to 806 Gb peak per second. Now, if we actually take a look at the Perfkit Benchmark for the n1-standard-4, we can achieve the same results, the same throughput with 132 instances.

Now let's go to the Google Cloud calculator.

In this case, we can see the costs were 576 single core machines versus 132 quad-core actually come in with about a $1,100 price difference. So that's almost $12 thousand per year.

Now sure, there's a little bit of work in actually adjusting and optimizing these, but as an auto-scaling template, this would be very easy to do.

It's not like you're updating all machines, you're actually updating one template and updating your auto-scaling instance, manage instance group.

So, actually this would be quite trivial, and we could start saving money immediately within the first 30 days.

Use Case – 28b Dealing with log files

The video transcription application service design is now set to auto scale and grow for the projected doubling of demand in the coming year. However, that means the log information will also double.

The current storage service is Bigtable. Will the additional demand both data and traffic put stresses on Bigtable?

Will the system need an additional Bigtable node to handle the demand in the coming year?

In our case, we're using 22 Bigtable nodes with SSD drops. We'll calculate the performance using queries per second or QPS, as well as throughput in megabytes.

We'll also look at the overall quantity of data stored each year which is going to double.

The first question is, do we need more Bigtable nodes?

We know from Google's performance benchmarks that each Bigtable node can handle about 10,000 queries per second and about 10 megabytes per second of throughput.

Looking at the size of the log payload for each of our workloads, the log data for the web, app, and data servers are all about the same size.

We're joining the log data of the app and data servers on a common field which reduces the combined log to 552 bytes per transaction. We then estimated the amount of logs at 300 million entries per day, which comes out to about 154 gigabytes per day. Multiplying that by 365, we get about 55 terabytes of log data per year at our current utilization.

Now comes the challenge, what would this service look like if the user base doubled in the coming year?

What would our bottlenecks be?

We ran the calculations to determine the number of queries per second our application will use. When we look at our request over time, we get 3,472 queries per second. We then calculated the throughput requirements to be 1.8 megabytes per second and our total disk capacity of the joint records will be 55 terabytes per year. If we were to double everything, we'd require 6,944 queries per second and 3.6 megabytes per second of throughput, which can be handled by a single Bigtable node. But we need to consider the storage capacity, which could reach 110 terabytes by the end of the second year.

Doing the math, 22 Bigtable servers using SSD drives won't be sufficient for the double growth that we're forecasting for the coming year as 110/22=5.5Tb per SSD. We could consider changing to HDD as their larger capacity would be more appropriate and our application is not latency of disk throughput sensitive.

Chapter 29 - Monitoring, Alerting, & Incident Response

In this Chapter we will discuss deploying, operating and maintaining your design.

A design team do not typically just design, deploy and commission and then immediately move on as there will be a period post deployment where they have to stabilise and perform a handover of the system to operations. This is because it is important to transfer the knowledge of the systems characteristics and operational best practices to the people who will be operating and maintaining the system.

This is where those SLO and SLI you've been developing and refining with each design iteration will provide an objective method to manage the newly deployed system. They will help to keep it running in production and meeting its operational objectives. Moreover, the practice of iteratively reviewing the service indicators and objectives also flags when perhaps the production environment and the assumptions of the original design no longer meet the market or production conditions. Then it will be time to revisit the design and evolve the system and refit for purpose. Therefore, a key point in system design is don't just design your service to meet the project specifications, design it for operational manageability. To achieve this means you're going to be thinking about continuous improvement and deployment, monitoring and alerting, and incident response.

In order to demonstrate these techniques and methods we will revisit our video transcription service as we are now well into the stabilization and operation period.

Hence, the design challenge for logging is to configure a full set of monitoring and alerting indicators for real world production conditions.

Deployment Checklist

Now, when it comes to deployment, the first thing you need to do is make a launch checklist that defines your dependencies, any shared infrastructure, not forgetting any external or third-party dependencies.

Secondly, we must ensure that all resiliency and redundancy issues for capacity overload and the appropriate handling procedures have been addressed and tested. To do this you should have followed the best practices of deploying n+2 everywhere that you can and ensuring there are no single points of failure.

Thirdly, you should have completed and verified your security audit and identified and mitigated any attack surfaces.

Fourthly, it will be time to develop the deployment strategy and define the roll out plan.

The roll out strategy could be one of several methods such as gradual, staged or a phased rollout, or perhaps a canary to only a limited percentage of the user base.

So once you've decided on that roll out strategy, then we create automations.

Finally, you will want to automate everything you can for rapid and continuous deployment tactics so the key here is reliability and consistency.

Ideally you are striving to create a self-service release process, which allows you to run a continuous improvement and continuous deployment strategy through high velocity development and operations (DevOps) teams so they can develop code and then automatically deploy new versions rapidly.

However we must not forget IAM we want to ensure that we only give the correct privileges to the correct teams and/or services as this is vital for access control over critical operations.

Fortunately Google Cloud Platform has a service, Deployment Manager, which can help us build this checklist and create the scripts necessary for automation.

Deployment Manager

This should be your tool of choice for deploying into Google Cloud, basically because your deployment configuration script is going to describe all the required resources for rapid deployment of the entire infrastructure.

Now, the way that Deployment Manager works is it uses templates written in YAML syntax, utilizing Jinja, which define all the resources and their properties. For example, the script could contain a segment of code for virtual machines with virtual machines types and templates another section will detail the properties for firewalls and firewall rules, and so on until the entire infrastructure has been defined.

Now to make this more manageably you will be utilizing templates, written in either Python or Jinja2, as these are the building blocks of an entire deployment configuration. They're also going to be referenced in the YAML configuration file. This means you can take this modular approach and leverage it for collaboration in so much as you can pass each service to a specialist team. For example you can pass any networking properties that need to be defined in the template to the networks team. That way the specialist teams can take responsibility for the correctness of the definitions.

Monitoring and Alerting

In operations and production everything really starts with monitoring. As once you start and activate a monitor and define its specific alerts, you have to respond to the incident and resolve the problem.
Of course once you have found the root cause you will then need to find a solution to prevent the problem reoccurring in the future. Depending on the results of your root cause analysis you may well need to change capacity planning, redeploy and/or update the product. Regardless, you will need to recreate testing and deployment releases that include your potential fix.
In production environments, you use monitoring to rapidly surfaces potential problems that need urgent attention and it can also help you in identifying any potential improvements.
Also, monitoring helps identify existing but perhaps illusive trends, which will help with forecasting and planning.

Now there are two approaches to monitoring namely, black-box and white- box monitoring. With the latter, white-box monitoring is going to work from the perspective of having full system knowledge and visibility so it can identify all the actual backend services themselves.

On the other hand the black-box style of monitoring works from a customer experience perspective and so doesn't assume any knowledge of any services or infrastructure in the backend.

It is important to remember the difference on focus when designing monitoring and alerts and how the two types are best suited and also how they can co-exist and complement each other by using different metrics.

There are two types of metrics you need to be aware of as you can have push-based metrics which will simply send out alerts or you can have pull-based, where you can do a pull from the outside. An example of a push metric is if you have a new item that's been uploaded to a cloud storage bucket so you're going to receive a web-hook notification.

An example of a pull-based metric is if you are trying to check at certain intervals to make sure everything is functioning this is typically because the service lacks the ability to notify you that something is down so you have to perform periodic checks yourself. This is where the pull type metrics and the black-box monitoring is important as it reflects the users' experience. As neither the black box nor the customer have any visibility into the chain of backend business logic and perhaps its supporting microservices, distributed storage, and private networks, and so on. The black box doesn't know about any of the backend because it doesn't need to know as it cares only about the user experience from the users point of view.

However, if black box monitoring alerts an issue then you will go to your white-box monitoring to identify where in your business logic there is a problem that is possibly affecting that user experience. Therefore you use white box to monitor the individual services and as the basis for your root cause analysis. If you remember the 5Ys then you will ask the five questions based upon your white box's service level indicators. This will help you to determine which part of the business logic is failing and potentially affecting the user experience.

An important design principle is to automate monitoring and alerting as much as possible in order to remove the human from the loop. Therefore we want to design thresholds into our indicators so that the system itself can take the required actions. After all this is why we built the system to have fail-over and auto-scale. Therefore, we would ideally like to stream alerts to the Stackdriver logging server.

The benefit of using Stackdriver Logging is that it has the capability to ingest these alerts in real time, which means we can readily query it. Also, it can export in real time to BigQuery and/or Google Cloud Storage for long-term archive.

Stackdriver can handle everything end to end from the monitoring, error reporting, Cloud tracing, and debugging. A caveat being that last three features are exclusive to Google App Engine and so are only available if you're using that service.

Stackdriver

Stackdriver is unique because it was a third party acquisition that was originally built for AWS. This is why you will find that it has AWS connectors so that you can monitor various products in AWS as well as multiple products within GCP.

Stackdriver is actually a collection of dozens of specialist tools that are integrated into a single package and user interface.

Resource Management with Stackdriver

Resource monitoring isn't just about billing and tracking budgets there are many other critical operational and performance criteria that we need to track. Therefore we will need a feature that provides monitoring, logging and diagnostics for your applications, resources and networks. The service that GCP provides to deliver this functionality is Stackdriver.

You learned earlier through a high-level introduction to Stackdriver that it integrates five services; Monitoring, Logging, Error Reporting, Fault Tracing and Debugging. In most enterprise environments, these monitoring services are typically handled by a collection of third party packages or by a loosely integrated collection of tools. However, with Stackdriver you can see these functions working together in a single comprehensive integrated service. By doing so you'll realize how important it is to creating reliable, stable, and maintainable applications.

The way that Stackdriver integrates with GCP is that the Stackdriver account is the root entity that holds all the monitoring and configuration information. However this account can monitor multiple GCP projects simultaneously so we need to place the account into a host project. This hosting project will then have available all the dashboards, uptime checks, and configurations, and the Stackdriver account will take its name.

Monitoring

Stackdriver dynamically configures the monitoring of resources after it is deployed, and it has intelligent defaults for many key performance metrics. This allows you to capture relevant data and then visualise the information gathered via charts for basic monitoring activities. Stackdriver provides the integrated tools that help you to monitor your platform, systems, and applications by ingesting data such as metrics, events, and metadata.

You can then generate insights from this data through dashboards, charts, and alerts.

For example, you can configure and measure uptime and health checks that send alerts via e-mail.

Monitoring is a critical discipline and Google places much importance on it as it underpins the concept of site reliability. Google founded the discipline of Site Reliability Engineering or SREs and the goals are to create ultra-scalable and highly reliable software systems. SRE incorporates aspects of software engineering, and applies that to operations. This discipline has enabled Google to build, deploy, monitor, and maintain some of the largest software systems in the world.

By deploying Stackdriver and following SRE principles you can monitor the GCP platforms, systems, and the deployed resources through individual hosted probes, actual application instrumentation, and third party and open source applications.

Uptime checks

A key metric for any service is uptime as this is directly related to availability and reliability. Without monitoring uptime we would not know whether we were receiving the SLA's for the resources or receiving the service that we were paying for. Stackdriver can verify that the service provider is indeed delivering the SLA on availability of your service by checking it responds correctly to requests from locations around the globe.

There are several types of Uptime check as they can be triggered using HTTP, HTTPS, or TCP and the resource to be checked can be an App Engine application, a Compute Engine instance, or a URL of a host. An example of an HTTP Uptime check for a web server VM instance may require that the resource is checked every minute with a 10-second timeout designated to be considered a failure. Stackdriver's monitoring feature can actually access some metrics without any monitoring agent being installed. For example, this may include VM CPU utilization, some disk traffic metrics, network traffic, and Uptime information. However, to monitor and access additional system resources and especially application services, you should install the specific monitoring agent.

App Engine includes built-in support for Stackdriver monitoring in both the standard and flexible environments as does the Google Compute Engine. However, the monitoring agent does not currently support Kubernetes Engine. Additionally, you can configure the monitoring agent to monitor many third party applications. Uptime monitoring can be based on different conditions like predefined metrics or lock based metrics. These conditions can trigger incidents that create notifications in the form of an email, SMS, Webhook or another third party service. For example, if your CPU utilization on your VM is too high, you can get an email notification with all the necessary details.

Groups

Groups allow you to aggregate metrics across a set of machines. These are dynamically defined in so much as groups are filtering driven, meaning any existing or future resources that match the criteria for group membership will be automatically included.

This means that you don't have to alter or update the group membership or related dashboards/alerts, every time that you add or move resources making groups useful for highly changeable environments.

Groups also serve another function in that they provide a neat way for you to separate your production from development services. In addition, you can filter Kubernetes engine data by name and custom tags for clusters.

Dashboards provide quick visualization of core metrics for insight. These dashboards are customizable, and are auto-generated for most common applications. For example there are many standard metrics that cover; Compute Engine, Cloud Pub/Sub, Cloud Storage and Cloud Datastore. If these standard metrics provided by Stackdriver Monitoring do not fit your needs, you can create your own custom metrics. For example, if you have a use case where a game server is going to be running your own gaming application but it has a known capacity of 1000 concurrent users. Then you might consider what metric indicator you would use to trigger a scaling event?

Possibly, you could take various perspectives, for example, if you were to take an infrastructure focus then you might consider monitoring the CPU load or the memory utilization. You might also consider looking at the network traffic load as these are all values that are somewhat correlated with the numbers of concurrent users. Nonetheless, you could use a custom metric where you could easily pass the current number of users directly from your application into Stackdriver.

Securing Stackdriver

We learned earlier that Stackdriver accounts have the capability to monitor all your GCP projects within a single account. But this in many situations can be problematic as it makes the account "a single pane of glass", which means that all Stackdriver users that have access to the account also have access to all the projects' data by default.

It also means that a Stackdriver role assigned to one person on one project applies equally to all projects monitored by that account. This is okay for an organization that monitors the network holistically from a centralised location such as a Network Operations Centre (NOC) as the agents can all be given access to Stackdriver in order to monitor all the projects and deny everyone else. But most organisations will still want some local project monitoring, logging and diagnostic capability.

In order to give people different roles per project, and to control visibility to data, consider placing the monitoring of those projects into a separate Stackdriver account that is configured to only monitor that host project/account.

Monitoring best practices

A recommended best practice when it comes to monitoring is to set alerting on symptoms and not necessarily causes. For example, you want to monitor failing queries of a database rather than alert when the database is actually down. This is because often the database may be showing up but the engine is no longer responding to requests. This is also a common issue with web servers as they will show the up status but the application will have crashed. Therefore, make sure you're monitoring the correct event triggers and using multiple notification channels on which to receive the alerts such as email and SMS. This prevents you experiencing a single point of failure in your alerting strategy. Similarly, make sure that you plan independence and redundancy into your notification and alerting process so that it isn't dependent on any of the monitored resources.

Another recommendation is to customize your alerts to the audience's needs by describing what actions need to be taken, or what resources need to be examined. This will give the person receiving the alert and tasked with resolving the issue a clear indication of where to start.

Finally, make sure you set thresholds at realistic and practical levels where there actually is an issue. Often people set the thresholds higher than they need be. The logic is that they wish to catch deteriorating performance so that they can catch it before it becomes a fault. However this just creates false alerts and additional noise and this will cause alerts to be ignored in the future. Specifically, adjust monitoring alerts so that they're necessary and actionable, and don't just set up alerts on everything possible.

Logging

While monitoring is the fundamental service of Stackdriver, the product also provides logging, error reporting, tracing and debugging. Indeed, Stackdriver logging allows you to store, search, analyse, monitor, and alert on log data and events from the Google Cloud platform. Furthermore, it is a fully-managed service that performs at scale and can ingest application and system log data from thousands of VMs.

The Logging feature of Stackdriver includes a function for the storage of logs as well as a user interface called the Log Viewer. It also has an API to manage logs programmatically, which is designed to let you read and write logs, search and filter logs, create log based metrics, and export logs to a cloud storage bucket, BigQuery data set, or to a Cloud Pub/Sub topic.

Why export to Stackdriver?

It is a best practice to install the logging agent on all your VM instances as Stackdriver logging allows you to export your logs and synchronise them for export. There is a logging agent for Google Compute Engine, App Engine and Kubernetes Engine, which is supported through inherent support for Stackdriver logging using their own software interface.

However, Stackdriver logs must have access to the resource that you're trying to export to, such as, for Cloud Storage, BigQuery, and Cloud Pub/Sub. Consequently, as new log entries arrive into Stackdriver logging service, they will be compared against the export syncs to see if an entry matches. If it does then it will be exported to the destination. However, log entries received before sync is created will not be exported through that method.

You should also be aware that log entries exported to Cloud Storage are batched and sent out approximately every hour. On the other hand the log entries exported to BigQuery and Cloud Pub/Sub are streamed to those destinations immediately.

When exporting logs to different storage classes of cloud storage you should consider how long and often you will need to access the data. This is because Stackdriver logging will only retain the logs for 30 days. Also, exporting the logs allows you to perform search and then analyse the logs in BigQuery, Google's data warehouse for analytics. Finally, exporting the logs also lets you create advanced visualizations using Cloud Datalab, and you can also stream logs to applications or endpoints using Cloud Pub/Sub messaging service.

Stackdriver Logging best practices

The best practices when it comes to Stackdriver logging are;
- Don't if you can avoid it use substring matches on service names or resource types. For example, searching for the text, 'abc', will match log entries containing abc, xyabcyx, and even ABC. Instead, for an exact match, use the equals operator.
- Perform faster searches by targeting specific values of indexed fields. For example, specify your search for a log entries name, resource type, or resource label. Using advanced filters will result in even more effective queries. You can add filters directly from log entries.
- Finally, get accustomed to using and learning the advanced viewing interface. Start by setting up selections and filters in the basic interface, and then switch to the advanced interface.

Error Reporting

Stackdriver has another in-built feature that is extremely useful – error reporting. Indeed Stackdriver error reporting will count, analyse and aggregate all of the errors in all of your active cloud resources. This works because the Stackdriver probe or agent acts as a distributed collection points that send the data to a centralized error management interface. The centralised error reporting node then collates and displays the results. Furthermore it does so with granular sorting and filtering capabilities, so that you can even configure and subsequently trigger notifications and alerts in real time when predetermined anomalies are detected.
Error reporting as a function is available for the App Engine Standard environment, the App Engine Flexible environment, and the Compute Engine services. Also it is available in terms of programming languages, using; Java, Python, JavaScript, Ruby, C#, PHP, and Go as the exceptions stack trace parser can handle these languages.

Tracing

Stackdriver Trace is a distributed tracing system that collects latency data from your applications and displays it in the GCP console. Tracing is another function that Stackdriver integrates into the GCP. Using Stackdriver trace you can track how requests propagate through your application and receive detailed new real-time performance insights.

Consequently, you can use the Stackdriver Trace to automatically analyse all of your applications' processes in order to produce in-depth latency reports. These latency reports can be used to detect deep rooted performance deteriorations over time. The service can also capture and analyse the traces from all of your VMS, containers or Google App Engine products.

Managing the amount of time it takes for your applications to handle incoming requests and perform operations is an important part of managing overall application performance.

Debugging

Stackdriver Debugger inspects the state of a running application in real-time without any interruption. The application and the users are not impacted while you capture the call stack and variables at any location in your source code. Indeed, you can use debugging to understand the behaviour of your code in production as well as analyse its state to locate those hard to find bugs. However, you should be aware that debugging can be strenuous on CPU activity. The Stackdriver Debugger is generally used with App Engine, both Standard and Flexible,

Compute Engine and the Kubernetes Engine. The debugger also supports multiple languages such as, Java, Python and Go.

Installing Stackdriver is also very easy and most basic built-in monitoring functions are available by default inside of the VM. But, should you need some of the additional capabilities then you need to do this via the startup script. Indeed you use this script to install the Stackdriver agent as well as the logging agent.

With the logging agent installed you can capture not just the system logs, but a number of custom applications such as Cassandra, MySQL, PostgreSQL, Java, different run-times, custom metrics, and all sorts of other things.

Istio for GKE

The open source service mesh Istio is integrated with GKE. When you create or update a cluster with Istio on GKE, the following core Istio components will be installed:

- Pilot, this is the component responsible for service discovery and for configuring the Envoy sidecar proxies within an Istio service mesh.
- Mixer, this is the component responsible for the Istio-Policy and Istio-Telemetry, Mixer enforces usage policies and gathers the telemetry data across the service mesh.
- Istio ingress gateway, this service provides an ingress point for traffic from outside the cluster.
- Istio egress gateway, provides a place for Istio monitoring and routing rules to be applied to traffic exiting the mesh. The Istio egress gateway is no longer installed by default in version 1.1 and later.
- Citadel, this Istio component is responsible for key and certificate management.
- Galley, this component provides configuration management services.

The installation also lets you add the Istio sidecar proxy (Envoy) to your service workloads, allowing them to communicate with the control plane and join the Istio mesh. However, for clusters with Stackdriver enabled, the Istio Stackdriver adapter is installed along with the core components described above. The Istio adapter then sends metrics, logging, telemetry and trace data from the Istio service mesh into Stackdriver. This integration provides the required observability into your services' behaviour, which is visible in the Stackdriver console. Thus you only need to enable a particular Stackdriver feature for your project and cluster, and the tight coupling between Istio and Stackdriver will ensure that the data is sent from your service mesh to the Stackdriver console by default.

Monitoring

If the Stackdriver Monitoring API is enabled in your GCP project, your Istio mesh will automatically send metrics related to your services (such as the number of bytes received by a particular service) to Stackdriver, where they will appear in the Metrics Explorer. You can use these metrics to create custom dashboards and alerts, letting you monitor your services over time and receive alerts when, for example, a service is nearing a specified number of requests. You can also combine these metrics using filters and aggregations with Stackdriver's built-in metrics to get new insights into your service behaviour.

Logging

If the Stackdriver Logging API is enabled in your GCP project, your Istio mesh will automatically send logs to Stackdriver, where they will appear in the logs viewer. See the Stackdriver Logging documentation to find out more about what you can do with the log data, such as exporting logs to BigQuery.
Caution: This feature may incur additional costs for usage, especially with a high volume of logs data. To find out how to disable this feature for your mesh, see Disabling Stackdriver Logging and Tracing.

Tracing

If the Stackdriver Trace API is enabled in your GCP project, your Istio mesh will automatically send trace data to Stackdriver, where they will appear in the trace viewer. Note that to get the most from distributed tracing to help find performance bottlenecks, you will need to change your workloads to instrument tracing headers. You can find out how to do this in the Istio Distributed Tracing guide.
Caution: This feature may incur additional costs for usage, especially with a high volume of trace data. To find out how to disable this feature for your mesh, see Disabling Stackdriver Logging and Tracing.

Incident Response

Planning Incident response brings together all the knowledge that you've learned so far.
That's the entire pyramid from monitoring to incident response, which is where we maintain our users' trust.

Incident response is defined as the human behaviour that results in system stability when things don't go as planned. After all, we've set up alerts, we're doing dashboards, and now we've got health checks, but how will we respond to an incident?

In responding to incidents you will need to be consistent as you need to be able to minimize the frequency and the duration of those outage downtimes. You also need to be transparent about the root cause of the incident and share with others what you have done to fix it. By sharing with the team what you have identified and how you responded lets them learn quickly from this outage. It is therefore imperative that you do so in a consistent and repeatable manner, and hence consequently we will want to create a structured incident response policy. This should result in the team being prepared, able to respond and fix rapidly as they will know what to do ahead of time.

To address consistency you will need to reduce the duplication of effort. We need to ensure that there is not multiple occurrences of the same thing going on which could delay our response. For a best practice we can look to Google and their Site Reliability Engineering (SRE) culture. Within SRE the focus is on collaboration and communication, learning, open source and sharing of designs. This culture is demonstrated by Google's willingness to publish best practices and anything they believe to be of value to the community under open source via the research.google.com site as well as through many other blog posts.

In developing a strict incidence response policy we must treat it in the same way as we consider the business logic for our app as having an organized flow, step by step following a flow of information and subsequent customer notifications. Therefore we must fully identify the flow and then put the steps in place to say this is our first level communication, this is our conclusion, then once we're back online you must take the time to follow up with a post-mortem, which will update the documentation and that's typically a three-step process.

Of course that's easier said than done so we must first determine what each step in the process will address.

For the first step we will require a monitoring service with alerting as well as a dashboard and have the metrics in place to understand the scope of what has been affected.

As we have already in place an alerting policy the question now is how are we are going to notify the support on-call, stakeholders, and the customers.

None of that can happen without you having planned the incident response policy and put in place the communication tools for responding to the issue. However you also have to consider if this needs to be done if you already have in place robust mechanisms for automated fail-over, auto-scale or even automated rollback mechanisms. Regardless, you will have to proactively put in place some method to prepare for these situations.

Our business logic layer is where we start to work through our root cause analysis.

Remember that 5Ys methodology that we used to work through the issues in our troubleshooting faults to understand what initially caused the failure? Well we utilise that same method to help us develop procedures that ensure that we have resiliency when we deploy our revision to production. Hence, we're going to implement some of the key things we can use to mitigate weaknesses that surfaced during the post-mortem.

So, now we can design not based on forecasting but for the future based on real production traffic and so we can budget and we can modify our development more accurately.

So, let us see how we can apply this to the way we can update our business logic layer in our video transcription service.

Initially we started out as a proof of concept as an application hosted on a single box but now it's evolved into a complex array of specialist microservices and network components with IAM and security. Moreover, this all came about as a result of an evolution by changing the product's capabilities to become a production ready system.

But the product itself hasn't changed as the business logic remains fundamentally the same even though we use different technologies to deliver it. In fact, there were very few changes to the product. Most changes were typically added to provide more capable and robust logging, but we did change to APIs, for example, to take advantage of the native Google Cloud Services.

There are a few practical items remaining that we need to cover. These deal with the implementation of the 12 factor guidelines on administration and management tasks as best practices suggest they should be a one-off process. Ideally, we want to automate and that means segregating the control plane functions from data plane functions and removing any unnecessary human intervention. When we contemplate isolation we create things like out-of-bound management utilizing the serial console, isolating internal VMS from the internet by using a bastion host and communicating with them only through a SSH connection. We can also deploy private sub-networks, so segregating the business and user logic from the outside world.

But finally we need to sit down and build an incidence response playbook. This is the great big book of tried and tested remedies to fix just about any failure. It will contain all the guideline for dealing with an outage such as; What to do if you get an alert notification? Such as advise on how to understand the severity of the issue and how to confirm the problem is still persisting.

After all intermittent faults are far more complex to deal with as the testing results are not consistent so neither is the process for diagnosing and how to fix the problem.

But of course when remediating problems there is always the question; are we going to do short-term versus long-term?

Maybe a long-term solution is going to be to update a potential flaw in our code, but then it might be more effective to immediate mitigate the infrequent outage by restarting the service rather than do a code rewrite. But then that's going to have to define what our deployment process will be like. Finally, we have to perform our post-mortem and identify the post-fix, clean it and escalate it to other support teams.

This is also key, document it, this is why documentation is a core element in incident response. But when it comes to outlining processes and procedures try and use automation and quick buttons. Use micro services with RESTful APIs to instigate a procedure. This way the support person doesn't really have to understand what's going on inside those processes, you can communicate these in the documentation. Moreover you can use Google Cloud APIs, a lot of these are thoroughly tested by Google, so why go to the trouble of reinventing the wheel?

Then of course make sure you set your alarm threshold realistically to reduce noise. This will prevent many false alarms – false negatives – but of course you mustn't miss those true alarms – false positives – that do require urgent additional levels of more detailed and deeper investigation. You can do this by reducing low-value work through automation as this is something the system can handle itself without the need for human intervention.

Use case - 29 Stabilizing & Commissioning

Now, basically, you have supervised the running of the video transcription application in production for three months. You are proud that it is working effectively, the stakeholders are happy, and although like any parent you still have some niggling doubts it is time to move on as you have delivered on all the project deliverables.

But, here lies that shadow of doubt, how once you leave will the operations team keep this service running?

After all you designed and evolved this video transcription service from our primitive prototype into a sophisticated, scalable, reliable, secure system. Therefore before you go you must responsibly have a final objective, which is to stabilize the system and make it maintainable and operable.

In order to do this we must address some pertinent questions; what elements of the service should be monitored? And to achieve this, what kinds of alerts and notifications should you set up?

So let's bring everything we have learned here into stabilizing our video transcription application so that we can responsibly hand over to an operations team.

What change in circumstance do we need to be concerned about and what should we be monitoring in the meantime to give us early warning of a change in production conditions?

In our design we have identified specific indicators and thresholds, which will determine some of the service disruptions that can occur, however, what if there's some kind of error loop, and that leads to a runaway consumptions of resources.

Now the problem is that we are trying to solve is that logging service isn't quite stable enough to support this so it also needs monitoring and alerting added.

So let's contemplate what might be important to monitor with regards a storage system and under what operational conditions the alerts and notifications should be sent.

Okay so we want to determine and identify any logs where the timestamp are out of date or are just failing to be delivered. Therefore, we will want to be able to troubleshoot the many different places that latency or a bottleneck could occur.

Say we're not getting the data storage logs, but we are getting web logs and the app logs, but we also want to be able to monitor for all of these different services. So we could do this by checking for the timeliness of all this incoming data. Therefore we would want to periodically query a big table or query our log data to make sure that its recorded in real time.

Now we could also potentially monitor the queue mechanisms in Pub Sub in which case if the ingress process began to get too far behind, perhaps for some reason, our cloud functions are not scaling quick enough to handle this particular processing, then we could detect this.

We could do this as a white box monitoring method, as what we would do is we'd monitor to determine if any of these logs are out of date. Then our black box would monitor for the network up time, and as we are already monitoring the queues and checking for any of this data being ingested we might discover anomalies between the two.

Okay this is only one single example application. But there are many different solutions available.

Google actually publish solution architectures which cover many diverse use cases. So, if you go to cloud.google.com/solutions, you're going to find a wide range of case studies and solutions designed for many different business and industry vertical markets.

So, you can see a lot of synergies between the two and how they take advantage of services, but there are custom tweaks specific to certain verticals.

48952926R00352

Printed in Poland
by Amazon Fulfillment
Poland Sp. z o.o., Wrocław